D1592725

MuleSoft for Salesforce Developers

A practitioner's guide to deploying MuleSoft APIs and integrations for Salesforce enterprise solutions

Arul Christhuraj Alphonse

Alexandra Martinez

Akshata Sawant

BIRMINGHAM—MUMBAI

MuleSoft for Salesforce Developers

Copyright © 2022 Packt Publishing

All rights reserved. No part of this book may be reproduced, stored in a retrieval system, or transmitted in any form or by any means, without the prior written permission of the publisher, except in the case of brief quotations embedded in critical articles or reviews.

Every effort has been made in the preparation of this book to ensure the accuracy of the information presented. However, the information contained in this book is sold without warranty, either express or implied. Neither the author(s), nor Packt Publishing or its dealers and distributors, will be held liable for any damages caused or alleged to have been caused directly or indirectly by this book.

Packt Publishing has endeavored to provide trademark information about all of the companies and products mentioned in this book by the appropriate use of capital. However, Packt Publishing cannot guarantee the accuracy of this information.

Group Product Manager: Alok Dhuri

Publishing Product Manager: Harshal Gundetty

Senior Editor: Nisha Cleetus

Business Development Executive: Uzma Sheerin

Technical Editor: Maran Fernandes

Copy Editor: Safis Editing

Project Coordinator: Manisha Singh

Proofreader: Safis Editing

Indexer: Subalakshmi Govindhan

Production Designer: Prashant Ghare

Marketing Coordinator: Rayyan khan and Deepak Kumar

First published: September 2022

Production reference: 1090922

Published by Packt Publishing Ltd.
Livery Place
35 Livery Street
Birmingham
B3 2PB, UK.

ISBN 978-1-80107-960-0

www.packt.com

To the memory of my father, Alphonse, and to my mother, Esther RajaRathinam, for their sacrifices and love.

– Arul Christhuraj Alphonse

To my wife, Ana, for being my biggest supporter, my best friend, and the best life partner I could've asked for. To my aunts, Elia and Vero, for believing in me unconditionally and for all of your love. To my mom, Lulu, for all your sacrifices, your long nights when I was sick, your hugs, your tears, your smiles, your warmth, and everything you gave me. Las amo, siempre.

– Alexandra Martinez

To my parents, I truly appreciate your efforts in bringing me up to be a better individual. To my best friend and my favorite human, Dan! I love you! To my little bro, Shubham, for being so mature and supportive.

– Akshata Sawant

Contributors

About the authors

Arul Christhuraj Alphonse works as a senior integration architect at Cognizant. Before working at Cognizant, he also worked at Akmin Technologies, Quinnox, IBM, and TCS. He has over 18 years of experience in the integration and API domain and has designed over 1,000 integrations. His educational qualifications include Master of Computer Applications and Master of Business Administration degrees, and his professional qualifications include MuleSoft Mentor, MuleSoft Certified Integration Architect, MuleSoft Certified Platform Architect, MuleSoft Certified Developer Level 1, and SoftwareAG webMethods Certified Professional. He was born and raised in Thoothukudi, Tamil Nadu, India, and currently lives in Singapore. He shares his knowledge through Udemy and the Tech Lightning YouTube channel.

I thank God because without God I wouldn't be able to do any of this. I would like to thank my loving and understanding wife, Sahaya Divya, my son, Rithwin, my daughter, Riya, and also my family for their continuous support, patience, and encouragement throughout the long process of writing this book. Big thanks to my team at Cognizant and DFS for being supportive.

Alexandra Martinez is a developer advocate at MuleSoft, creating technical content to enable developers and architects to get started with MuleSoft's products. Before this, Alex worked as a MuleSoft developer and was part of the MuleSoft community as an Ambassadress and meetup leader for the Toronto, Online Spanish, and Women Who Mule chapters. Alex has more than 10 years of experience in technology and has developed software in other languages, such as Java, Python, and PHP. Born and raised in Monterrey, Mexico, Alexandra's MuleSoft career was key to moving to a different country, and she currently lives in Niagara Falls, Canada. Alex volunteers at organizations such as Women Who Code and Olascoaga MX to help close the gender gap in STEM careers.

I want to thank my dream team at MuleSoft: Mariana Lemus, Sabrina Marechal, Sabrina Hockett, Isabella Navarro, David Norris, and Meghan Murphy. You have helped me in more ways than you'll ever know and I really appreciate it. I also want to thank Bits In Glass for changing my life, especially Aaron Wentzell and Graham Fraser for mentoring me.

Akshata Sawant is a developer advocate at MuleSoft. She's been evangelizing MuleSoft through her blogs, videos, and training sessions. She has around five years of experience as a MuleSoft developer. Apart from this, she's also a MuleSoft Certified Developer and an architect. Akshata has been an active member of the MuleSoft community and is also a former MuleSoft Ambassadress and a meetup leader for the London, Mumbai, and Manchester regions. Her roots go back to Mumbai but she's currently living her London dream. She's been a global speaker and mentors women in the integration ecosystem.

I would like to thank my parents, Dan, Shubham, Chetan Parekh Sir, family, and my mentors at Apisero and EPAM for always motivating me. Thanks to all my friends for their honest reviews on my content. Thanks to everyone at Packt for being so patient and Uzma Sherin for trusting me with this book. To my team at MuleSoft and my amazing MuleSoft Community, a big thank you from the bottom of my heart! Ambadnya!

About the reviewers

Gaurav Kheterpal is a well-known name in the Salesforce ecosystem, a Salesforce MVP since 2016, and he holds 40 Salesforce Certifications, 21 Salesforce AP Credentials and 5 MuleSoft Certifications – he is ranked among the top 3 globally certified experts in Salesforce & Mulesoft ecosystems.

Gaurav has been recognized by Salesforce as a Developer Success Story and a Trailblazer. He has delivered several sessions at leading events such as Dreamforce, TrailheaDX, Salesforce World Tour, London's Calling, and several others. Gaurav is passionate about evangelizing Salesforce and MuleSoft platforms in the broader community.

D Rajesh Kumar is a Lead MuleSoft Integration Architect with 17+ years of extensive experience in the IT industry. For the last 8 years, he has been working on the MuleSoft platform in various domains for end-to-end platform setups, architecture, design and Center for Enablement (C4E) setups and execution. He is a MuleSoft Certified Architect and a MuleSoft Ambassador recognized by MuleSoft for his expertise in Mule. He is currently working for TCS as Solution Architect and previously worked for Infosys, HCL, and Jamcracker.

Table of Contents

3

Exploring Anypoint Studio   55

4

Introduction to Core Components   89

5

Part 2: A Deep Dive into MuleSoft

6

Learning DataWeave   173

7

Transforming with DataWeave   217

8

Building Your Mule Application   257

9

Deploying Your Application   285

10

Secure Your API   313

11

Testing Your Application   339

Part 3: Integration with Salesforce and Other Connectors

12

MuleSoft Integration with Salesforce

13

MuleSoft Connectors and Use Cases

Preface

MuleSoft for Salesforce Developers will help you build state-of-the-art enterprise solutions with flexible and scalable integration capabilities using MuleSoft's Anypoint Platform and Anypoint Studio. If you're a Salesforce developer looking to get started with this useful tool, look no further. This book will get you up to speed in no time, leveling up your integration developer skills.

Complete with step-by-step explanations of essential concepts, practical examples, and self-assessment questions, this essential guide will first introduce you to the fundamentals of MuleSoft and API-led connectivity, before walking you through the API life cycle and the Anypoint Studio IDE. Once you have the IDE set up, you'll be ready to create Mule applications. We'll look at the core components of MuleSoft and Anypoint Platform, and before long, you'll know how to build, transform, secure, test, and deploy applications using the wide range of components available to you. Finally, you'll learn about using connectors to integrate MuleSoft with Salesforce and fulfill a number of use cases, which will be covered in depth, along with interview and certification tips.

By the end of this book, you will be confident in building MuleSoft integrations at an enterprise scale. Also, it'll help you to pass the fundamental MuleSoft certification – **MuleSoft Certified Developer (MCD)** – Level 1.

Who this book is for

This book is aimed at Salesforce developers who want to get started with MuleSoft. There's an increasing demand for cross-cloud solutions that involve integrating MuleSoft with the core Salesforce platform or one of the Salesforce cloud offerings, such as Service Cloud, Marketing Cloud, and Commerce Cloud. Salesforce architects will also find the concepts covered in the book useful in designing Salesforce solutions.

It's helpful if you have knowledge/prior experience with any programming language and some basic integration concepts.

Some basic familiarity with Salesforce development and experience with Salesforce APIs is expected – at least SOAP API, REST API, Bulk API, or Streaming API.

What this book covers

Chapter 1, *Introduction to APIs and MuleSoft*, covers what no-code and low-code technologies are, what APIs and integrations are, the different MuleSoft products, what application networks are, and what the API-led connectivity approach is.

Chapter 2, Designing Your API, explores the API life cycle and how to create an API specification and fragments using RAML, fundamentals of REST and SOAP API and HTTP protocol, capabilities of API Manager, and API Design best practices.

Chapter 3, Exploring Anypoint Studio, covers how to download Anypoint Studio from the official website, install it on the system, and perform the required configuration. After the installation, we will develop the new Mule application and run it inside Anypoint Studio.

Chapter 4, Introduction to Core Components, covers the basics of a Mule Event, the flow, and the sub-flow. It introduces us to several components, scopes, routers, transformers, and flow controls in Mule. It also examines error handling and batch processing in Mule 4.

Chapter 5, All About Anypoint Platform, delves into the Anypoint Platform components, such as Design Center – API Designer, Exchange, API Manager, Runtime Manager, and Anypoint Monitoring. At the end of this chapter, we will be familiar with how to create an API using Design Center, how to publish the API in Exchange, how to create the API in API Manager to enforce the policies, what Runtime Manager is, and how to monitor applications from Anypoint Platform.

Chapter 6, Learning DataWeave, covers an introduction to DataWeave if you're new to the language. We discuss what DataWeave is, how scripts are created, how to add comments, and what data types, data formats, operators, variables, functions, selectors, scopes, and conditionals are.

Chapter 7, Transforming with DataWeave, focuses on learning more about the DataWeave modules and some of the most used functions in real life. We also learn about the Transform Message component to use DataWeave in Anypoint Studio.

Chapter 8, Building Your Mule Application, explains how to build a Mule application using different configuration and properties files, and also covers Scheduler Endpoint, the APIkit router, and Object Store.

Chapter 9, Deploying Your Application, explores the different deployment options available in MuleSoft, how to deploy an application to CloudHub, how to download and install a Mule on-premises server, how to deploy a Mule application to an on-premises server, and also how to build a CI/CD pipeline using MuleSoft.

Chapter 10, Secure Your API, covers the need to secure your API with the help of policies, explores the capabilities of API Manager, and more about MuleSoft's security features.

Chapter 11, Testing Your Application, examines MUnit, MUnitTools, different operations, and how to create test suites and test cases using MUnit. We will also see how MUnit can speed up the development process and the test recorder.

Chapter 12, MuleSoft integration with Salesforce, covers how to leverage the capabilities of MuleSoft to integrate Salesforce with other end-systems. It also covers Salesforce connectors, accelerators, and templates and several capabilities of MuleSoft to make integration easy. It also covers about MuleSoft Composer to simplify integrations.

In the API-based approach, we will access the Salesforce objects via the API to access the information in real time. In the event-based approach, we will listen to the Salesforce topic to receive the message and process it synchronously to the required backend system.

Chapter 13, MuleSoft Connectors and Use Cases, delves into the different modules (File, FTP, SFTP, Database, Slack, SOAP, VM, and JMS) available in MuleSoft. In the File-based modules (File, FTP, and SFTP), we will connect to the system and read the file. We will also send the file through different connectors. In the Database module, we will perform the required connector configuration to a specific database and read/insert records from/to the database. This chapter also covers the different modules, such as Slack, Web Service Consumer (SOAP), VM, and JMS connectors.

Chapter 14, Best Practices, Tips, and Tricks, covers the MuleSoft best practices, guidelines, coding standards, tips, and tricks.

Chapter 15, Certification and Interview Tips, explores the different career paths you can choose in the MuleSoft ecosystem, what the different MuleSoft certifications are and some tips to get certified, what the different available trainings are, how to contribute to the MuleSoft community, and some interview tips for your first MuleSoft position.

To get the most out of this book

You will need a version of Anypoint Studio 7.x installed on your computer – the latest version, if possible. Examples have been tested using Anypoint Studio 7.12 on macOS. However, they should work with future minor version releases too.

You will need a web browser installed on your computer to access Anypoint Platform and the DataWeave Playground. Examples have been tested using Google Chrome on macOS. However, other browsers such as Safari or Firefox should work too.

You will need a REST client application installed on your computer to make requests to the APIs. Examples have been tested using Postman v9 on macOS and Windows. However, other tools such as an advanced REST client or curl should work too.

Software/hardware covered in the book	Operating system requirements
Anypoint Studio 7.12	Windows 11 or macOS
Anypoint Platform and MuleSoft Composer	Any browser
Postman or any similar API client tool	Postman v9 (Windows 64-bit), Mac (Intel chip/Apple chip), or Linux (x64)
Google Chrome	Windows 11 or macOS

If you are using the digital version of this book, we advise you to type the code yourself or access the code from the book's GitHub repository (a link is available in the next section). Doing so will help you avoid any potential errors related to the copying and pasting of code.

Download the example code files

You can download the example code files for this book from GitHub at `https://github.com/PacktPublishing/MuleSoft-for-Salesforce-Developers`. If there's an update to the code, it will be updated in the GitHub repository.

We also have other code bundles from our rich catalog of books and videos available at `https://github.com/PacktPublishing/`. Check them out!

Download the color images

We also provide a PDF file that has color images of the screenshots and diagrams used in this book. You can download it here: `https://packt.link/u7ZAp`.

Conventions used

There are a number of text conventions used throughout this book.

`Code in text`: Indicates code words in the text, database table names, folder names, filenames, file extensions, pathnames, dummy URLs, user input, and Twitter handles. Here is an example: "You want to compare whether `b is greater than a` or `a is greater than or equal to b`."

A block of code is set as follows:

```
a = 1
b = 5
if b > a:
    print("b is greater than a")
else:
    print("a is greater than or equal to b")
```

When we wish to draw your attention to a particular part of a code block, the relevant lines or items are set in bold:

```
asyncapi: '2.0.0'
```

```
info:
  title: MusicAsyncAPI
  version: '1.0.0'
```

Bold: Indicates a new term, an important word, or words that you see onscreen. For instance, words in menus or dialog boxes appear in **bold**. Here is an example: "Click on **Publish** and select the **Publish to Exchange** option."

Tips or Important Notes
Appear like this.

Get in touch

Feedback from our readers is always welcome.

General feedback: If you have questions about any aspect of this book, email us at customercare@packtpub.com and mention the book title in the subject of your message.

Errata: Although we have taken every care to ensure the accuracy of our content, mistakes do happen. If you have found a mistake in this book, we would be grateful if you would report this to us. Please visit www.packtpub.com/support/errata and fill in the form.

Piracy: If you come across any illegal copies of our works in any form on the internet, we would be grateful if you would provide us with the location address or website name. Please contact us at copyright@packt.com with a link to the material.

If you are interested in becoming an author: If there is a topic that you have expertise in and you are interested in either writing or contributing to a book, please visit authors.packtpub.com.

Share Your Thoughts

Once you've read *MuleSoft for Salesforce Developers*, we'd love to hear your thoughts! Scan the QR code below to go straight to the Amazon review page for this book and share your feedback.

https://packt.link/r/1801079609

Your review is important to us and the tech community and will help us make sure we're delivering excellent quality content.

Part 1:
Getting Started with MuleSoft

Part 1 covers an introduction to MuleSoft, Anypoint Platform capabilities, and how to design an API. This part also covers the core components of Anypoint Studio. We will explore various components of Anypoint Platform. At the end of this part, we will be familiar with the features and capabilities of Anypoint Platform and Anypoint Studio. We will also have hands-on experience in designing an API.

The following chapters are included in this part:

- *Chapter 1, Introduction to APIs and MuleSoft*
- *Chapter 2, Designing Your API*
- *Chapter 3, Exploring Anypoint Studio*
- *Chapter 4, Introduction to Core Components*
- *Chapter 5, All About Anypoint Platform*

1

Introduction to APIs and MuleSoft

The world is changing. Technologies keep emerging. There are more needs for technology now than there used to be, and it's not a coincidence. Earlier, there were simple problems and simple solutions: maybe not the best solutions, but they worked well enough for the needs at the time. Now, we are swamped with different technologies we can choose from to achieve the same goal. We are bombarded with new programming languages, frameworks, and methodologies. What was popular yesterday is obsolete today. How do we keep up?

Before, it was good enough to just have an engineering or computer science degree to be able to thrive in the **Information Technology (IT)** world. Now, you don't necessarily need a degree, but you do need to understand the basic terminology or learn the appropriate logic required to create software. A lot of people think this is a skill you are born with, that you either have what it takes to understand programming algorithms and patterns or you're doomed to never be able to work in IT. This is not true – especially nowadays, in the **no-code/low-code** era.

Today, we can find mobile applications that do our work for us. There are tools online to help us write, design, paint, sing, and build, even if that is not our strongest suit. Why would programming be any different? This is where technologies such as **Salesforce** and **MuleSoft** come into play. The simplicity they're based on helps you to thrive in this environment even if you don't come from an IT background.

In this chapter, we're going to cover the following main topics:

- No-code and low-code technologies
- Integrations
- APIs
- MuleSoft's products
- Application networks
- API-led connectivity approach

Let's start by understanding the need for an integration tool.

Understanding the need for an integration tool

If you come from a Salesforce background, you might not be 100% familiar with the usefulness of an integration tool such as MuleSoft. Before we dive into MuleSoft, let's first understand why we need an integration tool and what low-code or no-code technologies are.

Introducing no-code and low-code technologies

Programming and software development have been evolving over the years. At first, programmers needed to manually translate the behavior they wanted into computer code. You needed to study a programming language, practice it, and really polish it to be able to create unimaginable programs. Eventually, this transformed into human-readable words that you could input into the machine and it would automatically know what you meant.

Fast-forward to the year 2022 and you don't even have to input words for the computer to know what you want to do. Computers are now good enough to work with icons, buttons, or drag-and-drop components. You don't need to memorize commands; you just need an introduction to the tool and some practice to be proficient in it. What a blessing!

Of course, there might still be some need to write code in order to have more customized behavior that fits into more complex needs for the tool; but code in general, or a programming language, is easier to understand every time.

Let's now look into both no-code and low-code technologies in more detail.

No-code technologies

There are some applications that you can use that involve no coding whatsoever. A few examples that come to mind are Trello for project management, Canva for graphic design, or Zapier for integration/automation. You can use them without needing to know a programming language. It's all done through clicks and configurations.

For example, Zapier and other tools such as **If This Then That** (**IFTTT**) are very popular because you only need your browser to access them. There's no need to install an application on your computer or perform updates to your software. You can simply type the site name into your browser, create an account, and start using it right away. Of course, there is a learning curve to understanding how to use them. But this can be overcome in a matter of hours or days, not years of a professional career. With these kinds of integration tools, there are predefined apps that you can connect to through their **Graphical User Interfaces** (**GUIs**), such as Google Calendar, GitHub, and Philips Hue. You can create specific triggers to automate your day-to-day work. An example that comes to mind is sending a Slack message as soon as a commit is pushed in GitHub. You can just click through the flow to sign in to your accounts from these different services and you don't even need to understand how their code works. That is the beauty of no-code technologies.

Low-code technologies

In low-code tools, you can still take advantage of drag and drop, clicks, and configurations, but there might be some coding involved for more precise functionality. However, programming is not the majority of the work. The technology does not revolve around the programming language; rather, it is considered a feature of the overall product. This is the case for Salesforce with **Apex** and MuleSoft with **DataWeave**. You can use Salesforce and MuleSoft without the need to use their programming languages, but they are available for you in case you need custom functionality.

We will look into these in more detail later in the book, but if you're completely new to MuleSoft, picture this: you have a palette of **connectors** you can choose from. There is a Salesforce connector, a Workday connector, and a Slack connector, and they are ready for you to just drag and drop onto a canvas. Imagine these as building blocks that you take and start building something new. Alone they might not be super useful, but together they create utility applications. Well, you can take these connectors and build some logic. You're building a backend application without the need to know how to code. The learning curve is smaller than trying to learn a programming language from scratch, because the visual assets help you to get a better understanding of what you're building, instead of having to read actual code and understand what it does.

Let's say that you have two variables: a and b. You want to compare whether b is greater than a and print b is greater than a, or a is greater than or equal to b otherwise. To do this in Python, it would look like this:

```
a = 1
b = 5
if b > a:
    print("b is greater than a")
else:
    print("a is greater than or equal to b")
```

Python is one of the languages that has a more human-readable syntax. Even if you don't know Python, you'll be able to read this code. However, you do have to get familiar with the syntax to know how to create this piece of code.

Now, let's take a look at the same functionality, but using MuleSoft's **Anypoint Studio** (MuleSoft's **Integrated Development Environment** (**IDE**)). Remember that this is a visual flow where you can follow the components through icons, instead of just code. It would look something like this:

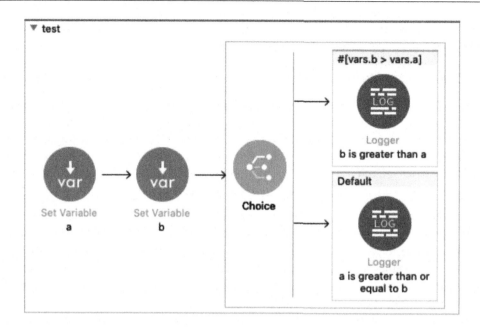

Figure 1.1 – Flow from Anypoint Studio

There is still some syntax involved. In Python, you wrote the condition as b > a, but in MuleSoft, our condition is vars.b > vars.a. So, MuleSoft is not completely free of code. But the majority of the components we used here did not involve writing code; they were connectors that can be configured in the canvas by drag-and-dropping.

Analyzing integrations

We can look at integration as some sort of translator that will allow *system A* and *system B* to talk with each other even if they both speak different languages. A quick analogy that comes to mind is if, for example, you speak English and need to speak with someone in Spanish; you can use a translator app on your phone to help you communicate with the other person. You don't need to learn Spanish and the other person doesn't need to learn English in order for you two to communicate effectively. This is achieved, thanks to your mobile device or the mobile application that you downloaded (the *integrator*).

Let's now look into a technical example to demonstrate what integration does. If you're not familiar with **JavaScript Object Notation** (**JSON**), it's a type of data that is widely used nowadays because of its simplicity and easiness to read.

Let's say that *system A* uses the following JSON object to describe a person. It contains the ID, FirstName, and LastName fields:

systemA-person.json

```json
{

"ID": 1,

"FirstName": "Alexandra",

"LastName": "Martinez"
}
```

However, *system B* uses a different JSON structure to describe a person. Instead of the ID field, it uses id, instead of FirstName, it uses firstName, and instead of LastName, it uses lastName:

systemB-person.json

```json
{

"id": 1,

"firstName": "Alexandra",

"lastName": "Martinez"
}
```

For a human, this might seem like a pretty straightforward transformation. The fields have the same names; they just have different upper- and lowercase letters. However, for a computer program, these fields are completely different. You need an integration that will help *system A* and *system B* to effectively communicate with each other even though their fields are different.

Of course, this example is simple compared to real use cases. This is just to give you a better idea of why you would need integration to connect different systems. In the real world, this data can be as short as what was just demonstrated or as long as 2,000 fields at a time.

Now imagine that we not only have to connect different data structures from *system A* to *system B* but also need to connect systems *C, D, E*, and *F*. All of them have their own data structures. Some of them don't even use JSON; they use other data types, such as CSV or XML. It would be a lot of work to manually create code to be able to talk within all of these systems. Instead of creating a huge, tightly coupled, and hard-to-maintain application to connect them all, you can create small and easy-to-maintain **Application Programming Interfaces** (**APIs**) that will help you to integrate all of these systems and even leave space for any changes to the integrations that can be easily done. You're not stuck with a ton of dependencies within the same project, but have different **microservices** to manage your whole **application network**, which brings us to our next topic.

Understanding APIs

The term *integration* is still an abstract concept without seeing some examples of technology that can implement it; but don't worry, we'll get there. Let's now switch gears and dive into another popular term we hear a lot nowadays: **API**.

If you're a visual person, we encourage you to watch this video, `https://youtu.be/s7wmiS2mSXY`, from MuleSoft to see an animation with a restaurant analogy that is widely used to explain APIs. This step is optional, but it might help you to understand this concept better. We will walk through the restaurant analogy in the following section.

Reviewing the restaurant analogy

When you go to a restaurant, after you sit down and get yourself comfortable, a server will come to ask for your order. You order your dish, the server writes it down, and then they proceed to communicate the order to the kitchen. The kitchen staff works their magic to cook your meal, and then let the server know when the meal is ready. The server picks up the dish and takes it to your table for you to enjoy.

Now, let's break this down into smaller pieces:

1. You order your food.
2. The server writes down your order and sends it to the kitchen staff.
3. The kitchen staff prepares the order and gives it to the server.
4. The server picks up the order and brings it to you.
5. You receive your food.

We can look at this process as if it were API calls:

1. You call the Server API, *requesting* some food.
2. The Server API forwards your order to the Kitchen API, *requesting* your food.
3. The Kitchen API processes this information and *responds* with your food.
4. The Server API takes the food and *responds* to your order with the food.
5. You receive the food and confirm it is correct.

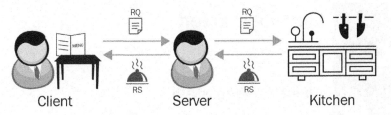

Figure 1.2 – API calls in restaurant analogy

The important things to understand from this analogy are as follows:

- You don't know what the server wrote down in their notebook that was sent to the kitchen
- You don't know all the ingredients that were put into your food or the exact process that the kitchen staff followed to prepare the order
- You don't know what the kitchen staff told the server to let them know your order was ready

All that you know is that you ordered something and you received what you had ordered. APIs are a lot like that.

Fun fact

In a restaurant, you are the **client** and the person who brings your food is the **server**. Guess what it is called in the API world? In API lingo, the application that calls an API is called the **client application**, and the application or API that responds is called the **server application**.

Let's now look into a real-life API to understand it better.

Exploring an API example

There are thousands of APIs that you can use in the real world. An example that we can use to demonstrate is the Twitter API. Twitter is a social network that is popular because of the maximum number of characters allowed in a single *tweet*. As of the time of writing, you can only post *280* characters at a time, which makes it ideal for short thoughts or quick updates about different topics. Once you have a Twitter profile and start *following* other accounts, you will be able to see the tweets from those accounts on your home page, or *timeline*.

If you go to the Twitter API documentation (`developer.twitter.com/docs/twitter-api`), you will be able to find all the different requests and responses that you can use to communicate with the API (the menu from the restaurant analogy, if you want to look at it that way).

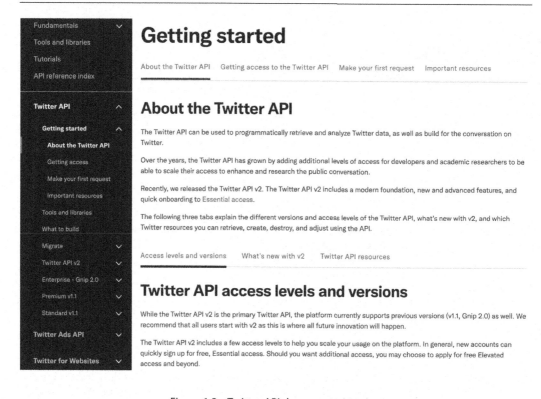

Figure 1.3 – Twitter API documentation site

You can find the technical details to call the API and receive a list of your own tweets, for example; or you can post a new tweet using this API. This is useful if you want to communicate with Twitter using a backend application, if you're developing your own app that can talk to Twitter, or if you want to integrate Twitter with other apps. For example, you can use social media tools (such as Hootsuite or Later) to schedule posts on your social networks. You give them the information you want to post and they take this information (or order) to the backend systems, which will make this possible (like the kitchen staff).

Any integration you create using the Twitter API can be written in any language or technology you decide. It doesn't have to be compliant with how Twitter developed their APIs. That is the beautiful thing about the APIs. They offer their documentation so you know what's available from them (like the menu from a restaurant) and you can make the appropriate requests to receive the data you need. The only thing you need to do is send the data in a format that the API is expecting, but any processing before or after the API request can be handled however you see fit.

To put it in more technical terms: you don't know exactly what programming language the Twitter API is built in or what kind of data type it uses internally to process the information, but you do know the type of data it accepts and the type of data it returns. This is all you need to know to communicate with it.

Analyzing API components

Now that we have a better idea of what APIs are, let's start looking into some components to define them. We won't get into the technical details just yet, but it is good for you to start familiarizing yourself with this terminology.

Implementation

The **implementation** is the body of the API, that is, the code you choose to build the API with, the part that does the processing of the **request** and the **response**. We will use this term interchangeably with API throughout the book.

Request

Whatever is sent to the API is called a **request**. This includes different kinds of information that will tell the API what needs to be done with the data that is received. In the restaurant analogy, this can be, for example, a hamburger with no pickles, in a combo, with a large soda, and some fries on the side.

Response

Whatever is received back from the API is called a **response**. This includes information to describe what happened in the processing of the requestor, for example, whether the request was successful or not or whether there was a problem with the request. In the restaurant analogy, this can either be the food you ordered (a successful response), the server telling you that the dish is no longer available but you can still order something else (a failed response with a workaround), or the server telling you that they're closed for the day (a failed response with no workaround).

API specification

This specification serves as a rule, standard, or contract – however you want to look at it – to tell the client application (the application that calls the API or sends a request to the API) what kind of information it needs to send to the API in order to be accepted and processed as needed. For example, if the **API specification** says the API only accepts JSON requests and the client application sends an **XML** request instead, then an error will be returned stating that this data type is not accepted by the API. This is also a contract in the sense that it lists what the API may or will return to the client application, for example, a JSON object containing the `id`, `firstName`, and `lastName` fields.

Listing the benefits of using APIs

We still haven't talked about the technical aspect of an API, but we've seen some examples and an analogy to help us get a better idea of this concept. Let's list some of the benefits of using APIs:

- **Loosely coupled**: We touched on this subject briefly, back in our explanation of integration technologies. When you have a lot of systems that you need to integrate, you can create an application network with loosely coupled APIs that communicate with each other. This is a better alternative to having a huge, tightly coupled system that can't let any more functionality in or out without having a dependency problem.

- **Governance**: With the APIs approach, you have a better chance of being able to govern your network. You can create API gateways, policies, and any sort of security to ensure that no unwanted intruder can get to your APIs. This can be a challenge with legacy systems sometimes because you need to create personalized code or external solutions may not be available for your system.

- **Discoverability**: APIs, as opposed to legacy systems, have a best practice of including documentation to use them. Since these are supposed to be open to the public, or easily discoverable, organizations also want their users (developers) to be able to find them and start using their APIs. Because of this, they try to generate better documentation with examples, use cases, descriptions, and even sample code.

- **Easier maintenance**: In hand with the loosely coupled and discoverability benefits, the developers that end up maintaining these APIs have a better understanding of their code. Because APIs are supposed to cover a small, specific use case for the developers, it is also easier for them to understand the code. Legacy systems, however, end up being a headache because of their millions of code lines and dependencies.

- **Efficiency**: From a project management perspective, we can also take this point into account. Because APIs have less code and their functionality is so specific, the time to deliver new features can be shortened compared to other architecture types or legacy systems.

- **Reusability**: As we mentioned earlier, we want to create an application network that connects all of our APIs to bring together a system that covers our needs. Since APIs are so small and functionality-specific, they are created with reusability in mind. The output response depends on the input request it receives. This is helpful to reuse specific functionality that is consumed by several services or systems and there's no need to create custom code since they're loosely coupled.

Introducing MuleSoft

Everything comes together. After understanding all of the previous concepts – no-/low-code technologies, integrations, and APIs – we can start talking about MuleSoft. In this section, we'll describe what MuleSoft is, what some of its products are, how it's useful, and how it is going to help you in your career as a Salesforce developer. First of all, MuleSoft is the name of the company that created the existing suite of products. When people talk about MuleSoft in a development context, they are referring to all of the products that this company has created. A clearer example of this can be seen now that Facebook has changed its name to Meta; we can more easily see the difference between the name of the company (Meta) and its corresponding products (Facebook, Instagram, and WhatsApp). The same is the case with MuleSoft. The name of the company is MuleSoft; it's not the name of a product. But when we refer to MuleSoft, it encompasses all of MuleSoft's products.

Listing MuleSoft's products

Let's take a look at some of the most popular products that MuleSoft has released so far (up to the time of writing this book). The suite of technologies can be broken down into three main products:

- **Anypoint Platform**
- **Anypoint Studio**
- **Composer**

Each of these products includes its own products and functionality as well. Let's review them in detail.

> **Note**
>
> There are more products on the way – such as MuleSoft **Robotic Process Automation** (**RPA**) and Anypoint Code Builder – but we will not be talking about those in this book since they're either not publicly available yet or have been just released.

Anypoint Platform

Anypoint Platform can be accessed through your browser. If you go to `anypoint.mulesoft.com`, you will see the login screen. You can create a free trial account that will last 30 days. Inside Anypoint Platform, you will find the following products:

> **Note**
>
> We will talk more about all these products in *Chapter 5, All about Anypoint Platform*.

- **Anypoint Design Center**: This is where you can manage your API specifications with **API Designer** and your **Async API Specifications** with **AsyncAPI Designer** and create quick Mule applications with Flow Designer.
- **Anypoint Exchange**: You can look at this product as an app store of sorts where you can find a catalog of published assets that you can reuse in your own code.
- **Anypoint DataGraph**: If you're familiar with DataGraph, MuleSoft created its own product to help you use this technology within its suite of products.

- **Access Management**: This is where mostly only the admins of the account will be able to change permissions or access for the users of the account.

- **Anypoint API Manager**: As its name says, you will be able to manage your APIs from here. You can manage alerts, contracts, policies, SLA tiers, and other settings.

- **Anypoint Runtime Manager**: The Mule applications are located in Runtime Manager. You can access logs, object stores, queues, schedules, and settings.

- **CloudHub**: If your Mule application is running within MuleSoft's cloud provider service, that means you're using CloudHub. Your Anypoint Platform free account will use CloudHub by default.

- **Anypoint Visualizer**: You can use this product to get a visual representation of your systems, such as autogenerated architectural diagrams or available policies, or perform some general troubleshooting of your applications.

- **Anypoint Monitoring**: Here, you can generate custom dashboards or use the built-in dashboards to get a better feel for how your apps are behaving.

- **Secrets Manager**: Here, you can store sensitive data such as passwords, tokens, certificates, or keys in Secrets Manager so they can be accessed and still be secured.

- **Anypoint Runtime Fabric**: This is not included in your free trial account, but this is where you would be able to deploy your Mule applications to different cloud providers, such as Microsoft Azure, Amazon Web Services, or Google Cloud Platform.

- **Anypoint MQ**: This is MuleSoft's message queueing service. It is a built-in solution that includes its own connectors to use within your code with no extra drivers or settings needed.

- **Anypoint Service Mesh**: This is not included in your free trial account, but with this product, you can manage non-Mule applications within the same suite of products, regardless of the programming language they're based in.

- **Anypoint Flex Gateway**: With this lightweight gateway, you can manage Mule and non-Mule applications. You can install Flex Gateway in Docker, Kubernetes, or Linux. This is included in your free trial account.

- **Anypoint API Governance**: Here, you can create standards for your API specifications, Mule or non-Mule applications, security policies, and more. This is included in your free trial account.

Let's now see the products inside Anypoint Studio.

Anypoint Studio

Anypoint Studio is MuleSoft's IDE (based on Eclipse). You install this application on your computer and this is where you're able to develop Mule applications. Studio has a nice GUI to find predefined connectors and use them to develop your Mule flows. Inside Anypoint Studio, you will find the following products:

- **MUnit**: MuleSoft's testing framework. MUnit is optimized to create tests visually. We can create tests using connectors such as Mock, Assert, and Spy. We will talk more about MUnit in *Chapter 11, Testing Your Application*.

- **APIkit**: With this product, you can take your API specification and create a basic structure for your Mule application instead of doing it from scratch. We will talk more about APIkit in *Chapter 8, Building Your Mule Application*.

- **DataWeave**: MuleSoft's functional programming language, optimized for transformations. We will do a deep dive into this language in *Chapter 6, Learning DataWeave,* and *Chapter 7, Transforming with DataWeave*.

Let's now see an overview of Composer.

Composer

Composer, as opposed to the other MuleSoft products, is a no-code tool. There's no need to create an API specification or implementation. Composer was specifically designed to have *clicks not code*, as its slogan says. If you're familiar with some of the no-code tools we mentioned earlier in this chapter, such as Zapier and IFTTT, Composer follows a similar approach. We will talk more about Composer in *Chapter 12, MuleSoft Integration with Salesforce*.

Now that we understand the variety of products MuleSoft offers, let's look into how all of these tools are useful.

Understanding why MuleSoft is useful

We just learned about the suite of products and functionality that MuleSoft offers. Besides being a low-code technology with a smaller learning curve than a regular programming language, MuleSoft can fulfill almost all the requirements you need to cover in the development life cycle. From designing to implementing and testing, to deploying, securing, and monitoring your solutions, MuleSoft most likely has a product for your needs. The best part is that because you're using all these products under the same sphere, they can be easily integrated or moved from one stage to the next.

Let's review what a Mule application or an API life cycle would look like within MuleSoft's products.

Design phase – API specification

We're first going to review what MuleSoft products can be used in the design phase of your API. This will result in an API specification that you can use as the foundation for the next phase. This phase takes place in Anypoint Platform:

1. **API specification design**: Using Design Center, you can start designing your API specification with the visual API Designer without having to know **RESTful API Modeling Language (RAML)** or **OpenAPI Specification (OAS)**.

2. **API specification testing**: Using the mocking service, which can be found in API Designer, you can create a mock of your current API specification and make calls to it. This is with the purpose of getting a feel for how the developers will experience your API before even implementing it. The idea is that you go back and forth between the design and testing until you feel comfortable with the specification you've created.

3. **API specification publishing and feedback**: From API Designer, you can publish your finished specification to **Exchange** for others in your organization to discover. Exchange will automatically generate basic documentation based on your API specification. You can share this Exchange asset with others in order to gather feedback on your design. If you still need to adjust things, you can just go back to API Designer and modify what's needed. After you do this, you can publish a new version of your API specification in Exchange.

We can iterate through these first three steps as long as needed until we feel comfortable that we have an API specification on which to base our implementation. Once we have the first draft, we can continue with the next phase.

Implementation phase – Mule application

Now that we have a first draft of the API specification, we can get started with the implementation. This phase takes place in Anypoint Studio:

1. **Mule application implementation**: This process is where you would be using the available connectors or **DataWeave** to start creating your Mule application's implementation. After you've finished any number of iterations and feel comfortable with the API specification you generated in the previous phase, you are now ready to start creating your Mule application. From Anypoint Studio, you can connect to your Anypoint Platform account and download the API specification from Exchange. This will generate the basic flows and error handling so you don't have to start creating everything from scratch. This process uses APIkit to route the different types of requests to their corresponding Mule flows. In addition, any request that is not recognized by the API specification will be routed to the corresponding error handling. For example, if we refer to our previous restaurant analogy, if you were to order food that was not available on the menu, the server would respond that what you requested does not exist.

2. **Mule application testing**: Once you generate the main functionality, you are ready for the next step, which is where you would start creating your unit testing using **MUnit**. Nothing is better than a high-quality application. Here, you can create mocks and use asserts to make sure the different scenarios for your code are indeed working as expected. A best practice is to aim for 90% of MUnit coverage, if not 100%, but this varies depending on each project.

Same as earlier, we can iterate through these steps as many times as we need to achieve good-quality code and functionality of the application. Once we're happy with the first draft of the functioning app, we can continue with the next phase.

Deployment and managing phase – API

Now that we have a functioning Mule application, we can start the deployment and managing phase. This phase takes place in Anypoint Platform:

1. **API deployment**: After you've implemented and tested the Mule application on your local machine, you are ready to deploy it to the cloud. You can deploy your application from Anypoint Studio directly to Anypoint Platform. Just a few clicks and we're done. You can see the progress of this deployment from Runtime Manager. You can host your app in different cloud providers, such as Amazon, Microsoft, or Google; but for now, we'll just focus on MuleSoft's CloudHub.

2. **API security**: Now that your application is running in CloudHub, you are ready to create API policies, contracts, SLA tiers, and so on. All of this is managed by API Manager.

3. **API monitoring**: Your API is secured and running. Now it's time to lay back and relax. You can monitor your API from Anypoint Monitoring or create alerts in case something goes wrong and you want to immediately get notified about it.

The whole life cycle doesn't end there, of course. This is just an example of what an API life cycle could look like. After deploying the application, the cycle starts again. Once the developers get a hold of your API and start testing it, some features or bugs will be on their way to you. This is where we'll restart the cycle from the design or implementation phase, depending on the case, and the cycle continues once again.

Now we have a better idea of what MuleSoft is and how it's useful in the API life cycle. This book was written for Salesforce developers and architects, so let's now see how MuleSoft is helpful for your professional career.

Analyzing how MuleSoft helps Salesforce developers

MuleSoft has long been helpful in integrating different technologies, including Salesforce. However, since Salesforce acquired MuleSoft, we can see more and more integrations between the technologies. Furthermore, the acquisitions of **Slack**, **Tableau**, and **Servicetrace** have also increased the use of MuleSoft throughout these platforms and vice versa. For example, there wasn't an official Slack connector in MuleSoft before, but one was created after the official acquisition. There is also a new product in the works called MuleSoft RPA, and guess what Servicetrace is? Yes, it's an RPA technology. We now also have Composer, which is a technology created by mixing both Salesforce and MuleSoft technologies.

While it might be true that you don't necessarily need to know MuleSoft in order to be a Salesforce developer, the past and the present are the foundation of what we predict the future will be like. What history's been telling us is that Salesforce will continue adding to its 360 products from other companies it acquires. We already have Composer in common between Salesforce and MuleSoft – who knows what else will be integrated in the future. But it all points to the fact that MuleSoft will be integrated more and more to the Salesforce suite.

From a professional career perspective, currently, there are not a lot of developers who are proficient in both MuleSoft and Salesforce – they are either Salesforce developers or MuleSoft developers, or they may know a little bit about the other but are not experienced developers in both. It wouldn't be a surprise if in some years job postings started requiring proficiency in both technologies.

The following summarizes what we have discussed in this section:

- MuleSoft is slowly being added to Salesforce's technology suite
- There is already a product created that combines both Salesforce and MuleSoft: Composer
- Career-wise, it would be smart of you to get ahead of the trend and become proficient in both technologies before it becomes a requirement

Exploring application networks and the API-led connectivity approach

This is where it all comes together. We understand that MuleSoft is a collection of low-code technologies that help us create APIs or microservices based on Mule applications. Integrations are important because we can connect different services with different data types or structures to create an application network.

Understanding what application networks are

Why do we create several APIs and connect them instead of creating one single system to do all of this? Remember the benefits of using APIs: loosely coupled, governance, discoverability, easier maintenance, efficiency, and reusability. We can't achieve these with a regular system. All the code is tightly coupled, it's hard to maintain, it can't be reused, and so on. This is why we want to create an application network to connect all of these different building blocks.

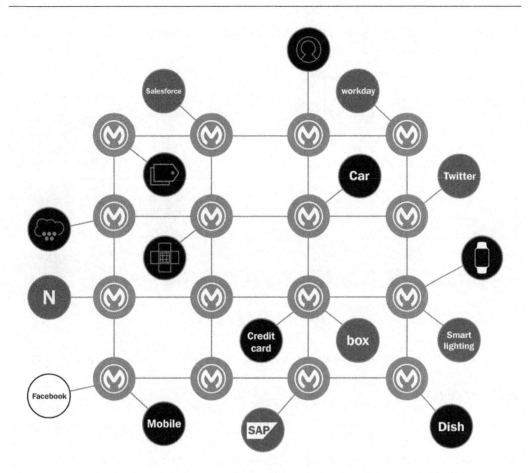

Figure 1.4 – Application network representation

We can connect services or platforms such as Salesforce, Workday, Amazon Web Services, NetSuite, Dropbox, Google Drive, SAP, and Twitter – the options are endless. Even if these don't have an API to connect to as easily, MuleSoft's products offer so many options for customization that you can really integrate almost anything with MuleSoft. The main vision when MuleSoft was created was to be able to work together and make more APIs to discover and reuse. This would essentially reduce time to delivery and IT demands would be easier to meet over time. But how exactly do we plan on doing this network? This brings us to our next point.

Analyzing the API-led connectivity approach

MuleSoft believes in an architectural approach in which you have a standard to give your APIs a specific purpose in your application network. This can help you create more reusability around your APIs so you can easily add new functionality or APIs, modify or upgrade existing ones, or remove any API that's no longer being used.

This **API-led connectivity** approach is based on three different layers in which we'll categorize our APIs: Experience, Process, and System.

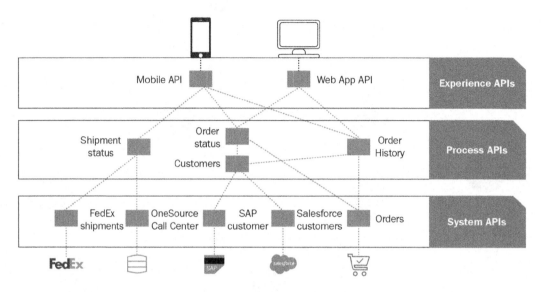

Figure 1.5 – The three layers of the API-led connectivity approach: Experience, Process, and System

Experience layer

This is the top layer. It is where we have the APIs that directly make contact with the client application, whether that's a mobile application or a desktop application. This is where we put the APIs that have direct contact with the outside world, that is, the APIs that are public. The sole purpose of these Experience APIs is to connect to the client application and send the information to the next layer. The only logic we may add here is any kind of security or filter to make sure the information that is received is correct and can indeed proceed with the rest of our application network. If anything is missing or looks suspicious, then it's the Experience API's responsibility to not let this data proceed further and raise this as an error immediately.

Process layer

This is the middle layer. It is where we, as its name suggests, process or transform the data we received from the Experience layer in order to be sent to the rest of the APIs. Just as we saw earlier on in this chapter when we talked about integrations, if we have *system A*, which processes certain information, and then we have *system B* with a different data structure, then it'd be the responsibility of the Process APIs to transform (or translate) these two data types in order to be understandable by their corresponding APIs.

Going back to our previous example, say now *system A* is the data that comes from the client application and *system B* is the data that we need to send to the server application; we end up with something like this:

client-application.json

```
{

"ID": 1,

"FirstName": "Alexandra",

"LastName": "Martinez"
}
```

server-application.json

```
{

"id": 1,

"firstName": "Alexandra",

"lastName": "Martinez"
}
```

It is the Process API's responsibility to do these two transformations both upstream and downstream. The Process API would first receive client-application.json as its input, then it would have to transform it to the server-application.json structure and send it to the corresponding API. After the downstream API responds, the Process API needs to transform the data from whatever it received from the server application to whatever data type or structure the client application is expecting to receive. In this case, the client application would be the Experience API that's calling the Process API, and the server application would be the System API.

System layer

This is the last layer. The Experience layer, the topmost layer, is the one that directly connects to the client application. Now that we're at the bottom, this is where we directly connect to the server application, whether that is Salesforce, Facebook, SQL, or Azure, you name it. These APIs are where we store any tokens, passwords, credentials, or URLs that are needed to connect to the underlying systems.

Since most of the filtering, security, cleanup, and transformations are done in the previous layers, this layer can focus solely on connecting and sending the data to its target. If there is more data transformation needed from this response, the Process API is responsible for doing so, not the System API.

We have a better picture now of how the API-led connectivity approach is helpful for our application network – when we separate the APIs into these three layers, we have a better standard to follow in our architecture. Now, let's summarize all we have learned in this chapter.

Summary

In this chapter, we learned how the learning curve for no-code or low-code technologies is smaller than learning a programming language. You mainly need to learn how to use the GUI, which may take some hours or days, and almost all the functionality is done through clicks instead of code.

When we have systems that need to exchange pieces of information, but they don't necessarily use the same data type or data structure, we create integrations to help translate this data. Using APIs is better for the developers who create or maintain the code, the developers who want to use a public API, and the companies behind them. APIs, as opposed to other systems, are loosely coupled, easier to maintain, discoverable, and reusable.

MuleSoft's products three main products are Anypoint Platform, Anypoint Studio, and Composer. Anypoint Platform is a tool you can access from your browser to design, deploy, manage, secure, and monitor your APIs or applications. Anypoint Studio is the IDE you download and install on your local computer to develop and test your Mule applications. Finally, Composer is a no-code product that was created by mixing both Salesforce and MuleSoft to help you integrate your systems faster.

The whole reason for creating APIs in the first place is that it makes it easier to have an application network made of smaller pieces that we can connect as building blocks. We can reuse the functionality for different purposes, instead of having to create custom code with the same functionality.

MuleSoft believes in using the API-led connectivity approach as the architecture pattern to connect our APIs. We have the Experience, Process, and System layers, which will help us create specific APIs that can be reused and maintained more easily throughout the application network: the Experience layer for client application-facing functionality, the Process layer for orchestrating and processing the information, and the System layer for connecting to external services.

In the next chapter, we will expand our API knowledge from the basics to the technical aspects. We'll review some best practices to design a better API specification and understand how exactly APIs connect with each other.

Questions

Take a moment to answer the following questions to serve as a recap of what you just learned in this chapter:

1. What's the difference between no-code and low-code technologies?
2. What are the API components we talked about in this chapter?
3. How do the API components relate to the API analogy we discussed?
4. What are the names of the three main MuleSoft products?
5. List some of the products or functionality that can be found inside those three main MuleSoft products.
6. What are the three phases we talked about when creating an API within MuleSoft?
7. What are the three API-led connectivity layers?
8. What purpose does each of the API-led connectivity layers serve?

Answers

1. The difference between no-code and low-code technologies are:

   - No-code technologies provide a user interface for you to use the product and don't require you to learn or know any type of programming language in order to use it.

   - Low-code technologies also provide a user interface, but they do involve some minor programming in order to create more personalized functionality. Although the use of the technology doesn't revolve around the programming language, it is a part of it.

2. The API components are as follows:

   - **Implementation**: The body of the API, where all the information is processed
   - **Request**: The data you send to the API with detailed information
   - **Response**: The data you receive back from the API with detailed information about what happened with your request
   - **API specification**: The standard, or contract, so you know what you can ask for in the request and what you might receive in the response

3. The API components relate to the API analogy as follows:

    - The implementation is like the kitchen staff: they receive your order, cook your food, and serve your order. You don't know how they cooked it or exactly what ingredients it has, but you receive what you requested.

    - The request is what you order, with any specific details, such as a hamburger with no tomatoes, extra pickles, in a combo, with an orange soda, and fries on the side.

    - The response is what you get back after you made your order, such as a hamburger with no tomatoes, extra pickles, and so on.

    - The API specification is like the menu when you arrive at the restaurant. You can't just order whatever you want; you have to order available dishes from the menu.

4. Anypoint Platform, Anypoint Studio, and Composer

5. The products or functionality that can be found inside the three main MuleSoft products are:

    - Anypoint Platform:

        - Anypoint Design Center

        - Anypoint Exchange

        - Anypoint DataGraph

        - Access Management

        - Anypoint API Manager

        - Anypoint Runtime Manager

        - CloudHub

        - Anypoint Visualizer

        - Anypoint Monitoring

        - Secrets Manager

        - Anypoint Runtime Fabric

        - Anypoint MQ

        - Anypoint Service Mesh

        - Anypoint Flex Gateway

- Anypoint Studio:
  - MUnit
  - APIkit
  - DataWeave
- Composer

6. Design phase, implementation phase, and deployment and managing phase.

7. Experience layer, Process layer, and System layer.

8. The purpose served by the API-led connectivity layers are:

   I.   Experience layer: The APIs that are exposed to the calling clients, such as a mobile application, a web application, or a desktop application. This is where you'd add any public-facing security, such as appropriate security policies.

   II. Process layer: The APIs that are in charge of orchestrating and processing the data. They receive the data from the Experience APIs, process it, and send it to the System APIs. Then they receive the data from the System APIs, process it, and send it back to the Experience APIs. This is where all the data transformation should take place.

   III. System layer: The APIs that connect to any downstream or external systems. Their sole purpose is to connect with external technologies and send back – to the Process APIs – the information that was received. This is where all the external systems' credentials are stored.

2
Designing Your API

In the previous chapter, we learned about MuleSoft and its capabilities. Also, we've gained some insights on APIs, API-led connectivity, and what we're trying to build – an API network.

After having a basic understanding of the fundamental concepts of MuleSoft, in this chapter, we shall learn about the life cycle of an API design, compare various API design modeling languages, and learn various aspects of API design and API fragments. We will also get hands-on practice designing an API specification using the **RESTful API Modeling Language** (**RAML**).

API design is a primary and crucial step toward building a successful application network; the goal of this chapter is to enable you to design an API using the best practices and industry standards.

Here is what you can expect from this chapter:

- The life cycle of an API
- An introduction to REST, HTTP, and SOAP
- Getting started with OAS and RAML
- The basics of API design
- Understanding the Anypoint Platform's Design Center
- Designing your first API using RAML
- Hands-on experience with your API design
- Best practices and guidelines to design an API

Before getting started with the actual API design, let's first understand the fundamentals of an API design life cycle.

Understanding an API life cycle

In order to build a complete API, we need to follow a systematic approach. Hence, we shall now learn about the life cycle of an API. It consists of four stages:

1. Design: This involves architecting the basic skeleton of your API. This is the first and the most crucial step, as we need to take into consideration all the functional and non-functional requirements to build a logical structure.

2. Simulate: After having a fair understanding of the initial requirements, we need to implement the API by using appropriate endpoints, methods, data types, and examples, and following the API design best practices.

3. Feedback: Once our API model is ready, we can simulate our API using the mocking service. Also, we can test our API to check if the response meets the initial requirements.

4. Validate: At this stage, we will share the API with other external/internal developers and collaborators and take into consideration the feedback received from them. Later, we shall introspect the received feedback and implement the API design changes accordingly.

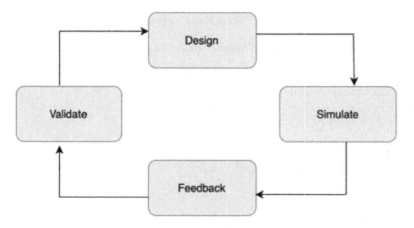

Figure 2.1 – API design life cycle

As we can see in *Figure 2.1*, this is an iterative process consisting of four stages until the API design is finalized.

After understanding the various stages of the API design life cycle, we shall now focus on the key elements pertaining to API design, which are REST, HTTP, and SOAP.

Introducing REST, HTTP, and SOAP

REST and SOAP are two different approaches to implementing an API design and HTTP is the data transfer protocol that supports REST APIs. In this section, we shall learn a bit more about them.

While we're mainly going to focus on the creation of a REST API, it's equally essential to know the difference between REST and SOAP APIs so that you can decide wisely what type of API suits your organization's requirements.

REST

REST stands for Representational State Transfer. It represents a modern architectural style for designing an API.

The features of a REST API are:

- A REST API accommodates stateless client-server architectural models, and the data is transferred over the HTTP/HTTPS protocol.

- It supports several data types such as XML, JSON, plain text, and HTML, which makes it easily consumable. JSON is the most widely used data type as it's a human-readable language.

- It is lightweight and compatible with most of the latest technologies.

Let's learn more about HTTP.

HTTP/HTTPS

HTTP, short for Hypertext Transfer Protocol, is a client-server communication protocol used to exchange data in a client-server architecture model.

HTTPS is identical to HTTP but has a security add-on. It supports **transport layer security (TLS)** protocol, which is a **secure sockets layer (SSL)** handshake – encryption to exchange data securely between a client and a server.

Figure 2.2 depicts what a typical HTTP request/response looks like:

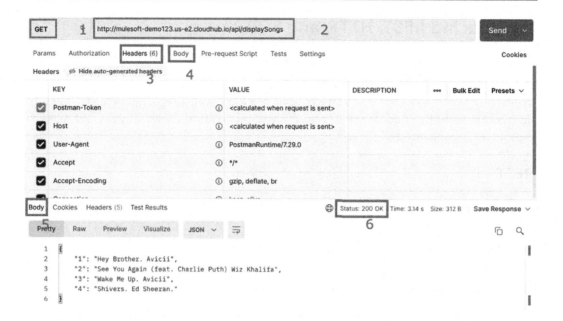

Figure 2.2 – A snapshot from the Postman tool depicting the HTTP request

Figure 2.2 tells us about the HTTP request triggered from the Postman tool. We shall now look at the various elements of the HTTP request-response with the help of the preceding figure.

The prime elements of an HTTP/HTTPS request-response are as follows:

1. Method: This is a verb that defines what action is to be performed. The most commonly used methods are GET, POST, PUT, PATCH, and DELETE.

2. URL: A Uniform Resource Locator, abbreviated as URL, is an address to send requests from a client to get service from a server. It contains all the information related to the host, port, domain, and endpoint.

3. Headers: This is an optional part of an HTTP request, which carries additional data/metadata related to the request.

4. Request body: Methods such as POST, PATCH, and PUT carry data in the form of the body. HTTP supports various formats such as text, JSON, XML, HTML, and so on.

5. Response body: This gives us the response returned by the server. Similar to the request body, it supports several formats.

6. Response status: The status code indicates the state of the response such as the 200 OK success status, 404 Not Found, and 500 Internal Server Error.

As we've now understood the REST API and the HTTP protocol, let's learn more about the SOAP API.

SOAP

SOAP stands for Simple Object Access Protocol. It's a protocol widely used to communicate between different applications. The SOAP API uses **Web Service Definition Language (WSDL)**, which is an XML-based contract between a client and a server. It contains all the relevant information related to a web service, endpoints, request-response, security, and so on.

The features of the SOAP API are:

- It can handle requests using several protocols such as HTTP, SMTP, and TCP

- SOAP supports only the XML format

- It is more secure as compared to REST and complies with ACID properties (Atomicity, Consistency, Isolation, and Durability)

- The structure of the SOAP API is a bit complex and there is an overhead to managing it.

- Most of the legacy applications use the SOAP API

After understanding the features of REST and SOAP APIs, and the HTTP protocol, we can select the respective API modeling language, which can be OAS or RAML, as per an organization's use case.

Let's now learn more about OAS and RAML.

Getting started with OAS and RAML

Open API Specification (OAS) and RAML are the two most extensively used API description formats. Anypoint Designer lets you create a REST API using RAML or OAS (previously known as Swagger).

Although they both have a lot in common, it's essential to understand the capabilities of both OAS and RAML so that we can choose our API specification language wisely.

OAS

OAS is an open source specification language founded in 2010 with huge community support. Its fundamental purpose is to keep API documentation, libraries, and code in sync:

- It supports both JSON and YAML to design API

- OAS is ideal if your application has response type-only JSON, as it takes a longer time to load other formats

- It is not very feasible in terms of code fragmentation and reusability

- It focuses more on the documentation of an API

Let's move on to RAML.

RAML

RAML was founded by MuleSoft in 2013 with the goal of providing all the relevant information pertaining to an API in one place, thus supporting the entire API life cycle stage:

- It uses YAML, which is a human-readable markup language and thus makes RAML easy to build and manage

- External files could be imported into RAML, and it supports several data formats with ease

- The reusable and composable nature of RAML makes it an appropriate choice for users who are working on a large enterprise project and would like to keep their API lightweight

RAML, being released by MuleSoft, supports the basic concept of API-led connectivity and API life cycle management. Hence, Anypoint Platform is more inclined toward MuleSoft. But on the other hand, if you're looking for industry-wide used specifications, then you can opt for OAS, as it has a large community base.

After understanding the fundamentals of API design, let's head toward designing our very first API.

Getting started with API design

In order to get started, go to the Anypoint Platform sign-up page, where you can create a free trial account for 30 days.

You can click here to create a free account: `https://anypoint.mulesoft.com/login/signup`.

> **Note**
>
> In case you're using your organization's enterprise Anypoint Platform account, make sure you have the correct access rights to design, publish, and deploy the API.

Follow these steps to get started:

1. Enter your details and sign up (see *Figure 2.3*).

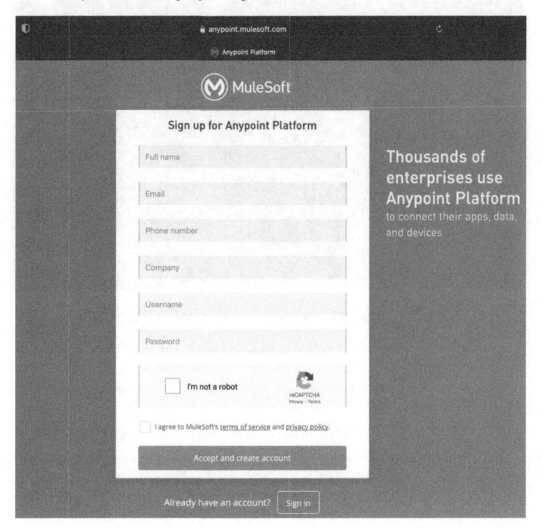

Figure 2.3 – The Anypoint Platform sign-up page

2. Once completed, you'll be taken to the homepage of Anypoint Platform – MuleSoft's iPaaS platform. Navigate to Design Center from the three dashes in the left corner of the home page (see *Figure 2.4*).

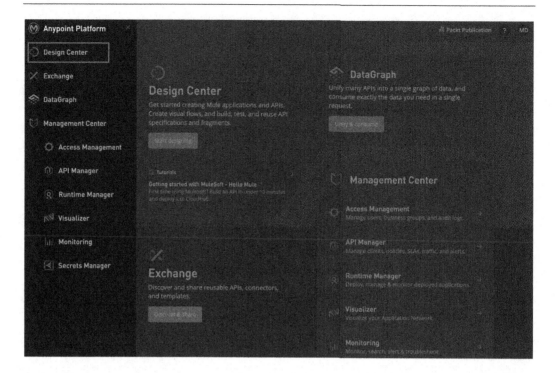

Figure 2.4 – The Anypoint Platform dashboard

You can start writing your API using any simple editor, but it becomes a bit hectic to manage the API and its dependency. Hence, we will design the API using Anypoint Platform's Design Center.

3. When you click on the + Create new button in Design Center (see Figure 2.5), it gives you multiple options to create:

    I.   **New API Spec**: This helps you build your API specification using RAML and OAS.

    II.   **New Fragment**: You can build reusable and composable API fragments to avoid redundancy.

    III. **New Mule App**: You can prototype your integration model similar to your Anypoint Studio (MuleSoft's Eclipse-based studio for developing integration). We will be talking more about this in *Chapter 3, Exploring Anypoint Studio*.

    IV.   **New AsyncAPI**: This helps you to design an asynchronous API.

    V.   **Import from File**: You can import an existing API specification/fragment or a Mule app into Design Center.

4. Once done, select the first option – that is, **New API Spec** – as shown in the following figure:

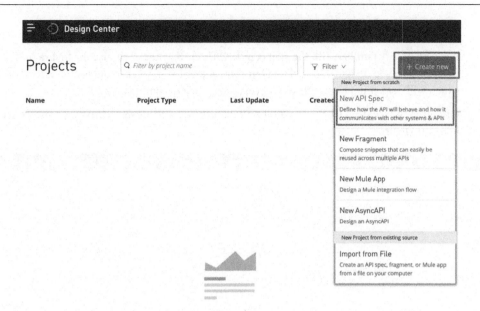

Figure 2.5 – Creating a new API spec

5. On selecting a new API spec, you'll get a dialog box, as shown in *Figure 2.6*, where you can enter the API title following the naming convention. In this case, we're designing a system API, which is evident from the title having keyword sys, denoting the system API.

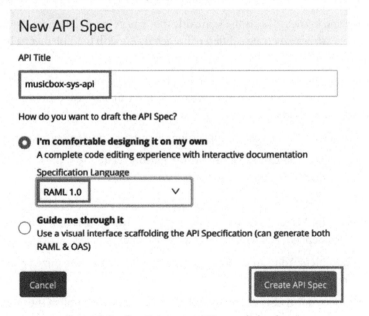

Figure 2.6 – Creating a new API spec dialog box

6. You can select the API specification language from the drop-down list.

    If you're already familiar with the syntax of RAML/OAS, you can choose the first radio button, which will let you design your API on your own; alternatively, you can opt for the second option, which will help you navigate through every step while designing an API.

7. On clicking **Create API Spec**, you'll be taken to the API design canvas, as shown in the following figure:

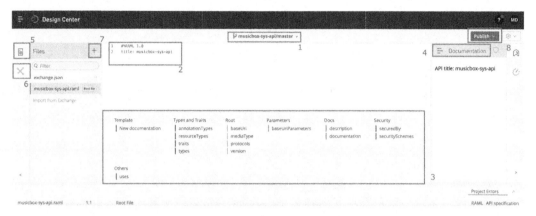

Figure 2.7 – The API Design Canvas

The API Design Canvas consists of several components. Let's learn more about them:

1. API name and branch: This is the same title that you've entered previously. You can also click on the down arrow and create a different branch if you wish to implement a branching strategy for RAML. By default, it's the master branch.

2. Editor: This is the space where you can edit the root file and enter the elements of APIs such as the root, security, methods, and endpoints. You can also edit other file fragments such as example.raml and datatype.raml here.

3. Suggestion palette: This gives you suggestions about various elements during your API design.

4. Documentation: You can see all the information related to a particular endpoint in the Documentation section. You can also mock an endpoint from this section.

5. Files: You can access all the newly created or imported files in the Files section.

6. Dependency: In this section, you can import pre-existing APIs or fragments from Exchange. The imported dependency will be eventually visible in the Files section.

7. Create files/folders: You can create a new file or a folder to reorganize your API into smaller reusable fragments.

8. Publish: Once your API is designed and validated, you can publish it to Exchange using the **Publish** button.

9. Settings: You can import pre-existing APIs; you can also import APIs/fragments from Exchange, download your API as a zip file, and share it with external collaborators, or rename/duplicate/ delete the API (see *Figure 2.8*).

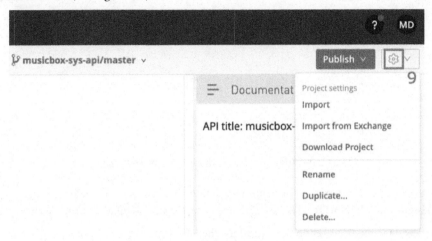

Figure 2.8 – API Design Center settings

We will now design an API using RAML as the modeling language. The following is the use case.

Music Box is an audio streaming platform that wants to build a mobile application for high-quality audio streaming, which will include songs as the main entity.

As per the initial requirement phase, design a REST API (system API) to achieve the following goals:

- Retrieve the list of all songs
- Add a new song based on the artist's code

Now, let's head to our Editor and start editing our API specification.

In the root section, as seen in *Figure 2.9*, along with the title, you can add a description, version, and other details:

1. To begin with, we'll start with a basic / songs endpoint and use a GET method. You can also refer to songs as a resource or an endpoint:

Figure 2.9 – Adding /songs endpoint in the API specification

At every stage, you can see the recommendations in the suggestion palette, which helps you to design your API quickly. Make sure you're taking care of indentation while designing your API.

We have described the /songs endpoint and added the GET method (see *Figure 2.10*). We have specified the response code and body with an expected response as an example.

Figure 2.10 – Simulate the GET endpoint using Try it

2. Similarly, you can try out designing a basic endpoint and later click on the **Try it** option (see *Figure 2.10*) at the top right of your documentation section to validate the response, if it meets your requirements.

> **Note**
>
> Here, we're just simulating the response based on the prototype we design. We will never receive an actual response from the backend systems, nor will the security validations be performed at the API design level.

3. Similarly, we'll add one more endpoint to post a new song based on the artist's code as a URI parameter.

Here, it's important to understand the difference between URI and query parameters, as they are often misunderstood, and it's equally important from an interview as well as a **MuleSoft Certified Developer (MCD)** certification point of view. Let's explore the URI and query parameters in detail.

URI parameter

A **Uniform Resource Identifier (URI)**, as the name suggests, is responsible for identifying a resource uniquely. For example, we can use it to search for songs based on the song ID – /song/{songId}:

```
/songs:
  /{songId}:
    get:
      description: To get all the songs based in the music-box
      displayName: Get all songs getSongsExample
      responses:
        200:
          body:
            application/json:
              example: {
                          "1": "Hey Brother. Avicii",
                          "2": "See You Again (feat. Charlie
                                Puth) Wiz Khalifa",
                          "3": "Wake Me Up. Avicii",
                          "4": "Shivers. Ed Sheeran."
                       }
```

This is what an actual request would look like: http://<host>/song/234.

So here, /{songId} is the URI parameter to fetch a particular song from the records.

Query parameter

A query parameter is used to query, filter, or sort data based on a particular condition. You can think of the query parameter as the WHERE clause used in SQL.

It is passed at the end of the URL, followed by ? and separated by &, if there is more than one query parameter. For example, we can use this to implement pagination and fetch a limited amount of songs per page that were released in a particular year.

So, here, year and limit are the query parameters: /songs?year=<year>&limit=<pageLimit>. This is what an actual request would look like: http://<host>/songs?year=2020&limit=20:

```
/songs:
    get:
        queryParameters:
            limit:
                required: true
                type: integer
                description: Enter the number of songs to be
                    displayed per page
            year:
                required: true
                type: date-only
                description: Enter the year for which you want the
                    songs
        displayName: Get all songs
        responses:
            200:
                body:
                    application/json:
                        example: {
                                    "1": "Hey Brother. Avicii",
                                    "2": "See You Again (feat. Charlie
                                        Puth) Wiz Khalifa",
                                    "3": "Wake Me Up. Avicii",
                                    "4": "Shivers. Ed Sheeran."
                                }
```

You can add more parameters, such as required, type, display name, and description, to further describe your query parameter.

Now that we have learned about the URI and query parameters, let's progress with our API design.

Getting back to our API design (see *Figure 2.11*), we've added a new endpoint, /song/{artistCode}, with the POST method. This is responsible for creating a new record in the backend system.

Figure 2.11 – Adding a new endpoint to post a new song

As it's a POST method, we also need to provide a request body, as mentioned in the example, and we can expect a 200 response after it has successfully created a new song entry. You can set multiple status codes and their corresponding responses.

Currently, in our RAML, we've added just two endpoints, and each has a single method; imagine if we had 20+ endpoints and each endpoint had at least two methods. In that case, the RAML would get pretty bulky.

Hence, to make RAML lightweight, flexible, and easily readable, we will externalize common, recurring components and then call them explicitly when required.

If you click on the + sign in the left panel of Design Center (see *Figure 2.11*), you get an option to create fragments and maintain a file structure.

Some of the commonly used API fragments are as follows:

- Examples: We can exemplify the expected request-response structure or the data type using example files.

- Data types: These define the properties or data schema of a particular resource.

- Resource types: Some of the resources have a common structure that recurs at multiple instances. We can group these commonly occurring elements into a resource type and call it at multiple instances.

- Trait: We can group together a particular method whose characteristics are occurring repeatedly.

- Library: We can club together different fragments in a single library file. This comes in handy when we're dealing with a concise API. We can include data types, traits, the security scheme, and so on in a library file.

- Annotation types: These help us to enhance the definition of endpoints by adding metadata and describing the API. They are defined in a similar fashion to data types. Annotation types are restricted by **allowedTargets**, which limits the usage.

- Overlays: These help to widen the API definition by further extending the details about the nodes. They focus on the non-behavioral aspects of an API.

- Extension: This is similar to an overlay, but they mainly focus on behavioral aspects of an API.

- User documentation: You can add documentation for your entire API specification or a particular resource.

- Security scheme: You can regroup all the security parameters and policies that will be applied throughout the API inside the security scheme.

In order to make it concise, we'll move the example into an example file and reference it explicitly in our root file:

1. Click on + in the right panel and create a new folder called `musicboxAssets` (see *Figure 2.12*).

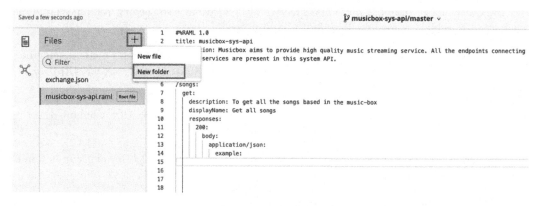

Figure 2.12 – Creating a new folder

2. Create a new folder named `examples` inside `musicboxAssets` (see *Figure 2.13*).

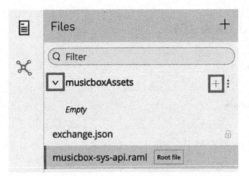

Figure 2.13 – Creating a new folder for example

3. Create a new example file with the name get-songs-example.raml inside the examples folder (see *Figure 2.14*).

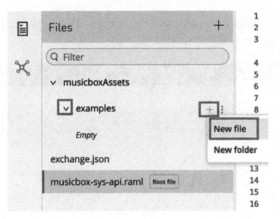

Figure 2.14 – Creating a new example file

4. Select your API specification type and file type (data type, example, traits, and so on) from the drop-down list and enter the filename, as shown in the following figure:

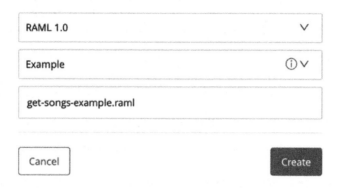

Figure 2.15 – Creating a new example file dialog box

You can now see an empty example file, `get-songs-example.raml`, where we will transfer our example from the root RAML file.

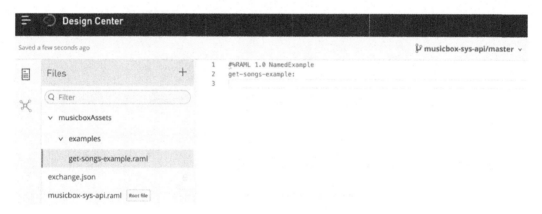

Figure 2.16 – The blank example file

5.   Cut and paste the example from the root RAML file to the `get-songs-example.raml` file.

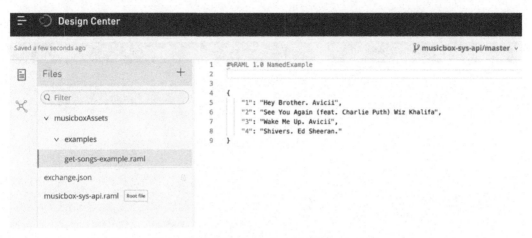

Figure 2.17 – The example added from root file

6. Now, let's reference our example file in our root RAML.

    We can reference any file in root RAML using `!include <file-path>`.

7. To get an accurate file path, copy the path by clicking on the **Copy path** option of the respective file, as shown in the following figure:

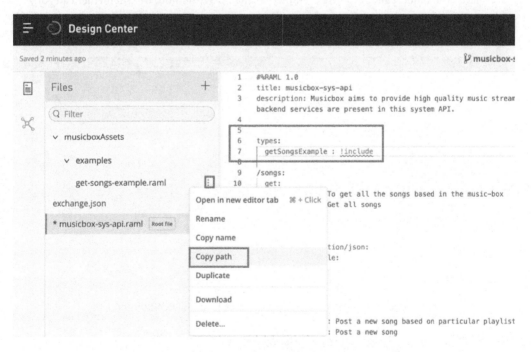

Figure 2.18 – A reference example file in the root RAML file

8. Once the path is copied, reference it in the root RAML file using `!include`.

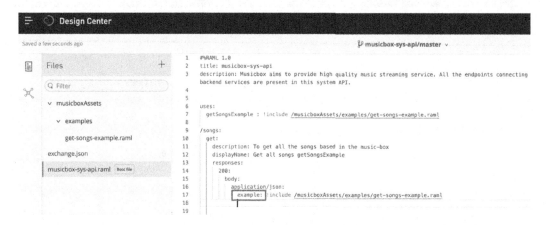

Figure 2.19 – An example file referenced in the root RAML file

Similarly, we can reference example files for the `/song/{artistCode}` endpoint with the POST method.

As we have both request and response examples for the POST method, we will further categorize the folder structure into `requestExamples` and `responseExamples`, save the corresponding files, and further reference them explicitly in our root RAML (see *Figure 2.20*):

Figure 2.20 - Referencing the example file for the POST method

We can follow a similar file structure for other fragments.

API mocking

As we're following a design-first approach, API mocking will help you simulate the API before implementing the API in Anypoint Studio.

Once we are done with the API design, we can simulate the API by mocking the endpoint. Let's follow the steps to mock our API:

1. Click on the endpoint you wish to mock on the right-side panel.

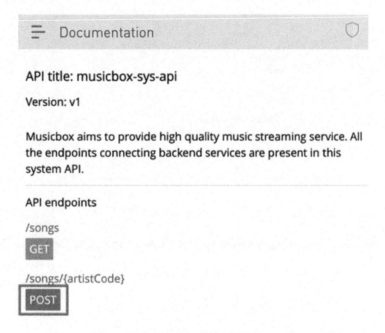

Figure 2.21 – Mocking the POST method

2. You can find all the details related to your endpoint here. Click on the **Try it** button to mock the endpoint.

Figure 2.22 – Reviewing the mocking endpoint information

3.   Next, you can review information about your endpoint and fill in the missing details.

Figure 2.23 – Entering the request details before simulating the endpoint

4. Click on the **Send** button once you've filled in all the missing elements and reviewed the endpoint.

Figure 2.24 – Sending details to mock the POST endpoint

5. Here, you can validate your response. Make any changes in the design specification if needed.

Figure 2.25 – Validating your API response

6. Once your API is finalized, you can publish the API to Exchange, as shown in *Figure 2.26*.

Figure 2.26 – Publishing your API to Exchange

7. Next, you can select the asset version and API version (if already not mentioned in the root file). Select a **LifeCycle State** option and click on **Publish to Exchange** (see *Figure 2.27*).

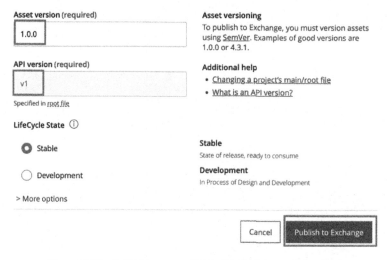

Figure 2.27 – Publishing your API to the Exchange dialog box

8. Once you've published your API, you can view your API in Exchange.

Figure 2.28 – The API successfully published to Exchange

We have successfully designed a simple API, mocked an API, and also published it to Exchange, thus completing the API design life cycle.

Now, we shall learn about some best practices and tips to standardize our API design.

Best practices and tips

We shall now learn some of the API best practices and tips. In order to get started, let's learn some commonly used API design naming conventions.

API design naming convention

Although every organization may have its own set of guidelines and best practices for API design, here are a few commonly used naming conventions while designing an API. Adhering to the naming conventions throughout the API makes it look consistent and standardized:

- Follow standard naming conventions for all the APIs. A commonly used format is `<project_ name><API-led-connectivity-layer>-api` – for example, `musicbox-sys-api`.

- Folder names should be in lower camel case – for example, `dataTypes`, `examples`, and `musicboxAssets`.

- Filenames should be in lower snake case for readability purposes – for example, `post-songs- datatypes.raml` and `get-songs-example.raml`.

- RAML declarations should be in lower camel case – for example, `musicDataType` and `musicTraits`.

- Add relevant **Create, Retrieve, Update and Delete (CRUD)** operations for your endpoints – for example, POST is equivalent to Create, GET denotes Retrieve, PATCH is for Update, and DELETE stands for Delete in CRUD.

- Use simple and short nouns instead of verbs for your endpoints – for example, /songs would be more accurate than /getSongs, as we already have HTTP verbs such as GET, POST, and PUT.

- Use plural nouns for endpoints such as /songs rather than /song. The latter could be correct if we wish to fetch a single object or delete a single object, but it's advisable to use the plural form for the endpoint.

Now that we've learned about the API design naming conventions, let's understand how we can optimize our API.

Optimizing your API design

APIs are considered an asset of an organization. They not only add technical value but can also be used for monetization purposes. API monetization is enjoying a boom period. Hence, a perfect API design is a stepping stone to a successful application network. By ensuring that the API design follows the best practices and standards, we're creating a sustainable API network. In order to design an optimized API, here are some tips, tricks, and best practices:

- First, and most importantly, make sure your design is consistent across the different API layers and fragments.

- Divide your API into smaller fragments, thereby making it reusable and easily consumable. A concise and lightweight API is easy to read, less bulky, and the changes are saved quickly.

- Follow the naming convention standards throughout your API design.

- Document your API so that it becomes easy for external collaborators and consumers to utilize it.

- Add a display name, a description, and examples to your endpoint.

- Make sure security parameters are taken into consideration at the API level.

- Mock your API service and get your request/response validated at an initial stage to avoid iterations in the latter stages of application design.

- Be clear with API versioning.

- Use custom error codes for your endpoints.

We have now learned about the best practices and tips involved in designing the API; let's make sure to implement them in our future APIs.

Summary

In this chapter, we learned the basics of the API life cycle and API designs and navigated through the REST and SOAP APIs, RAML, and OAS. This chapter also taught us the fundamentals of API design and the best practices to be followed.

As a MuleSoft developer and architect, I'd suggest you to not get overwhelmed by the different aspects of API design. It gets easier with practice. Make sure you're following the best practices and the industry standards. Try to get hands-on with API design, as this chapter is important from a MuleSoft certification perspective too.

In the next chapter, we shall learn about MuleSoft's Anypoint Studio – an Eclipse-based IDE for designing Mule applications.

You can now try out a practice API and answer a few quiz questions to boost your API design confidence.

Assignments

Music Box is an audio streaming platform that wants to build a mobile application for high-quality audio streaming, which will include songs and podcasts.

As per the initial requirement phase, design a REST API (system and process APIs) to achieve the following goals:

- Retrieve a list of all songs, podcasts, artists, genres, songs, and collections based on a particular artist
- Simulate a song by changing the artist's name
- Retrieve a paginated list of songs based on artists' names
- Delete songs added on a particular date
- Add a new song to the collection

Follow the API best practices and the industry standards. Make your API composable and concise by dividing it into smaller fragments. Try designing your own API and refer to GitHub for a solution: `https://github.com/PacktPublishing/MuleSoft-for-Salesforce-Developers`.

Questions

Take a moment to answer the following questions to serve as a recap of what you just learned in this chapter:

1. What are the different stages of the API life cycle?
2. What is the difference between data types, traits, and the library?
3. When should you use the query parameter and URI parameter?
4. How can you reference a file fragment in root RAML?
5. Why do we mock an API?

Answers

1. Design, simulate, feedback, and validate are the different stages of the API life cycle.

2. Data types help us to define properties for a particular endpoint. Traits help you to define properties for a method. The library consists of a mix of all fragments clubbed together.

3. If you want to filter or sort records based on some condition, then you use query parameters; if you want to fetch a particular resource, then you use the URI parameter.

4. By using `!include <filepath>`.

5. To simulate the API and validate the request and response of an endpoint.

Exploring Anypoint Studio

In the previous chapter, we looked at how we can design an API in API Designer. We'll now look at **Anypoint Studio**. Anypoint Studio is an Eclipse-based **integrated development environment (IDE)** tool used to design and develop Mule applications. We can also use this tool to test our applications.

Anypoint Studio enables users to drag and drop connectors and modules to create a Mule application. Many versions of Anypoint Studio are available, and it is recommended to practice in the latest version.

We will see how to download and install Anypoint Studio and what the different views, perspectives, and menu options available in Anypoint Studio are. Once familiar with the tool, we will learn how to create a simple *Hello World* Mule application and test the application using the **Postman** application.

After reading this chapter, you'll come away with an understanding of the following topics:

- What is Anypoint Studio?
- How to download and install Anypoint Studio
- Exploring the Mule Palette
- Getting familiar with various menu options and settings
- Creating and running a sample Mule application
- Exporting and importing the Mule application
- Exploring themes
- Installing software updates in Anypoint Studio

Technical requirements

You will need the following software for this chapter:

- Anypoint Studio: `https://mulesoft.com/studio`
- Postman application: `https://www.postman.com/downloads`

- We will use this tool to test the Mule application project.

- The exported JAR file of the first Mule application project, *Hello World*, is available in the following GitHub location

- `https://github.com/PacktPublishing/MuleSoft-for-Salesforce-Developers`

Let's get started by learning how to download and install Anypoint Studio.

Downloading and installing Anypoint Studio

In this section, we will learn how to download and install Anypoint Studio. The first step begins with downloading a software file to the computer, which may take a few minutes as the file size is around 2 GB. Afterward, we will install and launch Studio. Let's begin with downloading now.

Downloading Anypoint Studio

These steps can be followed for a simple and easy download:

1. Go to `https://mulesoft.com/studio`. Select the **operating system** (**OS**), Windows, Linux, or macOS, as per the computer's OS, and fill in the other required information.

2. Now, click **Download**.

The `.zip` (Windows/macOS)/`.tar.gz` (Linux) file of the latest version of Anypoint Studio is downloaded to the computer.

The Anypoint Studio file is bundled with the following components:

- **Mule runtime engine**

- **DataWeave**

- **MUnit**

- **MUnit Studio Plugin**

- **Eclipse**

- **Maven**

- **AdoptOpenJDK**

Now that we've downloaded the file, let's start the installation. The application can be simply installed by extracting the compressed `.zip/.tar.gz` file.

Installing Anypoint Studio

In this section, we will see how to install Anypoint Studio on the Windows OS. A similar procedure can be followed while installing it on other OSs, such as macOS and Linux:

1. Right-click the downloaded .zip file and click **Extract All**.

2. Provide the path where it needs to be extracted and click **Extract**. This extracts all the files into the mentioned folder.

> **Tip**
> For the Windows OS, do not extract the ZIP file in a large path. Try to place the file directly in C:/ or D:/. This helps avoid the *path is too long* error.

3. Once the extraction of the file is complete, check that all the components are in the installation folder, as shown in *Figure 3.1*, to confirm that the installation was successful:

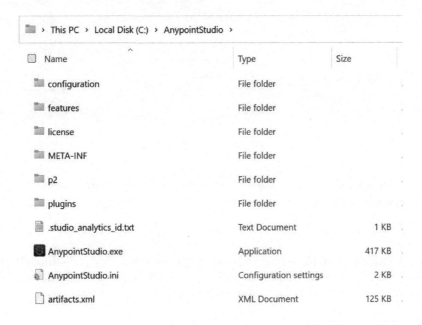

Figure 3.1 – Extracting Anypoint Studio for installation

We have extracted the folders to the chosen path. Next, we will see how to launch Anypoint Studio on our computer.

Launching Anypoint Studio

Follow these steps to launch Anypoint Studio:

1. Right-click on **AnypointStudio.exe** and select **Open**. The Anypoint Studio launcher will pop up.

2. Provide the workspace location by browsing the folder path and selecting where to store Mule projects (see *Figure 3.2*).

3. Check the **Use this as the default and do not ask again** checkbox so that the launcher doesn't ask for the workspace location the next time you open Anypoint Studio.

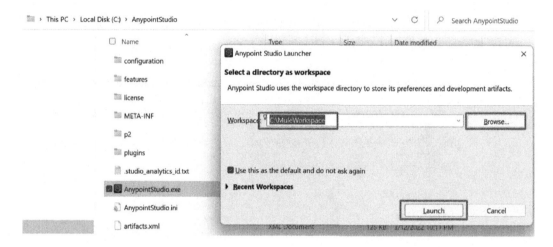

Figure 3.2 – Selecting a workspace location

4. After launching, we can change the workspace location anytime by selecting the **Switch Workspace** option under the file menu.

> **Note**
>
> A workspace is a location on your computer where all the work you do through Anypoint Studio is stored as files. It is easier to create one workspace and save it as the default so that the Anypoint Studio remembers the workspace next time.

5. Next, click **Launch** to open the welcome screen of Anypoint Studio.

6. Skip the introduction by clicking **Continue to Studio**. With this, we have launched Anypoint Studio successfully, as you can see in *Figure 3.3*:

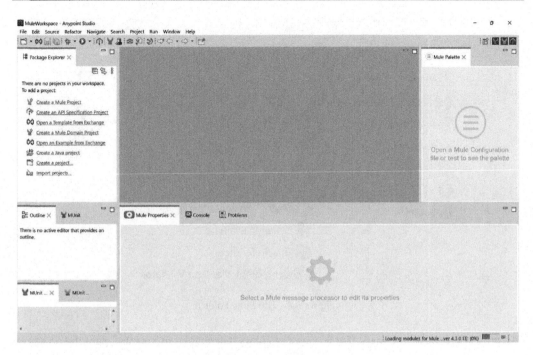

Figure 3.3 – Anypoint Studio: Home

Now that Anypoint Studio is all set, let us explore its various components and try building a Mule project. We will start by getting to know the Mule Palette.

Introducing the Mule Palette

The **Mule Palette** has modules and connectors that we can use in the flow. We can also download new modules or connectors from Anypoint Exchange, as shown in *Figure 3.4*. **Core**, **HTTP**, and **Sockets** are default modules in the Palette. Based on the project requirements, we can add modules to the Palette by using the **Add Modules** option. While developing a project, you can drag and drop the required components from the Mule Palette onto the canvas:

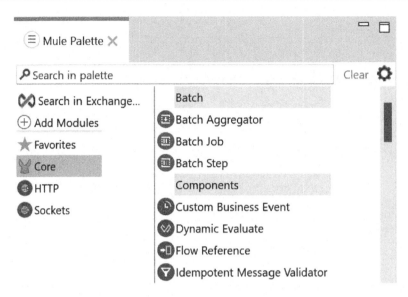

Figure 3.4 – The Mule Palette

An artist palette is a thin board that has a set of colors that enables mixing and painting on canvas. Similarly, the Mule Palette has collections of components that the developer can drag and drop onto the canvas to design or develop the Mule project.

With this, we have learned about the components available in the Mule Palette. Next, let's move on to learn about the Mule project structure.

Exploring the Mule project structure

Before getting into creating a Mule project, it is important that we get familiar with the Mule project structure. Let us see the project structure of a Mule application in Package Explorer. These are the main folders and files that are important for every Mule project:

- `src/main/mule` is for Mule configuration files. It is an `.xml` file that contains application logic where all the flow components reside. We can store *n* number of Mule configuration files to have different application logic, flows, or APIs and there is no limit enforced by Mule on the number of Mule configuration files. For example, we can store our API interface, API implementation, error handling, and the global configuration in separate Mule configuration files. This folder is for storing all your Mule XML code.

- `src/main/resources` is for Log4j configuration, any environment-specific properties files, DataWeave scripts, and API-related documents, such as the API specification and sample payload examples.

- `src/main/java` is for all Java programs.

- `src/test/resources` is for test files such as JSON, XML, and other formats that are required for testing.

- `src/test/munit` is for MUnit test cases.

- `mule-artifact.json` contains the `minMuleVersion` configuration, which specifies the minimum Mule runtime version that is required to deploy the application.

- `pom.xml` contains dependencies, shared libraries, repositories, and other project-related information.

Figure 3.5 clearly shows the project structure of a Mule application in which `helloworld.xml` is the Mule configuration file:

Figure 3.5 – Project structure

Similarly, we can see the other folders, as well as the `mule-artifact.json` and `pom.xml` files in the project structure.

Now that we've learned how Mule project folders are structured to store different folders and files, let's explore the different views and perspectives available in Anypoint Studio.

Introducing Mule views and perspectives

The **views** and **perspectives** of any IDE can be customized based on the user's preference. A perspective is nothing but a collection of views. Let's learn about different views and perspectives.

Views

Views in Anypoint Studio are the graphical representation of project metadata or properties for the active editor window. We can easily maximize, minimize, and remove views from the active window. The following are some of the views in Studio:

- **Mule Palette**: This manages modules and connectors.

- **Mule Properties**: This allows you to edit the properties of the module that is currently selected in the canvas.

- **Package Explorer**: This displays the Mule project folder and files.

- **Console**: This contains errors and other information about the embedded Mule runtime.

- **Problems**: This shows a list of issues that occurred in the project.

- **Outline**: This displays the structure of a Mule flow that is opened in the canvas.

- **MUnit**: This is a testing framework that helps to test the Mule application:

  - **MUnit Coverage**: This shows how much of a Mule application has been executed

  - **MUnit Errors**: This displays the errors that occurred during MUnit testing

- **Mule Debugger**: While in debug mode, this displays the Mule event structure, which consists of the payload (message), variables, and attributes.

- **Mule Breakpoints**: This shows a list of processors that are enabled with a breakpoint.

- **Evaluate DataWeave Expression**: While in debug mode, we can write any DataWeave expression to evaluate the results. We will be learning about DataWeave in detail in *Chapter 6*.

- **API Console**: This shows the generated API documentation.

These are the various views that we can see in the Anypoint Studio window. Each view gives information relevant to the particular view. On the whole, it gives a clear picture of what the user needs to see in the active window based on their preferences.

Perspectives

As mentioned earlier, a perspective is a collection of views and editors. The default perspective of Anypoint Studio is the **Design perspective**. We can create our own perspective and add any of the views.

The different perspectives already available in the Studio are:

- **Mule Design perspective**: This is the default perspective and is used while developing the Mule project
- **Mule Debug perspective**: This is the perspective used while testing the Mule project
- **API Design perspective**: This is the perspective used while writing the API specification

The user can change the perspective based on their role or activities. For example, a developer might choose the Design perspective, while a tester might choose the Debug perspective to test the application. By doing so, they can work easily with the required views. Now that we have explored the basics of Anypoint Studio, let's try and build our own Mule application.

Building, running, and testing a Mule application

We have explored various components, views, and perspectives of Anypoint Studio. Now it is time to put all of what we have learned together with a new project. The steps involved in every Mule project are *build*, *run*, and *test*. Let's elaborate on each step.

Building the Mule application

In this section, let us learn how to create a new Mule project:

1. Click the **Create a Mule Project** option from **Package Explorer** (see *Figure 3.6*) to create a new Mule application project, or go to the **File** menu, click **New**, and select **Mule Project**:

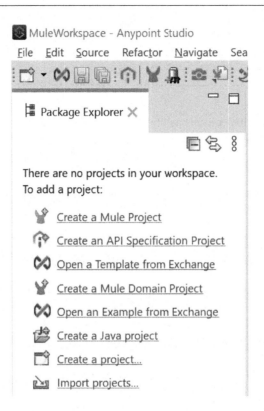

Figure 3.6 – Package Explorer

2. Provide the project name as *HelloWorld* and leave the remaining settings as they are, then click the **Finish** button (see *Figure 3.7*):

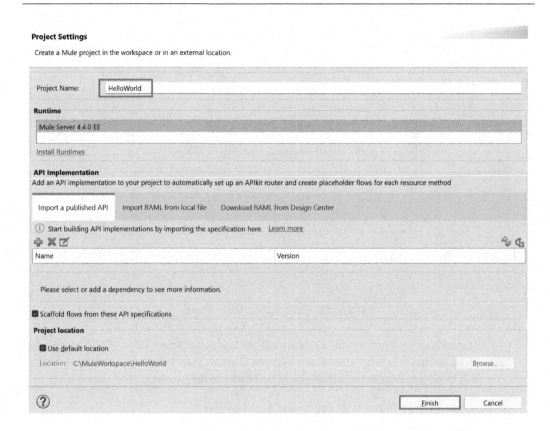

Figure 3.7 – Project Settings

- With this, we have successfully created the *HelloWorld* project.

- Whenever we create a new project, the **HTTP**, **Sockets**, and **Core** modules automatically get added to the project. We need to add the remaining required modules manually from the Mule Palette to the project. If the required module or connector is not available in the Mule Palette, we can search for it in Exchange and then add it to the project.

Figure 3.8 – Mule application – home

- In *Figure 3.8*, on the right, we can see the Mule Palette with the default **Core**, **HTTP**, and **Sockets** modules added. At present, the canvas is empty. Once we start building our Mule application, we will be adding components from the Mule Palette to the canvas.

3. Next, select **HTTP** in the Mule Palette and then **Listener**.

4. Drag and drop **Listener** onto the canvas.

5. Select **Listener** inside the canvas. In the **Listener** properties, add the connection configuration by pressing the **Add** symbol, as shown in the following figure:

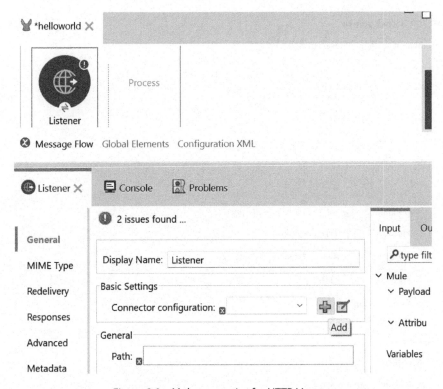

Figure 3.9 – Mule properties for HTTP Listener

6. Leave the host and port (8081) values as the default values and click the **OK** button on the connector configuration screen (see *Figure 3.10*):

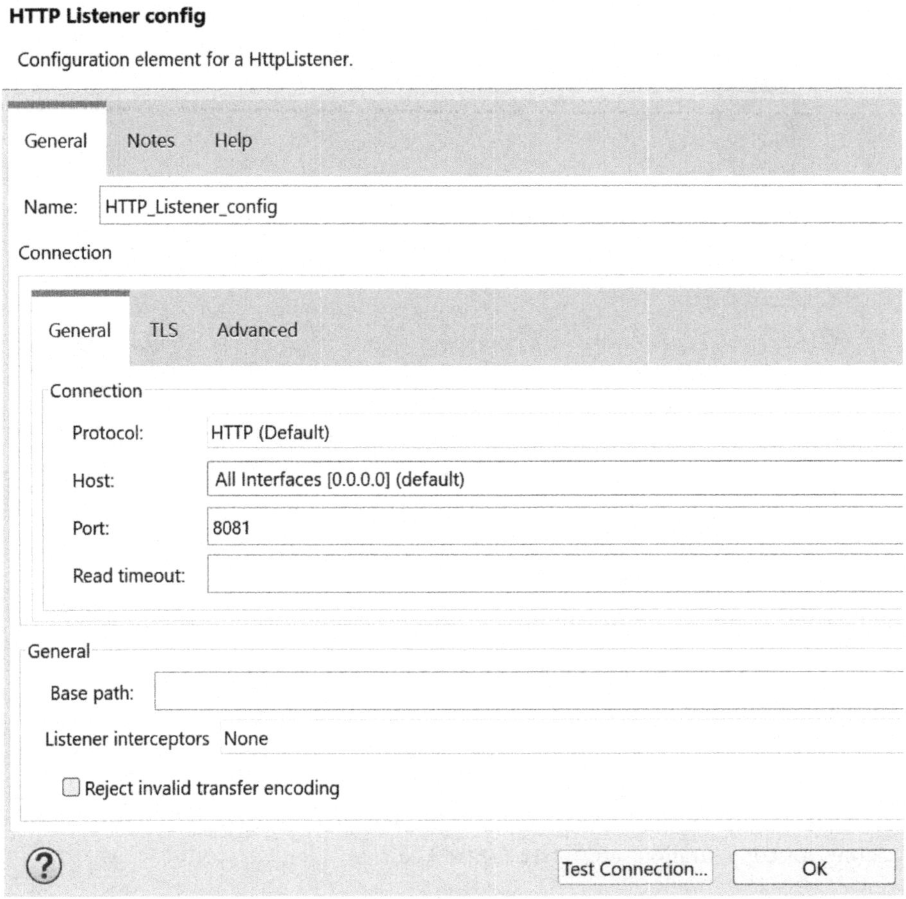

HTTP Listener config

Configuration element for a HttpListener.

| General | Notes | Help |

Name: HTTP_Listener_config

Connection

| General | TLS | Advanced |

Connection

Protocol: HTTP (Default)

Host: All Interfaces [0.0.0.0] (default)

Port: 8081

Read timeout:

General

Base path:

Listener interceptors   None

☐ Reject invalid transfer encoding

? Test Connection...   OK

Figure 3.10 – HTTP connector configuration

7.   Once done, set the **Path** value as /hello, as shown in *Figure 3.11*:

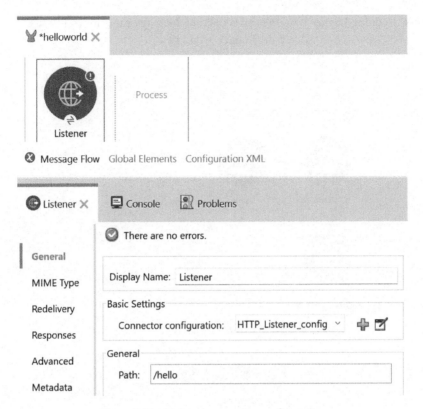

Figure 3.11 – Listener properties configuration

8. Next, search for Logger in the Mule Palette (see *Figure 3.12*). Drag and drop **Logger** on to the canvas, in the **Process** section. **Logger** is a Core component that logs the messages such as error messages, status information, request, response payloads and other important information.

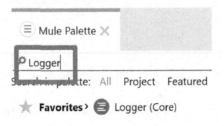

Figure 3.12 – Searching for Logger in the Mule Palette

- After dropping **Logger** onto the canvas, set the **Message** value to `Welcome to Hello world application` in the **Logger** properties.

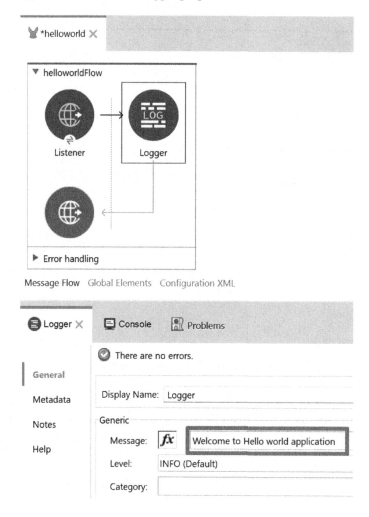

Figure 3.13 – Logger properties

9. Click on the **Core** module in the Mule Palette and select the **Transform Message** option.

Figure 3.14 – Mule Palette: Core module

10. Drag and drop the **Transform Message** selection to the canvas after the **Logger** step.

11. In the output section, change the output to `application/json` and also change the response as follows:

```
%dw 2.0
output application/json
---
{


"message" : "Hello World"
}
```

- **Transform Message** converts the structure from one format to another. In this example, we are converting the output format to JSON.

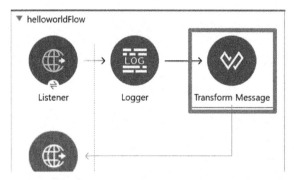

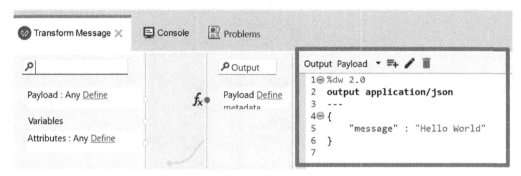

Figure 3.15 – DataWeave code in Transform Message

- Once we add the code in **Transform Message**, our code should look as in *Figure 3.15*.

12. Click the **File** menu -> Click Save button or press *Ctrl + S* to save the Mule application (see *Figure 3.16*):

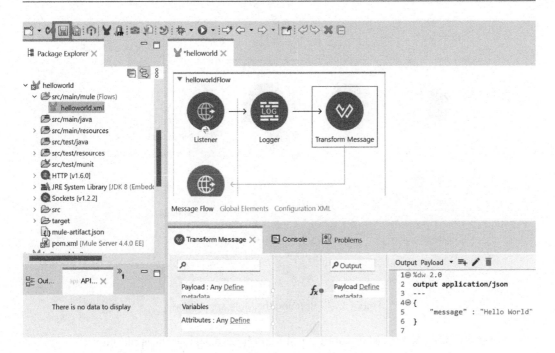

Figure 3.16 – Saving the Mule application

With this, we have created the Mule application successfully. The next step is to run the application, which involves nothing more than deploying the application into Mule runtime.

Running the Mule application

In this section, we will see how to run the Mule application from Anypoint Studio:

1. Go to the canvas, right-click on the empty space, and select **Run project helloworld**.

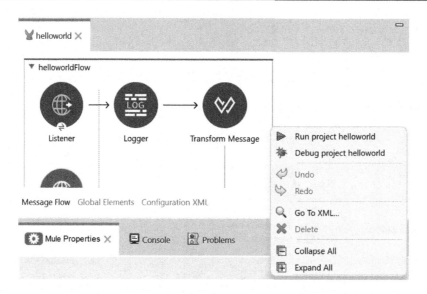

Figure 3.17 – Running the Mule application

2.   It starts the embedded Mule runtime inside Studio and deploys the application.

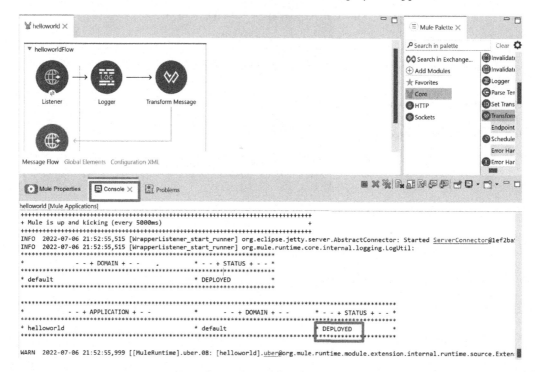

Figure 3.18 – Console view

- Once the application is deployed successfully, we will be able to see the logs showing the status as **DEPLOYED** in Console view (see *Figure 3.18*).

3. To terminate the project, we can right-click on **Console** and select the **Terminate/Disconnect All** option.

4. To clear the console log messages, right-click on **Console** and select the **Clear** option.

> **Tip**
>
> If the deployed status is **FAILED** due to **(java.net.BindException) or Caused by: java.net. BindException: Address already in use**, then try to use different ports, such as 8083, 8084, or any other port available in the system that is not used by any other applications.

Now that we have deployed the application in Anypoint Studio, the next step is to test the application.

Testing the Mule application

In this section, let us see how to test the Mule application using the API/web service testing tool (the **Postman** application).

> **Note**
>
> Postman is an application used for API/web service testing. It is an HTTP client that tests HTTP requests (GET, POST, and other methods) and receives the response. It is not related to Mule components. If you don't have a Postman application or any other web service testing tools on your computer, then install the Postman application by referring to the link that is referenced in the *Technical requirements* section of this chapter.

Once the application is deployed, you can follow these steps:

1. Open the Postman application.

2. In the URL box, enter http://localhost:8081/hello, provide the method name as **GET**, and then click **Send** (see *Figure 3.19*):

Figure 3.19 – Sending a request from the Postman app

We will receive a successful response with the **200** HTTP status code and the HTTP status description as **OK**. Also, we will be able to see the response message in JSON format, which we set in the **Transform Message** step (see *Figure 3.20*):

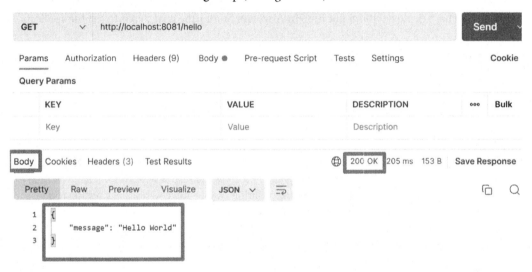

Figure 3.20 – HTTP successful response

3.   We can also see the message from the **Logger** step in the console (see *Figure 3.21*):

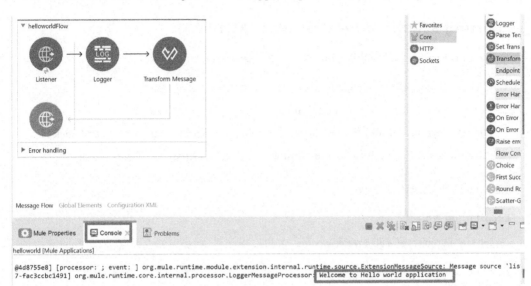

Figure 3.21 – Logger message in console

As you can see in the preceding figure, **Logger** has printed the required log message in the console. If the application is deployed into CloudHub, the **Logger** logs the message in the server log.

Good going! We are done with the very first Mule application project. In this *Hello World* project, the HTTP listener receives the incoming request, then, in turn, calls the logger to log the message, and finally, returns JSON output using the **Transform Message** step. Now, you should be confident enough to try other simple Mule projects using other components from the Mule Palette. As we move on, we will next explore how Mule files can be exported and imported.

Exporting and importing Mule files

In the previous example, we developed a new Mule project in Anypoint Studio. If we need to share the project with other developers or deploy this application into CloudHub or another deployment model, then we have to export the project.

We can export the project using the following options:

- Exporting a Mule application as a JAR file
- Exporting a Mule application as a filesystem

Let us look into each of these in detail.

Exporting a Mule application as a JAR file

Let's try exporting the Mule application as a .jar (Java Archive) file now:

1. Select the project in **Package Explorer**.
2. Click on the **File** menu and then **Export**.
3. Select **Anypoint Studio Project to Mule Deployable Archive** under **Mule** and click **Next**.
4. Browse to the file location on your computer and click **Finish** (see *Figure 3.22*):

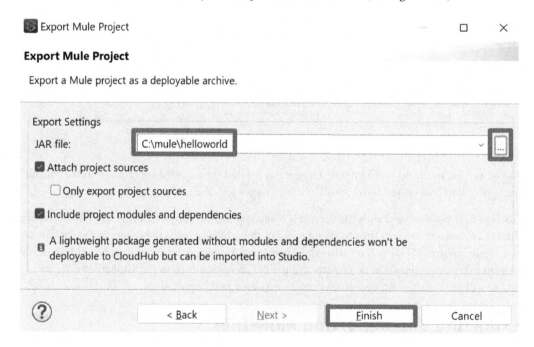

Figure 3.22 – Exporting settings as JAR

5. It packages the Mule application as a `.jar` file and exports the file to a given location. A success message pops up. Click **OK**.

6. We can see the exported `.jar` file in the location mentioned and the same `.jar` file can later be used to deploy the application directly into CloudHub.

We can share this `.jar` file with other developers to import into their Anypoint Studio. We can also use this `.jar` file to deploy the Mule application into CloudHub.

Now that we have got a clear idea of how to export a Mule application as a `.jar` file, let's try exporting it as a filesystem.

Exporting a Mule application as a filesystem

Let's try exporting a Mule application as a filesystem (as a folder and files) now:

1. Select the project in **Package Explorer**.

2. Click on the **File** menu and then **Export**.

3. Select **File System** under **General** and then click **Next**.

4. Browse to the folder location on your computer where the project needs to be exported and then click **Finish** (see *Figure 3.23*):

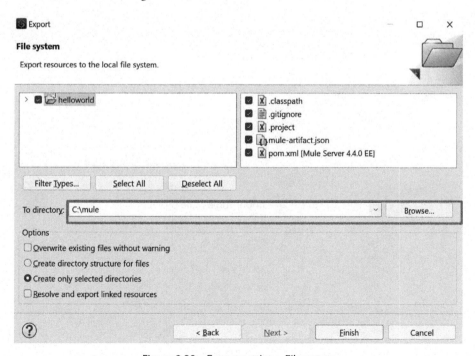

Figure 3.23 – Export settings: Filesystem

The Mule project is exported to the location specified as a filesystem.

By importing the filesystem into Anypoint Studio, it is easy to create a Mule application in Studio. This will be very useful when a user wants to share the Mule project with other users.

Now, let's see how to import a Mule application from a .jar file.

Importing a Mule application from a JAR file

Let's try importing a Mule application from a .jar file in Anypoint Studio:

1. Click on the **File** menu and select **Import**.

2. Under **Anypoint Studio**, select **Packaged mule application (.jar)** and click the **Next** button.

3. Browse to the .jar file that we want to import into Anypoint Studio. Provide the project name and click **Finish** (see *Figure 3.24*):

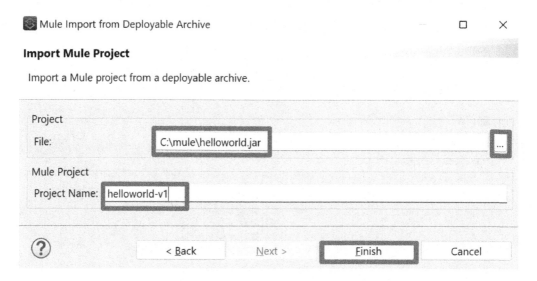

Figure 3.24 – Importing a Mule project

4. As you can see in the following figure, the project is imported into Anypoint Studio:

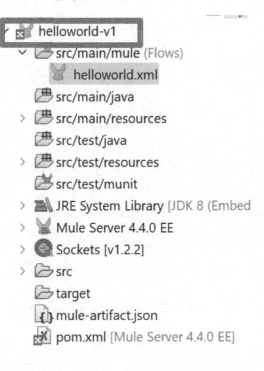

Figure 3.25 – Imported project from Package Explorer

As shown in *Figure 3.25*, we have imported the `.jar` file and created our Mule project successfully. Let's explore another option to import the Mule project.

Importing a Mule application from the filesystem

Let's try importing a Mule application from the filesystem (as a folder and files) now:

1. Click on the **File** menu and select **Import**.
2. Under **Anypoint Studio**, select **Anypoint Studio project from File System** and click **Next**.
3. Browse to the Mule application project from the filesystem that we want to import into Anypoint Studio. Provide the project name and click **Finish** (see *Figure 3.26*):

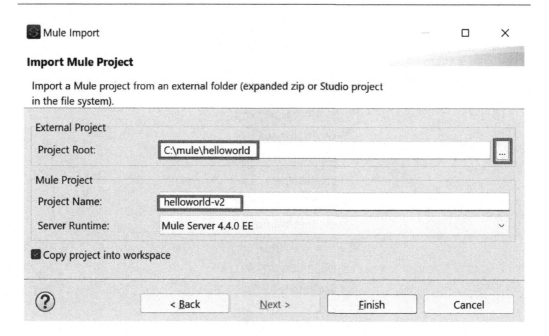

Figure 3.26 – Importing a Mule project

> **Note**
>
> If you don't uncheck the **Copy project into workspace** checkbox, shown in the previous screenshot, and you're using a Git repository, your changes won't be reflected in the original project folder. Instead, a copy of the project will be created under Anypoint Studio's current workspace. If you want to continue using the original project folder from your Git repository, then make sure you uncheck this option.

Now, the project is imported into Anypoint Studio (see *Figure 3.27*):

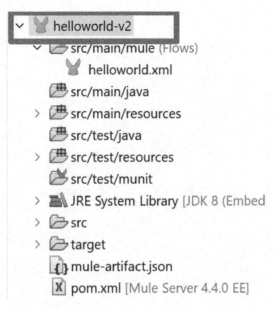

Figure 3.27 – Imported project in Package Explorer

As shown in the preceding figure, we have imported the filesystem and created our Mule project successfully.

With this, we can conclude that we have learned the concept of exporting and importing Mule applications.

We can also change or enhance the appearance of the Anypoint Studio user interface by updating the theme. Let's move on to learn more about themes.

Updating the theme in Anypoint Studio

Each developer prefers a different user interface. Some may prefer a dark theme, while others like a light theme. The theme sets the mood for the developer to help them focus. For example, a dark theme reduces strain on the eyes and makes it easier to notice the different syntaxes as they come with different colors. The look and feel of Anypoint Studio can be updated based on user preferences. Let's learn how to change the theme:

1. Click on the **Window** menu and select **Preferences**.

2. Type Theme. Select **Appearance** under **General**. In the right pane, choose the desired theme from the dropdown. In this example, let us select **Studio Dark Theme**. Now, select **Apply and Close** (see *Figure 3.28*):

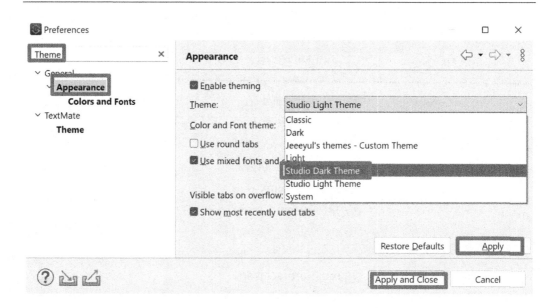

Figure 3.28 – Studio appearance

- The dark theme is applied to Anypoint Studio. A restart is required for the theme change to take full effect.

3.   If we need to revert the theme to the default theme, again type Theme, then select **Appearance** under **General**, choose **Studio Light Theme**, and select **Apply and Close**.

With this, we have learned how to customize the IDE experience by changing the theme in Anypoint Studio.

Now that we're familiar with multiple concepts and the working of Anypoint Studio, it is important to note the importance of updating the software in Anypoint Studio. Let's see how to do this in the next section.

Installing software updates in Anypoint Studio

Software updates are mandatory for bug fixing, getting new features, and avoiding performance issues. Let's see how to update the software in Anypoint Studio:

1. Click on the **Help** menu and select **Check for Updates**.

2. Check the available updates and click **Next** (see *Figure 3.29*):

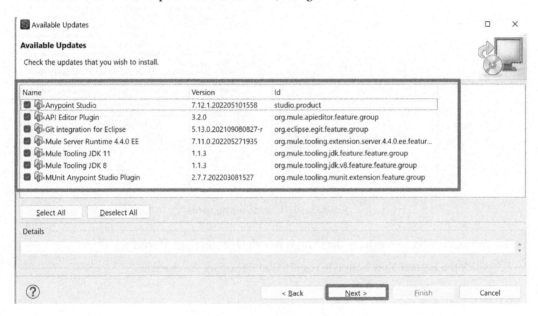

Figure 3.29 – Available Updates

3. Select the radio button for **I accept the terms of the license agreements** and click the **Finish** button (see *Figure 3.30*):

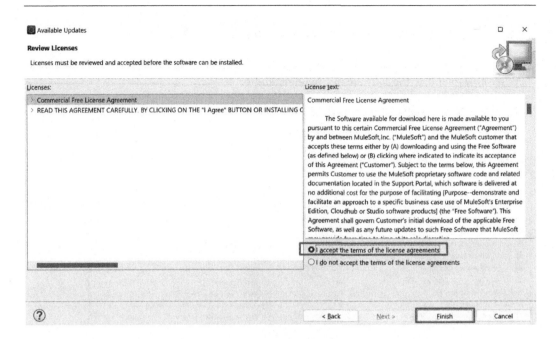

Figure 3.30 – License agreements

4. We will be able to see the update progress at the bottom right of Studio.

5. Click the **Restart Now** button to restart Studio to apply the changes.

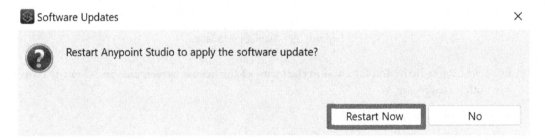

Figure 3.31 – Restart Now

It is always recommended to periodically check for any software updates.

Summary

In this chapter, we explored how to download and install Anypoint Studio. We also had a look into the various views and perspectives, as well as the Mule Palette. We created a *Hello World* Mule application using the HTTP connector, after which we tried to run it. Finally, we tested it using an external Postman application.

We also learned about exporting and importing a Mule application. This is important when we need to deploy these applications into different deployment models (CloudHub, on-premises, and so on) and also to share them with other developers. We next saw how to update the theme and software version of Anypoint Studio.

On completing this chapter, you have an elaborate enough knowledge of the Anypoint Studio IDE to feel confident in developing your own Mule application.

In the next chapter, we'll explore Core module components within Anypoint Studio to understand more about flow controls, scope, endpoints, transformers, batch, and error handling.

Questions

Take a moment to answer the following questions to serve as a recap of what you just learned in this chapter:

1. What's the default port for an HTTP listener in a Mule application project?
2. Can any other port be used as the HTTP listener port other than the default port?
3. Which file has the dependency details of the Mule application?
4. In which view can we see the Mule runtime startup logs and other logs logged by the **Logger** step?
5. Why do we use the Postman application?
6. Where can we find the modules and connectors in Anypoint Studio?
7. List some of the perspectives.

Answers

1. 8081.

2. Yes. We can use other ports that are not used by any other application in the machine while running an application in Anypoint Studio.

3. pom.xml.

4. Console view.

5. We can use the Postman application to test the web services.

6. The Mule Palette.

7. Mule Design perspective, Mule Debug perspective, and API Design perspective.

4

Introduction to Core Components

In the previous chapter, we learned about Anypoint Studio, its capabilities, and how to build a Mule Application using it. To utilize Anypoint Studio efficiently and get the most out of it, we need to have a basic understanding of the **Core** components in MuleSoft.

In this chapter, we will learn about various Core components, scopes, and routing strategies. To simplify integration and leverage the capabilities of Anypoint Studio, it's essential to study the Core components used. We will also learn about various error handling strategies, which is also an important topic from the MCD Certification perspective.

We will cover the following topics in this chapter:

- The flow and structure of a Mule event
- Understanding various flows, flow controls, transformers, routers, and scopes in MuleSoft
- Batch processing
- Error handling

Technical requirements

We need to install the following for this chapter:

- Anypoint Studio installation (refer to *Chapter 3*, *Exploring Anypoint Studio*, for installation guidance)

Before getting started with the Core components, we should have a basic understanding of a **Mule flow**. In the next section, we shall learn about the Mule flow and its components in depth.

Getting familiar with a Mule flow

Previously, we've built a simple Mule application consisting of the following:

- An HTTP Listener as an **event source**

- A Transform Message component and a Logger as an **event processor**

Here, the event source and event processor are the key elements of a Mule flow.

The Mule flow is responsible for the sequential execution of logical operations to achieve the desired outcomes, with the help of several Mule components and connectors.

You can consider it similar to a Salesforce flow.

A Mule flow is divided into two parts (see *Figure 4.1*):

- **Event source**

  - It consists of an inbound endpoint that listens to the incoming request from the client or an event-based trigger and further forwards the request to event processors. It also receives a response in the end, which is returned to the client.

  - Some of the commonly used message sources are HTTP, JMS, FTP, and Poller/Scheduler, based on a new event (for example, using Salesforce Connector on New Object).

- **Event processors**

  - They're mainly Mule-based connectors responsible for performing a logical transformation on the data or metadata received as a part of the incoming requests or the previous transformer, enhancing payload, connecting to end systems, and more.

  - **DataWeave** is mainly responsible for performing complex data transformations in Mule 4. We shall learn more about it in *Chapter 6*.

  - Event processors can be published by MuleSoft or third-party organizations. They need not be Mule-specific and can also be built into different services and languages such as **Enterprise Java Beans (EJB)**, Spring beans, **Plain Old Java Object (POJO)**, and Python.

Figure 4.1 shows the typical structure of a Mule flow:

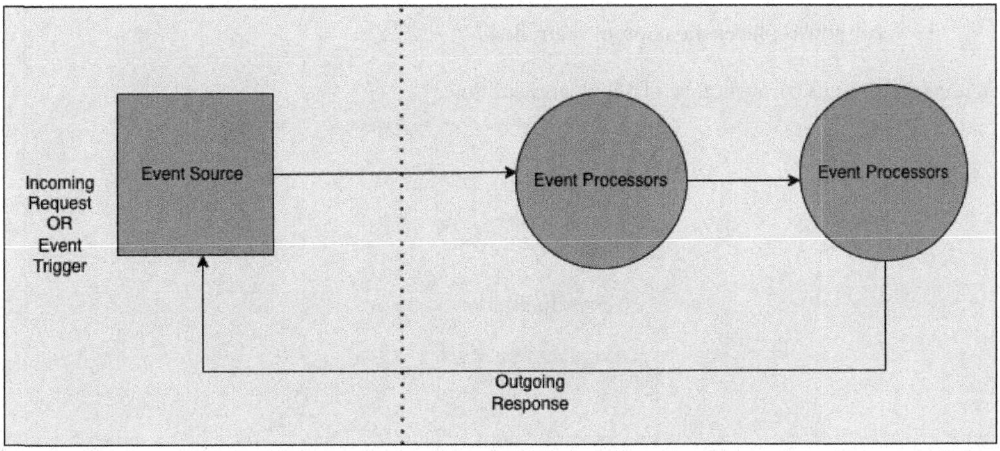

Figure 4.1 – A Mule Flow

To summarize, a Mule flow is based on event-driven architecture. Whenever an event is triggered at the Mule event source, it forwards the request to various event processors, performs tasks, and returns the response or acknowledgment to the event source.

We shall now learn about different types of Mule flows.

Exploring the types of Mule flow

You can use two types of Mule flow as per your requirements. Let us understand the types of flows used in Mule:

- **Main flow (flow)**

  - It consists of source and processor sections. We can trigger the flow using sources such as HTTP, JMS, FTP, and a Scheduler.

  - Each flow can have its own error-handling strategy.

  - By default, the flow is executed when the source is triggered. If you want the flow to be stopped initially or to be triggered manually, you can disable the flow on start and later trigger the flow manually from Runtime Manager.

- **Subflow**

  - A subflow doesn't have a source component and hence cannot be triggered by an event. It is referenced by the parent flow using a flow reference connector.

- They inherit the exception-handling strategy from the parent flow and do not possess their own exception scope.

- A subflow replaces the content main flow.

Figure 4.2 shows us the structure of a flow and subflow:

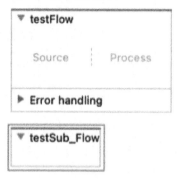

Figure 4.2 – The structure of a flow and subflow

In *Figure 4.3*, we can see the subflowB subflow is referenced by the flowA parent flow. We have also referenced a flowC main flow from the flowA parent flow.

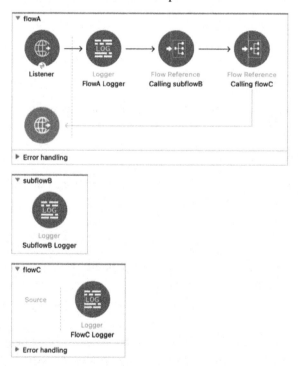

Figure 4.3 – The relation between a flow and subflow

Similarly, we can have a deeper nesting of flows and subflows to optimize the operations. However, it is always advisable to reference a subflow instead of a flow for better performance.

The execution sequence here would be the following:

```
FlowA -> Listener -> FlowA Logger -> Calling subflowB -> SubflowB
Logger -> Calling flowC -> FlowC Logger
```

If we are dealing with concurrent or multi-threading execution as with batch processing, we should avoid doing so inside a subflow, as this may lead to the creation of multiple events and thereby give incorrect results.

Now that we have seen that the Mule event is an atomic part of the Mule flow, let's understand the structure of the Mule event.

Understanding the Mule event structure

The Mule event structure is responsible for carrying all the information pertaining to a particular event. It is immutable, which means that whenever there is a change to an instance of a Mule event, a new instance is created. You can access all the properties of a Mule event and hence, it's important to understand its structure.

A Mule event is mainly divided into a **Mule message** and **variables** (see *Figure 4.4*):

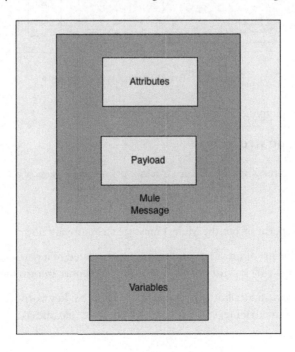

Figure 4.4 – A Mule event

A Mule message

The message structure in Mule 4 has undergone severe changes compared to Mule 3. Let's review both message structures now.

The Mule 3 message structure

Figure 4.5 depicts the message structure in Mule 3. It consisted of several components, such as a message object (message, header, and payload), variables, attachment, and exception payloads.

It is considered to be a bit complicated compared to that of Mule 4.

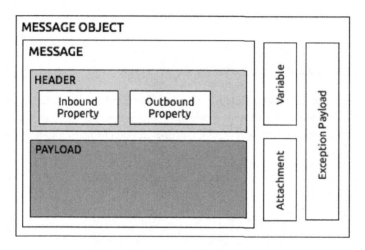

Figure 4.5 – The Mule 3 message structure

Let us now review the simplified Mule 4 message structure.

The Mule 4 message structure

Figure 4.4 shows us that the Mule 4 message structure primarily consists of attributes and the payload.

- **Attributes**

  - Inbound properties from the Mule 3 message structure are now attributes.

  - Attributes consist of metadata and information related to a particular Mule event such as headers, status codes, error details, and request-response information.

  - You can access an attribute using the `attributes` keyword. For example, to access a method in your attribute, you use `#[attributes.method]`.

- **Payload**

  - The payload consists of the data received as a part of incoming requests or the data set by the previous processor.

  - The payload can be a file (text or CSV, for example) or data supporting several formats (JSON or XML, for example) of varying sizes.

  - You can access the entire payload or a part of the payload using the `payload` keyword. For example, you use `#[payload]` to access the entire payload.

Now, we understand the Mule message structure and the changes undergone in Mule 4 as far as the message structure goes. We've also learned about its Core components: the attributes and the payload. Now, let's learn about the next component of a Mule event, which is the variables.

Variables

- Variables are used to store a value. You can define a variable consisting of the key as the variable name and the value as the value of the variable.

- Variables can be created using the Set Variable component, Transform Message connector, or by setting the target variable in any connector.

- You can access a variable using the `vars` keyword. For example, in order to access a particular variable, you can use `#[vars.<variable_name>]`, where `variable_name` denotes the name of the variable.

- Besides storing static values, a variable can also be used to write transformation logic using the DataWeave scripts.

The following screenshot (see *Figure 4.6*) of Anypoint Studio while debugging a Mule application depicts the information carried by a Mule event. You can retrieve all the components of the Mule event. In order to get better, more hands-on experience, try debugging a Mule component and study the Mule event structure.

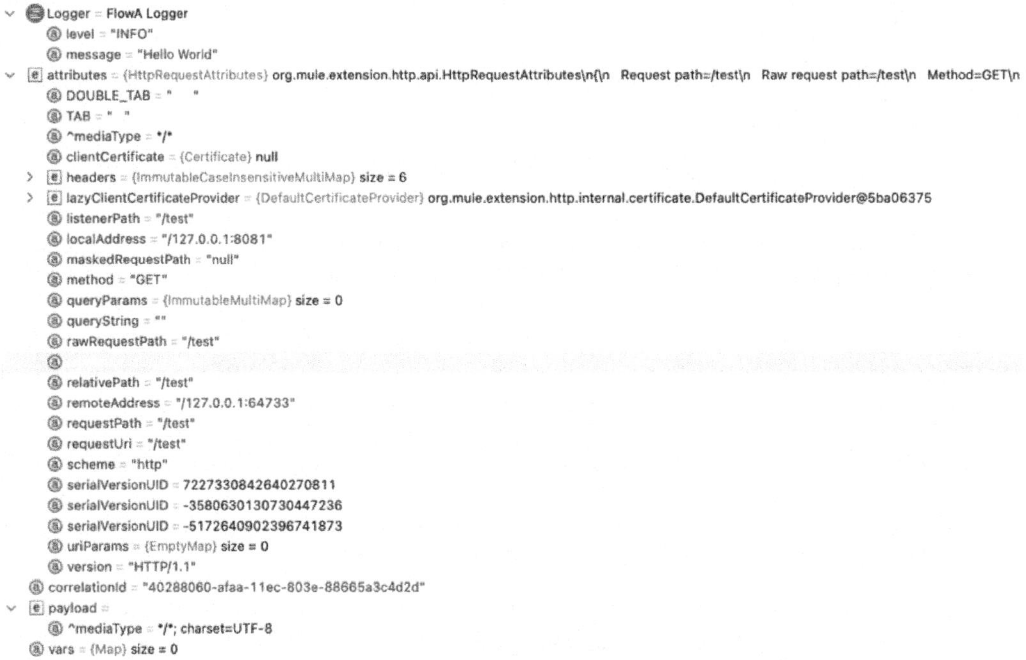

∨ ⊕ Logger = FlowA Logger
      ⓐ level = "INFO"
      ⓐ message = "Hello World"
∨ ⓔ attributes = {HttpRequestAttributes} org.mule.extension.http.api.HttpRequestAttributes\n{\n Request path=/test\n Raw request path=/test\n Method=GET\n
      ⓐ DOUBLE_TAB = "   "
      ⓐ TAB = " "
      ⓐ ^mediaType = */*
      ⓐ clientCertificate = {Certificate} null
   > ⓔ headers = {ImmutableCaseInsensitiveMultiMap} size = 6
   > ⓔ lazyClientCertificateProvider = {DefaultCertificateProvider} org.mule.extension.http.internal.certificate.DefaultCertificateProvider@5ba06375
      ⓐ listenerPath = "/test"
      ⓐ localAddress = "/127.0.0.1:8081"
      ⓐ maskedRequestPath = "null"
      ⓐ method = "GET"
      ⓐ queryParams = {ImmutableMultiMap} size = 0
      ⓐ queryString = ""
      ⓐ rawRequestPath = "/test"
      ⓐ
      ⓐ relativePath = "/test"
      ⓐ remoteAddress = "/127.0.0.1:64733"
      ⓐ requestPath = "/test"
      ⓐ requestUri = "/test"
      ⓐ scheme = "http"
      ⓐ serialVersionUID = 7227330842640270811
      ⓐ serialVersionUID = -3580630130730447236
      ⓐ serialVersionUID = -5172640902396741873
      ⓐ uriParams = {EmptyMap} size = 0
      ⓐ version = "HTTP/1.1"
   ⓐ correlationId = "40288060-afaa-11ec-803e-88665a3c4d2d"
∨ ⓔ payload =
      ⓐ ^mediaType = */*; charset=UTF-8
   ⓐ vars = {Map} size = 0

Figure 4.6 – A Mule event while debugging a Mule application

In this section, we've learned about the Mule flow, the types of Mule flow, and the Mule event structure.

Now that we've understood the basics of a Mule flow, in the next section, we will learn about the **Core** components in MuleSoft and their applications.

Core components

The **Core** components constitute a large section of the Mule palette. They are responsible for the logical transformation, routing, and processing of Mule events. You can find Core components by default in the palette section of Anypoint Studio, which means that you don't have to download them explicitly. In order to use these components, simply drag and drop the components from the Mule palette to the Canvas.

Figure 4.7 depicts the **Core** components in Anypoint Studio. We will learn more about them in this section:

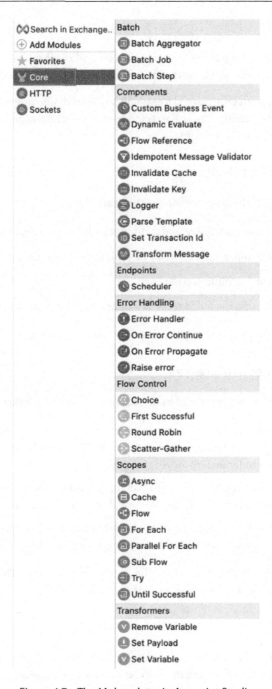

Figure 4.7 – The Mule palette in Anypoint Studio

We shall now dive deeper into the different **Core** components, starting with the **Batch** scope.

Batch

The prime functionality of the **Batch** scope is to process and synchronize a large number of records with ease, which makes it one of the most popular and widely used components.

Mule's **batch processing strategy** divides a large number of records into individual records and processes them asynchronously. By default, Mule's **Batch** scope processes 100 records per batch, which utilizes 16 threads – however, this is configurable.

Features of the Batch scope

A few prime features of the batch processing strategy are listed here:

- The capability to process large records and files with less processing time
- The parallel processing of records helps us achieve near real-time transformation
- It has its own error-handling section
- It helps us to reprocess the failed records and hence, achieve the maximum throughput

Now, we shall learn about the batch processing stages in the next section.

The batch processing stages

The batch processing strategy is executed in three stages, namely the following:

1. **Load and Dispatch**: This is an initial and implicit stage in batch processing. It is responsible for creating batch job instances, converting a payload into a collection of records, and splitting the collection into individual records for processing.

2. **Process**: This is a mandatory phase in batch processing wherein all records are processed asynchronously based on the number of threads and the batch size.

3. **On Complete**: This is the last phase of batch processing. It is also a mandatory or default phase. It summarizes the execution of batch processing and makes reports available for statistics.

See *Figure 4.8* to understand the structure of the **Batch** scope in Mule. The **Batch** scope comprises three components in the Mule palette. Let us look into each of these in detail.

A batch step

This is the smallest unit of the **Batch** scope and is a part of a batch job. It is divided into two sections, namely the **processors** and the **aggregators**. Processors are responsible for processing the records or carrying out the logical transformation. Once the records in a particular batch step are processed, their result is aggregated in the aggregator section.

We can have multiple batch steps within the **Batch** scope.

You can configure the acceptance policy of processed records by setting **Accept Policy** to:

- `NO_FAILURES`: The record which has been executed successfully in the previous steps will be processed. This is also considered the default acceptance policy.

- `ALL`: All the records will be processed.

- `ONLY_FAILURES`: The records which have failed in the previous steps will be processed.

We can see the layout of the **Batch** scope and batch step in *Figure 4.8*:

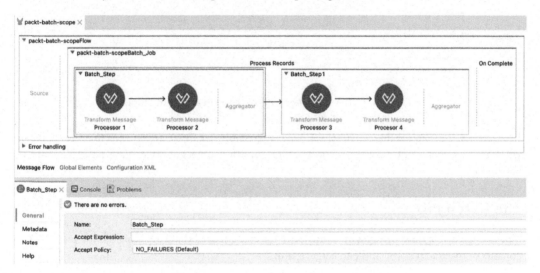

Figure 4.8 – A batch step in Anypoint Studio

Now, let's talk about the batch aggregator.

The batch aggregator

You can aggregate the records processed by the **Batch** scope using the batch aggregator. You can define the number of records to be added to form a collection and implement the task defined in the **Batch Aggregator** scope:

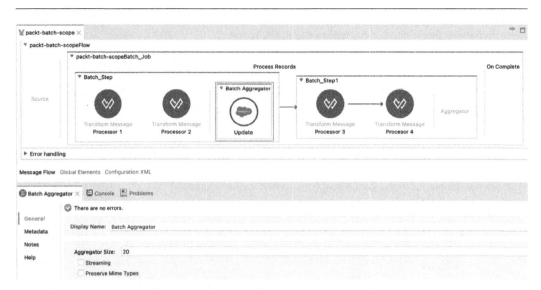

Figure 4.9 – The Batch Aggregator scope in Anypoint Studio

In *Figure 4.9*, you can see that we've set the batch aggregator size to **20**. This means that the aggregator will form a collection of records and update the Salesforce object at once. Now, let's talk about the batch job.

The batch job

This is responsible for creating a batch instance for every record that runs through the processors. It consists of the **Batch** scope and batch aggregator.

In order to configure it, you can set the following:

- **Max failed records**: You can set a threshold to allow the maximum permissible number of failed records. It can have three values:

  - 0: The default value is zero. It states that the execution of records is stopped whenever a record fails. This is the default value for Max failed records.

  - -1: A negative one denotes that the execution will continue even if there are infinite failures.

  - integer: A positive integer denotes the threshold value of the maximum number of permissible failed records. For example, setting Max failed records to 10 denotes that only 10 failed records will be allowed, and post 10 records, the execution terminates.

- **Scheduling strategy**: We can define our scheduling strategy for the batch process as one of the following:

  - ORDERED_SEQUENTIAL: This is the default strategy. The instances are executed sequentially based on their timestamps. We follow the **First In First Out (FIFO)** algorithm.

  - ROUND_ROBIN: In this strategy, the instances are executed using the round-robin algorithm.

- **Job instance ID**: This is a **unique ID (UUID)** created that gives us information about a batch job. You can access this ID using the batchJobInstanceId variable. It's helpful while debugging and logging the batch job execution.

- **Batch block size**: This denotes the number of records to be processed in a block by a single thread. By default, the block size is 100.

- **Max concurrency**: This defines the concurrent execution we want in our batch processing, as in, the amount of parallel execution. The default (and maximum) value is 16.

- **Target**: You can define an explicit variable to store the result of batch execution.

Figure 4.10 shows the configuration of the batch job:

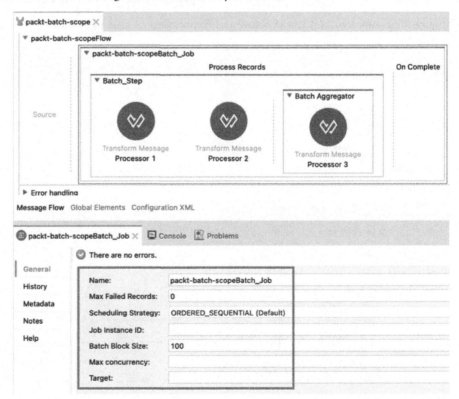

Figure 4.10 – A batch job in Anypoint Studio

A few examples of batch processing include the following:

- Synchronizing data from Salesforce or any other end system

- Processing or reading records from a large file or end system

However, it is not ideal to use the batch scope if the number of records is small, as it involves a large overhead.

We have covered all the important aspects of batch processing. Let's move ahead with the **Components** scope in Mule.

Components

Components consist of scopes to enhance your data or metadata of your Mule event. Let us learn about a few components used in Mule, starting with **Custom Business Event**.

Custom Business Event

Custom Business Event is used to add metadata and **key performance indicators (KPIs)** to your flow.

To configure the component, set **Event Name** and **Expression / Value** to evaluate the event (see *Figure 4.11*):

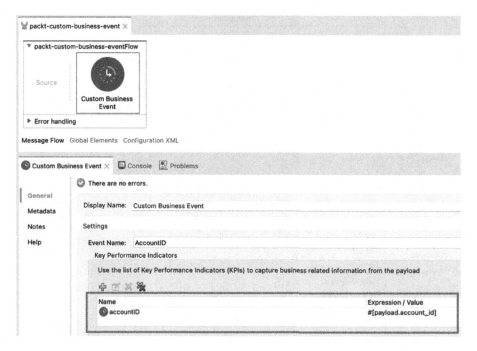

Figure 4.11 – Custom Business Event in Anypoint Studio

Figure 4.11 shows us the configuration of **Custom Business Event**.

In order to enable insights into the metadata (see *Figure 4.11*), do the following:

1. Go to **Runtime Manager**.

2. Choose your environment.

3. Select the application deployed, **Insights**, select the radio button, **Metadata**, and select **Insight** on the left-hand tab.

4. Configure the flow name to view the metrics.

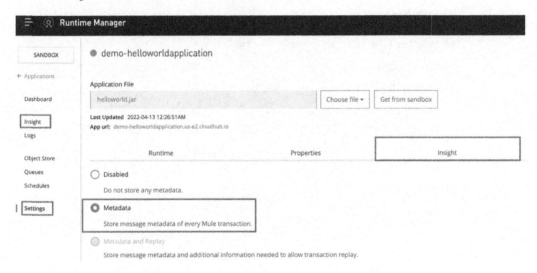

Figure 4.12 – The configuration of Insights in Anypoint Platform

We can now configure metadata inside the **Insight** section, as shown in *Figure 4.12*.

Let's move on to the next component, which is **Dynamic Evaluate**.

Dynamic Evaluate

Dynamic Evaluate is helpful when you want to evaluate a DataWeave file (a `.dwl` file) dynamically while running a Mule application.

In *Figure 4.13*, we can see that we've configured a simple DataWeave expression, `#[payload.dataweaveFile]`, which helps us evaluate a DataWeave file dynamically at runtime:

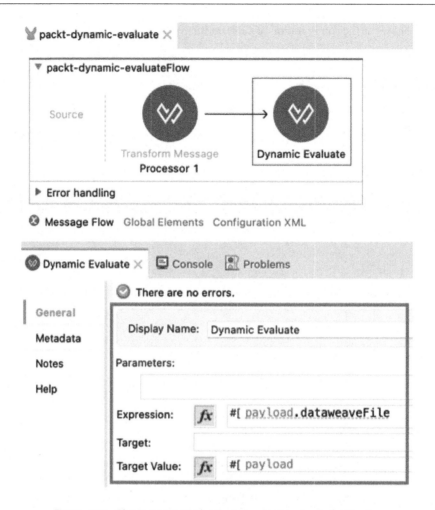

Figure 4.13 – The Dynamic Evaluate component in Anypoint Studio

Figure 4.13 shows us the configuration of the Dynamic Evaluate component.

The next component is **Flow Reference**, which we covered in the *Exploring the types of Mule flow* section (see *Figure 4.3*). So, let's jump to **Idempotent Message Validator**.

Idempotent Message Validator

Idempotent Message Validator helps you to validate that the flow processes only use unique messages. It raises an error, DUPLICATE_MESSAGE, if a duplicate message is spotted.

In order to configure it, you need to provide the Id and Value expressions to fetch the unique identifiers. By default, the Id expression is set to #[correlationId] (see *Figure 4.14*):

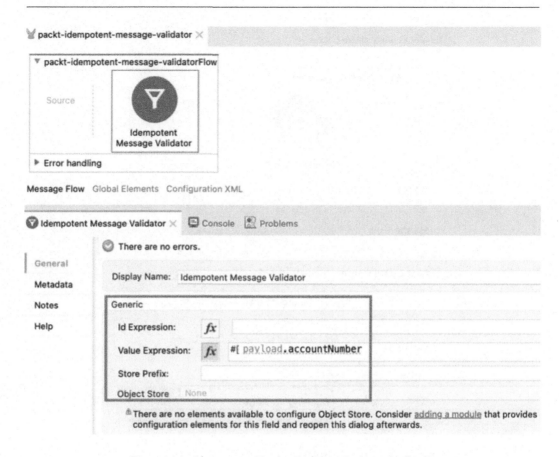

Figure 4.14 – Idempotent Message Validator in Anypoint Studio

Figure 4.14 shows how you can configure **Idempotent Message Validator**. The next component is **Invalidate Cache**.

Invalidate Cache

Invalidate Cache helps you to clear the cache entries by resetting the cache. In order to configure it, you need to fill the **Caching strategy** field in (see *Figure 4.15*):

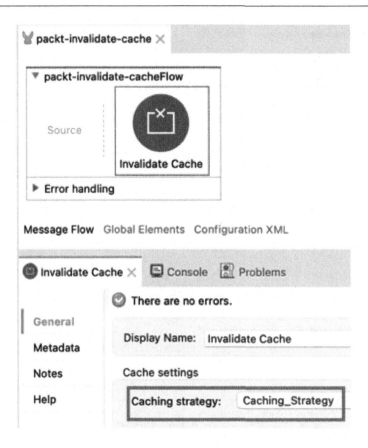

Figure 4.15 – The Invalidate Cache component in Anypoint Studio

Figure 4.15 shows the configuration of the **Invalidate Cache** component. After **Invalidate Cache**, let's take a look at a similar component named **Invalidate Key**.

Invalidate Key

Invalidate Key helps you clear the cached key referenced in your caching strategy. In order to configure this, select **Caching strategy** and the key that you wish to invalidate (see *Figure 4.16*):

Figure 4.16 – The Invalidate Key component in Anypoint Studio

Figure 4.16 shows the configuration of the **Invalidate Key** component. Let's move on to one of the most widely used components, **Logger**.

Logger

The **Logger** component helps you log important messages, errors, and the status of an application. It's helpful when debugging and monitoring your application.

You can simply drag and drop the **Logger** component from the Mule palette into any flow or subflow, as shown in the following figure. To configure **Logger**, you need to fill in **Message**, which could be with a simple `String` or a DataWeave script. Make sure you do not log any sensitive information, as it'll be retained.

You can view the application logs here: `MULE_HOME/logs/<app-name>.log`. You can also configure the path and customize the logging tools (Splunk or ELF, for example) explicitly in `log4j.xml`.

As you can see in the following figure, INFO (default) is the default **Level** input – the other levels are DEBUG, ERROR, TRACE, and WARN. Setting log levels will help you to filter out certain logs while debugging.

You can also club logs into a different category. In order to categorize logs, you can set **Category** to String. *Figure 4.17* shows the configuration of the **Logger** component:

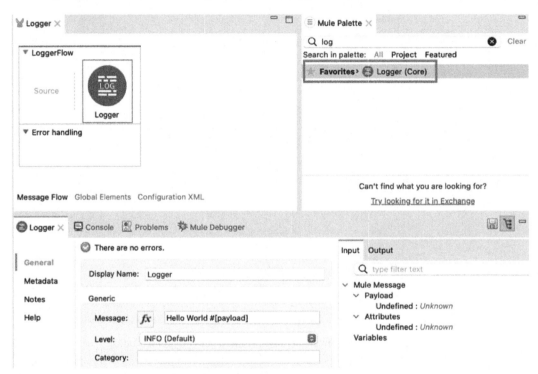

Figure 4.17 – The Logger component in Anypoint Studio

The next component in our list is **Parse Template**.

Parse Template

This component helps you to process an embedded Mule expression or an external file.

To configure it, you need to provide content or an external file (see *Figure 4.18*). As you can see, we're getting the user information from Salesforce and later passing it through an HTML template:

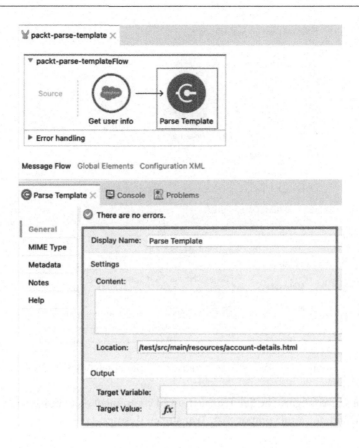

Figure 4.18 – The Parse Template component in Anypoint Studio

Figure 4.18 shows the configuration of the **Parse Template** component. Let's go ahead with our next component, which is **Set Transaction Id**.

Set Transaction Id

This helps you set a **Transaction ID** value, which helps you keep a track of a record when logging, monitoring, or analyzing data.

You can configure it by adding **Set Transaction Id**, which could be a `string`, integer, or DataWeave expression, as in the following, which helps you generate a universally unique identifier:

```
    %dw 2.0
output application/json
---
uuid()
```

Figure 4.19 – The Set Transaction Id component in Anypoint Studio

Figure 4.19 helps us configure the **Set Transaction Id** component. Let's move on to one of the most frequently used and powerful components, **Transform Message**.

Transform Message

Transform Message helps you with the conversion of a data format and with the logical transformation of data. **Transform Message** can perform complex data transformations. It uses the DataWeave expression language in order to perform the transformation.

We shall learn more in depth about **Transform Message** and DataWeave in *Chapter 7*, *Transforming with DataWeave*.

Now that we have studied the various components, let's learn more about the **Endpoints** scope in the Mule palette.

Endpoints

Endpoints help you to trigger a Mule event to start the execution of a Mule flow. They are present in the message source part of the Mule flow.

Let us learn more about one of the endpoints in the Mule palette, Scheduler.

A Scheduler

A **Scheduler** component is one of the components that can act as a trigger to start a Mule event.

You can use a **Scheduler** component when you want to poll or synchronize data from Salesforce or any other end system, poll **change data capture events (CDC events)**, or enable watermarking.

You can schedule an event based on two scheduling strategies:

- **Fixed frequency**: You can set a fixed frequency, defining the regular interval at which you want your Mule event to be triggered.

In *Figure 4.20*, we've configured the frequency to every 1000 milliseconds. We have other unit options, such as minutes, seconds, and so on, under **Time unit**:

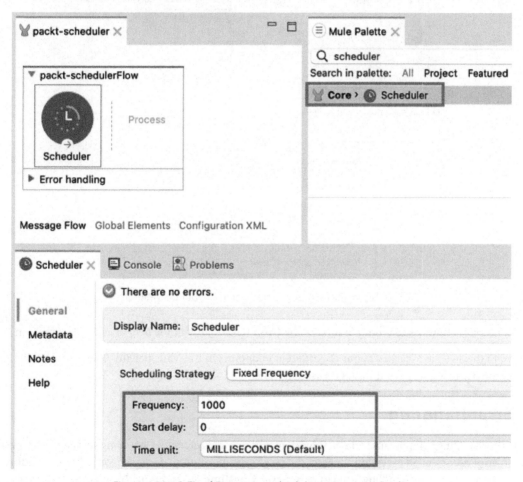

Figure 4.20 – A Fixed Frequency scheduler in Anypoint Studio

Figure 4.20 shows the configuration of the **Fixed Frequency** scheduler. The next component is the **Cron** scheduler:

- **Cron**: You can use a `cron` expression to schedule an event. You can generate it with the free cron expression tools available online.

As we can see in *Figure 4.20*, we've configured a `cron` expression to trigger a Mule event every 5 minutes and as per the `Europe/London` time zone. Similarly, we can set **Cron** schedulers to be triggered weekly, monthly, or at any time fixed interval, and within any time zone. The default time zone is UTC:

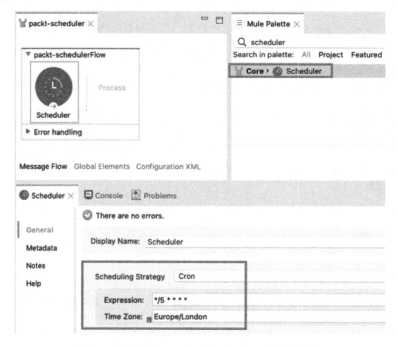

Figure 4.21 – A Cron scheduler in Anypoint Studio

Figure 4.21 shows us the configuration of the **Cron** scheduler with the help of a CRON expression.

With this, we have learned about the different endpoints in the Mule palette. Let us now study the **Error Handling** scope and strategies used in Mule.

Error handling

Error-handling components form an important part of Mule's exception-handling strategy. Whenever an error occurs, or an exception is raised, the flow's execution control is moved to the **Error Handling** scope and the error-handling strategy (**On Error Continue** or **On Error Propagate** is executed) is implemented (see *Figure 4.22*):

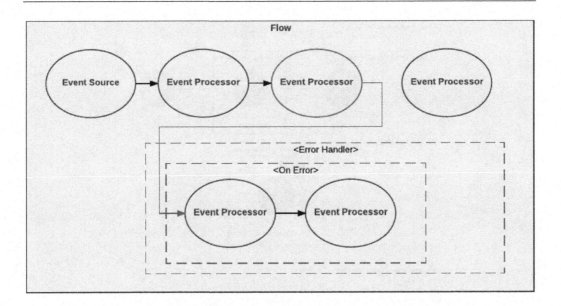

Figure 4.22 – Mule's error-handling mechanism

Figure 4.22 shows us the Mule's error-handling mechanism. Let us now learn about different **Error Handling** scopes, starting with **On Error Continue**. Apart from **On Error Continue**, there is **On Error Propagate**, **Raise Error**, and **Error Handler**.

On Error Continue

If an error occurs and the **On Error Continue** scope is defined in the **Error Handling** section, then the flow's normal execution is stopped and the processors inside the **On Error Continue** scope are executed.

A success response is returned in the case of **On Error Continue**.

As seen in *Figure 4.23*, if an error occurs at **Processor 2**, then flow control is moved to the **On Error Continue** scope, and **Processor 4** is executed. A success message is returned to the source.

The order of execution is: Processor 1|Processor 2|an error occurs| Processor 4.

You can also select the error type from the drop-down list in the **Type** section. ANY includes all error types:

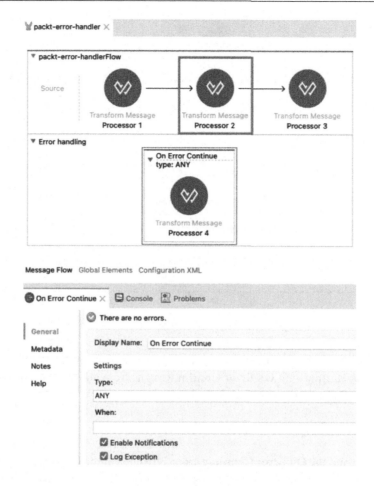

Figure 4.23 – The On Error Continue scope in Anypoint Studio

Figure 4.23 helps us with the configuration of the **On Error Continue** scope.

On Error Propagate

If an error occurs and the **On Error Propagate** scope is defined in the **Error Handling** section, then the flow's normal execution is stopped and the processors inside the **On Error Propagate scope** are executed.

An error response is returned in the case of **On Error Propagate**.

In *Figure 4.24*, if an error occurs at **Processor 2**, then the flow control is moved to the **On Error Propagate** scope, and **Processor 4** is executed. A success message is returned to the source.

The order of execution is: Processor 1|Processor 2|an error occurs| Processor 4.

You can also select the error type from the drop-down list in the **Type** section. ANY includes all error types:

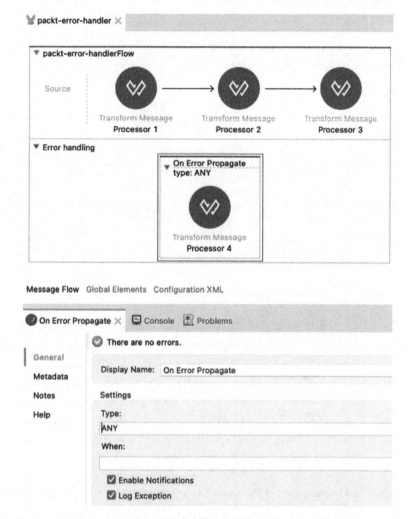

Figure 4.24 – The On Error Propagate scope in Anypoint Studio

Figure 4.24 shows us the configuration of the **On Error Propagate** scope. The next **Error Handling** scope is **Raise Error**.

Raise Error

The **Raise Error** component helps you throw an error deliberately. You can compare it to the throw keyword in common programming languages such as C++ or Java.

In order to configure **Raise Error**, we can select the error type in the **Type** section, but it's optional.

In *Figure 4.25*, we can see that an error is raised when the `#[!isEmpty(payload)]` condition is not met:

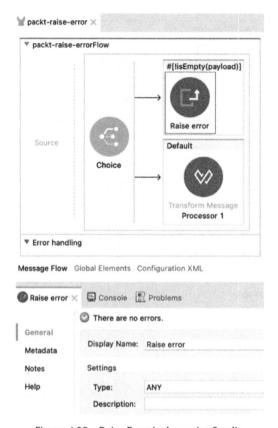

Figure 4.25 – Raise Error in Anypoint Studio

Figure 4.25 shows the configuration of the **Raise Error** scope.

We can handle the raised error using any error-handling strategy, such as **On Error Continue** or **On Error Propagate**, in the **Error Handling** section of the flow.

The next **Error Handling** scope is **Error Handler**.

Error Handler

Whenever an error is raised or an exception occurs, the Mule error event is forwarded to the Mule **Error Handler** scope. **Error Handler** can contain multiple error handlers such as **On Error Continue** and **On Error Propagate**. It matches the raised exception to behave as per the error-handling strategy mentioned.

By default, it's an empty scope. We can add one of the error-handling strategies (**On Error Continue** or **On Error Propagate**), as shown in *Figure 4.26*:

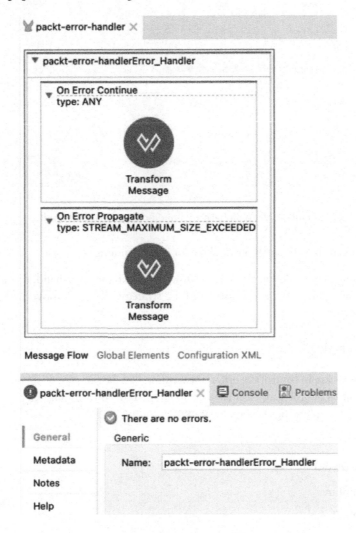

Figure 4.26 – A global error handler in Anypoint Studio

You can have a dedicated file for managing all the errors in one place, usually named `global-error-handler.xml`.

To create a global file for error handling, in the **Global Elements** section of `global-error-handler.xml`, go to **Create | Global Configuration | Global Element Properties**, set **Default Error Handler** as `<name of your global error handler file>`, and hit **OK** (see *Figure 4.27*):

Figure 4.27 – A global error handler file in Anypoint Studio

Figure 4.27 shows us how to create a global file for error handling.

We have now studied the different **Error Handling** scopes and the error-handling mechanism, which form an important part of the exception-handling strategy. Now, let's move ahead with the **Flow Control** mechanism.

Flow control

Flow control helps you to control the order of execution of a flow or subflow by routing the message to the same or different processors. Let us learn about the flow control components used in Mule. We will be exploring the following components in this section:

- **Choice**
- **First Successful**
- **Round Robin**
- **Scatter-Gather**

Let's get started with the first one, **Choice**.

Choice

The **Choice** router helps you select the route based on the condition satisfied. It is similar to the `if-else` block or the `switch` block in common programming languages.

To configure a **Choice** router, just drag the component from the Mule palette. By default, it consists of two routes, namely, the one that satisfies the criteria, and the default route to take if the condition is not met. You can drag and drop any other processor from the Mule palette to build upon the route (see *Figure 4.28*):

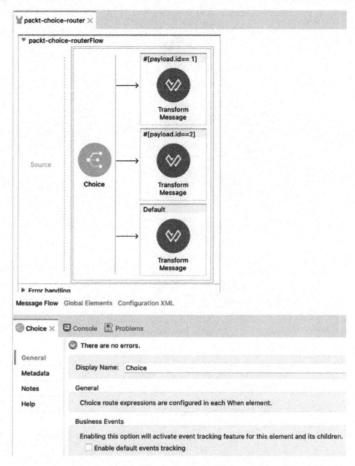

Figure 4.28 – A Choice router in Anypoint Studio

Figure 4.28 shows us the configuration of the **Choice** router.

First Successful

The **First Successful** router iterates through all the routes in sequence until one of the routes executes successfully. If none of the routes execute successfully, it throws an error.

To configure it, you can set the initial state to `started` or `stopped`. You can also set the maximum concurrency to the number of processes to be executed concurrently. Both the values are optional.

In *Figure 4.29*, we can see there are three routes. Here, the first route throws an error – hence, the second route is executed. The second route is the first successful route – hence, the flow terminates here, and the third route is not executed:

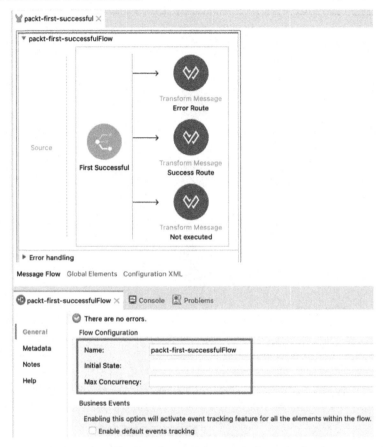

Figure 4.29 – The First Successful router in Anypoint Studio

Figure 4.29 shows us the configuration of **First Successful**.

Round Robin

The **Round Robin** router helps you to execute each route at a time, in a circular manner, every time the flow is executed. It keeps track of previously executed flows and executes the next route. If the currently executed route is the last one, it traverses back to the first route in the next iteration.

In *Figure 4.30*, we can see that every time the Mule flow is triggered, the order of execution will be the following:

```
Processor 1|Processor 2|Processor 3|Processor 1
```

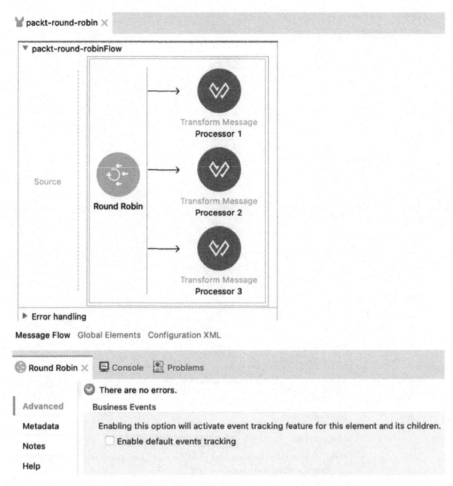

Figure 4.30 – The Round Robin router in Anypoint Studio

Figure 4.30 helps us to understand the configuration of the **Round Robin** router. The next router is **Scatter-Gather**.

Scatter-Gather

The **Scatter-Gather** router routes the Mule event through parallel routes simultaneously. The parallel execution of the Mule event speeds up the processing.

All three transformers will execute in parallel whenever the Mule event is triggered (see *Figure 4.31*).

Updating multiple Salesforce objects or end systems simultaneously are some of the applications of a **Scatter-Gather** router. To configure it, you can set **Initial State** and **Max Concurrency** values, but that is optional:

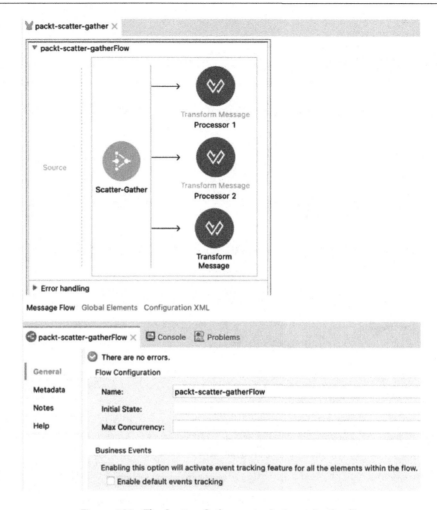

Figure 4.31 – The Scatter-Gather router in Anypoint Studio

Figure 4.31 shows us the configuration of the **Scatter-Gather** router.

We've now learned about several **Flow Control** scopes, which will help us in choosing the right flow control scope or router when building our integrations.

We shall now study several other **Scopes** options in Mule Palette and their applications.

Scopes

Scopes usually represent a block of code that executes several Mule processors, as per the characteristics of the scope. We shall now learn about the various scopes which are a part of the **Core** components in Mule.

Async

The **Async** scope helps you add an asynchronous block of code into your flow.

If the processors in the main flow are taking a long time to execute and there is no dependency on the response from those processes, we can club them together in the **Async** scope.

You can configure the scope by simply setting the **Max concurrency** value as equal to the number of messages that you wish to be executed concurrently (see *Figure 4.32*):

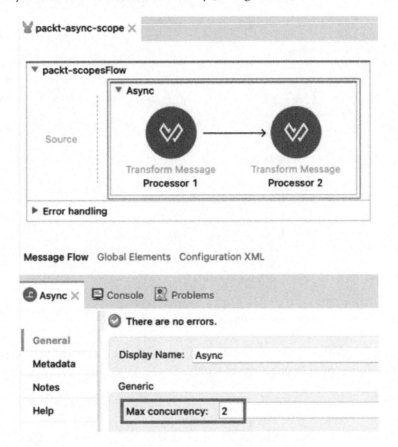

Figure 4.32 – The Async scope in Anypoint Studio

Figure 4.32 shows us the configuration of the **Async** scope. The next scope is **Cache**.

Cache

The **Cache** scope helps you to store frequently recurring data. It helps the processing time of similar events by reusing the cached event.

You can select a default caching strategy or a customized one (see *Figure 4.33*):

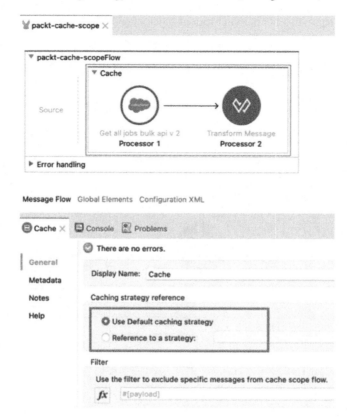

Figure 4.33 – The Cache scope in Anypoint Studio

Figure 4.33 helps us to understand the configuration of the **Cache** scope. The next scope in our list, **Flow**, is another of the most frequently used scopes.

Flow

Flow helps you carry out the sequential execution of Mule processors. You can trigger a flow with the help of a Message source or invoke it using a **Flow Reference** component (see *Figure 4.3*).

For Each

The **For Each** scope helps you to iterate over an object. It is similar to the `for` loop used in basic programming languages.

To configure the **For Each** scope, you need to specify a collection over which the loop will iterate, the name of the counter variable, and the batch size to group the messages (see *Figure 4.34*):

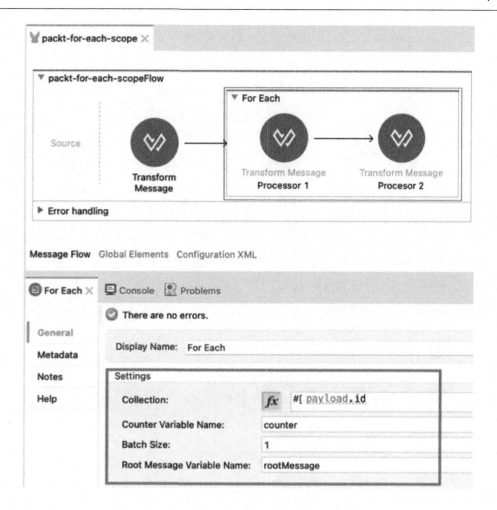

Figure 4.34 – The For Each scope in Anypoint Studio

Figure 4.34 shows us the configuration of the **For Each** scope. The next scope in our list is the **Parallel For Each** scope.

Parallel For Each

Parallel For Each splits the message into smaller batches, processes them concurrently, and aggregates them later to give a consolidated result.

As we can see in *Figure 4.35*, the configuration of **Parallel For Each** is similar to that of each scope:

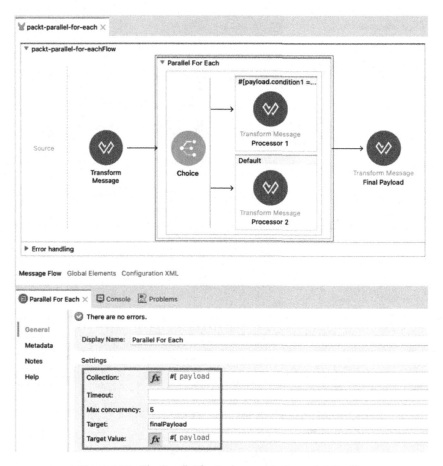

Figure 4.35 – The Parallel for Each scope in Anypoint Studio

Figure 4.35 helps us with the configuration of the **Parallel For Each** scope. Let's learn about the next scope in our palette, which is **Sub Flow**.

Sub Flow

Sub Flow helps you to execute the sequential execution of Mule processors. It does not consist of a Message source. It is invoked by a Mule flow (see *Figure 4.3*).

Try

The **Try** scope enables you to handle an error that may result while executing a processor inside a `try` block. The **Try** scope supports transactions. It is similar to the `Try-Catch` block in the basic programming language.

It is useful when we want a customized error-handling strategy for a particular component.

You can configure **Transactional action** and **Transactional type**. In *Figure 4.36*, we're going ahead with the default options:

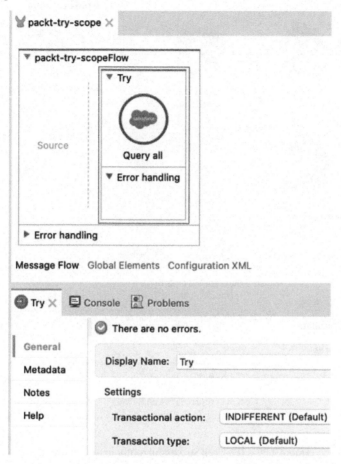

Figure 4.36 – The Try scope in Anypoint Studio

Figure 4.36 shows the configuration of the **Try** scope. Let's move ahead with our next scope, which is **Until Successful**.

Until Successful

As the name suggests, the **Until Successful** scope lets you retry a processor until it succeeds or the maximum number of retries is exhausted.

To configure the **Until Successful** scope, you need to define the maximum number of retries and milliseconds between two consecutive retries (see *Figure 4.37*):

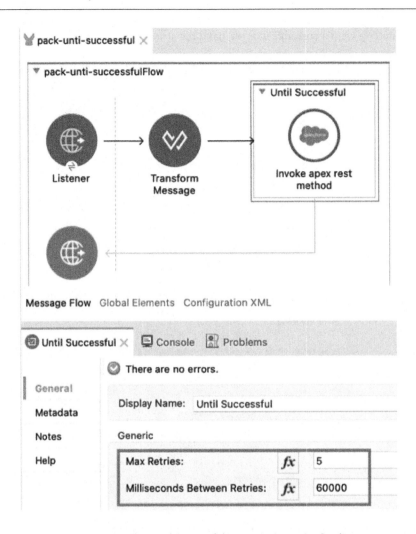

Figure 4.37 – The Until Successful router in Anypoint Studio

Figure 4.37 shows us the configuration of the **Until Successful** scope.

We have now studied the selection of scopes available in Mule, which are helpful from a routing perspective.

Let's move ahead with learning more about **Transformers**.

Transformers

Transformers are the processors mainly responsible for enhancing or transforming the Mule event. They're responsible for carrying out all the logical transformations. Let us learn about a few transformers.

Set Variable

You can configure a new variable in a Mule event with the help of the **Set Variable** component. To configure the variable, you need to assign a name and value to the variable (see *Figure 4.38*):

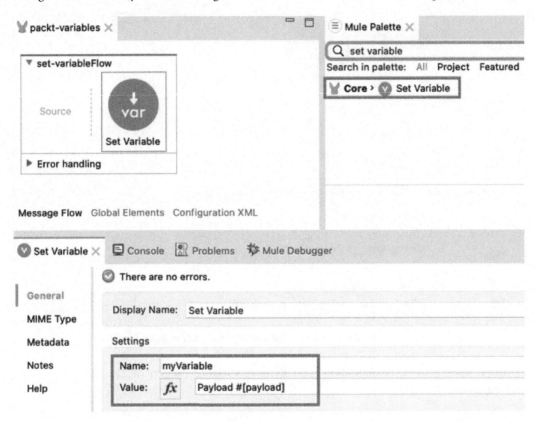

Figure 4.38 – The Set Variable component in Anypoint Studio

Figure 4.38 shows us the configuration of the **Set Variable** component. The next component is **Remove Variable**.

Remove Variable

This component helps you to remove an existing or default Mule variable from the Mule event.

To configure the **Remove Variable** component, you need to enter the name of the variable that needs to be removed from the Mule event (see *Figure 4.39*):

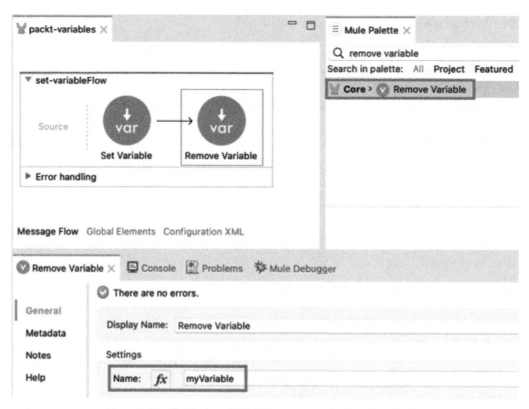

Figure 4.39 – The Remove Variable component in Anypoint Studio

Figure 4.39 shows us the configuration of the **Remove Variable** component. The next component is **Set Payload**.

Set Payload

It helps to override the existing payload and sets a new payload. To configure the **Set Payload** component, just drag and drop the connector from the Mule palette and enter the value of the payload.

The value could be a `String` or a DataWeave expression. You can also set the MIME type and encoding details in the **MIME Type** section, but that's optional (see *Figure 4.40*):

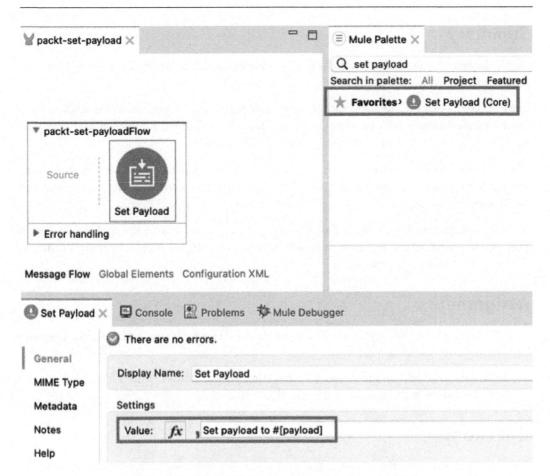

Figure 4.40 – The Set Payload component in Anypoint Studio

Figure 4.39 shows us the configuration of the **Set Payload** component.

> **Note**
> In this chapter, we've mostly used **Transform Message** as the processor, but you can use any processor any number of times, as per the use case.

We have learned about the transformers in Mule – now, let's solve a few assignment problems to get hands-on experience with the Core components.

Summary

In this chapter, we've learned about all the Core components in Mule's Anypoint Studio. We have also understood the architecture of the Mule event.

The Core components tell us about various routing strategies, scopes, flow control strategies, event-processing mechanisms, error handling, and so on. To become a proficient MuleSoft developer or an architect, it's essential that we know about these Core components.

Choosing the right component as per your use case helps you achieve the maximum throughput and optimum results. Learning about these Core components is also important from a MuleSoft certification perspective.

In the next chapter, we'll learn about the capabilities of Anypoint Platform, the configuration of the platform, and the different entities in Anypoint Platform. We will also get a better understanding of the entire iPaaS tool in the next chapter.

Assignments

- Create a simple Mule application that logs a unique ID every 10 min. Add **On Error Continue** as the error-handling mechanism.

- Create a batch job that processes a file containing 10,000 records (use the file on GitHub). Sort the records by account ID and log payload.

Questions

Take a moment to answer the following questions to serve as a recap of what you just learned in this chapter:

1. What is the difference between **For Each** and **Parallel For Each**?
2. What is the difference between the **Async** scope and a subflow?
3. When should you use batch processing and when to use **Parallel For Each**?
4. What is the difference between a **Choice** router and **Scatter-Gather**?

Answers

1. **For Each** splits the collection into records and processes them sequentially in iteration, whereas **Parallel For Each** processes them simultaneously.

2. Async flows run parallel with the main flow without obstructing the other operations of the main, whereas a subflow is a part of the main flow that continues the execution of the main flow.

3. When you have a large number of records to be processed you should go ahead with batch processing – otherwise, you can continue using **Parallel For Each**, as it has less overhead.

4. The **Choice** router evaluates the condition and routes the request to a particular route that satisfies this condition, whereas **Scatter-Gather** processes multiple routes in parallel.

All About Anypoint Platform

The terms Anypoint Studio and Anypoint Platform may sound similar and thus confusing. However, they are completely different and serve different purposes. Anypoint Studio is an **integrated development environment** (IDE), which we use to build, test, and run Mule applications. We thoroughly explored it in *Chapter 3, Exploring Anypoint Studio*, and *Chapter 4, Introduction to Core Components*. **Anypoint Platform**, on the other hand, is a **user interface** (UI)-based control plane, which manages a variety of components such as **Design Center**, **Exchange**, **Runtime Manager**, and so on. We will be learning all of this in depth in this chapter.

After reading this chapter, you'll know more about the following topics:

- Different components in Anypoint Platform
- What an API specification, an API Fragment, and AsyncAPI are in API Designer
- How to develop a Mule application in Flow Designer
- How to publish assets from an Exchange portal to a public portal
- How to deploy a Mule application from Runtime Manager
- How to create Runtime Manager alerts
- API Manager, Anypoint Monitoring, and Visualizer
- Access Management (organization and business groups)

Technical requirements

We will be using the Anypoint Platform that we already configured in *Chapter 2, Designing Your API*.

Here is the login link: `https://anypoint.mulesoft.com/login/`.

The `.jar` file used for deployment later in this chapter in the *Deploying to CloudHub* section is available in the following GitHub path in the `Chapter3` folder: `https://github.com/PacktPublishing/MuleSoft-for-Salesforce-Developers`.

Introducing Anypoint Platform

Anypoint Platform is a single platform that facilitates designing an API, storing assets, deploying any application to the cloud/on-premises, getting real-time visibility, and troubleshooting issues. It helps organizations to connect applications, data, and devices. It consists of the following components:

- Design Center
- Exchange
- Runtime Manager
- API Manager
- Anypoint Monitoring
- Anypoint Visualizer
- Access Management (organization and business groups)
- Data Group
- Data Gateway
- MQ
- Secrets Manager

In the upcoming sections, we will explore some of these components in detail.

Getting started with Design Center

Design Center is a tool that is used to design and build APIs in Anypoint Platform. Here, we design and test the API specification first, before the actual development. This is called the API design-first approach. We can share the API specification with other developers to consume the API even before we start the development. The two main components of Design Center are API Designer and Flow Designer.

API Designer

API Designer is a platform for designing, documenting, and testing APIs in **RESTful API Modeling Language** (**RAML**) or **OpenAPI Specification** (**OAS**) with code-based or visually guided experience. It also generates interactive API documentation in the API console, which provides information on APIs and their methods. Before the actual implementation, an API developer can also test their APIs in the API console itself.

> **Note**
> RAML is a YAML-based language for describing RESTful APIs. OAS, an open API specification formerly known as Swagger specification, is a standard for defining RESTful interfaces.

In the API Designer, we can design an API specification, fragment, and AsyncAPI. Let us learn more about them.

API specification

An API specification is API documentation that helps developers/consumers understand the API. This specification has API requests, response structures, methods, endpoints, examples, and other required details to consume the API. This is used in synchronous/real-time web service integration.

We have learned how to design the API specification in *Chapter 2, Designing Your API*. So, let's move on to an API fragment and AsyncAPI.

API fragment

An API fragment is a reusable component of RAML. It is not a complete RAML but a portion of the RAML specification. It can be created separately as an API fragment in API Designer and can be reused in multiple API specifications. We explored this in detail in *Chapter 2, Designing Your API*.

AsyncAPI

An AsyncAPI specification is used for creating the specification for a messaging-based interface. This specification is **protocol-agnostic**. That means it can support many protocols such as amqp, amqps, http, https, ibmmq, jms, kafka, kafka-secure, anypointmq, mqtt, secure-mqtt, solace, stomp, stomps, ws, wss, and mercure. In a nutshell, AsyncAPI is protocol-independent. We use AsyncAPI in any event-driven architecture, which deals with asynchronous/near-real-time integrations.

Let's follow these steps to create an AsyncAPI specification:

1. Log in to **Anypoint Platform** and click **Design Center**. Here, click **Create new**, and select **New AsyncAPI**.
2. Provide the project name. Project language can either be YAML or JSON. In this example, let's set the language as YAML, as shown in *Figure 5.1*, and then click on **Create AsyncAPI**.

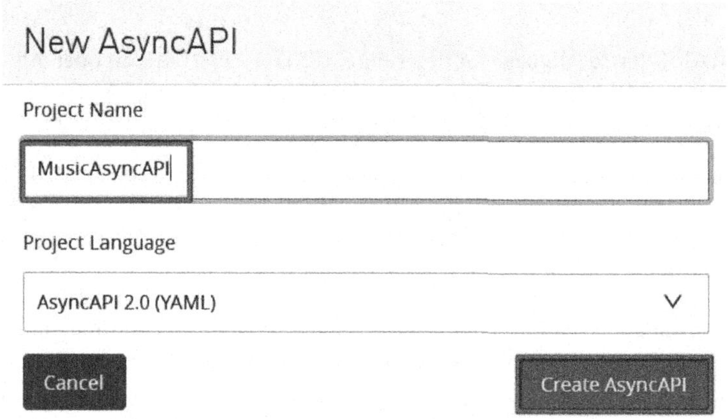

New AsyncAPI

Project Name

MusicAsyncAPI

Project Language

AsyncAPI 2.0 (YAML)   ∨

Cancel   Create AsyncAPI

Figure 5.1 – New AsyncAPI

Once created, it shows the following code block to describe the AsyncAPI version and other details:

```
asyncapi: '2.0.0'
info:
  title: MusicAsyncAPI
  version: '1.0.0'
channels: {}
```

In this example, to publish the song data to a queue/channel by an external application/ organization, they need the following: a queue name, a payload structure, and server details. These details will be available in the AsyncAPI specification provided by MuleSoft developers. Using this specification, external applications or organizations can publish (send) or subscribe (receive) data from the required queue/channel. Let's consider songs-request and songs-response as channel names (see *Figure 5.2*).

In the **PUBLISH** method section, we can define the fields that are required for publishing the message to the songs-request channel. Similarly, in the **SUBSCRIBE** method section, we can define the fields that we expect while subscribing to the message from the songs-response channel. If we need to reuse any code, then use the component object in AsyncAPI and refer to it using $ref.

The email and name are in the contact information section. Server details for different environments are in the servers section.

Figure 5.2 – AsyncAPI specification

Figure 5.2 shows the structure of an AsyncAPI specification, which includes the **info**, **servers**, and **channels** sections.

3. After successfully creating the AsyncAPI specification, click on **Publish** and select the **Publish to Exchange** option. On the dialog box that appears, provide the asset version and click **Publish to Exchange** to publish the AsyncAPI specification to Exchange (see *Figure 5.3*). Versioning is important because when the API version changes, it gives flexibility to clients on whether to update or continue with an older version of the API.

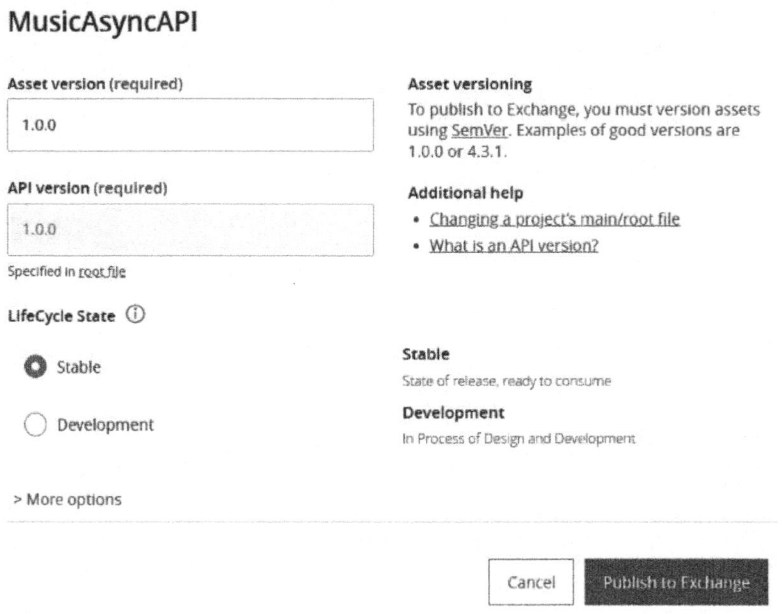

MusicAsyncAPI

Asset version (required)

```
1.0.0
```

Asset versioning

To publish to Exchange, you must version assets using SemVer. Examples of good versions are 1.0.0 or 4.3.1.

API version (required)

```
1.0.0
```

Specified in root file

Additional help

- Changing a project's main/root file
- What is an API version?

LifeCycle State ⓘ

⬤ Stable

◯ Development

Stable

State of release, ready to consume

Development

In Process of Design and Development

> More options

Cancel   Publish to Exchange

Figure 5.3 – Publishing the AsyncAPI

Once published to Exchange, the AsyncAPI specification is available for users in the same organization. If we need to make it available for external partners/consumers, then we need to publish it to the public portal from Exchange.

With this, we have understood how to design the API using an API specification, an API fragment, and an AsyncAPI specification from Design Center. After we design the API, we can share it with other developers/external partners/consumers to start their development. This way, they can consume the API before the actual development of the API.

Now, let's explore more about Flow Designer in Design Center.

Flow Designer

Anypoint Flow Designer is a low-code *drag and drop* tool. It allows anyone, even people with minimal programming knowledge, to build Mule integrations, such as receiving customer data from Salesforce and sending it to other backend systems (database or legacy applications).

In the following example, let's create a Mule application using **HTTP Listener**, **Logger**, and **Transform Message**. After creating it, let's deploy the application into CloudHub:

1. In the **Design Center**, click **Create new**, and select **New Mule App**.

2. Set the Mule app name as `SongsMuleApp`, as shown in *Figure 5.4*, and click **Create App**.

Figure 5.4 – Creating a new Mule app

3. Next, click on **Go straight to canvas** to open the canvas.

4. Click **trigger** and select **HTTP Listener**. Set the path value as /songs and click the *cross* button (see *Figure 5.5*).

Figure 5.5 – HTTP Listener path configuration

5. Click the *add* (+) symbol in the canvas beside the **HTTP listener** to add a new card (see *Figure 5.6*).

Figure 5.6 – Adding cards

6. Add the **Transform** component and select the configuration. Then, click on the **Scripts** tab and fill in song's JSON data, as shown in *Figure 5.7*. Next, click the *cross* button to close the window. The Mule application gets auto-saved.

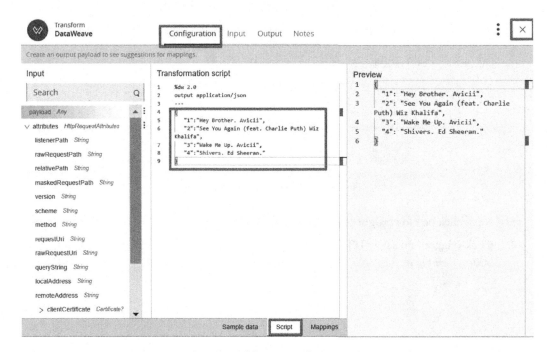

Figure 5.7 – Adding a transform message

7. Rename **New Flow** getSongsFlow (see *Figure 5.8*).

Figure 5.8 – Renaming the flow

With this, we have successfully created our Mule application, `SongsMuleApp`. Now, let's try to deploy it in CloudHub to run our application.

Deploying to CloudHub

There are a few ways to deploy an application in Mule, one of which is deploying to CloudHub. CloudHub is a MuleSoft **Platform as a Service (PaaS)** cloud environment, which is fully managed by MuleSoft. It is highly available, with 99.99% uptime.

Let's begin by deploying our application to CloudHub:

1. Click **Deploy application** (see *Figure 5.9*). In the dialog box, select the target environment as **Sandbox** and click **Deploy**.

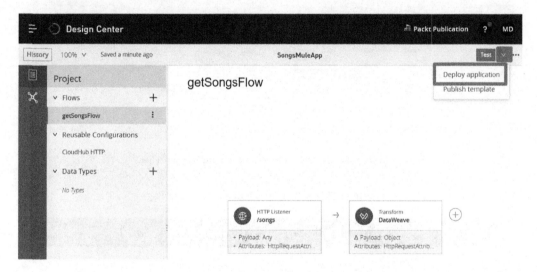

Figure 5.9 – Deploying an application in CloudHub

2. It will deploy the application and the following dialog box appears.

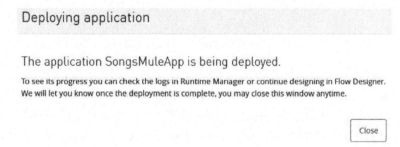

Figure 5.10 – Deploying an application

Once the application is deployed successfully into CloudHub, the following dialog box appears at the bottom right of the page:

Figure 5.11 – The Deployment success dialog

3.   Next, go to **Runtime Manager**. It shows the status of songsmuleapp-wtjz as **Started** (see *Figure 5.12*).

Figure 5.12 – Runtime Manager – the application list

4.   Click the application name and copy the application URL (see *Figure 5.13*).

Figure 5.13 – Runtime Manager – Dashboard

5.   Now, it is time to test the application we just created using Postman to check whether it is working. While typing the URL in Postman, add the /songs path, which we configured earlier in the **HTTP Listener** configuration, and select the **GET** method. Then, click the **Send** button.

6.   The application deployed in CloudHub will then receive the request and send the response, with the status as **200 OK**, which means our application is working. The response received in Postman is shown in *Figure 5.14*.

Figure 5.14 – The send request from Postman

Similarly, we can call this web service URL from any system (mobile, web, and legacy applications) to get the response.

In this section, you have understood how to create a simple Mule application and deploy it to CloudHub. Try creating a new Mule application with different components in Flow Designer for different use cases/requirements.

In this section, we have explored Design Center in Anypoint Platform. We learned more about API specifications, API fragments, and AsyncAPI in API Designer. We also created a Mule application in Flow Designer and deployed the same in CloudHub.

Next, let's learn more about the Exchange component.

Introducing Exchange

Exchange is an online catalog that stores all the reusable assets, such as APIs, connectors, templates, examples, policies, API groups, DataWeave libraries, AsyncAPIs, HTTP APIs, API specification and fragments, and custom assets. This is mainly used for exchanging/sharing assets with others in Anypoint Platform within an organization.

From Exchange, we can discover and see the assets available in the organization. We can access these Exchange assets from different components (both Anypoint Platform and Anypoint Studio) for our reuse. For example, in Anypoint Studio, we can access the connectors, templates, and examples by using the **Search in Exchange** option in the Mule palette. Similarly, in API Manager of Anypoint Platform, we can access the API assets by using the **Manage API from Exchange** option.

Assets are grouped under **Provided by MuleSoft** and the respective organization name in the Exchange. **Provided by MuleSoft** has all the assets shared by MuleSoft and its partners and certified by MuleSoft.

Figure 5.15 shows the assets under **Provided by MuleSoft**. These assets are publicly available for all MuleSoft customers.

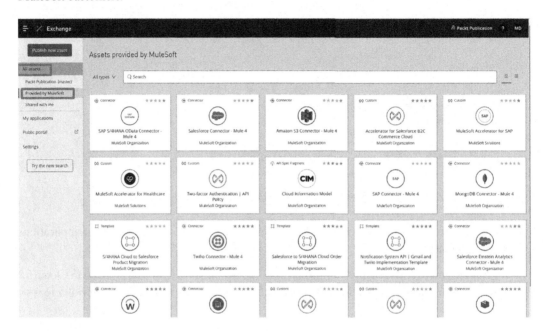

Figure 5.15 – Exchange assets provided by MuleSoft

Assets published/shared within the organization appear in the respective organization section. These assets are not accessible outside the organization. In this example, **Packt Publication** is an organization name.

This organization has a `musicbox-sys-api` REST API asset in the Exchange (which we designed and published earlier in *Chapter 2, Designing Your API*), and this is discoverable for other developers in the same organization, as shown in *Figure 5.16*.

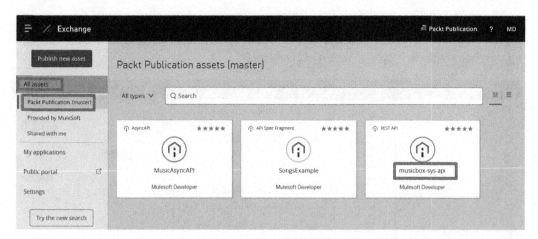

Figure 5.16 – Exchange assets from the current organization

On clicking the `musicbox-sys-api` asset, the asset page opens, as shown in *Figure 5.17*.

Let's try to download, view/edit, and share the API specification.

We can download the assets either as RAML, as OAS, as a Mule 3 connector, or as a Mule 4 connector by clicking the **Download** option.

The **View code** option allows you to view/edit the API specification from the Design Center.

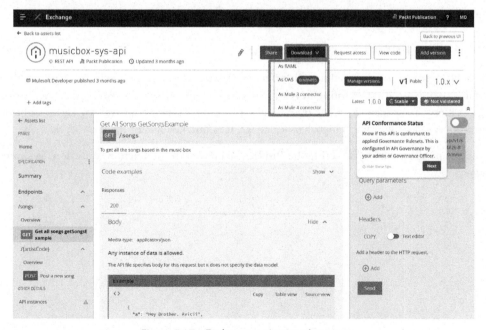

Figure 5.17 – Exchange – viewing the asset

We can share the assets with other developers within the organization and also publish the asset to the public portal by selecting the **Share** and then the **Public** option on the asset page. Check the checkbox for the version and click **Save**, as shown in *Figure 5.18*.

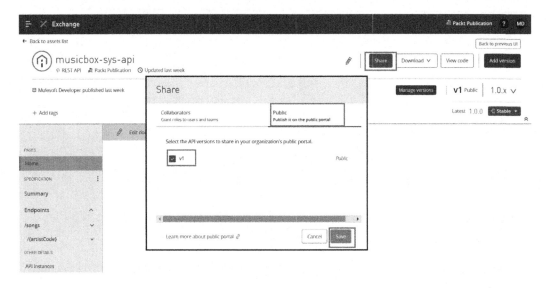

Figure 5.18 – Exchange – sharing assets to the public portal

Now, let's explore more about the public portal in Exchange.

The public portal

The public portal is a web-based **user interface** (**UI**) where developers can view the company's API, and it is mainly used for enabling developers/consumers to access the assets published by other organizations. The Exchange public portal is also called the **developer portal**. We can customize the portal appearance by adding a logo, banner image, text, and favicon for the browser tab.

Open the public portal by selecting the **Public portal** link in the **Exchange** section, as shown in *Figure 5.19*.

Figure 5.19 – Public portal

All assets published to the public portal are available, as displayed in *Figure 5.20*. Anyone with an internet connection can view these APIs. Open the public portal in **Private/Incognito** mode from the browser. If we open the public portal in a normal browser window, it might use the same login credentials that you logged in with already. Just to show that the public portal will work without any credentials, I have opened it in Private/Incognito mode. It doesn't require any credentials to see a list of APIs published to the public portal.

Figure 5.20 – Public portal

Previously, we tried to publish the API specification to the Exchange (In *Chapter 2*, *Designing Your API*). From the Exchange, we can publish the assets using the **Publish new asset** option. Try to publish various asset types (REST, SOAP, HTTP, and AsyncAPI) from Exchange using this option.

In this section, we learned about the assets provided by MuleSoft and also assets shared by our organization in Exchange. Then, we learned how to download, view/edit, and share/publish the asset to the public portal.

Let's move on to learning more about Runtime Manager.

Exploring Runtime Manager

Anypoint Runtime Manager is the single place to view and manage the Mule applications that are running in Mule Runtime. Mule Runtime is an integration engine that runs Mule applications. We can see and manage the application deployed in on-premises mode, CloudHub (MuleSoft-managed), and the public cloud from Runtime Manager. Earlier, we developed an application from Flow Designer and deployed it to CloudHub. We can also deploy a Mule application using a .jar file from Runtime Manager. A .jar file is a compressed version of an application.

Let's get familiar with some terms related to Runtime Manager before we deploy the Mule application into CloudHub using the .jar file.

- **Workers**: A worker is nothing but a small, dedicated server that can run a Mule application on CloudHub.

- **Worker size**: Different types of workers are available based on vCore size. Worker sizes come with different compute, memory, and storage capacities. A core can be a physical or **virtual core / vCore** (a virtual core denotes virtual CPU and allows the users to choose the physical properties (number of cores, memory and storage size) of hardware). In computers, we use a physical core, but in CloudHub, it's preferable to use vCore. vCore is partitioned from a physical core. For example, 1 physical core is partitioned up to 10 virtual small cores with 10 * 0.1 vCores. 0.1 vCore is the smallest size in CloudHub.

- Increasing the number of workers provides **horizontal scaling** for the application, whereas increasing the worker size provides **vertical scaling** for the application.

> **Horizontal and Vertical Scaling**
>
> Horizontal scaling means adding additional machines to accommodate new infrastructure demands. For example, if there is Black Friday/Christmas sale, we expect more traffic to our e-commerce server; in that case, we can add an additional server to share the load of incoming traffic.
>
> Vertical scaling means increasing additional resources to the same machine to get more power (CPU, memory, and disk). For example, if we need to process more records from a file/database, then we can add an additional CPU or memory to handle the load.

While deploying the Mule application, we can choose the worker size from the dropdown (see *Figure 5.21*). Let's look at the available worker size in the following table.

Worker Size	Heap Memory	Storage
0.1 vCores	500 MB	8 GB
0.2 vCores	1 GB	8 GB
1 vCore	1.5 GB	12 GB
2 vCores	3.5 GB	40 GB
4 vCores	7.5 GB	88 GB
8 vCores	15 GB	168 GB
16 vCores	32 GB	328 GB

Table 5.1 – Worker sizes

Heap memory is memory allocated to our Mule application. When the application runs, it uses this memory to process the requests received.

For example, if we choose 0.2 VCPU as a worker size, then the heap memory and storage allocated will be 1 GB and 8 GB respectively.

We are now familiar with the concepts of workers and worker size in Runtime Manager. Next, let's see how to deploy a Mule application into CloudHub using a .jar file.

Deploying a Mule application into CloudHub

Now that we have a basic understanding of common terms, let's deploy the Mule application using Runtime Manager. In this example, we are going to deploy the Hello World Mule application that we developed in *Chapter 3*, *Exploring Anypoint Studio*. In that chapter, we exported the application as a .jar file. The application has HTTP Listener with a /hello endpoint, Logger to log the Welcome to Hello world application message, and Transform Message to output { message: "Hello World" }. We will now use the same .jar file to deploy the application in CloudHub.

Follow these steps to deploy the application:

1.   Click **Runtime Manager** under **Management Center**.

2.   Choose **Sandbox** as the environment.

3.   Click the **Deploy application** button to deploy the application.

4.   Provide a unique application name, select the deployment target, and choose the .jar file. Now, select the worker size and the workers, and then click **Deploy Application** (see *Figure 5.21*).

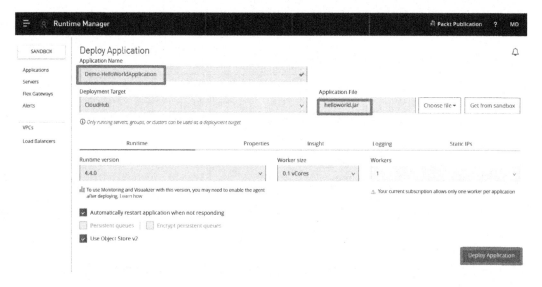

Figure 5.21 – Deploying an application in Runtime Manager

- A progress bar will appear on the same page while deploying in CloudHub. In this step, it will procure a **virtual machine (VM)**/system, install a lightweight Mule runtime, and also deploy the application.

5.   Now, we can see the following log page that shows the latest status of deployment (see *Figure 5.22*).

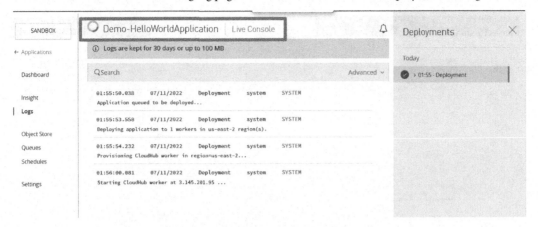

Figure 5.22 – Deployment status – logs

6.   Once the Mule application is successfully deployed, a *green* mark appears on the log page (see *Figure 5.23*).

Figure 5.23 – Runtime Manager – deploy application status

7.   Click on **Applications** on the left-side navigation to view the list of applications. You can see that the application is in a **Started** state (see *Figure 5.24*).

8.   Click the application named `demo-helloworldapplication`.

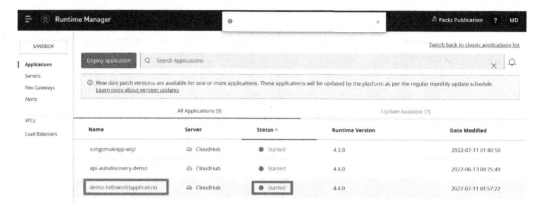

Figure 5.24 – Runtime Manager – deployed application status

- This shows the application URL in a domain column, the number of Mule messages received, **CPU** usage, and **Memory** usage in **Dashboard** (see *Figure 5.25*).

Figure 5.25 – Runtime Manager – Dashboard

9.   Copy the application URL from Dashboard, add a path (`/hello`), which we have specified in HTTP Listener (refer to *Figure 3.14 – Listener Properties Configuration* in *Chapter 3, Exploring Anypoint Studio*), and send the request from the Postman application. Once we click **Send**, the application that is running in CloudHub receives the request. It then gets processed through various steps (Logger, Transform Message, and so on) before getting the response. Send a

few more requests from the Postman application to see the number of Mule messages in the **Dashboard** (see *Figure 5.26*).

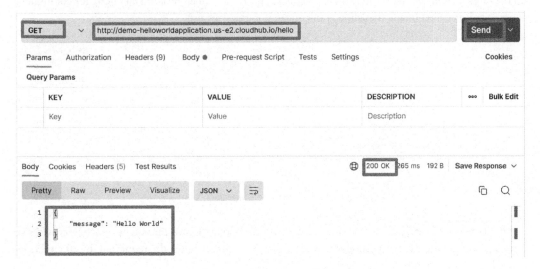

Figure 5.26 – A send request from Postman

As shown in the preceding figure, we can see the status is **200 OK**, which means that the application has received and processed the request successfully.

With this, we have successfully deployed the application in CloudHub using Runtime Manager. Now, let's learn how to manage a Mule application.

Managing a Mule application

After deploying the Mule application, typically the operation/support teams need to monitor/manage the application by checking the logs, the number of Mule messages received, CPU usage, and memory usage. This is done to check whether the Mule application is working or not. This kind of managing the application is facilitated by a list of options available such as **Dashboard**, **Insight**, **Logs**, **Object Stores**, **Queues**, **Schedulers**, and **Settings** in Runtime Manager.

By clicking the application name on Runtime Manager, we can see these options on the left-side navigation. Let's learn about those options one by one.

Dashboard

Dashboard displays the full details of the application (see *Figure 5.25*). It shows the number of Mule messages received, **CPU** usage, and **Memory** usage for that worker/application. We can also view the report for different time ranges, such as the last hour, the last 24 hours, and the last week.

Logs

In the **Logs** section, we can see logs related to the application. If an application has a **Logger** component, whenever it is called inside the Mule application, it logs a message.

Figure 5.27 – Runtime Manager – Logs

In the `demo-helloworldmuleapplication`, we logged a `Welcome to Hello world application` message using **Logger**. When this application receives the request, it logs the message from **Logger** (see *Figure 5.27*).

Insights

To learn the **Status**, **Processing Time**, and **Date** information for each run or transaction, we can check out the **Insights** tab.

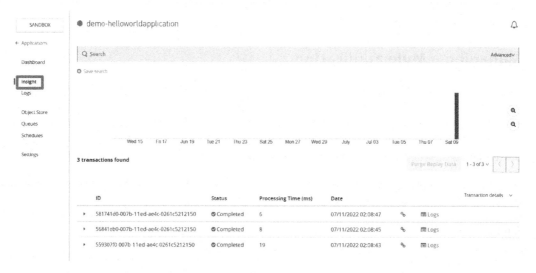

Figure 5.28 – Runtime Manager – Insights

We have called a `hello world` Mule application three times; hence, we can see three transactions in *Figure 5.28* with their status, processing time, and date. This helps with efficient monitoring.

To enable **Insight**, in the **Settings** tab, click **Insight** and enable the metadata.

Object Store

The **Object Store** connector is a Mule component that allows you to store a simple key-value pair. A key-value pair is a combination of two simple values where one is the key and the other is a value. The key is the unique identifier of the values stored.

If the application uses the **Object Store** connector, we can view the keys from the **Object Store** option. Let's look at *Figure 5.29* for a better understanding:

Figure 5.29 – Runtime Manager – Object Store

Here, `lastProcessedSongID` is a key name. For example, a Mule application processes songs from one system to another every few minutes. When it runs, it picks the records and stores `lastProcessedSongID` in the Object Store. Each time it runs, it checks for `lastProcessedSongID` from the Object Store so that it can process the succeeding records.

We will learn more about the Object Store in *Chapter 8, Building Your Mule Application*.

Queues

The **Queues** tab in Runtime Manager shows the queues within the flows of your deployed applications. For example, if we are using the VM Connector with a persistent queue enabled, then it appears in this **Queues** tab. We can see the number of messages in the queue and the number of messages that have been processed in the last 24 hours. We can also clear the messages if they are not required.

Schedules

The scheduler is a component that helps schedule the jobs. For example, if we need to run a specific program at 8 PM every day, then we can configure it based on a specific time. This is useful if we need to run a Mule application at a specific time.

The **Schedules** tab in Runtime Manager shows the scheduler details (the name, the time of the last run, and the frequency of the schedule) of the application. We can use the **Enable**, **Disable**, and **Run now** options as per requirements (see *Figure 5.30*). We will learn more about schedulers in *Chapter 8, Building Your Mule Application*.

Figure 5.30 – Runtime Manager – Schedules

In *Figure 5.30*, the scheduler is configured to run every 10 minutes, and we can see the previous run details in the **Last Run** column.

If the scheduler component is not applicable for a particular application, then it will not be displayed.

Settings

From the **Settings** page (see *Figure 5.31*), we can perform the following functions:

- For any application changes, we can update the .jar file to redeploy the application
- Change the Runtime version of the application
- Add/modify the application properties
- Enable the **Insight**
- Increase/decrease the logging level
- Allocate the static IP for the application

Figure 5.31 – Runtime Manager – Settings

In *Figure 5.31*, the Runtime version is **4.4.0**. If we need to change the version of the Mule runtime, then we can change it to the latest or previous version. Similarly, worker size, the number of workers, properties, and the logging level can be changed.

With this, we have learned about the various options such as **Dashboard**, **Logs**, **Insights**, **Object Store**, **Queues**, **Schedules**, and **Settings** in the Mule application that are useful to manage the application. Now, let's learn how to configure the alerts in Runtime Manager.

Runtime Manager alerts

Runtime Manager alerts enable you to set up an email alert whenever any event (condition) occurs in a specific application or all applications.

We can setup alerts for CloudHub as well as local servers in Runtime Manager. Now let's see various alert conditions for CloudHub:

- CPU usage – CloudHub
- Custom application alert
- Exceeds event traffic threshold
- Memory usage – CloudHub
- Deployment failed
- Deployment success
- Secure data gateway connected

- Secure data gateway disconnected

- Worker not responding

For applications running in local servers (on-premises), we can configure different types of alert conditions. Now let's look at those:

- Number of errors

- Number of Mule messages

- Response time

- Application undeployed

- Deployment failure

- Deployment success

Here's how we can create an alert.

Creating an alert

Let's create a new alert for the **Deployment Success** condition:

1. Click on **Create your first alert** if you are creating an alert for the first time. Otherwise, click on **Create Alert**.

2. Type the name of the alert and the application type that needs to be monitored, and then specify the condition. Then, provide the recipient's email ID in the **Recipients** field. This is the email address that the alert will be sent to. Finally, click on **Submit**.

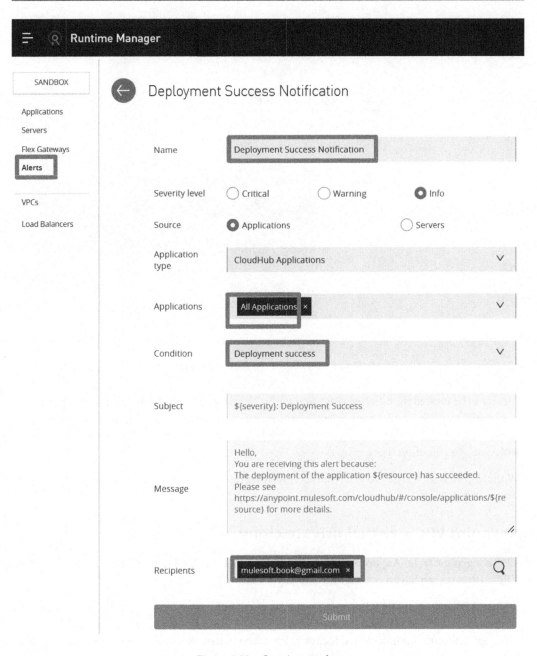

Figure 5.32 – Creating an alert

With this, the alert has been created. Going forward, if any application is deployed successfully, then an email alert will be sent to the email address you specified (see *Figure 5.33*).

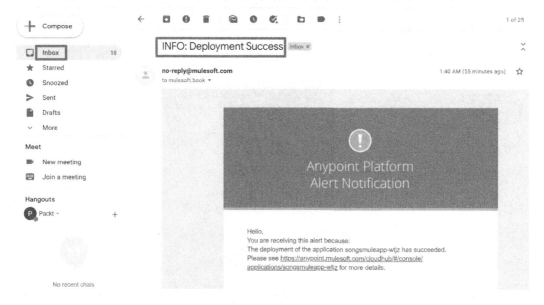

Figure 5.33 – An email alert in the inbox

Alerts can be created for different condition types. Try creating alerts for those different conditions. For example, create a deployment failure alert to notify you if there is any failure in the deployment. Similarly, create an alert if the memory/CPU threshold exceeds. Apart from these, try to create alerts with different condition types.

With this, we have learned to create an alert in **Runtime Manager**. Next, let's move on to explore Anypoint VPC.

Anypoint VPC – virtual private cloud

VPC is a generic term. **Anypoint VPC** is the VPC hosted inside CloudHub. Let's try to understand VPC so that we can have a clear idea about Anypoint VPC.

A **Virtual Private Cloud** (**VPC**) is a set of servers present in a protected environment. Communication with these servers can only be established through a VPC firewall. In the absence of Anypoint VPC, Mule applications run in a shared location. This means that the Mule applications in CloudHub belonging to all the customers run in the same location/space. This may raise security concerns among the customers.

Large organizations want their applications to run in a private and protected environment. This can be achieved by creating a VPC in Runtime Manager. After creating a VPC, we can connect to an on-premises environment using a **virtual private network** (**VPN**). A VPN ensures secure connectivity to your on-premises network from your Anypoint VPC.

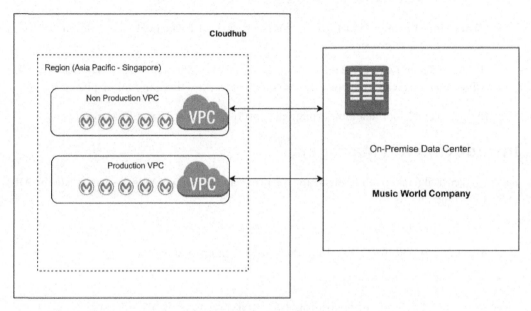

Figure 5.34 – Anypoint VPC

In *Figure 5.34*, the Music World Company has a backend system in an on-premises data center and a MuleSoft application in CloudHub. For security reasons, they run those Mule applications inside Anypoint VPC in CloudHub. We can group all MuleSoft applications into either one or more VPCs. Here, the customer has all the non-production MuleSoft applications in one non-production VPC and their production application in another VPC.

Now that we have learned about **Anypoint VPC**, let's learn more about load balancers in **Runtime Manager**.

Load balancer

A load balancer is one of the options available in **Runtime Manager** that enables the handling of the external HTTP/HTTPS traffic to multiple applications deployed in CloudHub workers in a VPC. CloudHub provides two types of load balancers:

- **Shared load balancer** (**SLB**): This provides a basic load-balancing functionally and is shared across multiple customers.
- **Dedicated load balancer** (**DLB**): This is an optional component of Anypoint Platform. This allows handling load balancing between different workers that run Mule applications.

Next, let's take a quick look at another component of Anypoint Platform, API Manager.

Introducing API Manager

API Manager facilitates creating, managing, securing, and analyzing APIs. We can create the APIs in the following ways:

- Manage from Exchange
- Create a new API from a RAML/OAS/SOAP definition or an HTTP API
- Import an API from a `.zip` file

Once we create the API, we can apply the policies to secure our APIs. We will explore how to apply policies and custom policies in *Chapter 10, Secure Your API*.

Exploring Anypoint Monitoring

Anypoint Monitoring provides visibility to all the integrations across an application network. From the built-in dashboard (see *Figure 5.35*), we can check the following metrics:

- Number of Mule messages received
- Average response time of the API
- Number of errors received
- CPU utilization
- JVM heap memory used
- JVM thread count

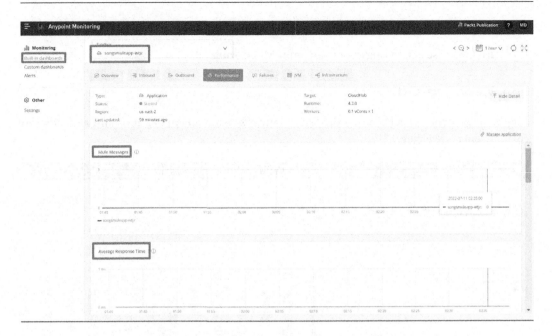

Figure 5.35 – Anypoint Monitoring – Built-in dashboards

This dashboard gives a clear picture of application performance and failure details.

If we need to enable alerts for Mule applications, then we can set an alert in Anypoint Monitoring. Let's learn how to create an alert in **Anypoint Monitoring**.

Alerts

From Anypoint Monitoring, we can configure an alert based on the metrics and send an email alert to a specific email ID or Anypoint user (see *Figure 5.36*).

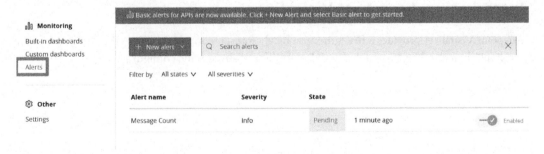

Figure 5.36 – Anypoint Monitoring – Alerts

We can monitor the state (success/failure) of the alert. Alerts can be either enabled or disabled.

Let's learn how to search the logs from **Anypoint Monitoring**.

Log Management

Log Management helps to search the log for any text from all applications and also different environments (see *Figure 5.37*).

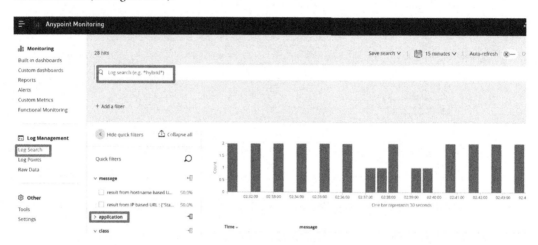

Figure 5.37 – Anypoint Monitoring – Log Management

One of the features of **Log Management** is that our search can be saved for future reference. This helps the operation team to quickly search the logs from the saved search.

Let's learn more about Visualizer, which is one of the components of **Anypoint Platform**.

Introducing Anypoint Visualizer

Anypoint Visualizer provides a real-time, graphical representation of the APIs. The data displayed in the graph dynamically gets updated and doesn't require any specific configuration.

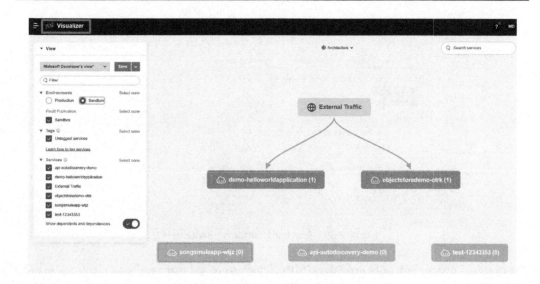

Figure 5.38 – Anypoint Visualizer

From this graphical view, we can easily understand how APIs are connected to each other (see *Figure 5.38*).

We now know how we can visualize a Mule application using Anypoint Visualizer. Let's now explore Access Management, which is one of the components of **Anypoint Platform**.

Exploring Access Management

Access Management is used to manage an organization, business groups, users, roles, environments, identify providers, client providers, and audit logs in Anypoint Platform. Let's see how each of them is managed.

Organization and business groups

When we create an Anypoint Platform account, a root **organization** gets created. The root organization can contain multiple business groups.

A **business group** is the child of the root organization. It is a self-contained resource group that contains resources such as Mule applications and APIs.

Invite user

From the **Users** link on the left-side navigation, we can invite users to our Anypoint Platform, as shown in *Figure 5.39*. By default, users are stored in Anypoint Platform.

Figure 5.39 – Anypoint Platform – Invite user

We can also configure **identify providers** (**IdPs**), which store and manage digital identities, in order to store the users.

Roles

Anypoint Platform comes with the following default roles, which are assigned to predefined permissions. We can assign the users to the roles (see *Figure 5.40*), based on their responsibilities. We can also create a new role and set the required permission for different components.

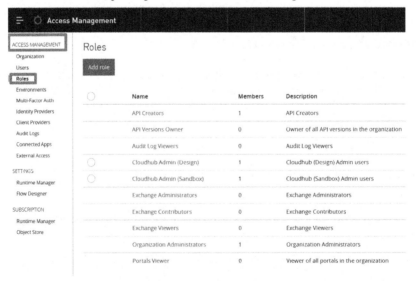

Figure 5.40 – Anypoint Platform – Roles

A user can also be assigned multiple roles, based on their responsibilities.

Environments

This tab enables you to add a new environment. For example, if we need more test/non-production environments, then we can create an environment such as **System Integration Testing (SIT)**, **Quality Assurance (QA)**, **User Acceptance Testing (UAT)**, and so on.

Audit logs

Audit logs track user activity with date/time, product, action, IP address, and other details (see *Figure 5.41*).

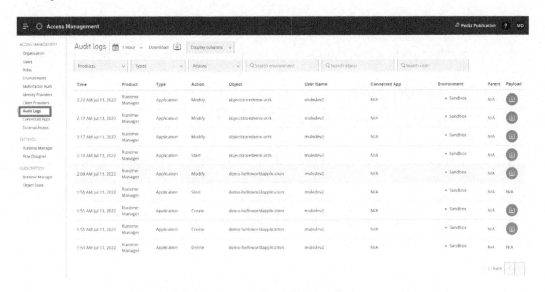

Figure 5.41 – Anypoint Platform – Audit Logs

We can download audit logs as a `.csv` file using the **Download** option.

SUBSCRIPTION

This provides validity and subscription information for different environments, static IPs, VPC, and load balancers in Runtime Manager, and also Anypoint MQ and Object Store subscription/usage details.

With this, we have learned how to manage the access-related functions in Access Management.

Summary

This chapter is all about Anypoint Platform and its components: Design Center, Exchange, Runtime Manager, API Manager, Anypoint Monitoring, Anypoint Visualizer, and Access Management (organization and business groups). We have learned about each component's functionalities. On completing this chapter, you now have sufficient knowledge of Anypoint Platform and can feel confident enough to design, manage and monitor Mule applications.

In the next chapter, we'll explore DataWeave, an expression language used for transforming data from one format to another and performing complex logical transformations.

Questions

Take a moment to answer the following questions to serve as a recap of what you just learned in this chapter.

1. What is Anypoint Platform?
2. Are Anypoint Platform and Anypoint Studio the same?
3. What is a reusable component of RAML?
4. A is a business analyst, with minimal coding experience. Can A build his Mule application? Justify your answer.
5. What is the minimum worker size in CloudHub?
6. What are the components in which we can configure alerts?

Answers

1. Anypoint Platform helps organizations to connect applications, data, and devices.
2. No. They are not the same. Anypoint Studio is an IDE, which we use to build, test, and run a Mule application. Anypoint Platform is a UI-based control plane with which we can manage all the components of Anypoint Platform.
3. An API fragment is a reusable component of RAML. It is not a complete RAML but a portion of a RAML specification. It can be created separately as an API fragment in API Designer and can be reused in multiple API specifications.
4. Yes. Business analysts can easily design and build Mule applications from Flow Designer using drag and drop.
5. The minimum worker size is 0.1 VCPU in CloudHub.
6. We can configure alerts from the following components in Anypoint Platform:
    *   Anypoint Monitoring
    *   Runtime Manager
    *   API Manager

Part 2:
A Deep Dive into MuleSoft

Part 2 covers the concepts of DataWeave and various stages of an application life cycle, such as building, deploying, securing, and testing your Mule application. This part focuses on how to ensure security for your Mule API, how to choose your deployment environment, and how to perform unit testing with the help of MUnit.

At the end of this part, we will be familiar with how to build, transform, secure, test, and deploy applications using different components in Anypoint Studio and Anypoint Platform. We will also have a deep understanding of DataWeave.

The following chapters are included in this part:

- *Chapter 6, Learning DataWeave*
- *Chapter 7, Transforming with DataWeave*
- *Chapter 8, Building Your Mule Application*
- *Chapter 9, Deploying Your Application*
- *Chapter 10, Secure Your API*
- *Chapter 11, Testing Your Application*

6
Learning DataWeave

DataWeave is a very powerful programming language created by MuleSoft. It's widely used in Mule applications to transform the data inside your integrations or APIs. It's mostly used with the **Transform Message** component in Anypoint Studio, but it is also used with other components such as **Choice** or **For Each** (inside the # [] syntax).

DataWeave keeps evolving because of its popularity. Earlier, you would only be able to explore DataWeave inside the Transform Message component in Anypoint Studio, but now there are more products such as the Visual Studio Code (or VSCode) extension, the DataWeave **command-line interface (CLI)**, DataWeave for Apex (from Salesforce), and the very popular DataWeave Playground (which we will use for this chapter).

In this chapter, we're going to cover the following main topics:

- Introducing DataWeave
- Writing DataWeave scripts

This chapter is focused on getting you started with the very basics of the language so you can understand more advanced transformations in later chapters (or in real life!). If you are familiar with DataWeave, you could also benefit from this chapter since we provide some tips and additional information that you may not be aware of.

Technical requirements

You will need the following technical requirements for this chapter:

- An internet browser: Google Chrome will be used throughout this chapter for the DataWeave Playground located at https://developer.mulesoft.com/learn/dataweave/. To learn how to use the DataWeave Playground, you can follow this guide: https://developer.mulesoft.com/tutorials-and-howtos/dataweave/learn-dataweave-with-the-dataweave-playground-getting-started/.

- GitHub repository: It's not required for you to open this repository, but it'll be easier for you to copy and paste the examples and scripts. You can access it through the following link: `https://github.com/PacktPublishing/MuleSoft-for-Salesforce-Developers`.

Introducing DataWeave

Before we dive into all the DataWeave syntax and start doing some programming, we'll first understand what DataWeave is and how it's different from other programming languages you may be familiar with – such as Java or Python. Then, we can start with the basics of the language.

There are two major versions of DataWeave so far:

- DataWeave 1 is used with the Mule runtime version 3 (Mule 3)
- DataWeave 2 is used in Mule 4

Since Mule 3 is mostly used by companies who have not yet migrated to Mule 4, and Mule 4 is the language chosen in new projects nowadays, we'll focus on DataWeave 2 in this chapter, specifically, version 2.4.

> **Note**
> The full list of differences between DataWeave 1 and DataWeave 2 will not be covered in this chapter since they're out of scope. However, you can read the following documentation page to learn how to migrate your code from version 1 to version 2: `https://docs.mulesoft.com/mule-runtime/latest/migration-dataweave`.

Analyzing DataWeave

DataWeave is a functional programming language created by MuleSoft. It is not only used within the Transform Message component from Anypoint Studio, but it is also the language that is used in other Mule components such as the Choice router or the Set Variable component.

If you come from an imperative programming background, and you haven't worked with other functional programming languages before, then this might be a bit strange for you at first. The biggest difference is that the lines of code are not executed in a sequential manner. Certain functions such as `for` and `while` are not available in DataWeave. However, similar outcomes can be achieved with other functions, as we'll see later in this chapter.

These are the most important points to remember when learning DataWeave:

- *DataWeave was created as a transformation language.* This means that there is generally some input data that needs to be transformed into an expected output structure. The goal is not to create applications, run command-line commands, or modify files; the goal is to transform data. For example, you can transform given data to a different data format (such as XML, JSON, CSV) or just a different data structure (for example, from an array to an object).

- *The execution of the code is not sequential.* This is the main pain point for developers that are not familiar with functional programming. You not only need to get familiar with the language's syntax, but you also need to change your whole thinking pattern to accept the fact that solutions in C++, Java, or Python will not be translated into DataWeave just by modifying the syntax.

- *All data is immutable.* Even if you use functions or operators to apparently modify the data, you're only creating new data, not modifying the existing data.

- *Variables can't be modified.* In line with the previous statement, all data is immutable, including the values that are assigned to the variables. Once you assign a value to a variable, you can't re-assign a new value. You must create a new variable.

- *DataWeave uses the call-by-need strategy.* Also called *lazy evaluation*. This means that *[...] expressions are evaluated only when they are needed and their result is stored to avoid evaluating an expression multiple times if the input parameters are the same.* (`https://docs.mulesoft. com/dataweave/2.4/dataweave-language-guide`)

- *There are no loops.* There are some DataWeave functions to get the outcomes of a `for` or a `for each` operation, but it is not the exact same functionality. However, loops that are generated by a `while`, for example, are not possible with DataWeave functions.

- *There are no classes.* We mentioned earlier that all data is immutable. If you come from an object-oriented programming background, you might be used to creating getters and setters to modify your objects. In this case, since data is immutable, you are only creating new data.

- *DataWeave syntax is not tab- or new-line-based.* Some programming languages depend on tabs, spaces, new lines, or other characters to define their functionality. This is not the case for DataWeave. Unless strictly defined (as is the case for some operators and data types), you can choose to add/remove spaces, continue on a new line, use parentheses, and more.

Taking these facts into account, we can get started on learning about DataWeave. Let's first talk about the anatomy of a DataWeave script.

Diving into a script's anatomy

There are two main parts of a DataWeave script: the **header** and the **body**. These two are separated by three dashes (- - -). The following script is an example of a DataWeave script that outputs a Hello World string in a JSON format:

basic-script.dwl

```
%dw 2.0
output application/json
---
"Hello World"
```

Let's talk about the script's header to understand what can go in here.

Script header

These are the components that can go in the header of a DataWeave script:

- **DataWeave version**: Using %dw, you can define whether the script is for DataWeave 1.0 or DataWeave 2.0. If this is not provided, the default is version 2.0. Even if you're on a different minor version (such as 2.4), you just have to specify 1.0 or 2.0 since those are the major versions.

- **Output MIME type**: Using output, you can specify which data format the output is going to be in. For example, JSON, XML, CSV, and so on. We will talk more about data formats in a bit. If no output is specified, it will be determined by DataWeave.

- **Input MIME type**: Using input, you can specify which data format the input for the script is in. This is almost never needed since DataWeave is very good at analyzing input data. However, you can use this directive to specify additional details about the input's format. For example, when your input is a CSV, you can specify the separator character, whether the data is using quotes, whether it has a header, and so on.

- **Import modules**: Using import, you can choose from the variety of built-in DataWeave modules and functions to create more complex transformations. You can also use this to import custom modules that you create within your Mule project.

- **Import namespaces**: Using ns, you can define the namespaces you want to import to make reference to them on the script. This is mostly used with XML data formats.

- **Custom types**: Using type, you can define your own data types or data structures for your data. This is helpful to catch possible errors before reaching runtime.

- **Global variables**: Using var, you can define any global variables to use on the script. We will talk more about variables in this chapter.

- **Function definitions**: Using fun, you can define custom named functions to use on the script. We will talk more about functions in this chapter.

Now that we have a better understanding of what goes in the header section of a DataWeave script, let's now look into the body section.

Script body

This section is easier to describe than the header. Here is where you create all your transformation code. In the header, you're defining what your script may use, but you don't actually use some of this information until you create a script. For example, you can create variables and function definitions in the header, but you don't actually use them until you call them in the body with some data. It's like having a factory all ready to create some products but not having any materials to work with. All the machinery would be the header and the actual tangible materials to create products would be the body.

All programming languages have ways of adding comments to your code. Let's now see how comments work in DataWeave.

Adding comments to your code

You can't always assume that anyone who looks at your code will be able to understand how it works right away. Even we forget, with time, what our code is doing. It's best practice in a lot of programming languages to leave comments in your code for the next person to discover and get a better idea of what it does. DataWeave is not an exception to this rule.

There are two ways of adding comments to your code:

- Single-line
- Multi-line

If you want to add **single-line comments**, you just need to use // and whatever comes to the right of these will be a comment. Let's see an example:

single-comments.dwl

```
%dw 2.0
output application/json
---
"Hello World" // this is a comment
```

Here, we are using the same example we saw before to output a Hello World string in JSON format. It's still doing exactly the same thing, but now we have added a comment next to the code that says this is a comment.

For **multi-line comments**, the first line needs to start with /* right at the beginning, the last line needs to end with */ after your comment, and any line in-between needs to start with *. Let's look at an example to illustrate this better:

multi-line-comments.dwl

```
%dw 2.0
output application/json
---
/* This is a comment
 * ...a multi-line comment.
 * And it ends here */
"Hello World"
// this is a single-line comment
```

> **Warning**
>
> In Anypoint Studio, the Mule configuration files are created in XML format. If you have DataWeave code inside these files, the multi-line comments might sometimes produce an error. If this happens, you can either use single-line comments or create an external .dwl file and refer it from the Transform Message component. We will learn how to do this later in the chapter. For more information, see the documentation:
>
> https://docs.mulesoft.com/dataweave/latest/dataweave-language-introduction#dataweave-comments

Now that we know how to add comments to our code, let's dive into the available data types in DataWeave.

Understanding data types

Data types in DataWeave are separated into three main categories:

- Simple
- Composite
- Complex

The purpose of this book is to get you started with the basics of MuleSoft. We won't be covering complex data types in this book because they are used in more advanced examples, but we will look into simple and composite types. Let's start with the simple data types.

> **Note**
>
> You can confirm a value's data type by using the `typeOf` function as we will learn in the next chapter (*Chapter 7, Transforming with DataWeave*). For example, `typeOf(1)` will result in `Number`.

Simple data types

These data types are considered simple because they don't have any underlying values. These types are just composed of one single value:

- **String**: This type is specified by surrounding quotes (i.e., `"Hello World"`). There can also be empty strings if you just have quotes with no characters inside (i.e., `""`).

- **Boolean**: This type can only have two values: `true` or `false`. It is mainly used together with conditions or to define flags (i.e., `isActive`).

- **Number**: This type includes all the available numbers. In other programming languages, you can have different number types such as `Integer` and `Float`. In DataWeave, all numbers fit within this type (i.e., `1`, `250`, `34.7`, or `3.14159265359`).

- **Regex**: This type is used to define regular expressions. It's specified by surrounding forward-slashes (i.e., `/([A-Z])\w+/`). This is mostly used as an input parameter to other functions to search for specific data. To learn more about regular expressions, visit `https://regexr.com/`.

- **Null**: This type can only have one value: `null`. Note that the name of the type is specified with a capital *N*, whereas the actual value is written in all lowercase. If you're not familiar with the `null` value, it is used to specify *no data*. It's different than `0` or `""`, because `0` is still of type Number and `""` is still of type String. `null` means there was no data found, returned, or specified. Or simply put, it's a different data type than the expected one.

- Date and Time-related types: There are different data types to define date and time formats and they're defined by surrounding `||`. These are as follows:

  - **Date**: Includes year, month, and day; no time (i.e., `|2020-01-01|`).

  - **DateTime**: Includes year, month, day, hours, minutes, seconds, milliseconds, and a given time zone (i.e., `|2020-01-01T10:00:00.172144Z|`).

  - **LocalDateTime**: Includes year, month, day, hours, minutes, seconds, and milliseconds in the current time zone (i.e., `|2020-01-01T10:00:00.607214|`).

  - **LocalTime**: Includes hours, minutes, seconds, and milliseconds in the current time zone; no date (i.e., `|10:00:00.607214|`).

  - **Time**: Includes hours, minutes, seconds, milliseconds, and a given time zone; no date (i.e., `|10:00:00.172144Z|`).

  - **TimeZone**: Indicates the time zone for a time (i.e., `|-04:00|`).

- **Period**: Indicates a period of date or time. The number of years, months, days, hours, minutes, seconds, or milliseconds can be included (i.e., |P1Y2M30D|).

Now let's look into the composite types.

Composite data types

As opposed to the simple types, these contain other values or are made of other values:

- **Array**: This type is specified by surrounding square brackets (i.e., [1, 2, 3]). It is a list or a collection of other data types. The values inside an array don't have to be of the same data type and they're not limited to simple types. There can also be empty arrays if you just have square brackets with no values inside (i.e., []).

- **Object**: This type is specified by surrounding curly brackets. Each object is composed of key-value pairs separated by a comma. A *key* is what is specified before the colon and a *value* is what is specified after the colon. The same as the array type, the values don't have to be of the same data type and they're not limited to simple types. There can also be empty objects if you just have curly brackets with no values inside (i.e., {}). In the following example, we have an object with two key-value pairs: the first is the key a with the value 1 (of type Number) and the second is the key b with the value "Hello World" (of type String):

```
{
    a: 1,
    b: "Hello World"
}
```

Let's take a quick look at an additional data type that is important to understand even though it's not a simple or composite type: the Range data type.

The Range data type

There is an additional data type that we will use later in this chapter called **Range**. This data type is not part of the simple or composite types, but we need to mention it for later concepts. You can look at ranges as "arrays of numbers" for the purpose of this book, however, Range is not the same as Array. You can create a range by using the keyword to. For example, 1 to 5 results in [1, 2, 3, 4, 5].

> **Note**
>
> The purpose of this book is to get you started with the basics of MuleSoft. There are more DataWeave data types that we are not covering right now because they are used in more advanced examples. For a complete list, please visit the following official documentation pages:
>
> https://docs.mulesoft.com/dataweave/latest/dataweave-type-system
>
> https://docs.mulesoft.com/dataweave/latest/dataweave-types

Now that we have a better understanding of the basic DataWeave data types and how they are used, let's now talk about data formats.

Understanding data formats

We mentioned earlier that DataWeave is a transformation language. It usually takes input data and transforms it into a different output format or structure. Sometimes the code is created right from the script and there may be no input data, but there is always output data. We talked about the anatomy of a script and we mentioned the `output` directive that can be used in the script's header to specify a **Multipurpose Internet Mail Extension (MIME)** type. This is the data format of the output data.

Let's list some of the most popular data formats in DataWeave:

- **CSV**: You can refer to this MIME type as `application/csv` in your script's header. This format is translated to an array of objects in DataWeave. Each row represents an object, each value is separated by a specified character (it usually is a comma, but it can be any character), and each key comes from the header row (if provided).

- **DW**: You can refer to this MIME type as `application/dw` in your script's header. This format helps you to understand how the information is processed in DataWeave before being transformed to a different format. Please note that this should never be used in production environments because it will cause performance issues. It is intended to be used to debug or for learning purposes only.

- **Java**: You can refer to this MIME type as `application/java` in your script's header. This format translates DataWeave and Java data types.

- **JSON**: You can refer to this MIME type as `application/json` in your script's header. This format requires minimal transformation since DataWeave's data types are the same as JSON's data types.

- **XML**: You can refer to this MIME type as `application/xml` in your script's header. This format is translated to DataWeave objects. One difference from the other formats is that there always has to be one single root key in your script.

> **Note**
>
> For a complete list of all supported data formats in DataWeave, please visit the official documentation:
>
> `https://docs.mulesoft.com/dataweave/latest/dataweave-formats`

We are now ready with the basics of the language. We know about a DataWeave script's anatomy and its parts: the header and the body. We learned how to add comments to our code and we now have a list of data types and data formats that can be used in DataWeave. Let's now learn some more language basics in the next section.

Writing DataWeave scripts

Now that we understand the basics of the language, let's get started on learning how to write DataWeave scripts. In this section, you'll learn about operators, selectors, variables, functions, and scope and flow control. These will give you the basics to start transforming your data.

Using operators

If you come from a different programming language background, you probably already know what operators are – those characters that help you transform or compare data. Let's take a look at the different types of operators in DataWeave and their purpose.

Mathematical operators

These operators transform two values into one. They are mostly used for numbers but they can also be used with other data types:

- + **Addition**: This operator adds two values. It can be used to add date and time-related types and numbers or to append a new item to an array (i.e., 1 + 2).

- - **Subtraction**: This operator subtracts two values. It can be used to subtract date and time-related types, numbers, items from an array, or key-value pairs from an object (i.e., 1 - 2).

- * **Multiplication**: This operator multiplies two numbers (i.e., 1 * 2).

- / **Division**: This operator divides two numbers (i.e., 9 / 3).

Here you can find some examples with the different mathematical operators:

---

mathematical-operators.dwl

```
%dw 2.0
output application/dw
---
{
    Addition: |2020-01-01| + |P2D|, // = |2020-01-03|
    Subtraction: ["a", "b", "c"] - "a", // = ["b", "c"]
    Multiplication: 3 * 3, // = 9
    Division: 9 / 3 // = 3
}
```

Now let's look into the equality and relational operators.

Equality and relational operators

These operators compare two values and return Boolean values (`true` or `false`) with the result of the comparison:

- **< Less than**: This operator compares whether the value on the left is less than the value on the right. It can be used to compare date and time-related types (except Period), booleans, numbers, and strings (i.e., `1 > 2` would return `false`).

- **> Greater than**: This operator compares whether the value on the left is greater than the value on the right. It can be used to compare date and time-related types (except Period), booleans, numbers, and strings (i.e., `5 > 3` would return `true`).

- **<= Less than or equal to**: This operator works the same as the < (less than) operator, but includes values that are equal to each other (i.e., `1 < 1` would be `false`, but `1 <= 1` would be `true`).

- **>= Greater than or equal to**: This operator works the same as the > (greater than) operator, but includes values that are equal to each other (i.e., `1 > 1` would be `false`, but `1 >= 1` would be `true`).

- **== Equal to**: This operator compares whether both values and data types are equal. It can be used to compare all simple and composite data types except Regex (i.e., `1 == 1` would be `true`, but `1 == "1"` would be `false`).

- **~= Similar to**: This operator compares whether both values are equal regardless of the type. If the types are different, the operator will attempt to coerce one of the values to the type of the other and then compare them. It can be used to compare all simple and composite data types except Regex (i.e., both `1 ~= 1` and `1 ~= "1"` would be `true`).

Here you can find some examples with the different equality and relational operators:

equality-and-relational-operators.dwl

```
%dw 2.0
output application/dw
---
{
    LessThan: 1 < 2, // true
    GreaterThan: "a" > "b", // false
    LessOrEqualTo: |2020-01-01| <= |2020-01-01|, // true
    GreaterOrEqualTo: 1 >= 1, // true
    EqualTo: 1 == "1", // false
    SimilarTo: 1 ~= "1" // true
}
```

Now let's look into the logical operators.

Logical operators

These operators are used to manipulate or compare boolean values or expressions. They are mostly used together with conditionals (such as `if`/`else`) to control the flow of the script and/or modify the outputs dynamically:

- **not**: Negates the given boolean after the operator (i.e., `not true` results in `false`). This operator negates the complete logical expression and not just the first value (i.e., `not true or true` will first execute `true or true` and then negate the result; the final result would be `false`).

- **!**: The same as `not` but with different precedence. This operator negates the boolean next to it first and then executes the rest of the logical expression (i.e., `! true or true` will first execute `! true` and then complete the expression; the final result would be `true`).

- **and**: Compares two booleans and returns `true` only if both values are `true`. Otherwise, it returns `false` (i.e., `true and true` would return `true` but `true and false` would return `false`).

- **or**: Compares two booleans and returns `true` if either (or both) of the values are `true`. Otherwise, it returns `false` (i.e., `true or false` would return `true` but `false or false` would return `false`).

Here you can find some examples with the different logical operators:

logical-operators.dwl

```
%dw 2.0
output application/dw
---
{
    "not": not 1 == 2, // true
    "!": ! (1 ~= "1"), // false
    "and": (5 > 2) and (4 < 9), // true
    "or": (1 >= 5) or (3 >= 3), // true
    Precendence: {
        not: not true or true, // false
        // not true or true = not (true or true) = not
            (true) = false
        "!": ! true or true, // true
```

```
        // ! true or true = (! true) or true = (false) or
            true = true
        "!()": ! (true or true) // false
        // ! (true or true) = ! (true) = false

    }
}
```

Finally, let's look into some operators to manipulate arrays and time zones.

The prepend and append operators

These operators take two values to transform them into one. They are mostly used with arrays but prepend can also be used with DateTime and TimeZone:

- **>> Prepend**: When used with arrays, the item on the left will be added to the first position of the array on the right (i.e., `1 >> [2, 3]` would result in `[1, 2, 3]`). When used with DateTime and TimeZone, the DateTime must be located on the left side and the TimeZone on the right side. This will transform the given DateTime to a new DateTime with the given TimeZone (i.e., to convert a DateTime from Eastern Time to Pacific Time, you can either do `|2020-01-01T10:00:00-05:00| >> "America/Los_Angeles"` or `>> |-08:00|`; both would result in `|2020-01-01T07:00:00-08:00|`).

- **<< Append**: This operator can only be used with arrays. The item on the right will be added to the last position of the array on the left. Note that this is the same behavior as the + operator (i.e., `[1, 2] << 3` and `[1, 2] + 3` both result in `[1, 2, 3]`).

Here you can find some examples with the `Prepend` and `Append` operators:

---

prepend-append-operators.dwl

```
%dw 2.0
output application/dw
---
{
    Prepend: {
        Array: 1 >> [2, 3], // [1, 2, 3]
        EmptyArray: 1 >> [], // [1]
        TimeZoneWithName: |2020-01-01T10:00:00-05:00| >>
            "America/Los_Angeles", // |2020-01-01T07
                :00:00-08:00|
        TimeZoneWithNumber: |2020-01-01T10:00:00-05:00| >>
```

```
            |-08:00| // |2020-01-01T07:00:00-08:00|
    },
    Append: {
        Array: [2, 3] << 1, // [2, 3, 1]
        EmptyArray: [] << 1 // [1]
    }
}
```

> **Reminder**
>
> You can use the - operator to remove an item from an array.

There are more operators to discuss but we will talk about those later in this chapter because of their complexity (if/else, do, and using).

> **Note**
>
> For a complete list of all DataWeave operators and more information about them, please visit the official documentation: https://docs.mulesoft.com/dataweave/latest/dw-operators.

We now have a better idea of the different operators that can be found in DataWeave. With these, you can transform values or you can create conditionals to dynamically control the flow of your script. Now let's learn about one of the most basic concepts of programming languages: how to create and use variables.

Creating and using variables

Having the ability to create and use variables is needed in programming languages because it helps us save specific information in them and the ability to reuse them in other parts of the script. This is especially helpful when there are big expressions to retrieve specific data and we don't want to repeat the same expensive expression over and over again; instead, we want to reference the value that resulted from the expression. We can achieve this with variables.

Before we begin talking about the syntax, let's do a quick summary of what variables are in DataWeave:

- Because of DataWeave's nature, variables behave like functions.
- Lambda (anonymous) functions can be assigned to a variable (we will discuss functions after this section).

- Variables are defined with the `var` keyword.

- Variables need to have a value. No empty variables can be created.

- Variables are immutable – their value does not change.

- Variables can have data types manually assigned to them, although it's not required.

- Variables can be local or global. We will learn about global variables in this section, but we will talk about local variables later in the chapter when we talk about the `do` keyword.

Now let's understand how to use variables with some code examples.

Defining a simple variable

The first thing we need to learn is how to define a variable and how to call it from the rest of the script. To define a variable on the header of the script, you can use the following syntax:

```
var variableName = value
```

After you define your variable in the header, you can reference it in the body of the script. Here's an example:

simple-var.dwl

```
%dw 2.0
output application/dw
var hello = "Hello World"
---
hello // outputs "Hello World"
```

In a lot of programming languages, variables need to have a data type assigned to them to avoid mistakes. While this is not necessary in DataWeave, it can be added for extra peace of mind. Let's see how.

Assigning a data type to a variable

As we previously said, variables can have data types manually assigned to them. This is helpful when you want to check for mistakes in your script before getting to runtime. It's an additional layer of quality you can add to your code. The syntax to assign a data type would be like this:

```
var variableName: type = value
```

The type can be any of the predefined data types we learned about (String, Null, Boolean, Array, etc.) or it can also be a custom type created and defined by you. Custom types are out of the scope of this book, but you can create them using the keyword `type`. To learn more about custom types, please visit the official documentation: `https://docs.mulesoft.com/dataweave/latest/dataweave-type-system`

Now let's see an example of a variable with a data type:

var-with-type.dwl

```
%dw 2.0
output application/dw
var hello: String = "Hello World"
---
hello // outputs "Hello World"
```

Now if you try to assign any other value to this variable that's not a string, you will receive an error from DataWeave.

You may not see the full picture of how this is useful with this example because we already know the value is a string. However, when you're dealing with real-life transformations, variables' values tend to be dynamic data assigned from the input that is received. Or, you can also have very big DataWeave scripts with complex logic, and assigning a value to your variables helps you to make sure your code is bullet-proof and ready for any kind of data type that is received. Assigning types to your variables or functions is not always necessary, but it does help to have better-quality code.

Let's now see how to assign a lambda to a variable.

Assigning a lambda function to a variable

Finally, let's see how to define a variable with a lambda function. We won't get into the details of how lambdas work right now because we will talk about it in the next section, but it's good for you to have the syntax at this point:

```
var variableName = (params) -> body
```

Here's a very simple example that is taking just one argument and returning it as is:

var-with-lambda.dwl

```
%dw 2.0
output application/dw
var hello = (str) -> str
```

```
---
hello("Hello World") // outputs "Hello World"
```

This might look confusing to you if it's the first time you've seen a lambda expression, but don't worry, we will understand more about them in the following section.

> **Note**
>
> To read more about variables in DataWeave and some additional examples with lambdas, please visit the official documentation: `https://docs.mulesoft.com/dataweave/latest/dataweave-variables`.

Let's now talk about functions and the different ways they can be used in DataWeave.

Defining and calling functions

Another big part of programming languages is the ability to define pieces of functionality in functions or methods that can be reused in the rest of the code.

The same as we did with variables, let's first do a quick summary of what functions are in DataWeave:

- There are two ways of defining and calling a function: named functions and anonymous functions (lambdas).
- Named functions are defined with the `fun` keyword.
- Lambdas can be assigned to variables.
- Functions need to return a value. No *void* functions can be created.
- Functions' parameters and functions themselves can have data types manually assigned to them, although it's not required.
- Functions can be local or global. We will learn about global functions in this section, but we will talk about local functions later in the chapter (the `do` keyword).
- Parameters are optional but encouraged for pure functions.

Now we can jump into some code examples.

Creating named functions

To define a named function in the header of the script, you can use the following syntax:

```
fun functionName(arg0, arg1, argN) = body
```

After you define your named function in the header, you can call it from the body of the script followed by (). If no parameters are needed, leave the parentheses empty. If parameters are required, provide the values inside the parentheses. Here's an example without parameters:

simple-fun.dwl

```
%dw 2.0
output application/dw
fun echo() = "Hello World"
---
echo() // outputs "Hello World"
```

Although, that's not very useful if it's just returning the same value without parameters. In that case, it's better to use a variable. Let's add some parameters to return the value provided instead of a hardcoded message:

simple-fun-with-args.dwl

```
%dw 2.0
output application/dw
fun echo(msg) = msg
---
echo("Hello World") // outputs "Hello World"
```

Now we're talking! We have created our first named function.

You can also assign default values to the parameters if needed. These are called **optional parameters**. But note that you can only have optional parameters at the end of the function definition and the rest of the parameters need to be at the beginning. In simpler words: optional parameters always have to be at the right, inside of the parentheses:

simple-fun-opt-args.dwl

```
%dw 2.0
output application/dw
fun echo(msg1, msg2 = "!") = msg1 ++ msg2 //
    ++ concatenates the strings
---
{
    twoArgs: echo("Hello ", "World"), // outputs "Hello
```

```
        World"
    oneArg: echo("Hello") // outputs "Hello!"
}
```

Remember we can also assign types to the parameters or the function itself. We will learn how to add data types to the named functions later in this section when we talk about function overloading. Let's now learn how lambdas work.

Creating anonymous functions (lambdas)

Why are lambdas called anonymous functions? Because they don't have a name assigned to them. In our previous example, we created a function called echo, but with lambdas, there is no need to associate the function with a name. Let's see the syntax:

```
(arg0, arg1, argN) -> body
```

As you can see, you don't need the fun keyword or the name of the function. Just the parameters and the body of the function. Because of this, you can't create lambdas in the header of the script as you do with named functions. You can, however, assign lambdas to variables or use them in the body of the script. Let's see how we can create the previous named function as a lambda inside a variable instead:

lambda-in-var.dwl

```
%dw 2.0
output application/dw
var echo = (msg1, msg2 = "!") -> msg1 ++ msg2 //
    ++ concatenates the strings
---
{
    twoArgs: echo("Hello ", "World"), // outputs "Hello
        World"
    oneArg: echo("Hello") // outputs "Hello!"
}
```

We mentioned you can also use lambdas from the body of the script. You can do this directly in the body or as a parameter to another function. To use a lambda in the script's body, you can use the following syntax:

```
((arg0, arg1, argN) -> body)(arg0Value, arg1Value,
    argNValue)
```

Lambdas in DataWeave are mostly used as parameters to other functions and not so much in the body of the script, but here's an example to have the same functionality as before from the script's body:

lambda-in-body.dwl

```
%dw 2.0
output application/dw
---
((msg1, msg2 = "!") -> msg1 ++ msg2)("Hello ", "World")
// outputs "Hello World"
```

This looks more complex than the rest of the examples because we are not just defining the lambda but we are also calling it right after we define it. In the rest of the examples, we define the functions in the header and call them in the body. In this example, we do both actions within the same line. This, and the lack of reuse, is the reason why lambdas in the body of the script are not popular.

We will learn later how to call lambdas in a third way – from within a function. Let's now learn about function overloading in DataWeave.

Using function overloading

Here is where we will talk about defining types for the parameters and the functions because we need them to make use of function overloading. Let's look at a quick code example and then we can analyze it further to understand this concept:

fun-overloading.dwl

```
%dw 2.0
output application/dw
fun plus(str1: String, str2: String): String = str1 ++ str2
fun plus(num1: Number, num2: Number): Number = num1 + num2
fun plus(data1, data2): Null = null
---
{
    Strings: plus("Hello ", "World"), // "Hello World"
    Numbers: plus(1, 2), // 3
    Others: plus(1, "World") // null
}
```

In this example, we have three overloaded functions. We know they are overloaded because they share the same name: plus, but their parameters' types are different. Let's take a closer look at the first overloaded function (the third line from the previous script):

```
fun plus(str1: String, str2: String): String = str1 ++ str2
```

This function accepts two parameters: str1 and str2. They are both type String and we know this because they have a type assigned to them by specifying str1: String and str2: String. The function itself also has a type assigned to it, which is also String. We can see this after the parentheses and before the = character:): String =. This function takes two strings and concatenates them as one. Now let's see the second overloaded function:

```
fun plus(num1: Number, num2: Number): Number = num1 + num2
```

This function also accepts two parameters: num1 and num2. Both of these and the function itself are of type Number. This function is using the + operator to add the two numbers and return the results. Finally, here's the third overloaded function:

```
fun plus(data1, data2): Null = null
```

This function also accepts two parameters: data1 and data2. However, they don't have any specific type assigned to them. This means that the type they are accepting is Any. Any is the data type used to define all the data types. You could also explicitly assign this type to the two parameters by writing (data1: Any, data2: Any) and it will work the same way. The function itself is of type Null, which means that it will always return a null value.

You can see right away the advantages of using function overloading in your scripts. You can use the same named function but with different parameters and get different results. In the previous examples, all three of our functions contained two parameters, but you can add functions with more or fewer parameters and that also works.

> **Important**
> The order of how you define the overloaded functions matters. If you define the third function (using Any) before the other two, this will be the only function that will run every time since both String and Number are cataloged inside Any.

Now that we learned how to define data types for our parameters and functions, let's learn about the final concept: how to use recursiveness with functions.

Understanding recursive functions

A recursive function has the ability to call itself from within the same function. This is useful for a number of cases in which you need to work with trees. Let's see an example of a function that will execute a summation from a number:

sum-recursive-fun.dwl

```
%dw 2.0
output application/dw
fun sum(number: Number): Number =
    if (number > 0)
        number + sum(number - 1)
    else 0
---
sum(3) // 6
```

In the last line, we can see that we called the function sum with a parameter value of 3, which results in 6. This is the number of iterations this function does in this case:

1. The parameter number is 3, which is more than 0, so it executes `number + sum(number - 1)`, which means `3 + sum(2)`.

2. Now number is 2, still more than 0, so it executes `2 + sum(1)`.

3. Now number is 1, still more than 0, so it executes `1 + sum(0)`.

4. Now number is 0, which is not more than 0, so now it returns 0 instead of calling the sum function again.

5. Now that we have broken the recursiveness cycle, 0 goes back to the previous call (*step 3*) where we executed `1 + sum(0)`. Since our result from `sum(0)` was 0, we can now add `1 + 0` to get the result of 1.

6. We go back to the previous call (*step 2*) where `sum(1)` results in 1. We can now add `2 + 1` to get the result of 3.

7. Finally, we go back to the first step where we initiated the recursion. `sum(2)` results in 3, so we can now add `3 + 3` to get the final result of 6.

If you're more of a visual learner, here are some rough diagrams to show the previous steps.

> **Note**
>
> This was created with the purpose of aiding the understanding of this process and not as a formal flow diagram.

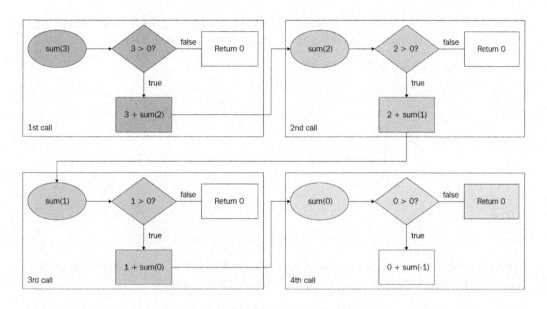

Figure 6.1 – Diagram showing steps 1-4

In this first diagram (*Figure 6.1*), we can see steps 1-4, from doing the first call of sum(3) up until getting the final result 0 from the fourth call sum(0). As you can see, we are creating a total of four calls to the function sum. This is important to notice and we will learn why it matters in a moment. Now let's see steps 5-7.

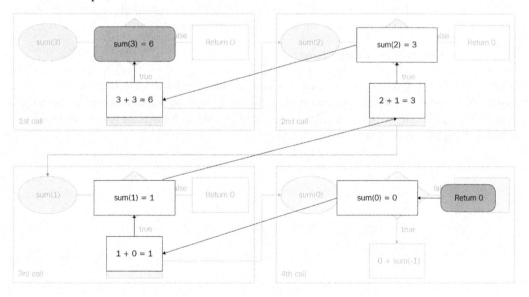

Figure 6.2 – Diagram showing steps 5-7

In this second diagram (*Figure 6.2*), we can see steps 5-7, from getting the result of our last call (0) up until returning the final result to the calling function (sum(3)), which is 6.

Here's another way to look at this set of calls:

```
sum(3)
3 + sum(2)
3 + (2 + sum(1))
3 + (2 + (1 + sum(0)))
3 + (2 + (1 + 0))
3 + (2 + 1)
3 + 3
6
```

In the preceding code, we can see the tree of calls we're creating in the background with this recursive function, right from calling sum(3) up until getting 6 as the final result.

This was a simple example with only four calls. It's not a big deal. The problem comes when we hit the memory limit. By default, there is a limit of 255 recursive calls that can be done at a time. This limit can be extended by modifying some configurations, but it might hurt your app's performance. You can try this out for yourself by using the previous code but instead of calling sum(3) in the body, try using bigger numbers. If you call sum(254), it'll work because we're exactly at the limit of the 255 calls. However, if we attempt to do sum(255) or a higher number, we will get a StackOverflow error.

There is a way to "bypass" this limit, and not only by adjusting your configuration but by actually rewriting your code. Let's learn how to do this using tail recursive functions.

Understanding tail recursive functions

These are still considered recursive functions because they continue to call themselves. However, instead of creating a tree of calls or a call inside a call inside a call, we will now be passing the result of each call in a parameter to the next call. Let's see this in action with the same functionality as before but now using a tail recursive function:

sumtail-recursive-fun.dwl

```
%dw 2.0
output application/dw
fun sumtail(number: Number, result: Number = 0): Number =
    if (number > 0)
        sumtail(number - 1, result + number)
    else result
---
sumtail(3) // 6
```

We still call the function with a parameter value of 3, which results in 6. Let's analyze how the iterations work in this case:

1. The parameter number is 3 and result is 0 (we are using this as an optional parameter so we don't have to pass it in the initial call, but we have the option to send it in the next calls). The parameter number is more than 0, so it executes sumtail(number - 1, result + number), which means sumtail(2,3).

2. Now, number is 2 and result is 3. number is still more than 0, so it executes sumtail(1,5).

3. Now, number is 1 and result is 5. number is still more than 0, so it executes sumtail(0,6).

4. Now, number is 0 and result is 6. number is no longer more than 0, so now it returns result (6) instead of calling the sumtail function again.

We can immediately notice there are fewer steps than for the previous function. Let's now look at some diagrams to picture this process better.

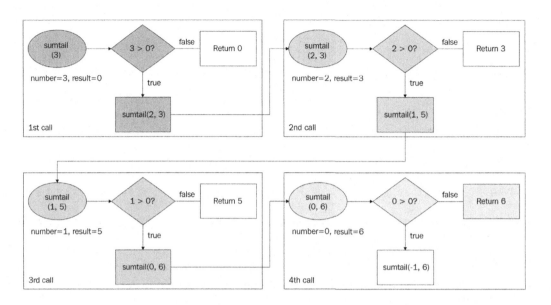

Figure 6.3 – Diagram showing all steps

We don't need two diagrams to explain all the steps as we previously did. When using tail recursive functions, there is no need to *go back* and report the result to the calling function. Since the result is saved and passed along to the next function, the final result can simply be returned to the initial caller.

Now let's look at the text representation of the set of calls as we previously did:

```
sumtail(3)
sumtail(2,3)
sumtail(1,5)
sumtail(0,6)
6
```

We can also immediately see there are fewer threads or steps in comparison to recursive functions. We also see the shape is not that of a triangle or an arrow, but they are just calls being made one after the other until we get to the final result. If we go back to the code example, you can try using bigger numbers now (i.e., sumtail(500)) and you won't get the StackOverflow error as we previously did because this function is being called one at a time as opposed to leaving the calls in memory.

> **Note**
>
> To read more details about functions in DataWeave and additional examples, please visit the official documentation:
>
> https://docs.mulesoft.com/dataweave/latest/dataweave-functions

We now have knowledge of some of the basic concepts of programming languages and how they apply to DataWeave. We still need to understand flow control statements such as `if/else`, but before that, let's take a look at what selectors are in DataWeave and why they are an important concept.

Retrieving data with selectors

We've mentioned a lot of times before that DataWeave is a transformational language. Often, there's an input that needs to be transformed into an output. Sometimes we need to retrieve specific information from that input, and we can achieve that with selectors. Let's take a look at the most popular selectors:

- **Single-value**: This selector can be applied to data containing key-value pairs and it's used to retrieve the first value that matches the given key in the first level. Its syntax is `<data>.key` or `<data>."key"` – the latter is used when there are reserved characters or keywords being used in the name of the key. Here are some examples – pay close attention to `SingleValue2` (only retrieves `"value2"` and not `"value2.1"`) and `SingleValue4` (`"key3.1"` is not found because it's on a deeper level):

single-value-selector.dwl

```
%dw 2.0
output application/dw
var objExample = {
    key1: "value1",
    key2: "value2",
    key2: "value2.1", // note this key is repeated (key2)
    key3: {
        "key3.1": "value3.1",
        "key3.2": {
            "key3.1": "value3.2"
        }
    }
}
---
{
    SingleValue1: objExample.key1, // "value1"
    SingleValue2: objExample.key2, // "value2"
    SingleValue3: objExample.key3, // {"key3.1":"value3.1",
        "key3.2":{...}}
```

```
        SingleValue4: objExample."key3.1" // null
}
```

- **Multi-value**: This selector can be applied to data containing key-value pairs and it's used to retrieve an array with the value(s) that matches the given key in the first level. Its syntax is `<data>.*key` or `<data>.*"key"` – the latter is used when there are reserved characters or keywords being used in the name of the key. Here are some examples – pay close attention to `MultiValue2` (retrieves both values and not just one) and `MultiValue4` (`"key 3.1"` is not found because it's on a deeper level):

multi-value-selector.dwl

```
%dw 2.0
output application/dw
var objExample = {
    key1: "value1",
    key2: "value2",
    key2: "value2.1", // note this key is repeated (key2)
    key3: {
        "key3.1": "value3.1",
        "key3.2": {
            "key3.1": "value3.2"
        }
    }
}
---
{
    MultiValue1: objExample.*key1, // ["value1"]
    MultiValue2: objExample.*key2, // ["value2","value2.1"]
    MultiValue3: objExample.*key3, // [{"key3.1":
        "value3.1", ... }]
    MultiValue4: objExample.*"key3.1" // null
}
```

- **Descendants**: This selector can be applied to data containing key-value pairs and it's used to retrieve an array with the value(s) that matches the given key at any level. Its syntax is `<data>..key` or `<data>.."key"` – the latter is used when there are reserved characters or keywords being used in the name of the key. Here are some examples – pay close attention to Descendants2 (retrieves only the first value if there are two keys with the same name on the same level):

descendants-selector.dwl

```
%dw 2.0
output application/dw
var objExample = {
    key1: "value1",
    key2: "value2",
    key2: "value2.1", // note this key is repeated (key2)
    key3: {
        "key3.1": "value3.1",
        "key3.2": {
            "key3.1": "value3.2"
        }
    }
}
---
{

    Descendants1: objExample..key1, // ["value1"]
    Descendants2: objExample..key2, // ["value2"]
    Descendants3: objExample..key3, // [{"key3.1":
        "value3.1", ... }]
    Descendants4: objExample.."key3.1", // ["value3.1",
        "value3.2"]
    Descendants5: objExample.."key3.2" // [{"key3.1":
        "value3.2"}]
}
```

- **Key-value pair**: This selector can be applied to data containing key-value pairs and it's used to retrieve key-value pairs that match the given key in the first level. Its syntax is `<data>.&key` or `<data>.&"key"` – the latter is used when there are reserved characters or keywords being used in the name of the key. Here are some examples – pay close attention to `KeyValuePair4` (`"key3.1"` is not found because it's on a deeper level):

key-value-pair-selector.dwl

```
%dw 2.0
output application/dw
var objExample = {
    key1: "value1",
    key2: "value2",
    key2: "value2.1", // note this key is repeated (key2)
    key3: {
        "key3.1": "value3.1",
        "key3.2": {
            "key3.1": "value3.2"
        }
    }
}
---
{

    KeyValuePair1: objExample.&key1, // {key1:"value1"}
    KeyValuePair2: objExample.&key2, // {key2:"value2"
        ,key2:"value2.1"}
    KeyValuePair3: objExample.&key3, // {key3:{...}}
    KeyValuePair4: objExample.&"key3.1" // null

}
```

- **Index**: This selector can be applied to data to retrieve the given index (Number) from it. Indexes start at 0 and can also be counted backward (i.e., the last item is -1). Its syntax is `<data>[index]`. Here are some examples:

index-selector.dwl

```
%dw 2.0
output application/dw
var objExample = {
    key1: "value1", // index 0 or -4
    key2: "value2", // index 1 or -3
    key2: "value2.1", // index 2 or -2
    key3: { //index 3 or -1
        "key3.1": "value3.1",
        "key3.2": {
            "key3.1": "value3.2"
        }
    }
}
var arrExample = [
    1, // index 0 or -6
    "Hello", // index 1 or -5
    key1: "value1", // index 2 or -4
    {key2: "value2"}, // index 3 or -3
    [2, 3], // index 4 or -2
    [4, [5, [6, 7]]] // index 5 or -1
]
---
{
    Index1: objExample[0], // "value1"
    Index2: objExample[-1], // {"key3.1":"value3.1",
        "key3.2":{...}}
    Index3: arrExample[1], // "Hello"
    Index4: arrExample[-1], // [4,[5,[6,7]]]
    Index5: "Hello"[-4] // "e"
}
```

- **Range**: This selector can be applied to data to retrieve the given range of indexes (Range) from it. Indexes start at 0 and can also be counted backward (i.e., the last item is -1). Its syntax is: `<data>[index to index]`. Here are some examples:

range-selector.dwl

```
%dw 2.0
output application/dw
var arrExample = [
    1, // index 0 or -6
    "Hello", // index 1 or -5
    key1: "value1", // index 2 or -4
    {key2: "value2"}, // index 3 or -3
    [2, 3], // index 4 or -2
    [4, [5, [6, 7]]] // index 5 or -1
]
---
{
    Range1: arrExample[0 to 3], // [1,"Hello",{key1:
        "value1"},{key2:"value2"}]
    Range2: arrExample[-1 to 0], // [[4,[5,[6,7]]], ... 1]
    Range3: "Hello"[-1 to 0], // "olleH"
    Range4: "Hello World"[0 to 4], // "Hello"
    Range5: "Hello World"[0 to -1] // "Hello World"
}
```

There are more selectors you can use in DataWeave, but they might be more complex to understand. For the purpose of this book, we want to mention the simpler concepts to get you started. However, there are a few more examples we want to show you so you are aware of their existence.

For the following example, we'll make use of three different variables: `objExample`, `arrExample`, and `dynamicKey`. Let's first see the definition of `objExample`:

additional-selectors-examples.dwl

```
var objExample = {
    key1: "value1",
    key2: "value2",
    key2: "value2.1",
```

```
    key3: {
        "key3.1": "value3.1",
        "key3.2": {
            "key3.1": "value3.2",
            key2: "value2.2"
        }
    }
}
```

There are several key-value pairs and `key3` contains nested key-value pairs. We will use these to demonstrate which selectors work with nested values and which don't. Next, we have the `arrExample` variable:

```
var arrExample = [
    1, // index 0 or -6
    "Hello", // index 1 or -5
    key1: "value1", // index 2 or -4
    {key2: "value2"}, // index 3 or -3
    [2, 3], // index 4 or -2
    [4, [5, [6, 7]]] // index 5 or -1
]
```

This is an array of different data types such as numbers, strings, objects, and arrays. The last array contains nested values to demonstrate how the selectors behave with them as well. Finally, we have the `dynamicKey` variable:

```
var dynamicKey = "key1"
```

This will be used to demonstrate how to retrieve values using dynamic data and not just hardcoded data.

Next, we created a function to retrieve a dynamic value to demonstrate this behavior as well:

```
fun getDynamicKey(value: Number | String): String =
    "key" ++ value
```

Now that we have defined our variables and functions, let's see some examples of other selectors. First, we have `Example1`:

```
---
{
    Example1: {
```

```
            MultiValue: objExample.*key2, // ["value2",
            "value2.1"]
            Descendants: objExample..key2, // ["value2",
            "value2.2"]
            Combined: objExample..*key2, // ["value2",
            "value2.1","value2.2"]
            "Descendants-KeyValue": objExample..&key2 //
                [{"key2":"value2","key2":"value2.1"},
                    {"key2":"value2.2"}]
        },
```

Here, you can see the differences between using the multi-value selector and the descendants selector and how by combining them, you can retrieve more values than using them separately. You can also combine other selectors such as the descendants selector and key-value pair to retrieve not only the values but also the keys (if needed).

Next, we have Example2:

```
    Example2: {
        Object: objExample[-1][1][0], // "value3.2"
        Array: arrExample[-1][-1][-1][0], // 6
    },
```

Here, you can see how the index selector can be combined to dive into the different levels of the data.

Now let's see Example3:

```
    Example3: objExample[-1].."key3.1", //
        ["value3.1","value3.2"]
```

Here, you can see another example of combining different selectors to get the required data.

Finally, let's look at Example4:

```
    Example4: {
        Dynamic1: objExample["key1"], // "value1"
        Dynamic2: objExample[dynamicKey], // "value1"
        Dynamic3: objExample[getDynamicKey(1)], // "value1"
        Dynamic4: objExample[getDynamicKey("1")] //
            "value1"
```

```
        }
    }
```

In `Example4`, while not previously mentioned, you can see a glimpse of how the **dynamic** operator can be used to retrieve data. You can pass different kinds of expressions to get the results you need.

> **Note**
>
> As mentioned before, the purpose of this book is to get you started with the basic concepts. There are more DataWeave selectors that we are not covering here. For a complete list, please visit the following official documentation pages:
>
> https://docs.mulesoft.com/dataweave/latest/dataweave-selectors
>
> https://docs.mulesoft.com/dataweave/latest/dataweave-cookbook-extract-data

We've covered some of the most used selectors. You now have a better understanding of how to retrieve specific data from an input source. You can then transform this data further if needed. Now let's take a look at our final basic concept that is also used in other programming languages: how to create scopes and how to control the flow of code.

Understanding scopes and flow control

When you are working on your transformations, you need to be able to control the flow of the code – whether it goes down one path or another – depending on some conditions. You may already be familiar with some of these operations from other programming languages. Using `if/else` is very popular among the most popular languages and you may also be familiar with `match/case` (or `switch/case` from other languages). We'll also learn about the `do` keyword to create scopes. Let's take a look at how to use these in DataWeave.

Adding conditions with if/else

Sometimes you need to create different outputs or code depending on other information you might receive as inputs. To create conditional statements or different routes for your data, you can use the `if/else` operators with the following syntax:

```
if (condition) expression else expression
```

An important thing to notice is that an `if` condition should almost always contain an `else` expression. This is because DataWeave knows there must be data being returned at all times. Remember we mentioned DataWeave is a transformational language and there are no `void` functions. Data must always be returned in every expression. Let's take a look at an example:

simple-if-else.dwl

```
%dw 2.0
output application/dw
var age: Number = 25
---
if (age >= 21) "Adult"
else "Minor"
// returns "Adult"
```

Here, we can see that there will always be data being returned. It's simple: if the age is more than or equal to 21, then it'll return the string `"Adult"`; if not, it'll return `"Minor"`. There's a problem with this example: what would happen if the `age` variable turns out to be negative numbers? We should return a different string. Let's see how to chain several conditions.

Chaining if/else statements

Following the previous example, we also want to verify that the given age is more than 0. Otherwise, it's invalid data. We mentioned an `if` condition must include an `else` expression to always return data regardless of the conditions. This also applies to chained statements. Let's see the syntax:

```
if (condition) expression
else if (condition) expression
else expression
```

See how what previously was an `else` now turned to `else if`? And the same rule applies. You can keep adding `else if` statements as long as there's a final `else` expression to take care of the data that doesn't match any condition. Let's see an example:

chained-if-else.dwl

```
%dw 2.0
output application/dw
var age: Number = -1
---
if (age >= 21) "Adult"
```

```
else if (age >= 0) "Minor"
else "Invalid data"
// returns "Invalid data"
```

Now, our age variable is -1 to test that our new functionality is working, and we can correctly see it returns "Invalid data" because it's not greater than or equal to either 21 or 0.

Another important thing to notice is that the order of the conditions matters. If you were to swap the first and second conditions' order, it wouldn't work as we expect. If our age was 25 but the first condition was if (age >= 0) "Minor", then it would return "Minor" because 25 is greater than or equal to 0.

Let's now see a case where an if case can be alone without an else condition.

Conditioning key-value pairs with if

Let's say we want to create an object but we want to dynamically decide to either show or hide certain key-value pairs from the output object. In this case, we can make use of the if operator without having to add an else. You can use the following syntax to achieve this:

```
(keyName: value) if condition
```

You just have to surround the key-value pair in parentheses and then add the if condition. If the condition is met, then the key-value pair will be returned, otherwise, it won't be shown. Let's see an example:

key-value-pair-if-condition.dwl

```
%dw 2.0
output application/dw
var value2 = 0
---
{
    key1: "value1",
    (key2: value2) if value2 != 0
}
// outputs {key1:"value1"}
```

Here, the key-value pair for key1 is correctly displayed in the output, but the key-value pair for key2 is not because our variable value2 doesn't meet the condition.

That's it for using if/else statements. But that's not the only way to create conditions or control the flow. Let's now see a different statement.

Using match/case for pattern matching

Some say this is a more elegant approach than if/else, but it is also harder to understand if it's the first time you're seeing syntax like this. The main difference between the two is that if isn't necessarily based on data. You can create statements and conditions with the data you choose. But match *is* based on data. The conditions you create with match are *for* the data you first provided. Let's see the syntax so we can jump on to an example:

```
data match {
    case condition -> expression
    case condition -> expression
    else -> expression
}
```

Let's take our previous age example to understand how to use it with match statements:

simple-match-case.dwl

```
%dw 2.0
output application/dw
var age: Number = 25
---
age match {
    case a if a >= 21 -> "Adult"
    case a if a >= 0 -> "Minor"
    else -> "Invalid Data"
}
// outputs "Adult"
```

Granted, in this case, we are using the if operator inside the match statement. It might look like double work, but don't underestimate the power of match/case statements. Pattern matching is a more advanced topic with way more examples and other ways to use it that don't necessarily include the if operator. However, all these ways are beyond the scope of this book, which is to get you started with the basics.

> **Note**
>
> To read more details and examples about pattern matching in DataWeave with match/case statements, please visit the official documentation:
>
> https://docs.mulesoft.com/dataweave/latest/dataweave-pattern-matching

We caught a glimpse of how pattern matching works in DataWeave and the differences between using `if/else` and `match/case`. Let's finish this section by discovering how to create scopes.

Creating scopes with do

When we were learning about variables and functions, we mentioned we could use both local and global variables, but we only saw how to use them in a global context (in the script's header). Here is where we finally learn how to create local scopes with the `do` operator. Let's first take a look at the syntax:

```
do {
    header
    ---
    body
}
```

As you can see, we create a whole new `header` and `body` section, but they only live inside this expression. Any code outside of these brackets can't use what we define in this scope. The only thing *visible* externally will be the output of what is generated inside the scope. Now let's see an example:

local-context-do.dwl

```
%dw 2.0
output application/dw
fun sumtail(number: Number, result: Number = 0):
    Number = do {
    var newNumber = number - 1
    var newResult = result + number
    ---
    if (number > 0)
        sumtail(newNumber, newResult)
    else result
}
---
sumtail(255) // 32640
```

We are reusing a previous example used to demonstrate a tail recursive function but now creating a local context inside the `sumtail` function. After adding the `do` operator and opening the curly brackets, we are now inside of a local context. We created two new variables called `newNumber` and `newResult`, which are used in the body of the local context.

> **Note**
>
> There is also a `using` operator that can be used instead of `do`, but this is an old operator that is only supported for backward compatibility, so we don't recommend you learn about `using` unless it's for a previous Mule runtime version.

You can use not only the `do` operator inside a function definition as we just did but also to create contexts in several settings. It can be used inside variables, in the script's body, or inside other functions you're calling (which is one of the most used cases).

You can also create more contexts inside contexts if your use case requires it, but we strongly recommend against it. The cleaner your code looks, the easier it is to maintain for other developers. It can also lead to the creation of *spaghetti code* and that's the last thing we want since it can lead to more human error.

> **Note**
>
> To read more details about the `do`, `if`, and `else` operators in DataWeave and additional examples, please visit the official documentation:
>
> https://docs.mulesoft.com/dataweave/latest/dw-operators#scope-and-flow-control-operators
>
> https://docs.mulesoft.com/dataweave/latest/dataweave-flow-control

We've finished understanding the basic concepts of the language and how to perform some basic things such as creating and using functions and variables, using operators and selectors, creating local scopes, and making use of flow control operators.

Summary

In this chapter, we learned that DataWeave is a functional programming language and that a script has two sections: the header and the body. In the header, we keep global variables or functions, and additional directives to specify input, output, DataWeave version, and other information. In the body, we write the code that will be executed.

We learned two different ways to add comments to your code: on a single line (with `//`) or on multiple lines (with `/*...*...*/`).

There are simple, composite, and complex data types. However, we listed only the simple (**String**, **Boolean**, **Number**, **Regex**, **Null**, **Date**, and **Time-related**) and composite (**Array**, **Object**) ones to understand the basic or most used types.

We listed some of the most popular data formats, such as CSV, DW, Java, JSON, and XML, to get a better understanding of what these formats look like and how are they used in DataWeave to transform data.

We learned about several operators and their categories: mathematical, equality and relational, logical, and prepend and append. We saw different examples of each one of them to see how they can be used with different data types.

We talked about what variables are in DataWeave and how to define them with the keyword var. We defined a simple variable, we assigned a data type to it, and we assigned a lambda function to it too.

We talked about what functions are in DataWeave and how to define them with the keyword fun. We can create named functions, assign data types to the function itself or its parameters, and define optional parameters. We learned what lambdas are (anonymous functions) and how to create them. We saw examples of function overloading, recursive functions, and tail recursive functions.

We learned about several selectors and how to use them to retrieve data from an input source.

Finally, we saw how to add conditions and chain them with if/else statements, how to condition key-value pairs with the if operator, how to use match/case for pattern matching, and how to create scopes with the do operator.

In the next chapter, we'll expand our DataWeave knowledge from the basics to learning how to use DataWeave's functions and modules, practical use cases, and how to use DataWeave in Anypoint Studio.

Questions

Take a moment to answer the following questions to serve as a recap of what you just learned in this chapter:

1. How do you specify the DataWeave version inside a script if you're using version 2.4?
2. What operators can you use to add or remove values to/from an array?
3. How can you define and call a global variable named hello of type String with the value "Hello World"?
4. How can you define and call a global function named sum of type Number that accepts two parameters (both of type Number) and outputs the addition of both parameters?
5. Create a function called order of type String that accepts one parameter of type String called original. Open a local context inside the function and create a local variable called new of type String that reverses original (hint: use selectors). In the body of the local context – inside the variable – create some logic to return the following strings:

    A. <original> goes after <new> – when the value of new goes first in alphabetical order
    B. <original> goes before <new> – when the value of original goes first in alphabetical order

C. `<original>` is a palindrome – when it's a palindrome, meaning the original value and the reversed value are still the same string

Hint: Use ++ to concatenate values and remember to use operators.

Answers

1. Using `%dw 2.0` in the script's header because only major versions have to be provided, not minor versions.

2. Addition (+), subtraction (-), prepend (>>), and append (<<)

3. It can be defined as follows:

    ```
    var hello: String = "Hello World"
    ---
    hello
    ```

4. It can be defined as follows:

    ```
    fun sum(p1: Number, p2: Number): Number = p1 + p2
    ---
    sum(1,2)
    ```

5. *Solution 1: Using if/else*

    ```
    fun order(original: String): String = do {
        var new: String = original[-1 to 0]
        ---
        if (original > new) original ++ " goes after " ++ new
        else if (original < new) original ++ " goes before "
          ++ new
        else original ++ " is a palindrome"
    }
    ---
    order("abc")
    ```

    Solution 2: Using match/case

    ```
    fun order(original: String): String = do {
        var new: String = original[-1 to 0]

        ---

        original match {
    ```

```
            case o if o > new -> o ++ " goes after " ++ new
            case o if o < new -> o ++ " goes before " ++ new
            else -> original ++ " is a palindrome"
        }
}
---
order("kayak")
```

7
Transforming with DataWeave

In the previous chapter, we learned the very basics of DataWeave, including how to use functions, variables, conditions, operators, and selectors, but we didn't see any transformation examples. In this chapter, we are going to learn about DataWeave modules and some of the most used functions in real life. We will cover the following topics:

- Understanding modules in DataWeave
- Using the DataWeave core functions
- Using the Transform Message component in Anypoint Studio

We cannot cover absolutely everything that you can do with DataWeave, but we will provide a guide so you can get familiar with the functions that are widely used by developers in real life. Even if you are already familiar with DataWeave, maybe there are some popular functions you want to learn more about, such as map and reduce. This chapter will provide additional tips and tricks for your development experience.

Remember DataWeave is a functional programming language. Some of these functions might look familiar to you if you come from a functional programming background. If you're new to this programming paradigm, then this chapter is great for you to get started with DataWeave's syntax and use cases.

Technical requirements

You will need the following technical requirements for this chapter.

- **An internet browser**: Google Chrome will be used throughout this chapter for the DataWeave Playground, located at https://developer.mulesoft.com/learn/dataweave/. To learn how to use the DataWeave Playground, you can follow this guide: https://developer.mulesoft.com/tutorials-and-howtos/dataweave/learn-dataweave-with-the-dataweave-playground-getting-started/.

- **Anypoint Studio**: Make sure you have Studio installed on your computer. We'll mostly practice using the DataWeave Playground, but it's also good for you to know how to use DataWeave from Studio. Download Studio from `https://mulesoft.com/studio`.

- **GitHub repository**: It's not required for you to open this repository, but it'll be easier for you to copy and paste the examples and scripts. You can access it through the following link: `https://github.com/PacktPublishing/MuleSoft-for-Salesforce-Developers`.

Understanding modules in DataWeave

Some programming languages make use of libraries to import functions or methods from other pieces of code. This is helpful to reuse complex functionality that was written by someone else instead of trying to reinvent the wheel and wasting precious development time while trying to develop the code yourself. In DataWeave, these libraries of code are called **modules**. You can either use other existing DataWeave modules or create your own custom modules, which we will see later in *Using the Transform Message component in Anypoint Studio* section.

Let's see the syntax to import these modules in DataWeave.

Importing modules and functions

There are several ways of importing modules or functions to your DataWeave scripts, depending on your preference. But all of them make use of the `import` keyword and must be located within the header of your script. Let's see some examples:

- **Import the whole module**: You can import the whole module in your script's header and reference the function with its specified module from your script's body. This is the syntax for doing so:

import-example-1.txt

```
import Module

---

Module::function()
```

This is cleaner to look at from the script's header, but it makes it look busier in the script's body.

- **Import all functions**: Another way is to import all the functions from a module and then directly reference the function from the script's body. This is the syntax for doing so:

import-example-2.txt

```
import * from Module

---

function()
```

Now, it might look busier in the script's header, but the script's body looks cleaner. However, this might make it difficult for new developers to understand where your function is coming from, especially if they are not familiar with the different available DataWeave modules and you have several modules being imported in the same script.

- **Import specific functions**: To make things more explicit, you can import specific functions from each module, like so:

import-example-3.txt

```
import function from Module
---
function()
```

Now, everyone will be able to see where each function comes from. Plus, if you're working on a very big and heavy project, making these little adjustments to the code might help with the performance of the Mule application.

You can also import several functions from the same module by separating them with a comma. See the following example:

import-example-4.txt

```
import function1, function2, function3 from Module
---
function1()
```

- **Precedence**: If you have more than one function with the same name but from different modules, whichever function/module was defined first will take precedence. See the following example:

import-example-5.txt

```
import function from Module1
import function from Module2
---
function() // from Module1
```

If you end up with something like this and want to make things less confusing, you can import just the module and not the functions. This will help you to clearly see which module the function is being used from:

import-example-6.txt

```
import Module1
import Module2
---
Module2::function()
```

- **Create aliases**: Alternately, if you want to create an alias for your functions or modules, you can use the as keyword followed by the alias. Here's the syntax:

import-example-7.txt

```
import Module1 as Mod1 // alias Mod1 for Module1
import function1 as f1 from Module2 // alias f1 for
    function1
import function2 as f2, function3 as f3 from Module3
    // aliases f2 and f3 for functions from the same
        module (Module3)
---
// Mod1::function
// f1()
// f2()
f3()
```

- **Import from folders**: Finally, when you have modules separated by :: and you want to import the whole module, you don't need to reference the whole path in the script's body, only the module name. Here's what this syntax looks like:

import-example-8.txt

```
import folder1::folder2::Module
---
Module::function()
```

We are done understanding how to import modules or functions in DataWeave. Let's now talk about some of the existing modules you can find in DataWeave so you don't have to create code from scratch.

Analyzing the existing DataWeave modules

As mentioned earlier, the focus of this book is to get you started with the basics of MuleSoft's features and products. Understanding all of the existing DataWeave modules is out of the scope of this book, but we can get a glimpse of what modules are available so you can have a better idea of them. Here's a list of some of the existing DataWeave modules:

- `dw::Core`: We will talk more about this module in the next section. All the functions within this module are imported to your script by default so you don't have to explicitly import them in the script's header.

- `dw::core::Arrays`: Here, you can find functions to work with the *Array* type (defined by `[]`). Some functions are `countBy`, `every`, `join`, `slice`, and `splitAt`. There are still more functions, but we mentioned a few so you can get a better idea of what the module does.

- `dw::core::Binaries`: Here, you can find functions to work with the *Binary* type. Its functions are `fromBase64`, `fromHex`, `readLinesWith`, `toBase64`, `toHex`, and `writeLinesWith`.

- `dw::core::Dates`: Here, you can find functions to work with the *Date* type (defined by `||`). Some functions are `atBeginningOfWeek`, `dateTime`, `today`, `tomorrow`, and `yesterday`. There are still more functions, but we mentioned a few so you can get a better idea of what the module does.

- `dw::core::Numbers`: Here, you can find functions to work with the *Number* type. Its functions are `fromBinary`, `fromHex`, `fromRadixNumber`, `toBinary`, `toHex`, and `toRadixNumber`.

- `dw::core::Objects`: Here, you can find functions to work with the *Object* type (defined by `{}`). Some functions are `divideBy`, `keySet`, `mergeWith`, `takeWhile`, and `valueSet`.

- `dw::core::Periods`: Here, you can find functions to work with the *Period* type (defined by `|P<...>|`). Some functions are `between`, `days`, `duration`, `months`, and `years`. There are more functions but we mentioned a few so you can get a better idea of what the module does.

- `dw::core::Strings`: Here, you can find functions to work with the *String* type (defined by `""`). Some functions are `camelize`, `capitalize`, `dasherize`, `isAlphanumeric`, `isLowerCase`, `pluralize`, `substring`, and `words`. There are more functions but we mentioned a few so you can get a better idea of what the module does.

- `dw::core::Types`: Here, you can find functions to work with data types. Some functions are `arrayItem`, `functionParamTypes`, `functionReturnType`, `isBooleanType`, `literalValueOf`, and `nameOf`. There are more functions but we mentioned a few so you can get a better idea of what the module does.

- `dw::core::URL`: Here, you can find functions to work with URIs. Its functions are `compose`, `decodeURI`, `decodeURIComponent`, `encodeURI`, `encodeURIComponent`, and `parseURI`.

- `dw::Crypto`: Here, you can find functions to encrypt data through common algorithms. Its functions are `HMACBinary`, `HMACWith`, `MD5`, `SHA1`, and `hashWith`.

- `dw::Mule`: Here, you can find functions to interact with the Mule runtime. Its functions are `causedBy`, `lookup`, and `p`.

- `dw::Runtime`: Here, you can find functions to interact with the DataWeave runtime. Some functions are `eval`, `fail`, `orElseTry`, `props`, `run`, `try`, and `wait`. There are more functions but we mentioned a few so you can get a better idea of what the module does.

- `dw::System`: Here, you can find functions to interact with the operating system. Its functions are `envVar` and `envVars`.

- `dw::util::Math`: Here, you can find functions to make use of mathematical functions. Its functions are `acos`, `asin`, `atan`, `cos`, `log10`, `logn`, `sin`, `tan`, `toDegrees`, and `toRadians`.

- `dw::util::Timer`: Here, you can find functions to measure time. Its functions are `currentMilliseconds`, `duration`, `time`, and `toMilliseconds`.

- `dw::util::Tree`: Here, you can find functions to handle tree structures. Some functions are `filterArrayLeafs`, `filterTree`, `mapLeafValues`, and `nodeExists`. There are more functions but we mentioned a few so you can get a better idea of what the module does.

- `dw::util::Values`: Here, you can find functions to make changes to certain values. Its functions are `attr`, `field`, `index`, `mask`, and `update`.

Note

At the time this book is being written, the latest DataWeave version is *2.4*. If there are more advanced versions by the time you read this chapter, you may want to take a look at the release notes to see what changes were implemented. To review this, you can use the following link: `https://docs.mulesoft.com/dataweave/latest/whats-new-in-dw`.

To find the complete list of modules and their corresponding functions, please refer to the official documentation: `https://docs.mulesoft.com/dataweave/latest/dw-functions`.

As you can see, there is a wide variety of modules you can take advantage of instead of having to come up with the most efficient way of doing something. We can't discuss all the modules, but we will focus on the *Core* module and its most used functions.

Using the DataWeave core functions

These functions come from the `dw::Core` module but there's no need to explicitly import it into your script. All of these functions are added to DataWeave by default so you can make use of them right away.

We will mention whether the functions are *null-safe*. This means that you can send a `null` value as the input and it won't result in a DataWeave error. Instead, it will simply give a `null` value in return so you can handle the data in further steps.

One important thing for you to understand about calling functions with two parameters is that you can use two different syntaxes to call them. This only applies to two-parameter functions. The syntax is as follows:

- **Prefix notation**, which looks like this:

```
function(arg0, arg1)
```

- **Infix notation**, which looks like this:

```
arg0 function arg1
```

You can choose whichever notation or syntax you feel more comfortable with, but most people prefer to use the infix notation whenever possible because the functions become easier to understand (without all the parentheses). This is especially helpful when working with functions that make use of lambdas as one of their parameters, such as `map`, for example. In this chapter, we will make use of the infix notation when we have two-parameter functions.

We talked about *lambdas* – or anonymous functions – in the previous chapter. However, we haven't learned how to use them as another function's parameter. We will see some examples throughout this chapter, especially with the functions for objects and arrays. To give you a quick reminder, this is the syntax to use `map` (with the infix notation), which we will see later in the chapter in the *Transforming arrays* section:

```
<Array> map ((value, index) -> <code>)
```

The first parameter is the array we use as input and the second parameter is a lambda with the `value` and `index` parameters. We can then create the transformation code to make use of these two parameters inside the lambda.

There is another syntax to use lambdas in DataWeave: the *dollar-sign syntax*. This is helpful with functionality or functions that may be more straightforward than creating the whole lambda expression. The number of dollar signs represents the number of the parameter in the lambda. For example, when using `map`, we have two parameters in the lambda: `value` and `index`. Since `value` is the first parameter, it'd be represented with $, while `index` would be represented with $$. You can now use these characters in the lambda code instead of having to explicitly declare both parameters in the lambda expression. This syntax would change to the following:

```
<Array> map (<code>)
```

We will see some more examples when talking about the functions to transform objects and arrays.

In the following sections, we will learn how to transform different data types, such as numbers, strings, objects, and arrays. We will see an overview of some of the most used functions for each specific data type and brief examples to see how these functions work.

Let's start with some functions that can be applied to more than two data types.

Transforming multiple types

Let's first take a look at some of the functions that can be used with either several data types or no parameters since they're more general:

- ++ **(plus plus)**: This function is used to concatenate two given parameters. It can be used with Array, String, Object, or some of the Date and Time-related types. For example, `[1, 2] ++ [3, 4]` results in `[1, 2, 3, 4]`.

- now: This function is used to generate a DateTime data type with the information from today's date and time. For example, `now()` can result in `|2022-06-17T15:06:37.953742Z|`.

- random: This function is used to generate a random number from `0.0` to `1.0`. For example, `random()` can result in `0.5071719753789186`.

- read: This function is used when DataWeave can't determine the type of format that is being parsed. For example, `read("[1, 2, 3]", "application/json")` results in `[1, 2, 3]`. Note that the array is first being passed as a string and is then transformed into an actual array.

- readUrl: This function is used to retrieve the data from a URL and parse it to the given data format. For example, `readUrl("https://jsonplaceholder.typicode.com/posts/1", "application/json")` results in the JSON data retrieved from the URL.

- sizeOf: This function is used to retrieve a number with the size of the given parameter. It can be used with Array, String, Object, and Null (null-safe). For example, `sizeOf([0, 1, 2, 3])` results in 4.

- typeOf: This function is used to retrieve the type of the given parameter. It can be used with any data type – which makes it null-safe. For example, `typeOf("abc")` results in `String`, `typeOf(typeOf("abc"))` results in `Type`, and `typeOf(sizeOf)` results in `Function`.

- uuid: This function is used to generate a **Universally Unique Identifier (UUID)**. For example, `uuid()` can result in `"ffe58a18-06d9-47f5-be1e-c6fb1e7cf197"`.

- with: This is a helper function that is used along with other functions, such as replace, update, or mask. We will see some of these main functions later in this chapter, in the *Transforming strings* section. For example, `"hello world" replace "world" with "muley!"` results in `"hello muley!"`.

We listed some of the functions previously, but there are more functions that we'll look at separately because they are more complex, starting with the `isEmpty` function.

isEmpty

This function returns a Boolean indicating whether the given parameter is empty or not. It can be used with Array, String, Object, and Null (null-safe). Let's see some examples:

isEmpty.dwl

```
%dw 2.0
output application/dw
---
{
    Array: isEmpty([]), // true
    String: isEmpty(""), // true
    Object: isEmpty({}), // true
    Null: isEmpty(null) // true
}
```

If there were at least one item in the array, at least one character in the string, or at least one key-value pair in the object, the result would be `false` – indicating the provided parameter is not empty.

> **Tip**
> You can use the `default` keyword to set default values in certain transformations when a `null` value is received. For empty values (`[]`, `{}`, or `""`), however, it is better to use the `isEmpty` function. To learn more about the `default` keyword, see the official documentation:
> `https://docs.mulesoft.com/dataweave/latest/dataweave-cookbook-defaults#example-of-using-the-keyword-default-to-set-a-default-value`.

log

This function doesn't affect any values or transform any data. This is used to debug the DataWeave code and log certain values to a console or the **LOG VIEWER** tab in the DataWeave Playground. It is very helpful especially when you have long pieces of code and you want to see what's happening in specific steps within it. See the following example:

log.dwl

```
%dw 2.0
output application/json
---
```

```
[1, 2, 3] map log($)
```

In this case, we're using the map function just to demonstrate (we will talk more about this function in the *Transforming arrays* section). This code is iterating through the input array and logging each item in the console. From the DataWeave Playground, it would look like this:

Figure 7.1 – View from the DataWeave Playground

There is not a way to formally debug DataWeave code yet but using this function is a close workaround. For example, you can use console.log in JavaScript to achieve the same functionality.

then

This is a helper function that is more useful in larger code. It essentially replaces the use of parentheses for certain use cases. For example, consider the following code:

```
[1, 2] + [3] // [1, 2, [3]]
```

You have an array of numbers (1 and 2) and then added a third item [3]. This results in an array containing both numbers and arrays. Let's say you wanted to flatten this array to be just an array of numbers ([1, 2, 3]). To achieve this, you can use the flatten function, which we will see in detail in the *Transforming arrays* section, but you need to surround the whole code in parentheses in order to use it, like so:

```
flatten([1, 2] + [3]) // [1, 2, 3]
```

It doesn't seem like a big deal now because we just have a line of code, but when you have hundreds of lines and lots of other parentheses, it gets harder to identify exactly where to start. This is where the then function comes in handy:

then.dwl

```
%dw 2.0
output application/json
---
[1, 2] + [3] then flatten($) // [1, 2, 3]
```

The result from the previous execution gets passed after the then function is called and becomes a lambda. We will learn how to use lambdas as a parameter to another function in the *Transforming objects* and *Transforming arrays* sections. For now, you can see the difference in the syntax and why using then can be better than adding surrounding parentheses to the code.

Now that we know some of the more general functions, let's take a look at the functions that are specifically for transforming numbers.

Transforming numbers

These functions work specifically for the Number data type. Remember that a number in DataWeave can be either a decimal or integer number. For example, say you have a decimal number such as 5.6 that you want to round up to the nearest number; so, you'd transform it to 6.

The functions are as follows:

- abs: This function is used to retrieve the absolute value of a given number. For example, abs(-9) results in 9.

- ceil: This function is used to round up the value of a given decimal number. For example, ceil(5.1) results in 6.

- floor: This function is used to round down the value of a given decimal number. For example, floor(7.9) results in 7.

- isDecimal: This function is used to indicate whether a given number is a decimal value or not. It returns true if the parameter is a decimal number or false if it isn't. For example, isDecimal(4.5) results in true and isDecimal(4) results in false.

- isEven: This function is used to indicate whether a given number is an even value or not. It returns true if the parameter is an even number or false if it isn't. For example, isEven(4) results in true and isEven(5) results in false.

- `isInteger`: This function is used to indicate whether a given number is an integer value or not. It returns `true` if the parameter is an integer number or `false` if it isn't. For example, `isInteger(5)` results in `true` and `isInteger(5.5)` results in `false`.

- `isOdd`: This function is used to indicate whether a given number is an odd value or not. It returns `true` if the parameter is an odd number or `false` if it isn't. For example, `isOdd(3)` results in `true` and `isOdd(2)` results in `false`.

- `mod`: This function is used to retrieve the modulo of a given dividend (first parameter) and divisor (second parameter). This is the remainder of dividing the two parameters. For example, `5.5 mod 5` results in `0.5`.

- `pow`: This function is used to retrieve the result of raising a given base number (first parameter) to a given power (second parameter). For example, `5 pow 3` results in `125`.

- `randomInt`: This function is used to retrieve a random integer from 0 to the given number (excluding the given number). For example, `randomInt(5)` can result in 0, 1, 2, 3, or 4.

- `round`: This function is used to round up or down the value of a given decimal number into the nearest whole number. For example, `round(4.1)` results in 4 and `round(4.5)` results in 5.

- `sqrt`: This function is used to retrieve the square root of a given number. For example, `sqrt(100)` results in `10`.

- `to`: We mentioned this function briefly in the previous chapter when we talked about ranges. This function is used to retrieve a range that falls within the two given numbers (including both numbers). For example, `1 to 5` results in `[1, 2, 3, 4, 5]`. Note that this result is not an array of numbers but a Range type.

We now know some of the functions we can use to transform numbers. Let's continue with the functions for strings.

Transforming strings

These functions work specifically for the String data type. Remember that in DataWeave, a string is conformed by using quotes around it. For example, say you have a string such as `"hello"` that you want to transform into all uppercase to be `"HELLO"`.

The functions are as follows:

- `contains`: This function is used to indicate whether a given string (first parameter) contains a given string or regular expression (second parameter). It returns `true` if it does or `false` if it doesn't. For example, `"Hello world!" contains "hi"` results in `false` and `"Hello world!" contains /\w+ \w+!/` results in `true`. This is a null-safe function – `null contains "a"` returns `false`.

- endsWith: This function is used to indicate whether a given string (first parameter) ends with a given string (second parameter). It returns true if it does or false if it doesn't. For example, "Hello world!" endsWith "orld!" results in true. This is a null-safe function – null endsWith "a" returns false.

- find: This function is used to find the indexes of a given string or regular expression (second parameter) from the given string (first parameter). If no match is found, it returns an empty array. For example, "Hello world!" find "o" results in [4, 7]. This is a null-safe function – null find "o" returns [].

- indexOf: This function is used to find the first index of a given string (second parameter) from the given string (first parameter). If no match is found, it returns -1. For example, "Hello world!" indexOf "o" results in 4. This is a null-safe function – null indexOf "o" returns -1.

- isBlank: This function is used to indicate whether a given string is blank (including empty spaces or null values). It returns true if it is or false if it isn't. For example, isBlank("   ") results in true but isBlank("   a") is false.

- lastIndexOf: This function is used to find the last index of a given string (second parameter) from the given string (first parameter). If no match is found, it returns -1. For example, "Hello world!" lastIndexOf "o" results in 7. This is a null-safe function – null lastIndexOf "o" returns -1.

- lower: This function is used to transform the given string to lowercase. For example, lower("Hello") results in "hello". This is a null-safe function – lower(null) returns null.

- match: This function is used to retrieve the matches of a given regular expression (second parameter) from the given string (first parameter). If no match is found, it returns []. Note that you will receive more items if your regular expression is separated into capture groups. For example, "Hello world!" match /\w+ \w+!/ results in ["Hello world!"] and "Hello world!" match /(\w+) (\w+)!/ results in ["Hello world!", "Hello", "world"]. This is a null-safe function – null match /\w+/ returns null.

- matches: This function is used to indicate whether a given string (first parameter) matches a given regular expression (second parameter). It returns true if there is a match or false if there isn't. For example, "Hello world!" matches /\w+ \w+!/ results in true. This is a null-safe function – null matches /\w+/ returns false.

- replace: This function is used to replace a given string or regular expression (second parameter) from the given string (first parameter). If no match is found, it returns the original string. The with function is used along with replace. For example, "Hello world!" replace "world" with "team" results in "Hello team!". This is a null-safe function – null replace "a" with "b" returns null.

- scan: This function is used to retrieve all the matches of a given regular expression (second parameter) from the given string (first parameter). If no match is found, it returns []. Note that you will receive more items if your regular expression is separated into capture groups. For example, "Hello world!" scan /\w+/ results in [["Hello"], ["world"]]. This is a null-safe function – null scan /\w+/ returns null.

- splitBy: This function is used to split a given string (first parameter) into an array of strings, separated by the given string or regular expression (second parameter). For example, "a b c" splitBy " " results in ["a","b","c"]. This is a null-safe function – null splitBy " " returns null.

- startsWith: This function is used to indicate whether a given string (first parameter) starts with a given string (second parameter). It returns true if it does or false if it doesn't. For example, "Hello world!" startsWith "Hello" results in true. This is a null-safe function – null startsWith "a" returns false.

- trim: This function is used to remove blank spaces at the beginning or the end of a given string. For example, trim(" Hello world ") results in "Hello world". This is a null-safe function – trim(null) returns null.

- upper: This function is used to transform the given string to uppercase. For example, upper("Hello") results in "HELLO". This is a null-safe function – upper(null) returns null.

We now know some of the functions we can use to transform strings. Let's continue with the functions for objects.

Transforming objects

These functions work specifically for the Object data type. Remember that in DataWeave, an object is conformed by key-value pairs and it's surrounded by curly brackets. For example, in {a: "b", c: "d"}, a and c are keys and "b" and "d" are values.

The functions are as follows:

- -- (minus minus): This function is used to remove key-value pairs (second parameter) from the given object (first parameter). As the second parameter, you can send a key-value pair, an array of strings, or an array of keys. For example, considering the same input (first parameter) {a: "b", c: "d"}, you can achieve the same output {c: "d"} with both -- {a: "b"} and -- ["a"]. This is a null-safe function.

- distinctBy: This function is used to remove duplicate key-value pairs from the given object. The second parameter of this function is a lambda with the value and key parameters. For example, {a: "b", c: "d", a: "b"} distinctBy $ results in {a: "b", c: "d"}. This is a null-safe function.

- `entriesOf`: This function is used to describe the key-value pairs from a given object. For example, `entriesOf({a: "b"})` results in `[{ key: "a", value: "b", attributes: {} }]`. This is a null-safe function.

- `filterObject`: This function is used to filter the key-value pairs from the given object. The second parameter of this function is a lambda with the `value`, `key`, and `index` parameters. For example, `{a: "b", c: "d"} filterObject $$ ~= "a"` results in `{a: "b"}`. This is a null-safe function.

- `keysOf`: This function is used to retrieve the keys from a given object. Note that this returns an array of *keys*. For example, `keysOf({a: "b", c: "d"})` results in `["a", "c"]`. This is a null-safe function.

- `mapObject`: This function is used to transform the key-value pairs from the given object. The second parameter of this function is a lambda with the `value`, `key`, and `index` parameters. For example, `{a: "b", c: "d"} mapObject {($): $$}` results in `{b: "a", d: "c"}`. This is a null-safe function.

- `namesOf`: This function is used to retrieve the names of the keys from a given object. Note that this returns an array of *strings*. For example, `namesOf({a: "b", c: "d"})` results in `["a", "c"]`. This is a null-safe function.

- `pluck`: This function is used to transform the key-value pairs from the given object into an array. The second parameter of this function is a lambda with the `value`, `key`, and `index` parameters. For example, `{a: "b", c: "d"} pluck upper("$$:$")` results in `["A:B", "C:D"]`. This is a null-safe function.

- `valuesOf`: This function is used to retrieve the values from a given object. For example, `valuesOf({a: "b", c: "d"})` results in `["b", "d"]`. This is a null-safe function.

We now know some of the functions we can use to transform objects. Let's continue with the functions for arrays.

Transforming arrays

These functions work specifically for the Array data type. Remember that in DataWeave, an array is conformed by using square brackets around it. For example, `[1, 2, 3]` is an array of numbers and `["a", "b", "c"]` is an array of strings.

The functions are as follows:

- `--` **(minus minus)**: This function is used to remove items (second parameter) from the given array (first parameter). As the second parameter, you can send an array containing the items you want to remove from the original array. For example, `[1, 2, 3] -- [1, 2]` results in `[3]`. This is a null-safe function.

- `avg`: This function is used to retrieve the average of the given array of numbers. For example, `avg([1, 2, 3])` results in 2.

- `contains`: This function is used to indicate whether a given array (first parameter) contains a given item (second parameter). It returns `true` if it does or `false` if it doesn't. For example, `[1, 2, 3] contains 1` results in `true`. This is a null-safe function.

- `distinctBy`: This function is used to remove duplicate items from the given array. The second parameter of this function is a lambda with the `item` and `index` parameters. For example, `[1, 2, 1] distinctBy $` results in `[1, 2]`. This is a null-safe function.

- `filter`: This function is used to filter the items from the given array. The second parameter of this function is a lambda with the `item` and `index` parameters. For example, `[1, 2, 3] filter isEven($)` results in `[2]`. This is a null-safe function. Note that this function can also be used with strings instead of arrays, although it's not very popular to use it with strings.

- `find`: This function is used to find the indexes of a given item (second parameter) from the given array (first item). If no match is found, it returns an empty array. For example, `[1, 2, 1] find 1` results in `[0, 2]`. This is a null-safe function.

- `flatten`: This function is used to flatten nested subarrays into one array. Note that it only works with the first level of subarrays. For example, `flatten([1, [2], [3, [4]]])` results in `[1, 2, 3, [4]]`. This is a null-safe function.

- `indexOf`: This function is used to find the first index of a given item (second parameter) from the given array (first parameter). If no match is found, it returns `-1`. For example, `[1, 2, 1] indexOf 1` results in 0. This is a null-safe function.

- `joinBy`: This function is used to join a given array of strings (first parameter) into a new string, separated by the given string (second parameter). Note this is the opposite of `splitBy`. For example, `["a","b","c"] joinBy " "` results in `"a b c"`. This is a null-safe function.

- `lastIndexOf`: This function is used to find the last index of a given item (second parameter) from the given array (first parameter). If no match is found, it returns `-1`. For example, `[1, 2, 1] lastIndexOf 1` results in 2. This is a null-safe function.

- `max`: This function is used to find the highest-value item from the given array. For example, `max([8, 3, 5])` results in 8. Note that you can also use the `maxBy` function if you want to create custom mappings by using a lambda.

- `min`: This function is used to find the lowest-value item from the given array. For example, `min([8, 3, 5])` results in 3. Note that you can also use the `minBy` function if you want to create custom mappings by using a lambda.

- `orderBy`: This function is used to reorder the items from a given array. The second parameter of this function is a lambda with the `item` and `index` parameters. For example, `["c", "b", "d", "a"] orderBy $` results in `["a","b","c","d"]`. This is a null-safe function. Note that this function can also be used with objects.

- `sum`: This function is used to sum the items from the given array of numbers. For example, `sum([1, 2, 3])` results in 6.

We listed some of the functions previously, but there are three more complex functions that we'll look at separately, starting with the `groupBy` function.

groupBy

This function is used to group the given items by specific criteria. The second parameter of this function is a lambda with the `item` and `index` parameters. This is a null-safe function. Note that this function can also be used with strings or objects instead of arrays, although it's not very popular to use it this way.

Let's see an example that is used a lot in real-life scenarios. Consider the next variable that we'll use as the input array in our `groupBy` function:

groupBy.dwl

```
var arrayObject = [
    {
        id: 1,
        name: "alex",
        email: "alex@fakeemail.com"
    },
    {
        id: 2,
        name: "akshata",
        email: "akshata@fakeemail.com"
    },
    {
        id: 3,
        name: "arul",
        email: "arul@fakeemail.com"
    }
]
```

It's an array of objects containing data such as `id`, `name`, or `email`. Say we want to retrieve the information from a specific email, for example, `arul@fakeemail.com`. There are two main ways to achieve this: one with the `filter` function and one with the `groupBy` function. The `filter` approach is more straightforward: you can just filter the data by the email that matches the string, as follows:

```
arrayObject filter $.email == "arul@fakeemail.com"
```

However, if you were to do this operation (filter data by email) several times within the same script, it would cost you more resources because every time you use `filter`, the function reads the complete array to return the filtered data. To avoid this, you can group the data by email and then just retrieve the data you need with a selector. For example, let's create another variable with the grouped data:

```
var groupedByEmail = arrayObject groupBy $.email
```

Now, instead of having an array of objects, we have an object containing the emails as the first key and the value of each key would be the corresponding data, such as the following:

```
{
    "alex@fakeemail.com": [
        {
            id: 1,
            name: "alex",
            email: "alex@fakeemail.com"
        }
    ],
    "akshata@fakeemail.com": [
        {
            id: 2,
            name: "akshata",
            email: "akshata@fakeemail.com"
        }
    ],
    "arul@fakeemail.com": [
        {
            id: 3,
            name: "arul",
            email: "arul@fakeemail.com"
        }
```

```
    ]
}
```

Now, we can refer to this `groupedByEmail` variable and extract the specific data with a selector. Instead of having to filter the array *n* times, we just grouped the data once.

> **Note**
>
> To see more examples of the `groupBy` function, you can refer to this developer tutorial: `https://developer.mulesoft.com/tutorials-and-howtos/dataweave/groupBy-function/`.

For example, doing `groupedByEmail["arul@fakeemail.com"]` would result in the following output:

```
[
    {
        id: 3,
        name: "arul",
        email: "arul@fakeemail.com"
    }
]
```

Let's now look into the next function: `map`.

map

This function is used to iterate through and transform the items in the array. The second parameter of this function is a lambda with the `item` and `index` parameters. This is a null-safe function. This is one of the most used functions to work with arrays because of the freedom to transform the given data structure into something very different. A simple example would be the following:

map.dwl

```
%dw 2.0
output application/json
---
["a","b","c"] map {
    ($$): $
}
```

The output of this function would be the following:

```
[
  {
    "0": "a"
  },
  {
    "1": "b"
  },
  {
    "2": "c"
  }
]
```

This example transforms the input array of strings into an array of objects where the key is the index of the item and the value is the actual item.

> **Note**
>
> To see more examples of the map function, you can refer to this developer tutorial: https://developer.mulesoft.com/tutorials-and-howtos/dataweave/map-function/.

You can use map to transform input arrays into a different array structure. However, you will always end up with an array as the output. If you want to process and transform the given array into a different data type, you can use the reduce function, which we'll see next.

reduce

This function is used to iterate through and completely transform the given array (or a given string) into a different data type or structure. The second parameter of this function is a lambda with the item and accumulator parameters. This is a null-safe function. This is one of the most used functions to work with arrays because of the freedom to transform from an array to a different data type. A simple example would be the following:

reduce-simple.dwl

```
%dw 2.0
output application/json
---
(1 to 10) as Array reduce ($$ + $) // output is 55
```

First, we generate a Range data type from 1 to 10. Then, we coerce Range into Array to use it as the input array for the reduce function. Finally, we sum item (or $) and accumulator (or $$) to get the output of 55. There is a total of 9 iterations being made here instead of 10. If you add the log function to accumulator, you will be able to see how this value changes on each iteration, as follows:

```
reduce (log($$) + $)
```

This will output the values in the **LOG VIEWER** tab at the bottom of the online DataWeave Playground, or in the console if you're in Anypoint Studio. The results will be the following:

- 1
- 3
- 6
- 10
- 15
- 21
- 28
- 36
- 45

Here's a screenshot of what the previous results would look like from the DataWeave Playground once the log function is added to the code:

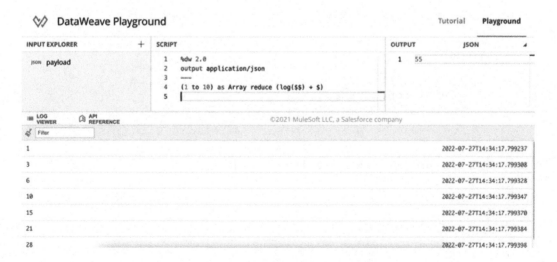

Figure 7.2: Preview from the DataWeave Playground

You might be wondering why the first value is 1 instead of 0. This happens when you don't assign a specific value for the accumulator to start with, so DataWeave assigns the first value from the input array as the initial accumulator's value. This functionality works perfectly when the output data type you want is the same for all the items – in this case, Number. Let's now see a more complex example. Consider the following variable:

reduce-complex.dwl

```
var arr = [
    {
        code: "ABC",
        isNewGroup: false
    },
    {
        code: "DEF",
        isNewGroup: true
    },
    {
        code: "GHI",
        isNewGroup: true
    },
    {
        code: "JKL",
        isNewGroup: false
    },
    {
        code: "MNO",
        isNewGroup: true
    }
]
```

Based on this data structure, we want to end up with the following array:

```
[
    "ABC",
    "DEF",
    "GHI,JKL",
```

```
    "MNO"
]
```

Every time the isNewGroup field is true, we want to add a new item to the array containing the value of the code field. If the isNewGroup field is false, we want to keep concatenating code into the previous item and separate each item with a comma. Let's see how we can solve this using the reduce function:

```
arr reduce (item, acc=[]) -> do {
    var previousItem = acc[-1]
    var previousItemIndex = acc find previousItem
    ---
    if (item.isNewGroup or previousItem ~= null)
        acc + item.code
    else
        acc update previousItemIndex with
            "$previousItem,$(item.code)"
}
```

Here, we make use of several other concepts we learned in this and the previous chapter, such as the do keyword, selectors, the find function, if/else conditionals, operators, and the update function, which we didn't see in detail but learned is a part of the dw::util::Values module.

First, we evaluate whether the isNewGroup field is true or whether this is the first item (as is the case with "ABC") to add a new item to the existing accumulator. If this is not the case, then we update the previous item from the accumulator to now include the current item's code.

This is why reduce is one of the most complex functions in DataWeave. This is the only function that can perform iterations in a line-by-line order, much like how forEach would work.

> **Note**
>
> To see more examples of the reduce function, you can refer to this developer tutorial: https://developer.mulesoft.com/tutorials-and-howtos/dataweave/reduce-function/.

We now have a better understanding of how some of the core functions work and some real-life transformations. Remember, you can also make use of some of the existing modules. There might already be a function that performs the functionality that you're trying to implement with just core functions.

> **Note**
> To find the complete list of core functions, including more details and examples, please refer to the official documentation: `https://docs.mulesoft.com/dataweave/latest/dw-core`.

So far, we've talked about these examples and how to learn DataWeave using the online DataWeave Playground. Now that we have a basic understanding, it's time we learn more about the Transform Message component or connector in Anypoint Studio.

Using the Transform Message component in Anypoint Studio

So far, we have been learning how to use DataWeave to transform data and we've been focusing on the use of the online DataWeave Playground to try out these concepts without having to install anything. However, the playground is used only to learn or experiment. To use DataWeave in Mule applications, we'd have to use Anypoint Studio; specifically, the Transform Message component. Let's explore this component in more detail.

Exploring the views

Go to Anypoint Studio and create a new Mule project. After you have it, drag and drop the Transform Message component from Mule Palette onto the canvas to create a new empty flow with Transform Message.

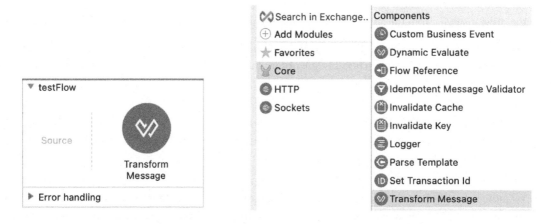

Figure 7.3: A flow with a Transform Message component in Anypoint Studio

If you double-click on the component in the flow, the component's configuration view will appear at the bottom of the screen with the predefined view.

Figure 7.4: The Transform Message component's configuration view

Let's start by exploring the views you can use for your DataWeave scripts (or the Transform Message configuration). These are located at the top right of the Transform Message configuration window.

Figure 7.5: A closer look into the Transform Message component's configuration view

There are three different views you can use for this configuration:

- **Graphics**: The default view is the first icon: the Graphics view. This view includes the inputs, a graphical mapping that you can use to drag and drop fields from the input into the output, the expected output, and the DataWeave script. Here's an example of what this view looks like when there is some data to map.

Figure 7.6: The Transform Message component's Graphics view

You can also press the **Preview** button to show how the output would look given the sample input that was given.

Figure 7.7: The Graphics view with the output's preview

- **Source with Trees**: The second view is the Source with Trees view. This one shows the same information as the previous one but without the graphical mapping. You can still drag and drop from the input structure into the output structure, but the mappings won't show in this view. Same as before, you can turn on or off **Preview** in order to see the sample output.

Figure 7.8: The Source with Trees view with a preview of the output

- **Source Only**: The third view is the most used one by experienced developers: the Source Only view. This one shows only the input and the script. You can't drag and drop data with this view. Same as before, you can turn on or off **Preview** in order to see the sample output.

Figure 7.9: The Source Only view with a preview of the output

We will work with this last view in the rest of the chapter. The first two views are useful for drag-and-dropping purposes, but that functionality is mainly used for very simple data structures or one-to-one mappings.

Let's now explore how we generated the sample data in the first place.

Defining metadata

When you first drag and drop the Transform Message component onto the canvas, it may or may not contain some metadata in either the input or the output structure. This depends on what other components are used before or after Transform Message. For example, if you first have a SOAP call, then Transform Message, then a REST call, Transform Message might be able to read the data structures from both the SOAP and REST calls and auto-populate the input and output metadata accordingly. Let's see a simple example of this in the following screenshot:

Figure 7.10: Transform Message's auto-populated input based on HTTP Request

Here, we have an HTTP Request connector before Transform Message. Because of this, the *attributes* structure was auto-populated based on the metadata from the Request connector. We can receive a `statusCode` number, a `reasonPhrase` string, and a `headers` object. However, it was not able to recognize the *payload*.

> **Note**
>
> *Payload*, *variables*, and *attributes* are concepts we learned back in *Chapter 4, Introduction to Core Components*, when we talked about the *Mule event* structure. These variables are not the same variables we use inside DataWeave (with the `var` keyword). *DataWeave variables* are only visible from the DataWeave script, while *Mule variables* are visible within the Mule application's components.

There are some connectors that will automatically return the output payload's structure and you will be able to see it from Transform Message's input structure. If this doesn't happen, you can also populate your own metadata to see a preview of the data. You just have to click on the **Define metadata** link that appears next to the data structure you want to populate.

Figure 7.11: A closer look at Transform Message's input

Let's see this step by step:

1. Click on the **Define metadata** link next to **Payload** to generate the payload's metadata and sample data. You will see a new window to select your metadata type.

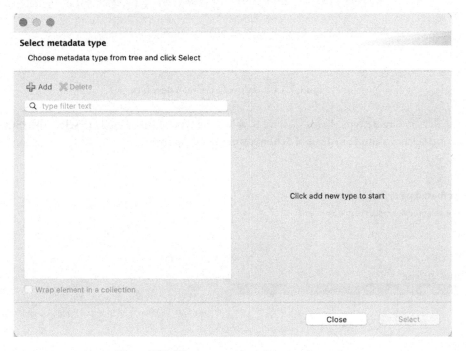

Figure 7.12: Window to select the metadata type

2.   Click on the green **Add** button and add a new type ID, for example, `authorsInput`.

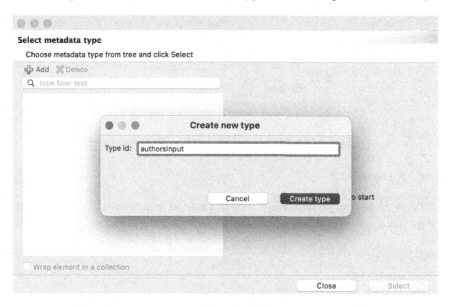

Figure 7.13: Window to create a new type

3.   Click on **Create type**. Now, we have to select the type of this data. Let's select the **JSON** type and select **Example** instead of **Schema** from the dropdown.

Figure 7.14: Window to modify the new type

You will be able to select the three-dots button next to the text box in order to choose a file with your metadata example. We are going to use the following file, which you can get from our GitHub repository, linked in the *Technical requirements* section at the beginning of this chapter:

authorsInput.json

```json
[
    {
        "id": 1,
        "firstName": "Akshata",
        "lastName": "Sawant"
    },
    {
        "id": 2,
        "firstName": "Arul",
        "lastName": "Alphonse"
    },
    {
        "id": 3,
        "firstName": "Alex",
        "lastName": "Martinez"
    }
]
```

4. Click the three-dots (**...**) button and select this file from your computer. Once you see the structure with the fields and their data types, you can click on **Select**.

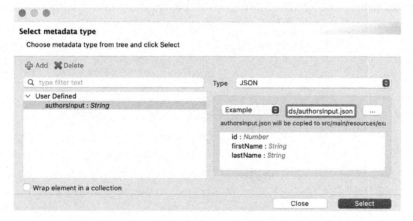

Figure 7.15: Window to finish creating the new type

Now your input payload contains metadata describing the data types of each field. `Payload` is an array of objects, `id` is a number, and `firstName` and `lastName` are strings.

5. Add the following script and click on **Preview**. You will be able to see the sample data in the preview window:

payloadScript.dwl

```
%dw 2.0
output application/json
---
payload
```

It will look like this:

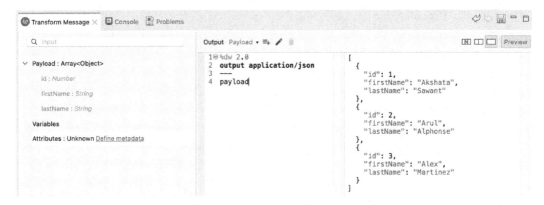

Figure 7.16: Payload preview in the output

6. Edit the sample data by right-clicking on the input payload and selecting **Edit Sample Data**.

Figure 7.17: Payload options after right-clicking on it

This will open a new tab called **payload** that is located next to the **Context** tab (the previous figure). Here, you can modify the sample data for the input payload to test different scenarios for your script and generate different output previews:

```
Transform Message ×    Console   Problems

list_json.json

[
    {
        "id": 1,
        "firstName": "Akshata",
        "lastName": "Sawant"
    },
    {
        "id": 2,
        "firstName": "Arul",
        "lastName": "Alphonse"
    },
    {
        "id": 3,
        "firstName": "Alex",
        "lastName": "Martinez"
    }
]

Context  payload  ×
```

Figure 7.18: Sample data from the payload tab

You can continue generating metadata for other fields, such as the *attributes* or *output* structure, if needed. For now, we just demonstrated the steps to generate new metadata for the *payload* structure.

The *Mule variables* should also appear automatically within the context. Here is an example of what that would look like:

Figure 7.19: Prepopulated Mule variables within the context

Same as before, you can right-click on each variable from the input structure to change the sample data. If you need additional variables that were not auto-populated, you can also right-click on **Variables** and select **New Variable**.

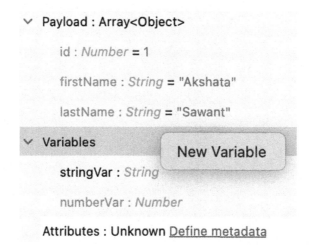

Figure 7.20: New Variable option after right-clicking on the Variables context

This will open the same window where we created our input payload type. We just need to repeat the same process as previously, but add the variable's name.

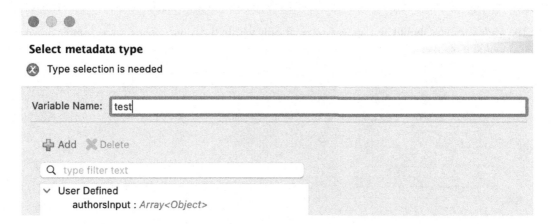

Figure 7.21: Creating new variable metadata

Whenever you want to reference the payload's data, you use the `payload` keyword. To use any of the Mule variables, you use the `vars` keyword. To use the attributes, you use the `attributes` keyword. Something that doesn't always appear in the context but is good to know is to reference an exception, you use the `error` keyword.

It is also worth noticing that any example file you use to create metadata will be stored under `src/main/resources/examples` and any sample data will be stored under `src/test/resources/sample_data`. If you chose to upload a schema instead of an example file, the schemas would be generated under `src/main/resources/schemas`. You can see a preview of the folder structure in the following screenshot:

Figure 7.22: View from Package Explorer

That is all we needed to learn about how the metadata works and how we can set it up to test our transformations and get a preview of the data. Let's now quickly get a glimpse at how we can create and use custom DataWeave modules in our Mule applications.

Creating custom modules

Earlier, we saw some modules we can use in DataWeave to get more functions that are not included in the core module, for example, `dw::core::Binaries` or `dw::Crypto`. But we can also create our own modules within a Mule application and reuse them in several scripts. Let's see the steps to create a custom module in Anypoint Studio:

1.   Create a new Mule project in Studio.

2.   Create a new folder called `dw` under `src/main/resources`. Then, create a new file in this new folder called `Utilities.dwl`.

Figure 7.23: New Utilities file in src/main/resources

3. Paste the following code into this new file and save it.

Utilities.dwl

```
%dw 2.0


fun getAuthorsNames(authors: Array): Array =
    authors map (
        ($.firstName default "")
        ++ " " ++
        ($.lastName default "")
    )
```

This function will get an array of objects with the authors' information and return an array of strings with the authors' full names. Our module would be dw::Utilities and our function would be getAuthorsNames.

Let's go back to our flow and add a Transform Message component.

4. Drag and drop the Transform Message component from Mule Palette onto the canvas.

5. Create the metadata for the payload using the authorsInput.json file we previously used to create the payload's metadata.

6. Paste the following code into Transform Message's script.

UtilitiesMapping.dwl

```
%dw 2.0
output application/json
```

```
---
import getAuthorsNames from dw::Utilities
getAuthorsNames(payload)
```

You should end up with something like this:

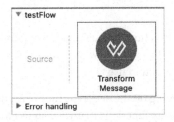

Figure 7.24: Transform Message using a custom module

Here, we can see the input metadata, the script we used to import the `getAuthorsNames` function from the `dw::Utilities` module, and a preview of the output based on the input payload's sample data.

> **Note**
>
> If you want to share DataWeave modules outside of your Mule application with other applications, you can create a DataWeave library and publish it in Anypoint Exchange (a subproduct of Anypoint Platform). Other Mule applications can pull your library from Exchange and use it in their own scripts. To learn how to do this, refer to the following developer tutorials:
>
> ```
> https://developer.mulesoft.com/tutorials-and-howtos/dataweave/
> dataweave-extension-vscode-getting-started/
> ```
>
> ```
> https://developer.mulesoft.com/tutorials-and-howtos/dataweave/
> dataweave-libraries-in-exchange-getting-started/
> ```

We now know how to use DataWeave in Anypoint Studio (or in a Mule application) with the Transform Message component. We explored the different views you can use to visualize your transformations, how to define metadata, which will be helpful if you want to see a preview of the output data, and how to create custom modules to reuse in your application.

Summary

In this chapter, we learned different ways to import a module or a function in DataWeave using the `import` directive. We listed some of the modules you can find in DataWeave with some of their functions so you can get a better idea of what is already available for you to use.

We learned how to use some of the most used core functions depending on the data type they're used with. We also reviewed multi-type, numbers, strings, objects, and array functions that you can use to transform the different data types.

Finally, we learned how to use the Transform Message component in Anypoint Studio. We explored the three views we can use depending on our needs or our personal preferences. We learned how to use **Preview** and sample data (metadata) to generate a sample output of our transformation. We also learned how to create and reuse custom modules within our Mule application.

In the next chapter, you'll learn more about building Mule applications and applying best practices to your projects.

Questions

Take a moment to answer the following questions to serve as a recap of what you just learned in this chapter:

1. List at least three different ways to import a module or a function in DataWeave.
2. Name at least five existing DataWeave modules.
3. Name at least two functions that are used with multi-type, numbers, strings, objects, and arrays.
4. In which folder should custom DataWeave modules be created?

Answers

1. The different ways to import a module or a function in DataWeave:

   - `import Module // Module::function()`
   - `import * from Module // function()`
   - `import function from Module // function()`

- `import Module as Mod // Mod::function`
- `import function as f from Module // f()`

2. The DataWeave modules are:

- `dw::Core`
- `dw::core::Arrays`
- `dw::core::Binaries`
- `dw::core::Dates`
- `dw::core::Numbers`
- `dw::core::Objects`
- `dw::core::Periods`
- `dw::core::Strings`
- `dw::core::Types`
- `dw::core::URL`
- `dw::Crypto`
- `dw::Mule`
- `dw::Runtime`
- `dw::System`
- `dw::util::Math`
- `dw::util::Timer`
- `dw::util::Tree`
- `dw::util::Values`

3. Functions that are used with multi-type, numbers, strings, objects, and arrays:

- **Multi-type**: `++`, `now`, `random`, `read`, `readUrl`, `sizeOf`, `typeOf`, `uuid`, `with`, `isEmpty`, `log`, and `then`.
- **Numbers**: `abs`, `ceil`, `floor`, `isDecimal`, `isEven`, `isInteger`, `isOdd`, `mod`, `pow`, `randomInt`, `round`, `sqrt`, and `to`.
- **Strings**: `contains`, `endsWith`, `find`, `indexOf`, `isBlank`, `lastIndexOf`, `lower`, `match`, `matches`, `replace`, `scan`, `splitBy`, `startsWith`, `trim`, and `upper`.

- **Objects**: `--`, `distinctBy`, `entriesOf`, `filterObject`, `keysOf`, `mapObject`, `namesOf`, `pluck`, and `valuesOf`.

- **Arrays**: `--`, `avg`, `contains`, `distinctBy`, `filter`, `find`, `flatten`, `indexOf`, `joinBy`, `lastIndexOf`, `max`, `min`, `orderBy`, `sum`, `groupBy`, `map`, and `reduce`.

4. Under `src/main/resources`. You can then create another folder to keep your modules as a best practice.

Building Your Mule Application

In the previous chapter, we learned how to use DataWeave to transform data from one format to another.

In this chapter, let us explore the different configuration files available in a Mule application and try using different components, such as **Schedulers**, **APIkit Router**, and **Object Store Connector**, to build a Mule application. In *Chapter 3*, *Exploring Anypoint Studio*, we created and tested a simple Mule application, `HelloWorld`. In this chapter, we will be learning how to build a Mule application with different components elaborately.

After reading this chapter, you'll come away with more knowledge on the following topics:

- Different configuration files in a Mule application
- How to create a Mule application with Schedulers
- How to create a Mule application with APIkit Router
- How to use Object Store Connector

Technical requirements

The prerequestive for this chapter are:

- **Anypoint Platform**, which we configured in *Chapter 2*, *Designing Your API*.

  The link to log in is `https://anypoint.mulesoft.com/login/`.

- The `musicbox-sys-api.raml` RAML file required to create a Mule application is available on GitHub at the following link, under `Chapter2`:

  `https://github.com/PacktPublishing/MuleSoft-for-Salesforce-Developers`

Exploring different types of configuration files

There are a few types of files that we will come across while developing a Mule application. Each file has its own purpose. The files are as follows:

- Mule configuration file

- Properties file

- Project Object Model – a `pom.xml` file

- API Specification file (Open API Specification and RAML)

We already learned about API Specification in *Chapter 2, Designing Your API*.

Let's begin by exploring the Mule configuration file.

Mule configuration file

A Mule configuration file is a `.xml` file that contains all the information related to Mule flows and connector configurations. Whenever we create a new Mule application project, it creates a Mule configuration file in the `/src/main/mule` folder in the **Package Explorer**. When you open the Mule configuration file, it opens in the editor, where you can see the following three tabs:

- **Message Flow**

- **Global Elements**

- **Configuration XML**

Message Flow contains the canvas, which helps with designing various flows. Canvas visually displays Muel flows. Inside the canvas, it is easy to drag and drop the required components from **Mule Palette**. Generally, a flow has two sections – **Source** and **Processor** – as you can see in the following figure:

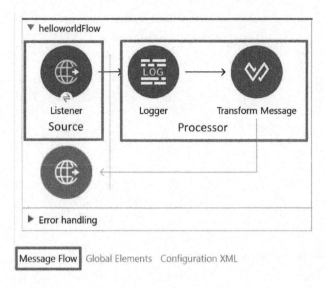

Figure 8.1 – Message Flow

The **HTTP Listener** component is available inside the **Source** area. **HTTP Listener** is the way to listen for incoming HTTP requests to any application. The **Logger** and **Transform Message** components are available inside the **Processor** section.

Global Elements is the place where we maintain all the configuration elements that are required for the particular Mule project. In this tab, we can add, edit, and delete the required configuration data for different connectors (see *Figure 8.2*):

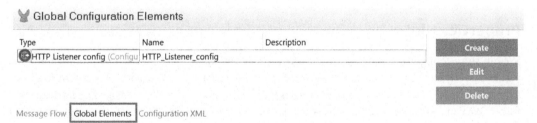

Figure 8.2 – Global Elements

Figure 8.2 shows **HTTP Listener config** in the **Global Elements** tab. This configuration will have details about the HTTP URL, port, and other required configurations for **HTTP Listener**. We can click the **Create** button to add other connector configurations, such as Salesforce and other systems.

Configuration XML, as shown in the following figure, is an XML file that contains the details of all the flows. In simple terms, the flow, which we design in the canvas, and the configuration in the global elements are written in XML:

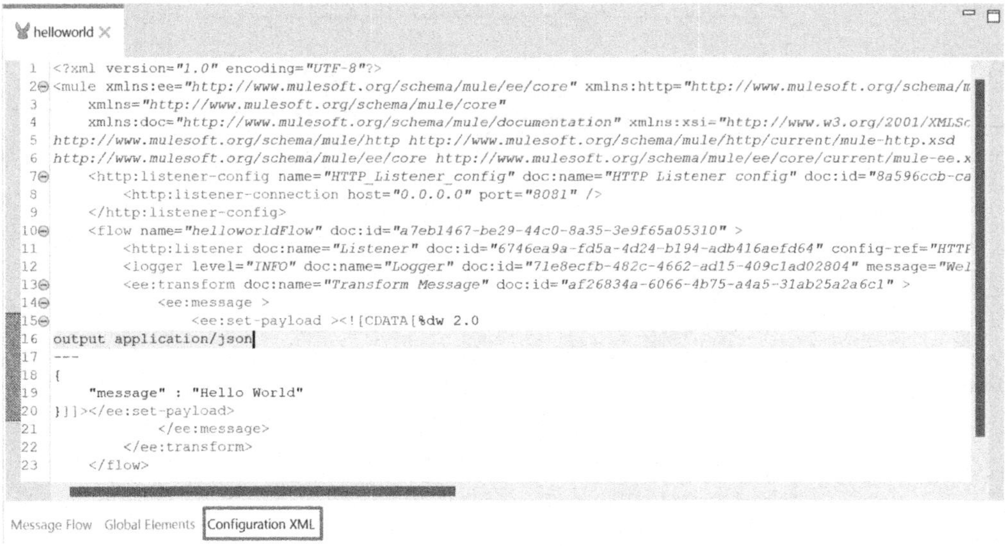

Figure 8.3 – Configuration XML

Figure 8.3 shows all the details of the flow, the **HTTP Listener** configuration, and the **Transform Message** configuration in XML format. These components come under the `<flow>`, `<http-listener-config>`, `<ee:transform>` tags/elements, respectively.

We can also directly edit the file to reflect the changes in the canvas.

With this, we have understood the list of tabs that are available in a Mule configuration file. Let's move on to the properties file, where we define the environment-related configurations.

Properties file

We can store configurations in `.properties` or `.yaml` files. To avoid hard coding (keeping the values directly in the program), we can store the values such as URLs, port, credentials, and any application-specific configurations in properties file. It is located under the `src/main/resources` folder. We can also store specific entries or the entire file in encrypted format instead of plain text in order to secure the configuration. For instance, while connecting to Salesforce, we have different URLs and credentials for development, test, and production environments. In this case, it is always best practice to keep the configuration separate instead of having it in the code. We can have the development environment configuration in `dev-properties.yaml`, **quality assurance (QA)** environment configuration in `qa-properties.yaml`, and production environment configuration in `prod-properties.yaml`. So, in future, if there are any changes to the URL or credentials, it will be easy to update them in the properties file directly.

We can define the configuration in two different file formats:

- The `.properties` file, where the key and values are on the same line
- The `.yaml` file, which follows indentation (syntax with few spaces) to store the key and values

The configuration data can be either plain or encrypted text. Let's see a few examples for better understanding. We can use the Secure Properties tool to generate the data in an encrypted format (part of or the entire file). We will be learning more about the Secure Properties tool in *Chapter 10, Secure Your API*.

Let us see few examples of properties file.

Example 1: In the following sample, the entire data is encrypted in the properties file:

salesforce_encrypted.properties

```
74wwCGyD/vw+eqVpwJ8M+bdfKMH08DbvcF+2mK9FwUZIOookgMDA7
MVJh0+dt0IIoVzpP0C5kNI8zBCaPItSIf7HwEGyDkKHDJepH6p/3Dam
ZlKpfyDJWXMGuq6+I951r8LG5JhXkAcuHvTeJaAGxz2L7dWRj/8fIfBCoB
MIhAw=
```

Example 2: In this sample, `username` is not encrypted. The `password` and `token` values are secured and encrypted. Encrypted values are stored in `![ ]` format. Here, `salesforce.username` is the key and `mulesoft.book@gmail.com` is the value of this key, `salesforce_partialencrypted.properties`:

```
salesforce.username=mulesoft.book@gmail.com
salesforce.password=![0+dCWnJ1QPg7/I6FpIGSEQ==]
salesforce.token=![2NjutvTeNH4tUfL/gC9V4bOnzlYFw
dqDQ8tJRD3TN/c=]
```

Example 3: In the following sample, the key and values are not encrypted or secured, and are stored in plain text format, `salesforce_plain.properties`:

```
salesforce.username=mulesoft.book@gmail.com
salesforce.password= B5SQZmHV4p5s5367
salesforce.token= iMoltMlDvfS5HlPIP3Vm12345
```

Example 4: In this sample, none of the key values are encrypted. As it is a `.yaml` file, follow the indentation (syntax with few spaces) in order to store the configuration values:

salesforce_plain.yaml

```
salesforce:
    username: "mulesoft.book@gmail.com"
    password: "B5SQZmHV4p5s5367"
    token: "iMo1tMlDvfS5HlPIP3Vm12345"
```

We have seen multiple ways to create the properties file. As we move on, we will become comfortable with generating encrypted data using the Secure Properties tool.

Now, let's move on to looking at the last file type, **Project Object Model** (**POM**).

Project Object Model

POM is an XML file that contains the project name, configuration details, runtime version, build, dependency, and repository details. **Maven** uses this `pom.xml` file to build and deploy the project. In **Package Explorer**, we can locate `pom.xml` under the Mule project.

> **Maven**
> Maven is a popular open source software (free software which anyone can modify it) developed by Apache Group, embedded in Anypoint Studio to build and deploy projects. Based on the information available in `pom.xml`, Maven can manage a project build.

Here is a sample POM file:

Sample pom.xml

```xml
<?xml version="1.0" encoding="UTF-8"?>
<project xmlns="http://maven.apache.org/POM/4.0.0"
  xmlns:xsi="http://www.w3.org/2001/XMLSchema-instance"
    xsi:schemaLocation="http://maven.apache.org/POM/4.0.0
      https://maven.apache.org/xsd/maven-4.0.0.xsd">

<modelVersion>4.0.0</modelVersion>

<groupId>com.mycompany</groupId>
```

```
<artifactId>helloworld</artifactId>

<version>1.0.0-SNAPSHOT</version>

<packaging>mule-application</packaging>

<name>helloworld</name>

<dependencies>
   <dependency>
   <groupId>org.mule.connectors</groupId>
   <artifactId>mule-http-connector</artifactId>
   <version>1.6.0</version>
   <classifier>mule-plugin</classifier>
</dependency>
</dependencies>
```

In pom.xml, <artifactId> contains the project name and the <dependencies> section contains all the dependencies, including all the connector details and its version. It also contains plugin details. Maven reads this POM file in order to build and deploy the project.

We have now learned about the different types of files that are available in the Mule application.

Let's move on to learn how to trigger or call our Mule application at a specific time using Scheduler.

Introducing Scheduler

Scheduler is a component that helps to schedule jobs at a specific time. For example, if we need to run a specific program at 8 P.M. every day, then we can configure it to run at this time.

We learned the basics of Scheduler and its scheduling strategies in *Chapter 4, Introduction to Core Components*.

Let us explore how to create a Mule application with the Scheduler component.

Creating a Mule application with the Scheduler component

In this section, we will be creating a new Mule project with the Scheduler component using the Fixed Frequency scheduling strategy. To do so, follow these steps:

1. Go to Anypoint Studio. Choose the **Create a Mule Project** option in **Package Explorer** to create a new Mule application.

2. Provide the project name as SchedulerDemo, leave the remaining settings as is, and click the **Finish** button.

3. Next, select the **Core** module and drag and drop **Scheduler** from **Mule Palette** to the canvas.

4. Click on **Scheduler** inside the canvas. Go to the **Scheduler** properties and set the **Scheduling Strategy** value to **Fixed Frequency** and the **Time unit** value as **MINUTES**. Set the **Frequency** value to 2, as seen in the following figure:

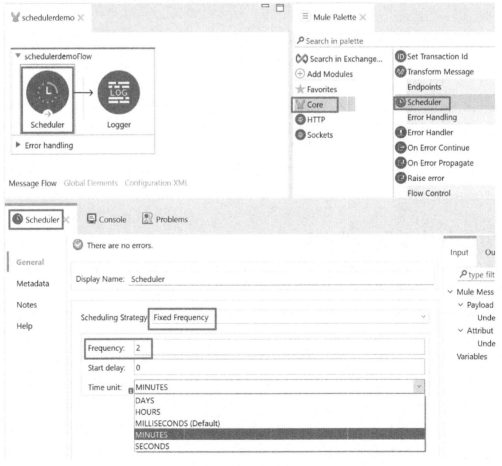

Figure 8.4 – Scheduler properties

In *Figure 8.4*, we have configured our Scheduler to run every 2 minutes. If we need to change **Time unit** to **DAYS, HOURS, MILLISECONDS,** or **SECONDS** as per the requirements, then we can configure the Scheduler timings accordingly.

> **Note**
>
> We can achieve similar **Fixed Frequency** scheduling using the **Cron** scheduling strategy. Cron is a job in the UNIX operating system that follows a specific syntax to mention the scheduling frequency/timing. It is used for scheduling specific tasks at a fixed time or specific intervals. If you are familiar with the Cron expression, then you can use the Cron scheduling strategy. For more information about Cron, refer to this link: `https://en.wikipedia.org/wiki/Cron`.

5. Next, select the **Core** module and drag and drop **Logger** from **Mule Palette** to the canvas.

6. In the **Logger** properties, specify **Message** as **Scheduler invoked**, as shown in the following figure:

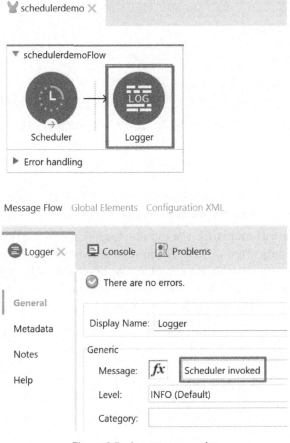

Figure 8.5 – Logger properties

In *Figure 8.5*, we have configured the **Logger** properties **Message** setting with **Scheduler invoked** for our demo in order to understand whether a Scheduler flow has been triggered or not at a specific time. In a real use case, instead of **Logger**, we will have other components or connectors to process the files or messages from one system to another at a specific time.

7. Click **Save**, or press *Ctrl + S*, to save the Mule application.

8. Go to the canvas, right-click, and select **Run project SchedulerDemo**.

9. Now embedded Mule runtime starts inside Anypoint Studio and deploys the application. Once the application is deployed successfully, then we will be able to see the logs with the status as **DEPLOYED**.

10. Watch the console for a few minutes. You will be able to see the Scheduler getting invoked every 2 minutes.

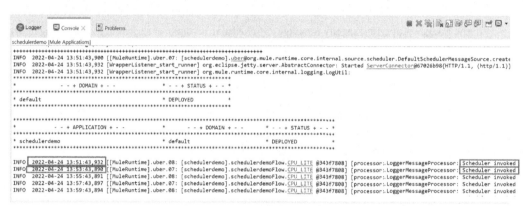

Figure 8.6 – Console

In *Figure 8.6*, the **Console** view is showing that the Scheduler was running every 2 minutes and printing the message **Scheduler invoked**, which we specified in the **Logger** properties.

With this, we have learned how to trigger or call a Mule application using the Scheduler component. Scheduler is used mainly when we have a requirement to handle or process the message in an asynchronous manner. For example, if we need to sync or send the sales order information from a CRM to an ERP system, then we can use the Scheduler component to run at a specific time to pick up the records from Salesforce and send them to the other system.

Let's move on to learning how to generate flows automatically using API specification and route them through **APIkit Router**.

Generating a flow using APIkit Router

APIkit Router generates the whole flow based on the API specification file. It receives the incoming request, validates it, and routes the incoming request to the flow.

If you have already created an API specification (or an API design) and you want to start developing the actual implementation, you can import your API specification into Anypoint Studio and APIkit will create the basic flows and error handling for your API based on the specification. By doing this, we need not create all the code from scratch.

It is always best practice to create the API specification first in API Designer. Once it is created, we can start building the Mule application with that API specification. This is called an **API design-first approach**. There is also the **code-first approach**, which mandates having an API specification but does not emphasize starting with the API design (specification) first. In the API design-first approach, the developer can consume the API to develop in parallel, which shortens the **time to market**. Hence, the API design-first approach is recommended over the code-first approach.

Now, let's create a Mule application using the API design specification.

Creating a Mule application using an API specification

Let's learn how to create a Mule application using an API specification to understand how APIkit Router will autogenerate the flows and route the request to different flows:

1. Go to Anypoint Studio. Click the **Create a Mule Project** option from **Package Explorer** to create a new Mule application.

2. Provide the project name as `APIkitRouterDemo`, select the **Import RAML from local file** option, and browse for the RAML file that we created in *Chapter 2, Designing Your API*. Leave the remaining settings as is and click the **Finish** button. This RAML file is also available on GitHub in the `Chapter2` folder, which is linked in the *Technical requirements* section.

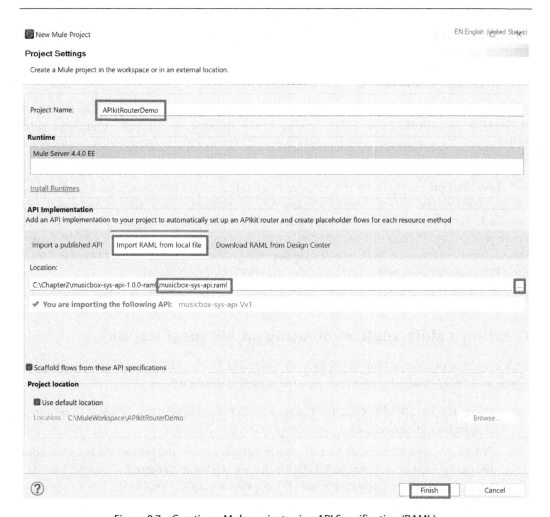

Figure 8.7 – Creating a Mule project using API Specification (RAML)

In *Figure 8.7*, `musicbox-sys-api.raml` is the RAML file that we will be using to create the Mule application.

Now, it will automatically generate all the required flows in our Mule application. It consists of flows such as `main` and `console` and also flows for each HTTP method, such as `get` and `post`.

When our application runs, the `main` flow is the one that actually receives the request.

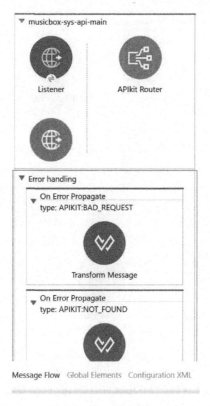

Figure 8.8 – main flow

In *Figure 8.8*, we can see that the main flow has **HTTP Listener** with the path as /api/* to receive the request and **APIkit Router** to validate and route the request to the get/post flow. If any validations fail, it will throw an exception, which will be handled by the error handler that is mentioned in this main flow. Error handling can handle the following error types:

- BAD_REQUEST

- NOT_FOUND

- METHOD_NOT_ALLOWED

- NOT_ACCEPTABLE

- UNSUPPORTED_MEDIA_TYPE

- NOT_IMPLEMENTED

Now, let's see the different components that are autogenerated as a part of the API console flow.

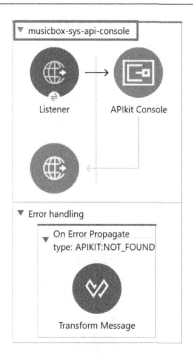

Figure 8.9 – Console flow

In *Figure 8.9*, the console flow has HTTP Listener with the path set to /console/* to receive the request and APIkit Console to validate and route the request. A console flow is mainly used for API documentation. This helps to test the API locally using interactive documentation.

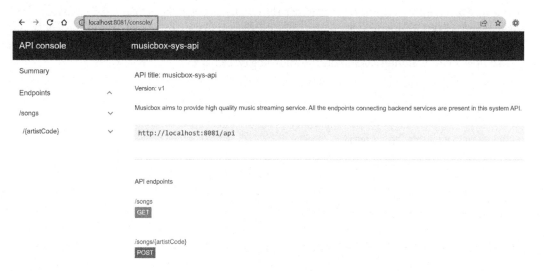

Figure 8.10 – API console documentation

Once we've run the Mule application, we can open the API documentation using the URL http://localhost:8081/console/ from the browser, as shown in *Figure 8.10*. Using this API console, we can explore the API documentation and test the API using different methods such as get and post.

Now, let us see the components that are autogenerated as a part of the get and post HTTP methods.

Figure 8.11 – Autogenerated HTTP methods

Our API specification had only two methods, get and post. Hence, it has generated two flows. Each HTTP method (get and post) has one flow with the **Transform Message** component, which sends the song sample response as defined in the API specification, which is highlighted in *Figure 8.11*. Now, we have seen different autogenerated flows for main, console, get, and post.

This way, we can easily create a Mule application using RAML, which in turn autogenerates all the flows and error handling. Now, our job is only to make minor changes to accommodate our requirements. For example, in our implementation of a get or post flow, if we need to fetch or create, respectively, the song data from the backend application, we just replace **Transform Message** with the required connectors.

With this, we have created a Mule application using an API specification (RAML) file. Now, let us see how to run and test the application.

Running and testing a Mule application

In this section, let us run and test the Mule application using Postman. While testing, we'll use different methods, such as get, put, and post, to check different scenarios:

1. Go to the canvas and right-click **Run project apikitrouterdemo**.

    Once the application has deployed successfully, we will be able to see the logs with the status as **DEPLOYED** in the Anypoint Studio **Console** view.

2. Go to Postman, set the method to **GET**, provide the URL as localhost:8081/api/songs, and click **Send**.

Figure 8.12 – Sending a request from a Postman application with the get method

In *Figure 8.12*, we can see that we have sent the request from Postman to our Mule application with the get method. On receiving the request, the Mule application processes the request and sends the response back.

Our `APIkitRouterDemo` Mule application receives the request in the `main` flow **HTTP Listener** and sends the request to APIkit Router, where it is validated. If the validation is successful, then it identifies the HTTP method and routes it to the appropriate flow. In our case, we have sent the request using the **GET** method from Postman, hence it invokes the `get` flow to process the incoming request.

A high-level sequence of processing will look as follows:

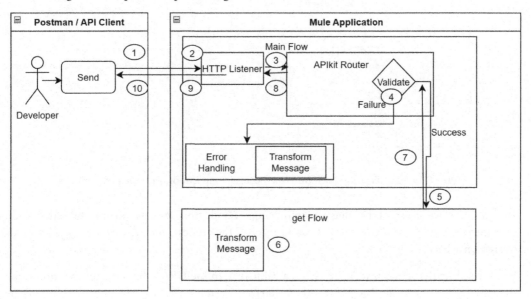

Figure 8.13 – High-level processing sequence

3. Now, let's try to send the request from the Postman application using the `put` method. We will get a response as `"message"`: `"Method not allowed"`. We are receiving this response because our `main` flow doesn't have a flow for the `put` method. This invokes error handling and matches with the corresponding error type `METHOD_NOT_ALLOWED` and sends the response.

4. Try to send the request from the Postman application with the `post` method to the URL `localhost:8081/api/songs/1`.

Figure 8.14 – Sending a request from the Postman application with the post method

In *Figure 8.14*, we have sent the song data in the request body from Postman to our Mule application with the post method, the Mule application receives the request, and after processing it, it sends the response back.

While sending the request, we are passing a value of 1 in the URL, which is nothing more than the URL parameter value. The post flow receives the request that we passed in the body of the request and sends the response back. In our example, the response, "Message": "Song added successfully", comes from the **Transform Message** setting of the post flow.

But in the actual implementation, Mule application extracts the value that comes in the URL parameters along with the request payload and sends it to the backend applications. Finally, the backend application generates the success or failure response message. In this test, we passed a value of 1, which is a songsid. When the application receives the request payload with 1, the Mule application creates the song data in the backend application with a songsid with the value of 1 and sends the success response back. If there is any failure while creating the song data in the backend system, it sends a failure response back. For a successful response, we will send 200 OK. Here, 200 is the HTTP status code and OK is the HTTP status description.

For a failure response, based on the error type, the Mule application will send a different HTTP status code and status description. For example, if we pass the put method, which is not there in our flow, then it will send a status code of 405 Method Not Allowed.

Now, we have understood how to build and run a Mule application using APIkit Router.

Let's move on to explore how to use Object Store Connector in a Mule application.

Exploring Object Store Connector

Object Store Connector is a Mule component that allows you to store a simple key-value pair. A key-value pair is a combination of two simple values where one is the key and the other is a value. The key is the unique identifier of the values stored.

The following are the operations of **Object Store Connector**. We can use these operations in order to manage our key-value pair:

- **Store**: To store the value using the key

- **Retrieve**: To retrieve the value stored using a specific key

- **Retrieve All**: To retrieve all the key-value pairs from the object store

- **Retrieve All Keys**: Lists all the keys that are available in the object store

- **Contains**: To check whether any value against the key is available in the object store or not

- **Remove**: To remove the value for a specific key from the object store

- **Clear**: To remove all the keys from the object store. In turn, all values will also be removed

Different types of Object Store

There are three types of Object Store:

- **Object Store v2**: This is only supported in CloudHub and is a cloud service. Use the **Object Store v2** option while deploying the application in CloudHub. Otherwise, based on the runtime version, the runtime manager will choose either **Object Store v2** or **Object Store v1**. Here, key-value pairs are stored externally to the Mule application. The **time to live** (**TTL**) is 30 days and after that, the key-value pair will get removed from the Object Store. The maximum size for a key value is 10 MB. The standard version supports 10 **transactions per second** (**TPS**) and the premium version supports 100 TPS as the API request limit. **Object store v2** is not recommended for multi-worker configurations, because **Store** operation will overwrite the key values in case of concurrent requests.

- **Object Store v1**: This is only supported in CloudHub and is currently deprecated. The **end of life** (**EOL**) is not confirmed. It is encouraged to use the latest version, Object Store v2. TTL is not configurable. The maximum size for a key value is 1 MB. There is no API request limit. Mule 4 does not support Object Store v1.

- **Object Store**: This is used in an on-premises environment and is a part of the Mule runtime. We can store the keys and values in memory for faster performance or disk (persistent) for reliability. There is no limit to the key-value size.

Let's apply some of these operations in a Mule application.

Creating a Mule application with Object Store Connector

Let's learn how to create a Mule application with Object Store Connector to understand how the object store uses the key to store and retrieve the data. We will be creating two different flows in this project. One is `StoreFlow`, which is used to store the key in the object store, and another one is `RetrieveFlow`, which is used to retrieve the key from the object store:

1. Go to Anypoint Studio. Choose the **Create a Mule Project** option in **Package Explorer** to create a new Mule application.

2. Provide the project name as `ObjectStoreDemo`.

3. Next, select **HTTP** in **Mule Palette** and then select **Listener**.

4. Drag and drop **Listener** onto the canvas.

5. Select **Listener** from the canvas. In the **Listener** properties, add the connection configuration by pressing the **Add** symbol, as shown in the following figure:

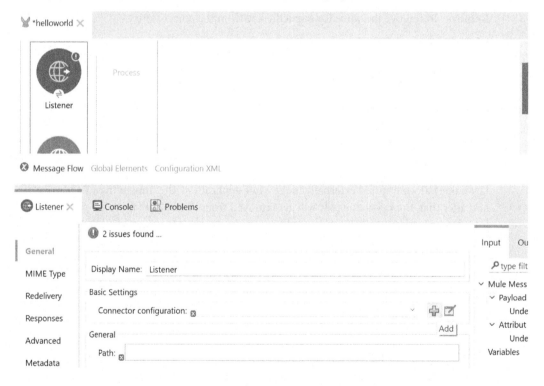

Figure 8.15 – Mule properties for HTTP Listener

6. Leave the host and port (8081) values at the default values and click the **OK** button on the connector configuration screen.

7. Once done, set the **Path** value as /store.

8. Click **Add Module** from **Mule Palette** and drag and drop **ObjectStore**, as shown in the following figure:

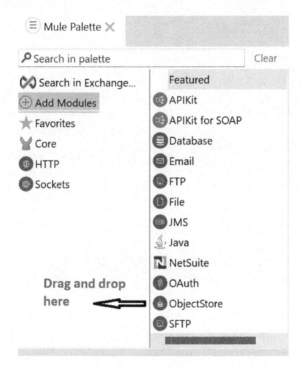

Figure 8.16 – Adding the object store to Project | Mule Palette

9. Click **ObjectStore** from **Mule Palette** and drag and drop **Store** onto the canvas. Configure the key as lastProcessedSongID with the value as 5 and the object store name as SongsObjectStore by clicking the plus symbol, as shown in *Figure 8.17*:

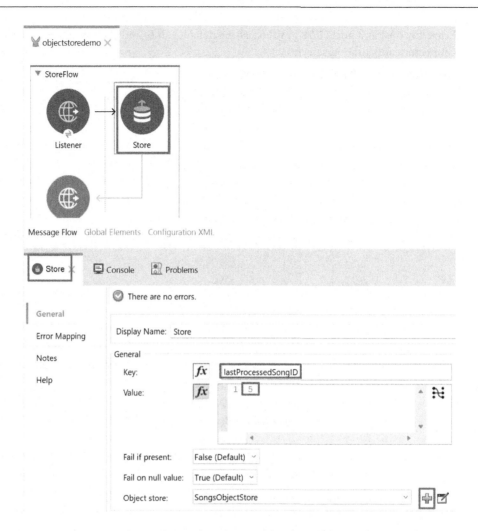

Figure 8.17 – Store configuration

10. Change the name of the flow to StoreFlow and save the Mule application. Now we have created a flow that stores the value in the object store. Let's create another flow in the same project to retrieve the value from the object store based on the key.

11. In the same project, create another flow with **HTTP Listener**, with the path set to /retrieve and the flow name set to RetrieveFlow.

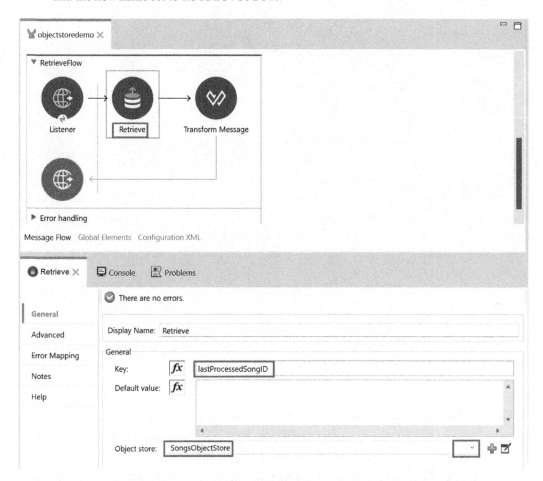

Figure 8.18 – Retrieve flow

As in *Figure 8.18*, provide the key as lastProcessedSongID in the Retrieve operation and set the object store name to SongsObjectStore, which we have already specified in StoreFlow.

12. Add **TransformMessage** after the **Retrieve** operation and add the DataWeave coding to the **Output** tab, as shown in the following figure:

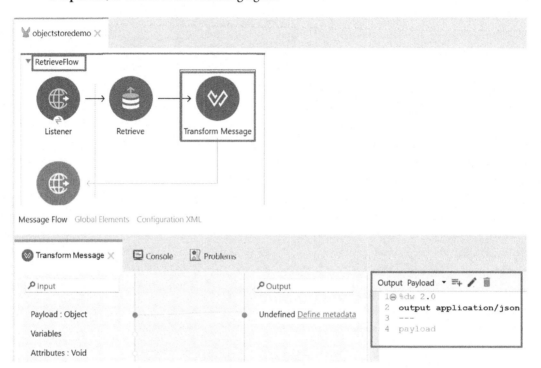

Figure 8.19 – Transform Message

13. Click **Save**, or press *Ctrl + S*, to save the Mule application.

14. Run the Mule application from the canvas. Once the application has deployed successfully, we will be able to see the logs with the status as **DEPLOYED**.

15. Open the Postman application. In the URL box, enter http://localhost:8081/store, then click **Send**.

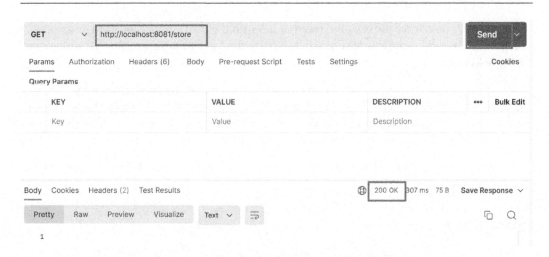

Figure 8.20 – Sending the request to the Store flow

In the preceding figure, we can see that the response received is 200 OK, which means that our application has received the request and stored the key (lastProcessedSongID with the value 5) in the object store successfully.

Let us try to retrieve the stored value from object store:

1. In the URL box, enter `http://localhost:8081/retrieve`, then click **Send**.

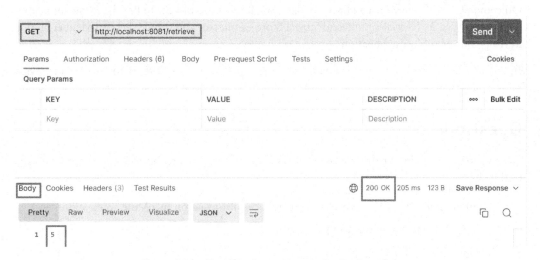

Figure 8.21 – Sending the request to the Retrieve flow

In *Figure 8.21*, we can see the response received is **5** with the HTTP status code and description as **200 OK**. This means we are able to successfully retrieve the `lastProcessedSongID` value stored in the object store.

For example, if we are synchronizing the song data from one system to another, then we need to store the last processed record value (`lastProcessedSongID`) in the object store. So, the next time the interface runs, it fetches the record from the system, which is yet to be processed to another system, with the help of the last processed record value (`lastProcessedSongID`).

With this, we have understood how to create an object store and store and retrieve values to and from the object store.

Summary

In this chapter, we had a look at various types of configuration files in the Mule application.

We created a Mule application using Scheduler, after which we tried to run it, and finally, we tested it using an external Postman application.

We also learned about creating a Mule application using the API specification. We saw how APIkit Router helps create flows automatically and route the flows into different HTTP methods. We tested methods such as `get`, `put`, and `post` to see the success and failure scenarios.

Our next topic was how to use Object Store Connector in a Mule application.

On completing this chapter, you have an elaborate knowledge of how to build a Mule application using Scheduler, API Specification, and Object Store Connector and should feel confident enough to develop your own Mule application.

In the next chapter, *Chapter 9*, *Deploying Your Application*, we'll explore further different ways to deploy our application.

Questions

Take a moment to answer the following questions to serve as a recap of what you just learned in this chapter:

1. Which `.xml` file will have project dependencies information in a Mule application?
2. What are the different types of scheduling strategies?
3. What is APIkit Router?
4. What is Object Store Connector?

Answers

1. `pom.xml`

2. There are two types of scheduling strategies:

   - Fixed Frequency

   - Cron

3. APIkit Router is a tool for creating a Mule application. It autogenerates the flow using a RAML file. It receives the incoming request, validates the URL, query parameters, and URI parameters based on the API specification, and also routes the incoming request to the Mule flow.

4. Object Store Connector is a Mule component that allows you to store a simple key-value pair.

9

Deploying Your Application

In the previous chapter, we learned how to build a Mule application using Anypoint Studio and about the different aspects of Anypoint Studio, different types of property files, and their configurations.

An optimized Mule application is the building block of a successful application network. We've previously built a simple Mule application by scaffolding RAML and learned about the different components and capabilities of Anypoint Studio.

MuleSoft has several alternatives to offer when it comes to deployment environments. Choosing the right deployment model is a crucial decision, as it involves investment cost and architectural strategy.

In this chapter, we'll learn more about the various deployment models and how to effectively choose a deployment model.

We will also learn about the steps involved in **CloudHub** and **on-premises** deployment. We shall also learn about the **Continuous Integration/Continuous Deployment CI/CD** deployment process with MuleSoft.

Here's what you can expect from this chapter:

- Getting started with deployment models
- Choosing the right deployment model
- Deploying your Mule application on CloudHub
- Deploying your Mule application on an on-premises server
- Building a CI/CD pipeline with MuleSoft

Technical requirements

The following requirements for this chapter are:

- Anypoint Studio installation (see *Chapter 3*, *Exploring Anypoint Studio*, for Studio installation guidance)

- An Anypoint Platform account (see *Chapter 2*, *Designing Your API*, to create a 30-day free trial account)

Getting started with deployment models

A **deployment model** basically tells you about the environment in which you'll be hosting your Mule application. In the previous chapter (*Chapter 8*, *Building Your Mule Application*), we deployed a Mule application to CloudHub.

We will study different types of deployment models in this chapter. Before getting started with the deployment models, let's understand some common terms.

The topology of Mule capabilities is divided into two fragments, namely the control plane and runtime plane (see *Figure 9.1*):

- **Control plane**: This consists of the components that are responsible for building and managing the Mule applications. Anypoint Exchange, Anypoint Design Center, and Anypoint Management Center are part of the control Plane.

- **Runtime plane**: This consists of the components mainly responsible for the deployment of your Mule applications. The Mule runtime engine, Anypoint connectors, and runtime services are part of the runtime plane.

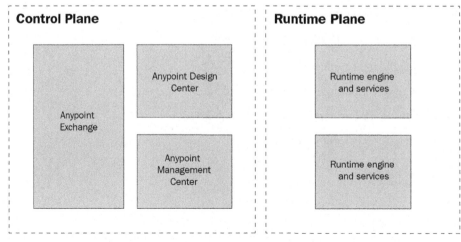

Figure 9.1 – The control plane and the runtime plane

Note to PD: Image to be redrawn

Now that we've understood the control plane and the runtime plane, let's understand the different deployment models.

Types of deployment models

MuleSoft has several deployment models to offer. Let's learn about the various deployment options available.

CloudHub

Let us now learn about CloudHub in brief:

- In this model, all the applications are hosted on MuleSoft's Anypoint Platform
- You can leverage the **Integration Platform as a Service (iPaaS)** capabilities of Anypoint Platform, such as troubleshooting, logging, monitoring, and so on
- Under the hood, your Mule application will be hosted on AWS's EC2 instance

Anypoint Runtime Fabric (RTF)

Let's understand the basics of RTF:

- RTF is a container-based service in which you can manage the deployment and scaling of Mule apps
- You can install Mule apps on customer-hosted infrastructures such as **Integration as a Service (IaaS)** platforms (AWS, Azure, and so on), virtual machines, bare metal (Microsoft Hyper-V, Citrix XenServer, and VMware ESXi), and so on using RTF
- It internally uses **Docker containers** and **Kubernetes** for orchestration on Mule apps
- You can leverage the capabilities of Anypoint Platform to manage apps deployed on RTF

Anypoint Platform Private Cloud Edition (PCE)

We shall now learn about PCE:

- Anypoint PCE allows you to manage Mule applications locally
- You can host Mule applications on a customer-hosted infrastructure
- With Anypoint PCE, you can have a control plane locally on your own network
- It helps you to leverage the capabilities of MuleSoft's Anypoint Platform combined with local infrastructure

Standalone Mule Runtime

Let us understand the concept of Standalone Mule Runtime:

- In this model, all the applications are hosted on the customer's infrastructure

- You may or may not leverage the capabilities of the cloud or Anypoint Platform, depending on your deployment environment (we shall learn more about the deployment environment further on in this chapter)

All these deployment models require a different subscription; therefore, it's essential to know the factors to be considered when choosing a deployment. We shall learn more about them in the next section.

Choosing the right deployment model

In order to efficiently execute your integration strategy, it's important to choose an accurate environment to host your applications. Let's understand the factors to be considered when choosing the right deployment environment:

- **Cost involved**: The organizational budget for implementing and maintaining the infrastructure

- **Security and compliance**: Organizational level security and regulation pertaining to the data/metadata

- **Existing infrastructure**: We need to analyze the existing network and IT infrastructure

- **Cloud-based approach**: The ability or willingness to adopt a cloud-based infrastructure

- **Size of the ecosystem**: We need to analyze and determine the current and futuristic applications and the number of APIs that we will have to host on the server

We have now taken into consideration the many factors involved when deciding on a correct deployment model. Let's now learn about the different deployment environments where we can host our Mule applications.

Understanding the different deployment environments

In this section, we will mainly focus on the different types of deployment environments and when to choose a particular environment. Also, let's understand the pros and cons associated with the deployment environments.

In *Table 9.1*, you can see a consolidated view of different deployment environments. We shall learn about them in brief in the subsequent sections.

	Fully cloud-hosted	Fully customer-hosted			Hybrid	
Deployment environment	CloudHub	Fully on-premises	Fully IaaS		iPaaS and IaaS	iPaaS and on-premises
	RTF and Mule runtime	RTF and Mule runtime	RTF, Mule runtime, and and Pivotal Cloud Foundry (PCF)		RTF, Mule Runtime, and PCF	RTF and Mule runtime
Control plane	MuleSoft-hosted	On-premises	Customer-hosted (Google Cloud Platform (GCP), AWS, Azure, and so on)		Mule-hosted	Customer-hosted (GCP, AWS, Azure, and so on)
Runtime plane	MuleSoft-hosted	On-premises	Customer-hosted (GCP, AWS, Azure, and so on)		Customer-hosted (GCP, AWS, Azure, and so on)	Customer-hosted (GCP, AWS, Azure, and so on)

Table 9.1 – A deployment environment in MuleSoft

With reference to *Table 9.1*, let's get started with our first deployment environment, which is **fully cloud-hosted**.

Fully cloud-hosted

Let us now learn about fully cloud-hosted environment:

- In this environment, all the applications are hosted on the cloud.
- You can leverage the capabilities of an iPaaS tool such as MuleSoft. We can also call a fully cloud-hosted environment as CloudHub (see *Figure 9.2*).
- Both the runtime plane and the control plane are hosted on CloudHub.

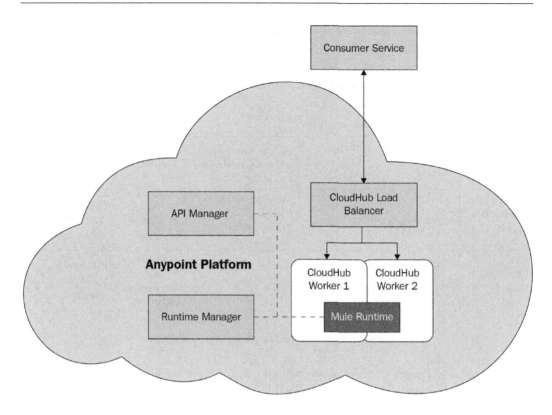

Figure 9.2 – A fully cloud-hosted environment model

In *Figure 9.2*, we can see both the runtime plane and the control plane are hosted in the cloud.

Let's understand when to opt for a fully cloud-hosted environment:

- If there is no existing infrastructure and you are willing to move toward the cloud

- When you don't want to spend time and resources on infrastructure management

- When there are no security regulations and restrictions on the data/metadata leaving your organization's network

- When you have a small ecosystem and a smaller number of applications/APIs to be managed

- If you want to take advantage of all the pre-existing capabilities of MuleSoft

Now that we know when to opt for a fully cloud-hosted environment, let's review the pros and cons of a cloud-hosted deployment environment.

Pros

Let us review the pros of a fully cloud-hosted environment:

- You will achieve high availability and reliability

- Easy configuration of load balancers, which are **Shared Load Balancers (SLBs)** and **Dedicated Load Balancers (DLBs)**

- Maintenance and support for Mule applications by using capabilities such as CloudHub logging, monitoring scheduling, and troubleshooting

- Easy and reliable security implementation

- Quick migration to the latest updates and patches

Cons

Let us review the cons of a fully cloud-hosted environment:

- A **domain project** is not supported by this model. It is supported by on-premises infrastructure.

- It could be expensive if you have a limited budget.

We now understand several aspects of a cloud-hosted environment. Let's move ahead with the next deployment model, which is fully customer-hosted.

Fully customer-hosted

In this deployment model, all the applications are hosted on the customer's network, leveraging the organization's current on-premises infrastructure.

We can categorize it as either **fully on-premises** or **fully infrastructure as a Service (IaaS)**. Let's learn about both models.

Fully on-premises

Let us learn more about fully on-premise infrastructure:

- We are hosting our applications on an organizational network

- The control plane and the runtime plane are hosted over an on-premises infrastructure

- When you want to opt for a fully on-premises infrastructure, you can deploy your application on the following:

  - **RTF**: We can opt for this deployment model when we have a large number of applications and also if we wish to use a **microservice architecture** and expand our application network

- **Customer-hosted Mule runtimes**: If you have only a limited number of Mule applications and a pre-existing network infrastructure

Let's understand when we should choose fully on-premises:

- When we have strict security regulations and do not want our data/metadata to leave the organizational network

- When you're an established organization that has legacy apps and you're not planning on cloud migration

- When you're planning to use your existing on-premises infrastructure

- When you don't have cost/resource-related obligations and you're perfectly fine managing your on-premises infrastructure

Fully IaaS

Let us now understand details about fully IaaS infrastructure:

- In this model, we have our control plane and runtime plane on a customer-hosted IaaS platform such as AWS, Azure, and GCP

- When you want to opt for a fully IaaS infrastructure, you can deploy your application on:

  - **RTF**: When we wish to use a microservice architecture and expand our application network

  - **Customer-hosted Mule runtimes**: If you have only a limited number of Mule applications

  - **Pivotal Cloud Foundry (PCF)**: When we have subscribed to a PCF infrastructure

Let's now understand when we should opt for fully IaaS:

- When you don't have many data regulations and also if you're fine with your data/metadata leaving your organizational network

- When you're a small organization planning toward cloud migration

- If your organization already has IaaS as the current infrastructure

- If there are some restrictions on data/metadata

- If you have a limited number of applications

- When you don't have a MuleSoft-hosted customer plane

- When you have cost-related obligations and don't want to switch completely to the cloud

Let's now look at the pros and cons of a fully customer-hosted deployment environment.

Pros

Let us review the pros of a fully IaaS environment:

- It provides reliable security, as your data resides within the organizational network

- You get complete control of your Mule applications, network, and security policies

- You can create a domain project to reference global configurations of several Mule applications

Cons

Let us review the cons of a fully IaaS environment:

- You need to manage a complete network infrastructure on your own.

- You need to manage your logs on your own. Also, you'll have to configure external logging and monitoring tools, which will be an additional job.

We now understand the different aspects of the customer-hosted deployment model. Let's now learn about our next model, which is the hybrid model.

The hybrid model

In the case of the hybrid model, you can leverage the capabilities of an iPaaS tool (MuleSoft) and your organization's current infrastructure.

As per your requirements, you can categorize this model as **iPaaS and IaaS** or **iPaaS and on-premises**.

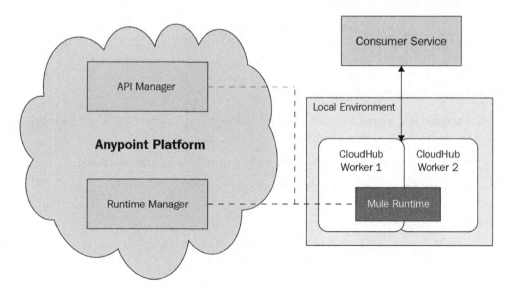

Figure 9.3 – A hybrid environment

As you can see in *Figure 9.3*, the control plane is hosted on the iPaaS platform, which is the Anypoint Platform, and the runtime plane is hosted on the customer's network, which could be on-premises or IaaS.

iPaaS and IaaS

Let's look at when we should opt for an iPaaS and on-premises hybrid model:

- When you want to leverage the capabilities of an iPaaS tool such as MuleSoft
- If you have no restrictions on your data and you're fine with data/metadata leaving your organizational network
- When you're planning to retain your existing cloud infrastructure and also reap the benefits of an iPaaS tool

iPaaS and on-premises

Similarly, let's learn about when should we opt for an iPaaS and on-premises hybrid model:

- If you want to leverage the capabilities of an iPaaS tool such as MuleSoft
- When there are fewer restrictions on data leaving an organizational network
- If you're fine with metadata leaving your organization but you still have data to reside on your premises
- When you're planning to retain your existing network infrastructure and slowly move toward a cloud-based infrastructure

Let's now discuss the pros and cons of a hybrid environment.

Pros

Let us review the pros of a fully hybrid model:

- You can utilize shared resources using a domain project, as you're still hosting an application on an on-premises infrastructure
- Latency is reduced, as the applications are hosted on an organizational network
- We can utilize the pre-existing load balancers

Cons

Let us review the cons of fully hybrid model:

- Scalability is difficult if you wish to add new servers
- You still need to maintain some part of the infrastructure
- You need to take care of updates/patches manually

We have studied the different deployment environments, their pros and cons, and when we should opt for a particular environment.

In the next section, we will learn how to deploy our Mule application to CloudHub.

Deploying your Mule application to CloudHub

We have previously seen how to deploy a Mule application using a JAR file (see *Chapter 8, Building Your Mule Application*).

There are several ways to deploy your Mule application on CloudHub:

- Anypoint Studio
- The **Anypoint CLI**
- Uploading an executable JAR file in Runtime Manager
- **CI/CD deployment**

We will now deploy our application on CloudHub using the most commonly used and easiest method, which is Anypoint Studio.

Let's follow some basic configuration steps in order to deploy our Mule application to CloudHub:

1. Configure your Anypoint Platform credentials by going to **Anypoint Studio | Preferences** (for Mac users) or **Windows | Preferences** (for Windows users). Once inside **Preferences**, navigate to **Anypoint Studio | Authentication |** the **Add** button (see *Figure 9.4*).

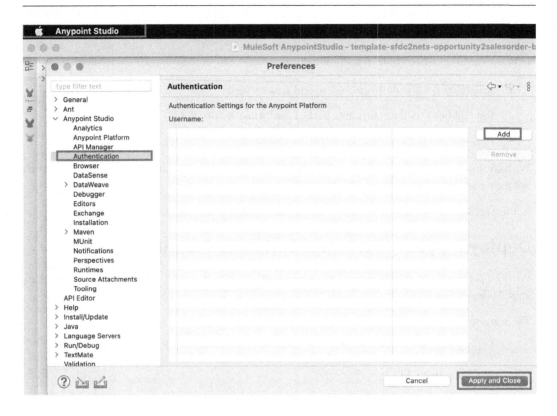

Figure 9.4 – Adding authentication in Anypoint Studio

2. Sign in to Anypoint Platform from Anypoint Studio by clicking **Add** and then **Configure**. Add your Anypoint Platform credentials and sign in (see *Figure 9.5*).

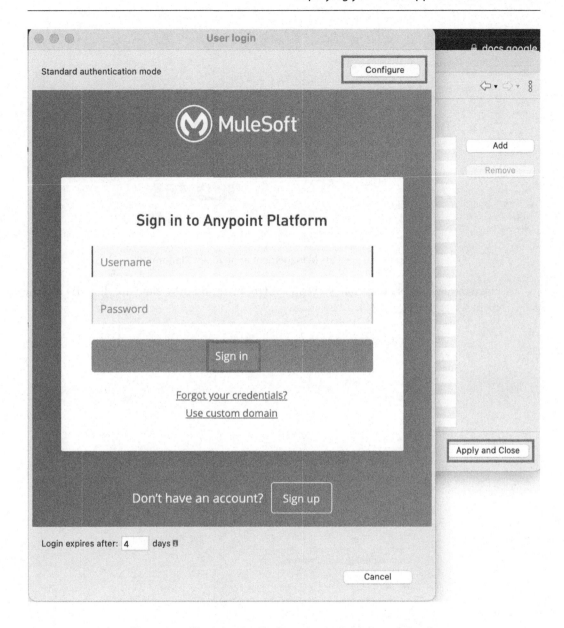

Figure 9.5 – The Anypoint Platform sign-in page through Studio

3.   Go to Anypoint Platform from the browser, click on **Organization**, and then the organization group (which is **Packt Publication** in *Figure 9.6*).

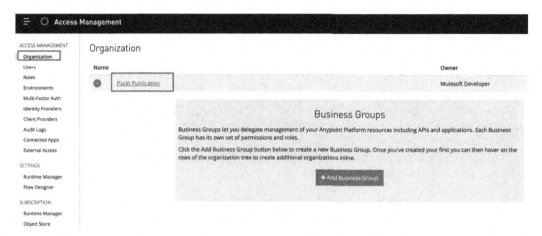

Figure 9.6 – Access Management in Anypoint Platform

Once inside your organization, you will see **Organization info**. Note the client ID and the client secret (see *Figure 9.7*).

Figure 9.7 – Organization info in Access Management

4. Configure the API manager details by going to **Anypoint Studio | Preferences** (for Mac users) or **Windows | Preferences** (for Windows users). Once inside **Preferences**, navigate to **API Manager**. Enter the client ID and client secret, which you noted earlier. Click **Apply | Apply and Close** (see *Figure 9.8*).

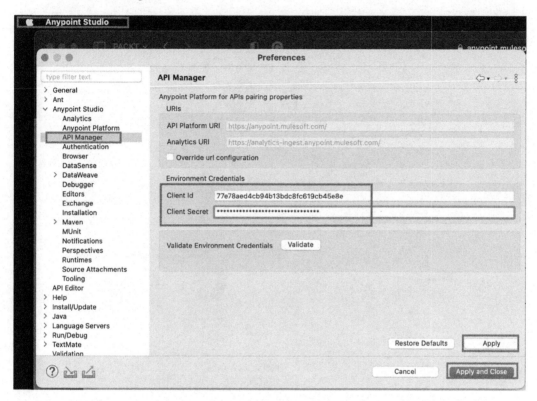

Figure 9.8 – Configuring the client ID and client secret in Anypoint Studio

> **Note**
>
> All the steps till *step 4* are one-time activities. You only need to configure it once before your first deployment. For every subsequent deployment, your configuration will be retained.
>
> You can skip all the previous steps (*step 1* to *step 4*) if you want to deploy to CloudHub just once or don't wish to save Anypoint Platform credentials.

5.   To deploy your application, follow these steps:

I.   Right-click on any application in Anypoint Studio that you wish to deploy to **CloudHub | Anypoint Platform | Deploy to CloudHub** (see *Figure 9.9*).

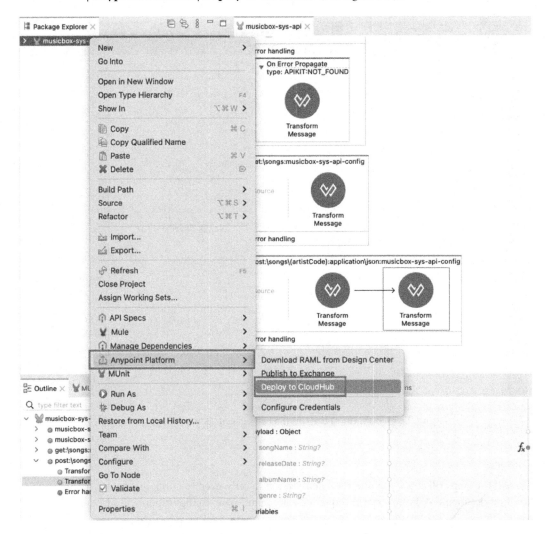

Figure 9.9 – Deploying to CloudHub from Anypoint Studio

II.   Choose a deployment environment – **Sandbox**, in our case (see *Figure 9.10*).

Figure 9.10 – Choosing Sandbox as a deployment environment

III.   Review the configurations and click **Deploy Application** (see *Figure 9.11*).

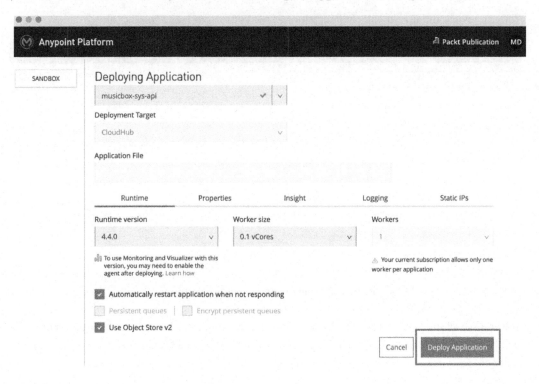

Figure 9.11 – Reviewing the deployment configurations

Note
Every time you wish to redeploy an application, follow *step 5*.

You will see the application is successfully deployed on CloudHub (see *Figure 9.12*).

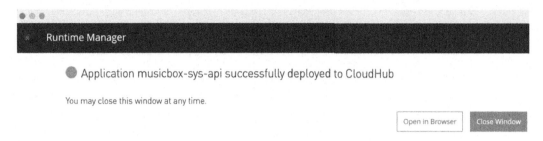

Figure 9.12 – Application successfully deployed on CloudHub

Let's now review our deployed application in Anypoint Platform's Runtime Manager.

You can review and update the configurations as per your needs (see *Figure 9.13*).

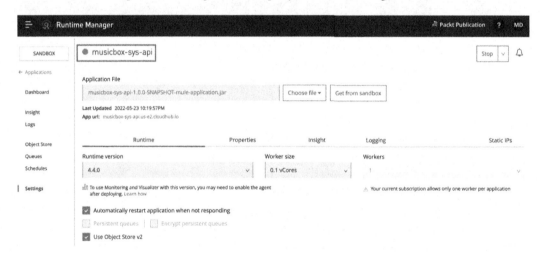

Figure 9.13 – The Anypoint Platform dashboard

You can see all the properties in the **Properties** tab auto-populated because we have configured the API Manager's configuration in the studio, which is the client ID and the client secret (see *Figure 9.14*).

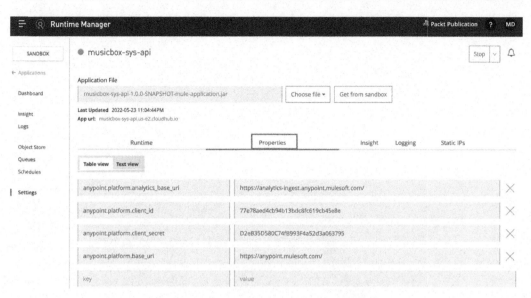

Figure 9.14 – Properties in Runtime Manager

We have now successfully deployed our Mule application to CloudHub. This is also considered the easiest way to deploy your application on CloudHub.

In the next section, let's now learn how to deploy it on standalone Mule runtime, also called an on-premises server.

Deploying your Mule application on an on-premises server

In an on-premise deployment, you host a Mule Runtime on your infrastructure. You have total control over the applications deployed on your network.

Let's understand how to set up an on-premises server and deploy a Mule application over it with some easy steps.

To download and unzip the Mule runtime, click on the following link: `https://www.mulesoft.com/lp/dl/mule-esb-enterprise`. Fill in the details as shown in *Figure 9.15* and click **Download**.

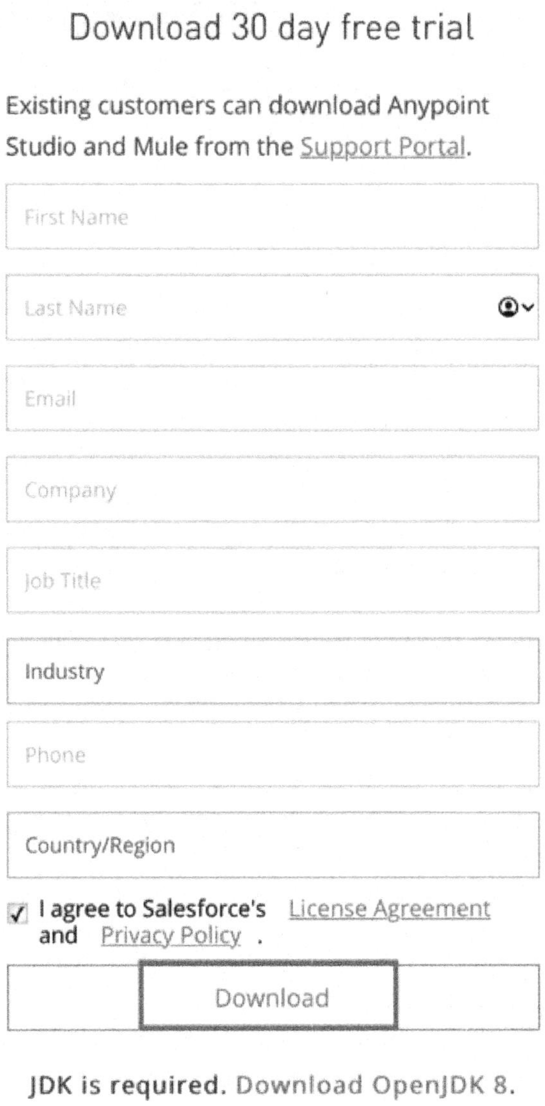

Download 30 day free trial

Existing customers can download Anypoint
Studio and Mule from the Support Portal.

First Name

Last Name

Email

Company

Job Title

Industry

Phone

Country/Region

☑ I agree to Salesforce's   License Agreement
and   Privacy Policy .

Download

JDK is required. Download OpenJDK 8.

Figure 9.15 – Downloading the Mule runtime

Extract the folder and review all the files in the package (see *Figure 9.16*).

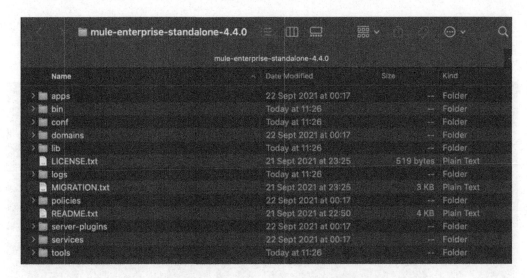

Figure 9.16 – The Mule standalone runtime's folder structure

To add a server, in Anypoint Platform, navigate to **Runtime Manager** | **Servers** | **Add Server**. Enter the server name of your choice and click **Copy command** (see *Figure 9.17*).

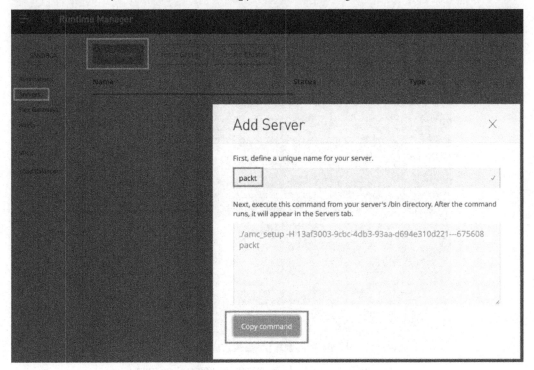

Figure 9.17 – Adding an on-premises server in Anypoint Platform

We can control and monitor our Mule servers with the help of a Mule agent. Open the terminal or Command Prompt (in a Windows OS). Paste the command copied in *step 2* and execute (see *Figure 9.18*).

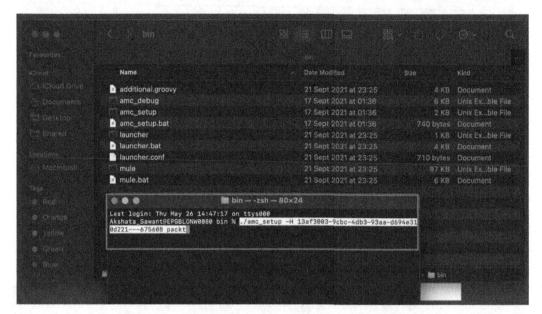

Figure 9.18 – Executing the command to install the Mule agent

You can see in *Figure 9.19* that the command is executed and the Mule agent is installed successfully.

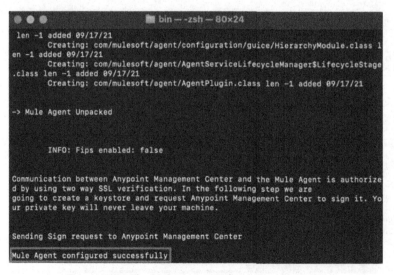

Figure 9.19 – The Mule agent configured successfully

You can also check the status of your server by logging in to **Runtime Manager**.

On logging into **Runtime Manager | Servers**, you can see that the status of the server is **Created** (see *Figure 9.20*).

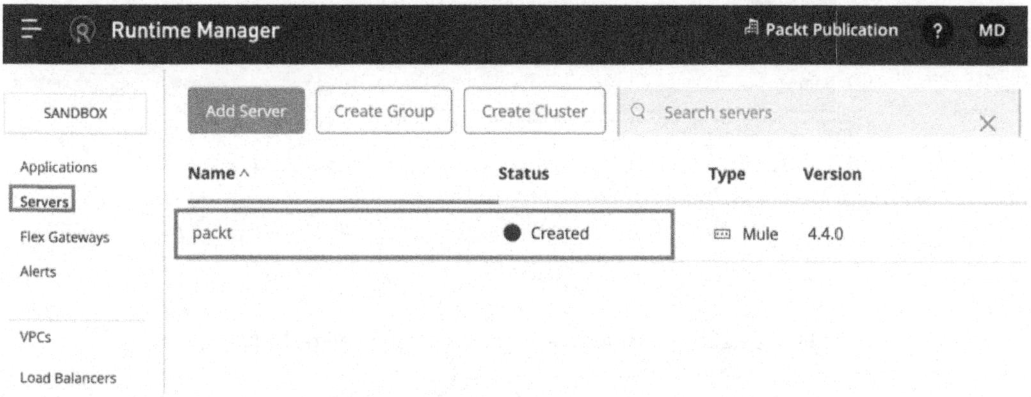

Figure 9.20 – A server created in Runtime Manager

To start the Mule standalone server, execute mule.bat under the /bin directory downloaded package. You can see the status as **DEPLOYED** on the terminal/Command Prompt (see *Figure 9.21*).

Figure 9.21 – The on-premises server started

You will also see the server in **Running** status in Runtime Manager (see *Figure 9.22*).

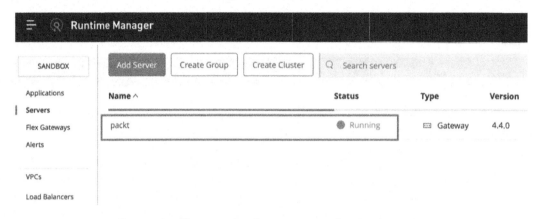

Figure 9.22 – The server in a Running state in Runtime Manager

To deploy the Mule application, go to **Runtime Manager | Deploy the application**. Select the **Deployment Target** to the server that you've recently set up. Choose the Mule application JAR file that you wish to deploy. Click **Deploy Application** (see *Figure 9.23*).

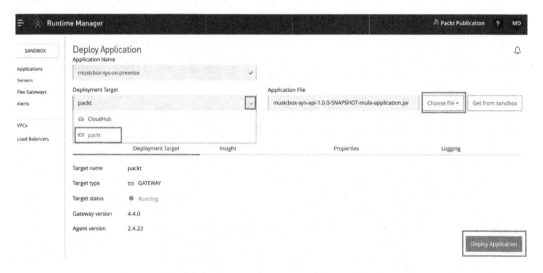

Figure 9.23 – Deploying a Mule application

Once the application is deployed successfully, you will see the status as **Started** (see *Figure 10.24*). Review the configuration of the application that is being deployed on your on-premises server.

Figure 9.24 – Reviewing the deployed on-premises application in Anypoint Platform

We know now how to deploy an on-premises application. In the next section, we'll learn more about the CI/CD process.

Building a CI/CD pipeline with MuleSoft

In the previous sections, we learned about the steps involved with manual deployment. In order to make deployment hassle-free and enable a faster release, we can automate the deployment process with the help of CI and CD.

This involves building a pipeline with predefined tasks to continuously build, test, and deploy our Mule application (see *Figure 9.25*). It automates the deployment process with or without any manual interventions.

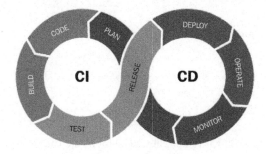

Figure 9.25 – The CI/CD process

To enable the CI/CD pipeline with a Mule application, we need to configure the **Mule Maven plugin** in pom.xml.

The Mule Maven plugin

This helps you to build and deploy a Mule application in various deployment environments. You can leverage the capabilities of Maven to perform different operations. The Mule Maven plugin has mainly three goals, namely package, deploy, and mule:deploy/mule:undeploy.

You need to enter deployment details in pom.xml pertaining to a specific environment. The following code snippet shows the configuration of the Mule Maven plugin in pom.xml for CloudHub deployment. We can similarly configure for other deployment models:

```
<plugin>
  <groupId>org.mule.tools.maven</groupId>
  <artifactId>mule-maven-plugin</artifactId>
  <version>3.5.4</version>
  <extensions>true</extensions>
  <configuration>
    <cloudHubDeployment>
      <uri>https://anypoint.mulesoft.com</uri>
      <muleVersion>${app.runtime}</muleVersion>
      <username>${username}</username>
      <password>${password}</password>
      <applicationName>${cloudhub.application.name}
          </applicationName>
      <environment>${environment}</environment>
      <region>${region}</region>
      <workers>${workers}</workers>
      <workerType>${workerType}</workerType>
      <properties>
        <key>value</key>
      </properties>
    </cloudHubDeployment>
  </configuration>
</plugin>
```

Also, you can integrate MuleSoft with different CI/CD tools, such as Jenkins, Azure DevOps, Bamboo, Bitbucket, GitLab, and so on.

We have learned about CI/CD configuration with MuleSoft and the Mule Maven plugin. It's essential to know about the basics of Maven before configuring the CI/CD pipeline with Mule.

Summary

In this chapter, we have studied different deployment models such as CloudHub, RTF, PCE, and standalone runtime. We have also learned about different deployment environments such as fully cloud-hosted, fully customer-hosted, and hybrid. We have explored the pros and cons of the deployment environment and when to opt for a particular environment and a model. Apart from this, we have also seen how to deploy a Mule application on CloudHub and on-premises systems.

We have also learned the basics of CI/CD integrations with the help of the Mule Maven plugin. We have seen the importance of the Mule Maven plugin while deploying a Mule application.

In order to automate and make your deployment process hassle-free, it's essential to be aware of the basics of deployment.

In the next chapter, we shall learn about API security and how to implement API security using MuleSoft.

Let's get some hands-on practice by solving an assignment and doing a quiz.

Assignments

Deploy a Mule Application from Anypoint Studio on a CloudHub and standalone Mule runtime server (on-premises).

Questions

1. What are the different ways to deploy an application on CloudHub?
2. What is the purpose of the Mule Maven plugin?
3. Where should you host your application if there are restrictions on your data/metadata leaving an organization?

Answers

1. You can deploy an application on CloudHub using Anypoint Studio, by uploading an executable JAR file in Anypoint Platform, using the Anypoint CLI, or using a CI/CD tool.
2. To enable the management of building and deployment of a Mule application in different deployment environments.
3. On a customer-hosted deployment environment.

10
Secure Your API

In the previous chapter, we have learned how to deploy a Mule application, what the different deployment environments are, and how to choose your deployment environment.

There are several factors that need to be considered while choosing a deployment model; hence, it's an important decision while building your application network.

We are also aware that APIs are responsible for carrying data/metadata and communicating with several end systems and, hence, are at a potentially high risk of being attacked. It's important to secure your API and thereby protect your integration ecosystem. In this chapter, we shall learn about API security and the need for securing your API and Mule application.

We shall also focus on how to implement API security using MuleSoft and study several techniques with which you can secure your APIs.

We will cover the following topics in this chapter:

- The need for API security
- API security with MuleSoft
- Introducing API Manager
- Policies in MuleSoft
- Implementing API security using policy
- Security capabilities of MuleSoft

Technical requirements

The requirements in this chapter are:

- Anypoint Studio installation (see *Chapter 3*, *Exploring Anypoint Studio*, for Studio installation guidance)
- An Anypoint Platform account (see *Chapter 2*, *Designing Your API*, to create a 30-day free trial account)

The need for API security

As we're aware, APIs are responsible for carrying data and critical information back and forth in an integrated system. Hence, it is essential for us to have control over the information being processed and transferred by the APIs.

Let's now understand the need for API security:

- To protect our APIs, applications, API network, and end systems from malicious attacks
- Prevent unauthorized use of APIs or data that is being processed by APIs
- To standardize rules and regulations across an API network
- To follow company-wide security protocols and standards
- Comply with government-laid security protocols and standards such as FedRAMP, FIPS 140, CIS Benchmarks, and so on
- To have control over incoming and outgoing data and metadata

We now know the need for and the importance of API security. Let's now see how we can secure API and applications that, in turn, will secure our application network.

API security with MuleSoft

In this section, let's simplify how we can achieve API security using MuleSoft.

In *Figure 10.1*, we can see that the application network is formed using reusable building blocks, such as Mule applications, end systems, and non-Mule applications. Here, the outer dotted line depicts the periphery of the Mule application, and the inner dotted line shows the integration between a Mule application and an external end system/non-Mule application.

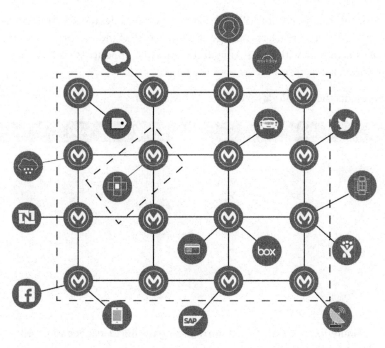

Figure 10.1 – A snapshot of Anypoint Platform depicting application networks

In order to achieve total security, you can apply security regulations on any of the following:

- On the periphery of the Mule application
- On one or more Mule applications and end systems
- On one or more non-Mule applications and end systems
- On an individual Mule/non-Mule and end system

You can implement the preceding security mechanism in any permutation and combination as per your organizational security needs. This is also called the **layered security** approach in MuleSoft. It helps us to achieve **zero-trust security**. It means trusting no one and verifying every incoming and outgoing request.

We've now understood how to achieve total security in MuleSoft. Let's now learn about the prime component responsible for securing our APIs, **API Manager**.

Introducing API Manager

In *Chapter 5*, *All About Anypoint Platform*, we saw a glimpse of API Manager. Let's now understand the prime capabilities of API Manager.

API Manager is mainly responsible for API governance, which includes tasks such as managing, securing, and governing the API. It's a place to manage all kinds of APIs and, in turn, our Mule applications under one roof. It is in sync with other Anypoint Platform components such as the Design Center, Exchange, Runtime Manager, and the Anypoint Studio.

Figure 10.2 represents the default dashboard of API Manager.

Figure 10.2 – Anypoint Platform depicting the API Manager dashboard

Let's now understand the core capabilities of API Manager.

Understanding the capabilities of API Manager

From *Figure 10.2*, we can see the navigation menu on the left-hand side of the dashboard. Let's learn in brief about each component in the menu:

- **API Administration**: It's mainly responsible for adding/importing a new/existing API into API Manager. It creates an API instance on which we can apply security policies. We shall learn about applying security policies in the upcoming section.

- **API Groups**: The main functionality is to consolidate the APIs into groups and apply security configuration to the whole group. The security configuration laid on a particular group will be applicable for all the applications in that group.

- **Automated Policies**: There are a few predefined policies pertaining to logging and monitoring. You can apply the same set of policies across all the APIs in the particular environment. They're known as automated policies. It saves time and makes your security configuration consistent, as you're applying the same set of common policies throughout the environment (a design, a sandbox, or any other).

- **Client Applications**: These are external services or applications that consume APIs.

- **Custom Policies**: You can publish your customized policy in this section. You can design your own policy in Anypoint Studio and configure it to match your organizational needs. Later, you can publish this policy and apply it over the API/APIs.

- **Analytics**: This provides you with information related to performance metrics. You can create your own customized dashboards, charts, and so on and analyze your application's performance.

Now that we've understood the capabilities of API Manager, let's move ahead and understand the underlying security architecture by learning about a **secure API gateway**.

Understanding the API gateway

An API gateway acts as a gatekeeper to keep a check on incoming and outgoing requests and responses.

Learning about the secure API gateway will give you an idea of how security mechanisms are enforced in MuleSoft.

We can see the architecture of the API gateway in *Figure 10.3*. Let's look at the flow of activities involved.

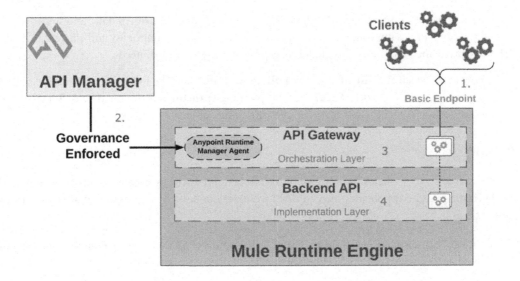

Figure 10.3 – The security architecture of the API gateway

With reference to *Figure 10.3*, let's understand the activities involved in implementing security with the help of the API gateway:

1. Whenever a request is sent to the **basic endpoint** or a **proxy endpoint**, the request is redirected to API Manager.

2. API Manager has a list of configurations enforced on a particular endpoint (security, performance, and so on).

3. The API gateway checks whether the configured parameters on API Manager and Anypoint Runtime Manager meets the requirements with the help of an **API Autodiscovery ID**. It's a number that helps to bind the activities of API Manager with Anypoint Runtime Manager. (We shall learn more about this in later sections.)

4. If all the conditions are satisfied, only then is the request allowed to reach the backend API. If the conditions are not satisfied, the API gateway rejects the request.

5. Once the request reaches the backend API, it continues the normal execution flow.

We have now learned about the API gateway and the steps involved in securing the APIs with the API gateway.

Now, let's learn about the most fundamental and easiest approach to securing your APIs, which are **policies** in MuleSoft.

Policies in MuleSoft

Policies help you to impose security regulations, control traffic, transform data, and improve the usability of an API. It's important to know about policies, as they are quite easy and efficient to apply. They are predefined and can also be tailored as per your organizational needs.

Let's now learn about the **out-of-the-box policies** in MuleSoft. The following policies are sorted as per their categories – that is, **Security**, **Compliance**, **Transformation**, **Quality of Service**, and **Troubleshooting**. We will also study in brief custom policies in MuleSoft.

Security

In this category, the policies mainly emphasize securing the API by means of authentication and authorization. Security policies protect an API from various security threats and attacks. Let's learn about them in brief:

- **Basic Authentication – Simple**: This is the simplest of all the security policies, which helps you authenticate your application using a username and password.

- **Basic Authentication – LDAP**: This is similar to simple authentication. Here, you can authenticate using **LDAP** (which stands for **Lightweight Directory Access Protocol**) credentials.

- **IP Blocklist/Allowlist**: You can allow or restrict IP addresses from accessing your APIs.

- **JSON/XML Threat Protection**: In the case of bulky and nested JSON or XML data, you can use this policy to limit the level of nesting. This way, you're protecting your API from a malicious payload.

- **JWT Validation**: **JSON Web Token** (**JWT**): helps you authenticate and authorize with the help of a valid JWT token. The token consists of claims, signature, a JSON payload, and so on.

- **OAuth 2.0 Access Token Enforcement Using Mule OAuth Provider Policy**: You can implement OAuth 2.0 as your security protocol to help you authorize your application. You can only use it with Mule OAuth 2.0 Provider. There are other provisions if you wish to use a different identity provider (for example, Okta or Salesforce).

- **OpenAM Access Token Enforcement**: This helps you secure your application by restricting access. It uses the OpenAM Access protocol and OpenAM as the authentication server to generate the OAuth token.

- **PingFederate Access Token Enforcement**: This allows you to secure your application by restricting access and validating the token. It uses PingFederate as a client management tool to generate an OAuth token.

- **Tokenization/Detokenization**: This helps you in securely transforming/de-transforming sensitive information such as **Personal Identifiable Information** (**PII**) and bank credentials.

We have now studied several security policies that will help us to enhance API security. Let's now learn about the different policies in the compliance category.

Compliance

In this category, we mainly focus on the API being compliant with an environment and obeying the regulations. Let's learn about the policies in the compliance category:

- Client ID Enforcement: This secures access to a resource by validating a client ID and secret. It ensures that only a request with a valid client ID and secret gets access to the resource. On registering an application in the Anypoint Platform, a client ID and client secret are generated.

- **Cross-Origin Resource Sharing** (**CORS**): This is also known as a CORS policy. As the name suggests, it helps to access resources from web applications that are in a different domain.

We have now learned about compliance-based policies. In the next section, let's learn about the transformation policies.

Transformation

Transformation policies help in modifying or enhancing metadata information:

- Header Injection/Removal: If you want to add/remove any data/metadata as a part of an inbound header, you can use the Header Injection/Removal policy.

We now understand the transformation policies. In the next section, let's learn about the Quality of Service.

Quality of service

As the name suggests, **Quality of Service (QoS)**-based policies help you to enhance the API experience. They also help with API performance optimization. Let's check out a few of the QoS-based policies.

- **HTTP Caching**: This helps you cache the API response for reusability purposes.
- **Rate Limiting**: This puts a limit on the number of requests that can be processed by an API during a particular duration. Once it reaches the maximum threshold value, all the other requests are rejected. This can prevent a **Distributed Denial-of-Service(DDOS)** attack.
- **Rate Limiting SLA**: This is similar to Rate Limiting, but with this policy, you limit the number of requests based on a **Service Level Agreement (SLA)**.
- **Spike Control**: This puts a limit on the number of requests that can be processed by an API during a particular duration. Once it reaches the maximum threshold value, it queues the requests and attempts a retry mechanism.
- **Message Logging**: You can log the information from an incoming/outgoing request/response.

Apart from these out-of-the-box policies, if your organization has any other different security regulations, you can design your own custom policy.

Now, let's learn in brief about custom policies in Mule.

Custom policies

As is quite evident from the name itself, you can customize a security policy to match your organizational security needs.

You can write your custom policy in Anypoint Studio, package it using Maven, and publish the policy on Anypoint Exchange. The following code snippet represents the structure of a custom policy:

```xml
<?xml version="1.0" encoding="UTF-8"?>
<mule xmlns:xsi="http://www.w3.org/2001/XMLSchema-instance"
    xmlns:http-policy="http://www.mulesoft.org/schema/mule
        /http-policy">

  <http-policy:proxy name="custom-policy-template">
    <http-policy:source>
        <http-policy:execute-next/>
    </http-policy:source>
  </http-policy:proxy>
</mule>
```

Once published, you can apply the policy to your APIs using API Manager. Along with basic transformation logic, you can also add form elements such as a text box or radio button to get user input.

Apart from this, we can also combine our custom policy with the out-of-the-box Mule policies. Custom policies give you better control if you have any particular requirements.

We now understand the different policies that we can apply to our APIs to achieve security. Let's learn how to implement these policies and secure our APIs.

Implementing API security using policy

We have learned about policies, types of policies, and categories of policies. Now, let's understand how to achieve security by applying a policy.

In this walkthrough, we shall apply a simple basic authentication policy:

1. Import any Mule application into Anypoint Studio or use your pre-existing Mule application.
2. Log in to the Anypoint Platform. Go to **API Manager** | **API Administration** | **Add new API** (as shown in *Figure 10.4*).

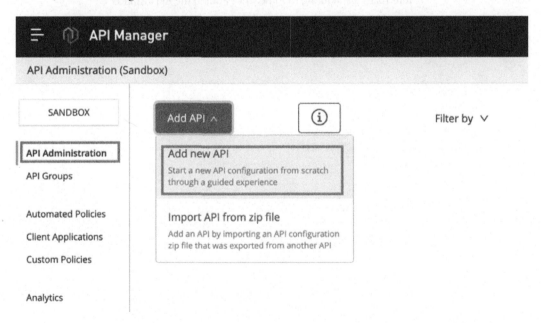

Figure 10.4 – Adding a new API instance on API Manager

3. In order to add a new API, we'll first configure **Runtime** (see *Figure 10.5*). Select **Mule Gateway** as the runtime, as we're connecting to a pre-existing application. You can also connect to a new Mule application as a proxy.

4. Select **Mule 4** as the Mule version. Click **Next**.

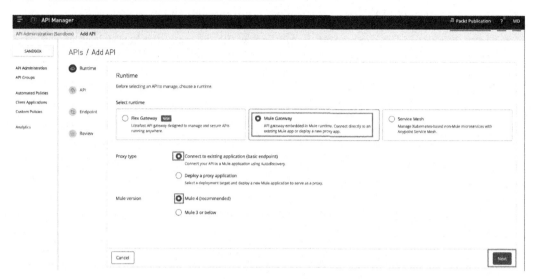

Figure 10.5 – Configuring runtime while adding the API instance

5. We will now configure the API. Select API from Exchange, the one we have already published, which is `musicbox-sys-api` (see *Figure 10.6*).

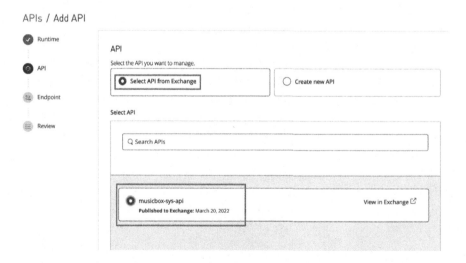

Figure 10.6 – Configuring the API while adding the API instance

6. Once you've selected the API from Exchange, details such as **Asset type**, **API version**, and **Asset version** will be auto-populated (see *Figure 10.7*). Review the information and click **Next**.

Figure 10.7 – Configuring the API from Exchange

7. We will now configure the endpoint. If you wish to have a customized URL for your endpoint, you can configure it; it's completely optional (see *Figure 10.8*). Click **Next**.

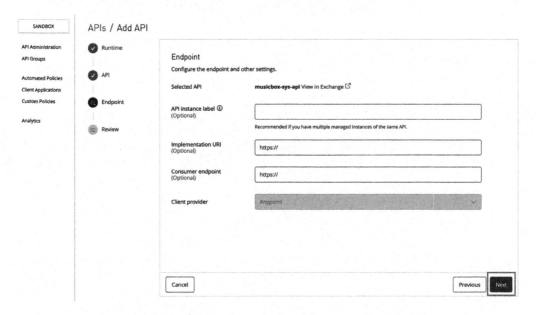

Figure 10.8 – Configuring the endpoint while creating the API instance

8. In this step, we will review all the information pertaining to our API instance (see *Figure 10.9*). Click **Save** in order to finalize our API instance.

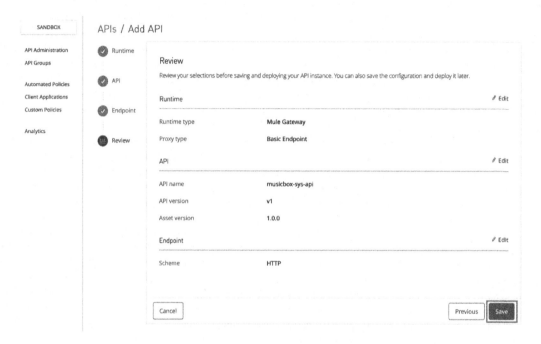

Figure 10.9 – Reviewing the API instance

You will now see a new API instance created. You can monitor and review your API performance metrics on this dashboard (see *Figure 10.10*).

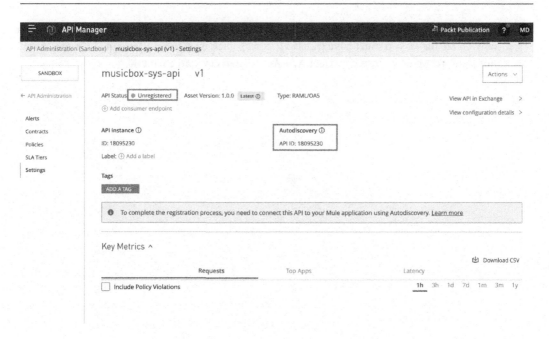

Figure 10.10 – The API instance dashboard

We have learned about how to create an API instance in API Manager. In *Figure 10.10*, we can see **Autodiscovery** and the API ID. Let's learn more about API Autodiscovery.

API Autodiscovery

API Autodiscovery binds the application deployed in Runtime Manager with the API instance created on API Manager.

The API **Autodiscovery** ID is a unique ID that helps you to connect the applications deployed on Runtime Manager to API instances on the API Manager. All the policies and other configurations that we apply on our API instance will be reflected on applications deployed in Runtime Manager.

Let's now understand how to configure API Autodiscovery.

Configuring API Autodiscovery

To configure API Autodiscovery, follow these simple steps:

1. Go to your Anypoint Studio, and open any of the previously built Mule applications or create a simple new Mule application on which you wish to configure API Autodiscovery (see *Figure 10.11*)

2. Inside your Mule application, go to `global.xml` (where you manage all configurations) or any `.xml` file (if you don't have `global.xml`), click on **Global Elements | Create**, search for `API Autodiscovery`, select **API Autodiscovery**, and click **OK**.

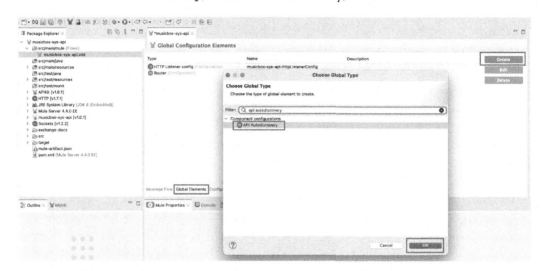

Figure 10.11 – Creating a new API Autodiscovery component

3. Copy and paste the Autodiscovery ID from the API instance in API Manager and select your main flow, which has an APIkit router in order to apply configuration across all the flows that are being routed (see *Figure 10.12*).

4. In this case, the API ID is `18095230` and the flow name is `musicbox-sys-api-main`. Once configured, click **OK**.

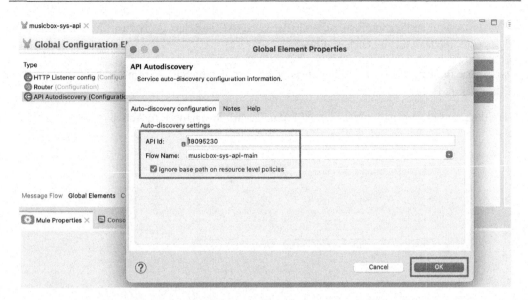

Figure 10.12 – Configuring the API Autodiscovery component

5. Deploy your application to CloudHub, as shown in *Figure 10.13*. (Refer to *Chapter 9, Deploying Your Application*, to learn more about deploying the Mule application.)

6. Right-click on your project, hover over **Anypoint Platform** and select **Deploy to CloudHub**.

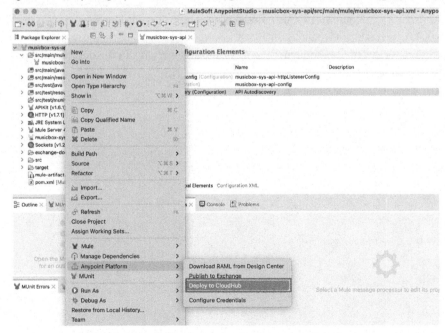

Figure 10.13 – Deploying your application to CloudHub

7. Once your application is successfully deployed to CloudHub, go to **Runtime Manager**, select your application, and click on **Logs**.

You can see in **Logs** that your API key ID is being logged, which is the same as the Auto Discovery ID (see *Figure 10.14*).

Also, the status of your API instance in API Manager will be changed to **Active**.

Figure 10.14 – API Autodiscovery logs in Runtime Manager

In this section, we saw how to configure the API Autodiscovery ID. In the next section, let's see how to configure a security policy.

Configuring a security policy

In the previous sections, we saw how to create an API instance and configure API Autodiscovery. Let's now configure a security policy using API Manager with the following simple steps:

1. In order to configure a policy, go to API Manager in Anypoint Platform, select the API instance, go to **Policies**, and click **Add policy** (see *Figure 10.15*).

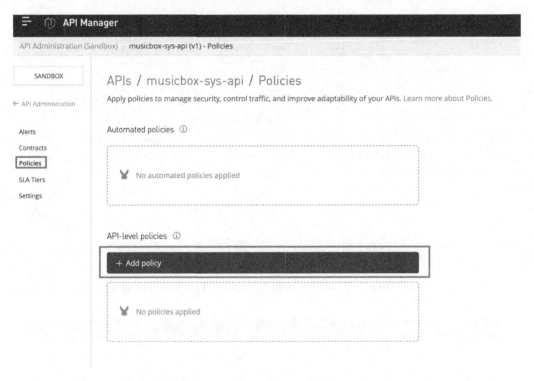

Figure 10.15 – Adding a new policy

2. You'll see a list of policies. Select the **Basic authentication - Simple** policy, which is the simplest policy (see *Figure 10.16*).

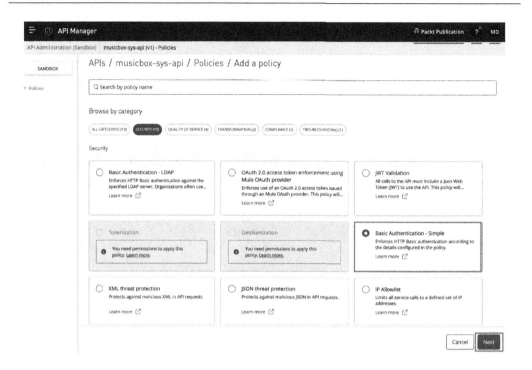

Figure 10.16 – Selecting the Basic authentication - Simple policy

3. Configure **User Name** and **User Password**. Click on **Advanced options** to configure further (see *Figure 10.17*).

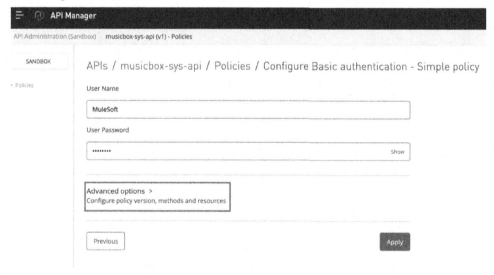

Figure 10.17 – Policy configuration

4. In the **Advanced options** section, select the latest policy version.

    You can apply the policies across all the methods and endpoints, or you can choose a particular endpoint over which you wish to apply the policy. Currently, we're applying it across all the API methods and resources. Once done, click **Apply**.

    Check the configuration in *Figure 10.18*.

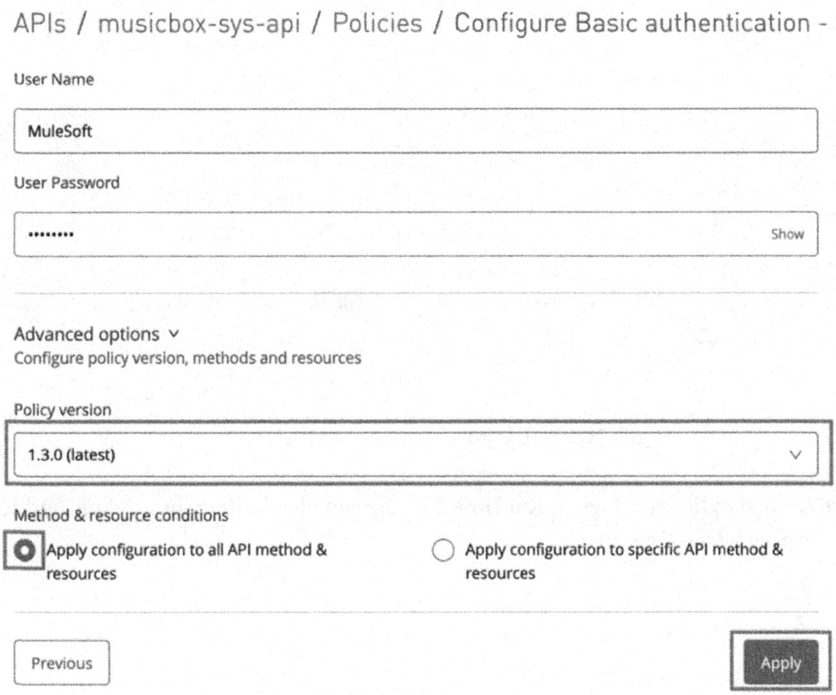

APIs / musicbox-sys-api / Policies / Configure Basic authentication - Simple policy

User Name

MuleSoft

User Password

....   Show

Advanced options ∨
Configure policy version, methods and resources

Policy version

1.3.0 (latest)   ∨

Method & resource conditions

⦿ Apply configuration to all API method &   ◯ Apply configuration to specific API method &
   resources   resources

Previous   Apply

Figure 10.18 – Advanced policy configuration options

You will see that your policy was successfully created (see *Figure 10.19*).

If you have multiple policies, you can rearrange the order of execution.

Figure 10.19 – The Policies dashboard

5. You can go to the application logs in Runtime Manager to check the policy details and logs related to the policy (see *Figure 10.20*).

```
14:45:20.463    08/27/2022    Worker-0    agw-policy-set-deployment.01    INFO

*********************************************************************
* Policy:                                                           *
* http-basic-authentication-mule-3133873-musicbox-sys-api-main      *
* OS encoding: UTF-8, Mule encoding: UTF-8                          *
*                                                                   *
*********************************************************************

14:45:20.467    08/27/2022    Worker-0    agw-policy-set-deployment.01    INFO
Applied policy http-basic-authentication-mule-3133873 version 1.3.0 to API musicbox-sys-api-v1-v1:18095230 (18095230) in application musicbox-sys-api
```

Figure 10.20 – Policy details in logs in Runtime Manager

6. Go to Postman or any other similar app and try triggering the endpoint on which you've applied the policy. You'll get an authorization error, as shown in *Figure 10.21*.

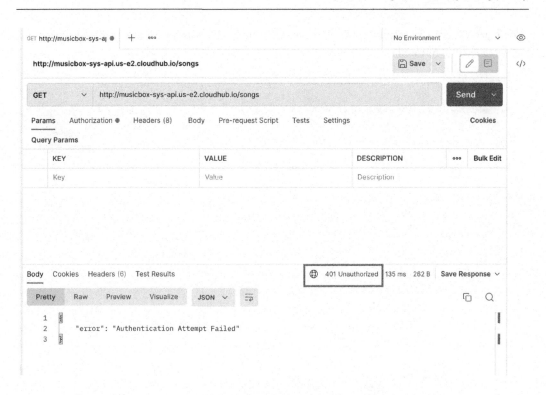

Figure 10.21 – A snapshot of Postman depicting an authentication error

7.   Go to the **Authorization** tab, select **Basic Auth**, and add a username and password (as defined in the policy). See *Figure 10.22* for reference.

You'll get a successful response, which means that the credentials have been validated successfully and you're authenticated.

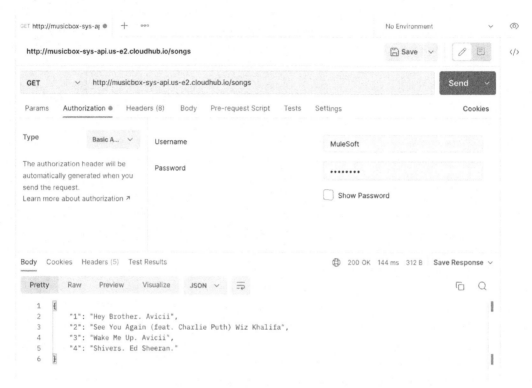

Figure 10.22 – A snapshot of Postman depicting a successful response

This is a simple demonstration of how we can leverage the security capabilities of MuleSoft by applying policies. We can further extend these capabilities to achieve zero-trust security.

Let's now learn more about the security capabilities of MuleSoft.

The security capabilities of MuleSoft

MuleSoft has a wide range to offer when it comes to security. In order to leverage the security capabilities of MuleSoft, let's learn about several security capabilities, starting with Anypoint Enterprise Security.

Anypoint Enterprise Security

In order to achieve enterprise-level security at an application level, you can install the Anypoint Enterprise Security suite. It offers you the following features to secure your Mule apps:

- **Mule Secure Token Service (STS) OAuth 2.0 Provider**
- **Mule Credentials Vault**
- **Mule Message Encryption Processor**
- **Mule Digital Signature Processor**
- **Mule Filter Processor**
- **Mule CRC32 Processor**

You can install Anypoint Enterprise Security on your Anypoint Studio to apply these capabilities.

We have learned about Anypoint Enterprise Security for Mule applications. Let's now learn about Anypoint Security, dedicated to applications deployed over **Runtime Fabric (RTF)**.

Anypoint Security

Anypoint Security offers a layered security approach in order to protect your APIs. It comprises the following:

- **Edge policies**: These are similar to the out-of-the-box MuleSoft policies
- **Secrets Manager**: This provides you with a secure vault to safeguard your security certificates and keystores
- **Tokenization service**: You can use this service to protect sensitive information like PII details, bank details, and so on

Anypoint Security helps us to secure apps deployed on RTF. Let's now learn more about Anypoint Flex Gateway, which is a capability from MuleSoft to level up API security.

Anypoint Flex Gateway

MuleSoft offers three types of gateway – namely, a Mule gateway, Anypoint Flex Gateway, and Anypoint Service Mesh. Anypoint Flex Gateway is an ultra-fast gateway for managing the security capabilities of Mule and non-Mule applications.

You can extend the security capabilities of MuleSoft beyond Anypoint Platform with the help of Anypoint Flex Gateway.

You can configure Flex Gateway in one of two ways:

- **Connected mode**: Use Anypoint Platform as a visual UI to secure, manage, and monitor your APIs.

- **Locally**: You can configure Flex Gateway on your local machine instead of connecting it to your Anypoint Platform account using YAML configuration files. You might need third-party providers if you want to have a UI to read logs.

In order to get started, you can create a free trial account with Anypoint Platform or you need to have an Anypoint Flex Gateway subscription. You can install Flex Gateway as a Linux service, in a Docker container, or as a Kubernetes Ingress controller. There is a predefined set of instructions that you can find in Runtime Manager that makes the installation and setup of Flex Gateway easy. For more information, see this article: `https://developer.mulesoft.com/tutorials-and-howtos/understanding-anypoint-flex-gateway-overview-introduction/`.

We have gone through several API security techniques. You can refer to the *Assignments*, *Questions*, and *Answers* sections at the end of this chapter to get more hands-on with API security.

Summary

In this chapter, we've learned about the security capabilities of MuleSoft. We have learned about different types of policies in MuleSoft and implemented a basic authentication policy.

We have also studied the API gateway, the security architecture of the API gateway, Enterprise Security, Anypoint Security, and Anypoint Flex Gateway.

In order to make your API network reliable and secure, it's essential to have a fair understanding of API security. It is also essential to have an understanding of various ways to achieve zero-trust security, which we have learned in this chapter.

In the next chapter, we'll learn how to test our Mule application and what the different testing tools are. We shall also study what MuleSoft has to offer when it comes to API testing.

Assignments

Apply Header Injection and Message Logging policies on an API instance. Add header values as `key` = `book` and `value` = `MuleSoft` for Header Injection policy. Log header using Message Logging policy. Verify logs in application logs on Runtime Manager.

Questions

1. What is the difference between Rate Limiting and Spike Control?

2. What is the purpose of using Anypoint Autodiscovery?

3. Which policy can we use to mask sensitive data?

Answers

1. Whenever a maximum threshold value is reached, Rate Limiting rejects all further incoming requests, whereas Spike Control controls queues of a request.

2. Anypoint Autodiscovery binds an application in Runtime Manager with an API instance in API Manager.

3. Tokenization.

11
Testing Your Application

In previous chapters, we learned how to build and deploy a Mule application. The next step is testing our application, which is important to ensure we deliver bug-free projects.

In this chapter, let us explore testing, types of testing, different testing tools, and ways to test a Mule application using **MUnit** and the **MUnit Test Recorder**. In *Chapter 3, Exploring Anypoint Studio*, we created and ran a simple Mule application called `HelloWorld`. Here, we will be learning how to test the `HelloWorld` Mule application using MUnit and the MUnit Test Recorder.

After reading this chapter, you'll come away with knowledge about the following topics:

- Different types of testing
- Different types of testing tools
- Commonly used testing tools, such as **Postman**, **SoapUI**, and **JMeter**
- How to create and run a test suite using MUnit
- How to create and run a test suite using the MUnit Test Recorder

Technical requirements

The prerequisites for this chapter are as follows:

- The `.jar` file used for creating a Mule application in the *Creating a test suite* section is available on GitHub, at the following link, in the *Chapter3* folder: `https://github.com/PacktPublishing/MuleSoft-for-Salesforce-Developers`
- Go to `https://www.postman.com/downloads` to download and install Postman
- Go to `https://www.soapui.org/downloads/soapui/` to download and install SoapUI
- Go to `https://archive.apache.org/dist/jmeter/binaries/?C=M;O=D` to download and install the latest version of JMeter (download the `.zip` file and extract it in `C:/`)

Introduction to testing

Testing is mainly done to check whether the software product is working as expected based on the requirements. The tester will verify the product, module, or code of the software product by running some test cases manually or automatically. This helps to identify bugs at the early stages of the product life cycle.

Before starting the actual testing, the tester will write the test cases and test suites. A **test case** is a sequence of steps that the tester wants to test and verify against the functionality to ensure the system is working properly. A **test suite** is a collection of test cases.

There are many types of testing available to test the software. Some of them are as follows:

- **Unit testing**: This helps to validate the smallest portion of the software product, for example, testing a specific program in an entire software product.

- **Functional testing**: This verifies the functionality of the product and whether it is working as expected or not based on the functional requirements.

- **Performance/load testing**: This validates the functionality by sending lots of requests (huge workloads) at the same time and at different intervals, for example, testing e-commerce platforms or websites with a large number of users (1,000+) at the same time to check the performance of the product.

- **Regression testing**: This is used to check whether any recent functionalities added to the product break the project functionality. When we are short on time to perform all the test cases again, this type of testing is preferred.

- **Stress testing**: This testing is used to check what the maximum volume/stress the system can accept is. For example, say we start testing with 500 concurrent users on an e-commerce platform. Assume it is working well with 500 users. Then, we will try a higher limit, such as 600 concurrent users, to verify whether the system can accept 600 requests at the same. If the system goes down, then we will know that the maximum volume that our system can accept is 500 and not 600 users.

- **Integration testing**: This is used to verify whether the different software products or components are functioning together or not. For example, our Mule application picks the data from the database and sends it to the partner system's web service. This testing ensures end-to-end functionality from the database to the partner's systems.

- **User Acceptance testing**: This testing is done to check if the system is as per user's requirements.

- **Vulnerability testing**: This is used to check whether any security-related issues are present in the software product.

We will use these types of testing while working on Mule projects.

Performing different types of testing provides us with the following benefits:

- Cost effective and saves money
- Customer satisfaction because of the quality of the product
- Addresses any design issues and poor design decisions at an early stage
- Improved security
- Better performance of the software product

With this, we have understood the basics of testing, its types, and its benefits.

Let's move on to learn about different testing tools.

Getting familiar with testing tools

There are many testing tools available to perform manual testing and automated testing. **Manual testing** is used for manually testing test cases. In **automated testing**, we script the test cases and execute them automatically.

Testing tools can be grouped as follows:

- **Test management tool**: To track test cases and execution
- **Defect/bug tracking tool**: To log the defects
- **Mobile testing tool**: To test different mobile devices that run on iOS, Android, and other **operating systems (OSs)**
- **Integration testing tool**: To test two or more modules together in order to verify, if all the modules are working together or not.
- **API testing tool**: To test web services
- **Load/performance testing tool**: To check the performance of the system
- **Security testing tool**: To check any security vulnerability in the software product

These tools help to reduce the time taken by the testers in their day-to-day testing activities. There are many useful tools on the market to perform manual and automated testing. Some of the most commonly used testing tools are as follows:

- Selenium (automation)
- Postman and Newman (API testing)
- JMeter (load testing)
- Gatling (load testing)

- HP ALM (test management)

- Jira and Bugzilla (test, defect, and bug tracking)

- Appium (mobile automation)

- Tricentis Tosca (automated testing) and Katalon Studio (licensed automation tool)

- BrowserStack (websites and mobile testing) and SeeTest (mobile testing)

- Load runner (load testing)

With this, we have understood the different types of testing tools and a few examples of tools that are commonly used by testers.

Let's deep dive into a few tools that are used in Mule projects, such as Postman, SoapUI, and JMeter.

Postman

Postman is an application used for API testing. It acts as an API/HTTP client to send a request to any web service endpoint. While sending the request, we can send the required standard or custom HTTP headers, such as content-type or accept. We can also configure different types of authorization, such as **basic authentication**, a **bearer token**, **OAuth**, and an **API key**.

As this tool is related to API testing, we can send the required value in the query parameters and URI parameters of the URL. This tool supports the testing of all types of HTTP methods, such as get, post, put, patch, delete, and head. If it is a post or put method, we can send the required payload in the body of the request.

After we have sent the request to the API URL, we will receive the response payload, the HTTP response status code, and the status description from the API. We can also check the response time to understand how much time it has taken to receive the response.

We can save each API request and group the related APIs into collections for future testing.

After configuring the API URL for testing, we can extract the code snippet in different languages to share it with the developer for development.

Postman also enables configuring environments in order to test the API using DEV, SIT, and QA endpoints. For any values specific to an environment, define them in the environment variable. Create the new environment variable in the **Environments** section for each environment.

While calling the API for each environment, the username and password differ. In that case, we can set the variables for **username** and **password** in the environment variable to specify their values. We can use those variables to call the API using the {{ }} syntax.

Figure 11.1 – Postman – environment variable

Figure 11.1 shows the Postman **Environments** section with two environment details, **DEV** and **TEST**. In **DEV**, it shows the **username** and **password** environment variables with their respected values. After adding variables and values, click **Save**.

While calling APIs, we can substitute the **username** and **password** variables by using `{{username}}` and `{{password}}`, as shown in *Figure 11.2*:

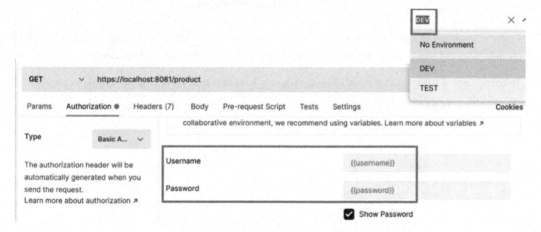

Figure 11.2 – Postman – Authorization

As shown in *Figure 11.2*, we need to select the appropriate environment to call the API. Here, we are calling the **DEV** environment API with its username and password.

Let us look at the Postman application home screen, which has many options/features as shown in the following screenshot.

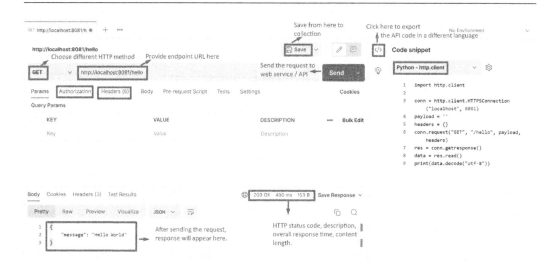

Figure 11.3 – Postman application

Figure 11.3 shows the Postman home screen, which shows endpoint details, the method, the HTTP request, the response, the HTTP status code, code snippets, and other information.

To change any settings in Postman, click the settings icon and select **Settings**, as shown in *Figure 11.4*:

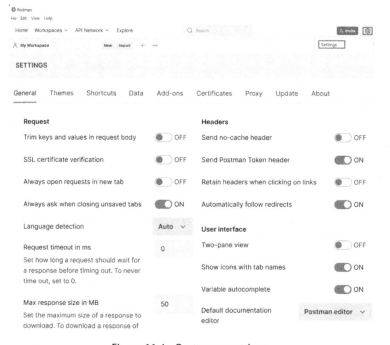

Figure 11.4 – Postman – settings

In the settings, we can set the request timeout value, set **SSL certificate verification** to on or off, configure certificates, configure proxy details, export data, and so on.

With this, we have understood the essentials of the Postman application.

Let us next explore how to create test cases in SoapUI.

SoapUI

SoapUI is an open source testing application, and it is commonly used for API manual and load testing. Using this tool, we can test SOAP, REST-based APIs, JMS, and other components.

Creating a SOAP project

In this section, let us create a SOAP project using the WSDL specification. **WSDL** refers to a **Web Service Definition Language** file, which will be in .xml format. This specification file has a request and response structure and endpoint details. Using a WSDL file, any developer can design, develop, and test their SOAP-based APIs.

Let's follow these steps to create a SOAP project:

1. Open the SoapUI application, click the **File** menu option, and select **New SOAP Project**.

2. Provide the project name, browse the WSDL file location, and click **OK**.

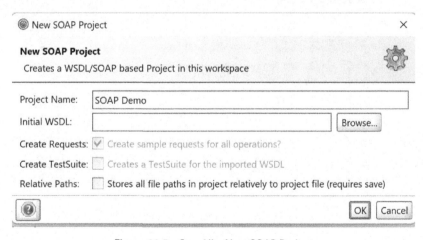

Figure 11.5 – SoapUI – New SOAP Project

We can browse the WSDL from a local file location or an HTTP/HTTPS URL. Once we click the **OK** button, it creates the SOAP project with all the operations, along with sample requests and endpoint details based on the information available in the WSDL file specification. In *Figure 11.6*, toward the left of the screen, **AddInteger**, **DivideInteger**, and the other operations that we can see under the project are SOAP operations:

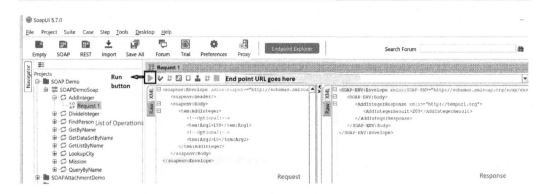

Figure 11.6 – SoapUI – SOAP project

As shown in the preceding figure, we can see the sample request structure and click on the **Run** button to send the request to the endpoint URL. Clicking **Run** invokes the actual endpoint URL and provides the response in SoapUI.

We can also create the test suite and test case by selecting the options from the sample request.

3. Select the **Request** option and choose **Add to TestCase** to create the test suite and test cases.

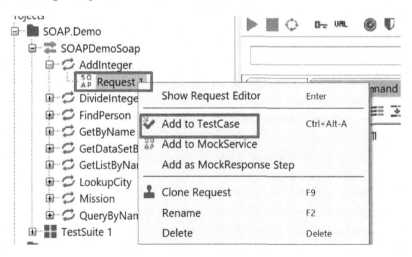

Figure 11.7 – SoapUI – test case

Upon clicking **Add to TestCase**, it will create a **Test Suite** with a **Test case**. Using these test cases, we can execute these cases to verify our functionalities are working as expected or not.

4. If you want to perform load testing for a specific API to measure the performance, then right-click on the **TestCase** and select **Load Tests**, then click **New LoadTest**.

The load test cases will be created now. We can specify the limit of transactions that we want to run within the specified time, and then we can execute the load testing.

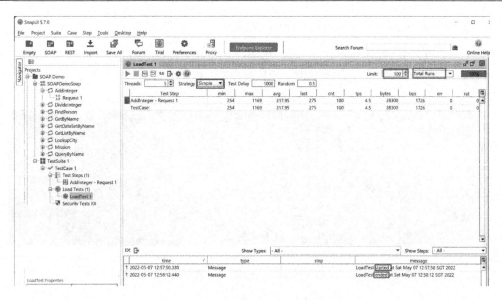

Figure 11.8 – SoapUI – load testing

As shown in *Figure 11.8*, we have tested sending 100 transactions to our API endpoint, a maximum of 5 messages at a time with a 1,000 millisecond (1 second) delay/interval after every 5 messages. This load test started at 12:57:50 P.M. and completed at around 12:58:12 P.M. This means we were able to complete 100 transactions within 22 seconds. In this test, the API response minimum, maximum, and average times were 254 milliseconds, 1,169 milliseconds, and 317 milliseconds, respectively.

We can change the values of **Limit**, **Total Runs**, and **Test Delay** to test more transactions to understand the API response and failure rates from the load testing.

With this, we have understood how to create a SOAP project, test case, and load test case, and also how to test using SoapUI.

Now, let's move on to learning how to perform load testing using **JMeter**.

JMeter

Performance is an important factor for any web- or mobile-based applications, as well as other applications. In order to measure the performance of the application, we need to send different workloads to our application so that we can measure the performance of our application. We use the JMeter tool to perform load testing and measure the performance. **Apache JMeter** is an open source application built on the Java platform. It is platform independent and works in Windows, Linux, and any other OS. It is mainly used for load, stress, and web service testing. This helps to ensure that our application performs well with different workloads.

Using JMeter, we can perform load testing for HTTP, FTP, JDBC, JMS, Java, and other components.

Let's follow these steps to create and execute a test plan:

1. If your OS is Windows, then open JMeter from the installation path, `C:\apache-jmeter-5.4.3\bin\jmeter.bat`, as shown in *Figure 11.9*:

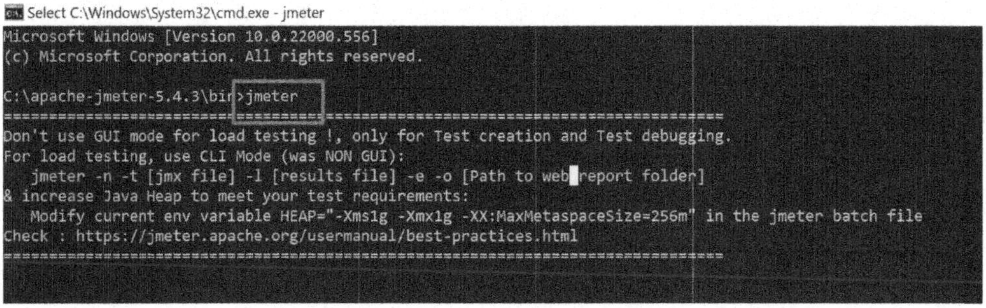

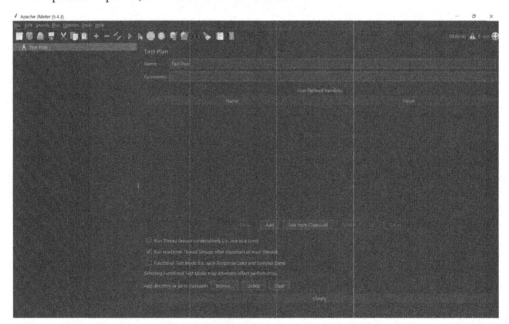

Figure 11.9 – Launching JMeter

It opens the Apache JMeter GUI in a new window.

Figure 11.10 – Apache JMeter – home window

When the JMeter GUI opens, it displays **Test Plan** on the left side of the user interface.

2. Change the name of **Test Plan** to `Test Plan Hello World` in the **Name** field.

3. Right-click **Test Plan Hello World**, then select **Add | Threads (Users) | Thread Group**.

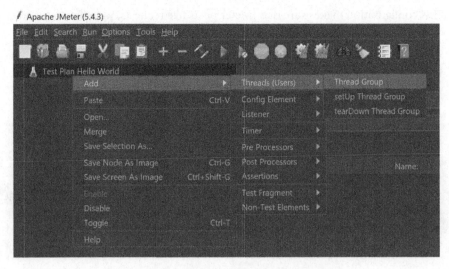

Figure 11.11 – JMeter – adding a thread group

A thread group in JMeter simulates concurrent requests to the API endpoint. After the execution, we can view the results in various formats, such as a graph, a table, a tree, or logs.

4. On the **Thread Group** screen, set **Action to be taken after a Sampler error** to **Continue**, **Number of Threads** to **5**, **Ramp-up period** to **1** second, and **Loop Count** to **4**. Then, click **Run**.

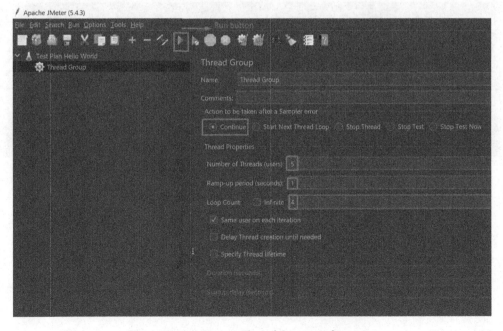

Figure 11.12 – JMeter – Thread Group configuration

This configuration makes sure that JMeter posts five requests, waits for 1 second, and then continues the loop four times in total. Overall, it calls the API endpoint 20 times.

Setting **Continue** in the **Thread Group** configuration means it will continue testing even when some test fails.

5.   Right-click on **Thread Group** and select **Add | Sampler | HTTP Request**.

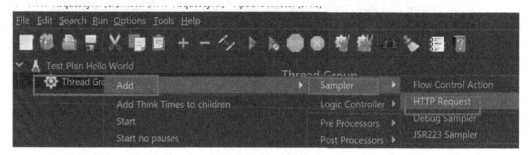

Figure 11.13 – JMeter – Sampler | HTTP Request

Here, we choose **HTTP Request** as we are going to invoke an HTTP-based web service for our testing. To test with a database, we would choose **JDBC request**.

6.   On the **HTTP Request** screen, provide the HTTP URL, method, and path details of our Mule application.

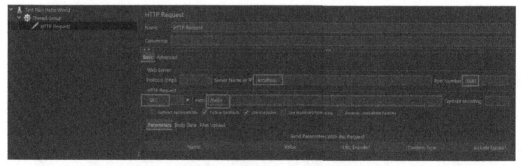

Figure 11.14 – JMeter – HTTP Request configuration

•   Right-click **HTTP Request** and select **Add | Listener | View Results in Table**.

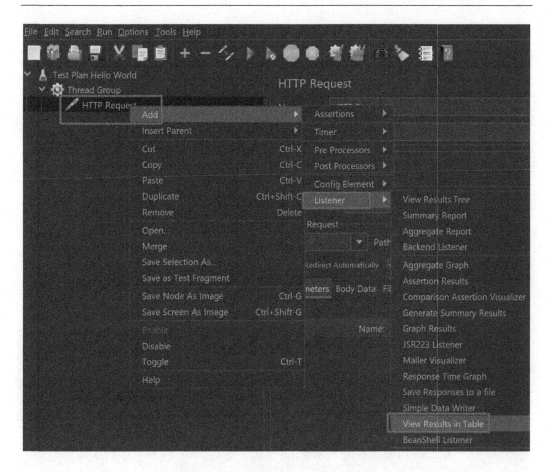

Figure 11.15 – JMeter – adding a listener

Here, we select **View Results in Table**. We can choose one of the other options to view results in graph or tree format, based on our preferences.

7. Click the **Save** button and choose the file location to save the test plan file.

8. Click the **Start** button to start the test plan execution.

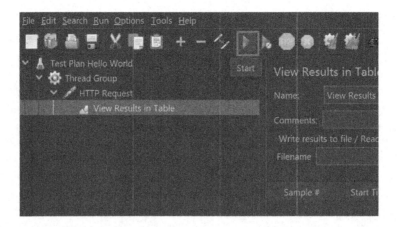

Figure 11.16 – JMeter – start the test

Now, we will be able to see that the test execution started and executed 20 times as per our **Thread Group** configuration.

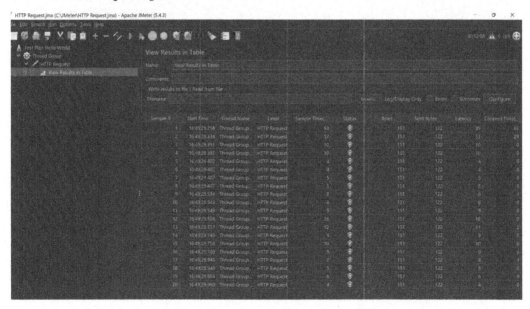

Figure 11.17 – JMeter – test execution results

In *Figure 11.17*, we can see that the overall execution was completed and each request took approximately a few milliseconds to get the web service response. This ensures our application is working fine with the workload of five concurrent requests for four loops. We can increase the workload by increasing the number of threads in our configuration to check the performance of our application.

With this, we have understood how to use JMeter to create and execute the test plan for load/performance testing.

Now, let's explore MUnit in Anypoint Studio.

Introducing MUnit

MUnit is a unit testing framework to test a Mule application. It provides complete unit testing capabilities within Anypoint Studio. MUnit has two modules, **MUnit** and **MUnit Tools**.

The MUnit module has the following operations:

- **Set Event**: To add a payload, variable, or attribute required for testing.
- **Set null payload**: To add a null value for a payload during testing.
- **After Suite**: This runs after all the test executions are completed. For example, if a test suite has 10 tests, then it gets executed just once after all 10 test executions are completed.
- **After Test**: Runs after each test.
- **Before Suite**: Runs only once before executing all the tests.
- **Before Test**: Runs before each test.
- **Test**: Used to create a new test.

The MUnit Tools module has the following operations to validate whether it is working as expected or not:

- **Assert equals**: To check whether the payload value is equal to a specific value or not.
- **Assert expression**: To check an evaluation based on a **DataWeave** expression.
- **Assert that**: To check whether a payload value is equal to a specific value by using DataWeave functions. For example, MUnit matchers have a set of DataWeave functions to validate the conditions. The `#[MunitTools::withMediaType('text/xml')]` condition checks whether the expression's media type is `text/xml`.
- **Clear stored data**: To clear all stored data.
- **Dequeue**: To remove the last event from the queue.
- **Fail**: To fail the test with an assertion error.
- **Mock when**: To mock the data when the flow calls the external system.
- **Queue**: To store the value in a queue during testing. The queue gets cleared after the test execution is complete.
- **Remove**: To remove the value of the specific key that is stored using the **Store** operation.

- **Retrieve**: To retrieve the value of the specific key that is stored using the **Store** operation.

- **Run custom**: To run the custom assertion.

- **Sleep**: To create a delay during a test.

- **Store**: To store the `value` against a `key` during a test. It is used for temporary storage. After the test, it is cleared.

- **Store oauth token**: To store the OAuth token during the test.

- **Verify call**: To verify whether the processor is called or not.

- **Spy**: To see what happens before and after the processors.

Using MUnit, we can perform the following actions:

- Create test suites and test cases

- Perform testing

- Check the code coverage after testing

Let's try to create a test suite to execute our test cases.

Creating a test suite

As we have learned, a test suite is a collection of test cases. In order to create a test suite, we need to create a Mule application first. Instead of creating a Mule application from scratch, we will use the `HelloWorld` Mule application, which we developed in *Chapter 3, Exploring Anypoint Studio*. The application has **HTTP Listener** with the `/hello` endpoint, **Logger** to log the **Welcome to Hello world application** message, and **Transform Message** to output { `message: "Hello World"` }. If you did not create this Mule application earlier, then you can use the `.jar` file to import the application into Anypoint Studio using the **File** menu option. Select **Import** and then click **Packaged mule application (.jar)** to create the Mule application.

Now, let us create the test suite using MUnit:

1. Open the Mule application, right-click on **Flow**, select **MUnit**, and choose **Create blank test for this flow**.

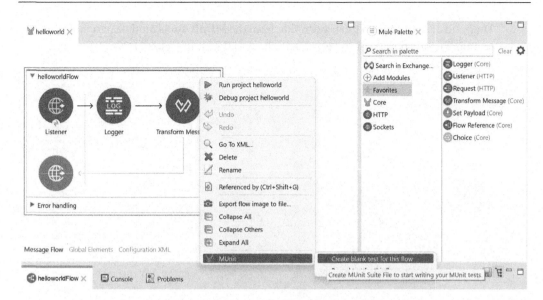

Figure 11.18 – MUnit – creating a blank test

This creates a new test suite in /src/test/munit/. The test suite contains **Behavior**, **Execution**, and **Validation**. In the test suite, **Behavior** sets the input for the test suite. The **Execution** step calls the actual flow in the Mule application. In the **Validation** step, we can write any kind of condition to validate the Mule application output. We can also see two different modules (**MUnit** and **MUnit Tools**) added in Mule Palette, as shown in *Figure 11.19*:

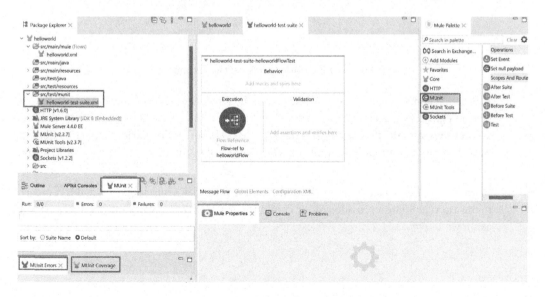

Figure 11.19 – MUnit – test suite

2. Drag and drop the **Asset equals** operation from the **MUnit Tools** module into the **Validation** section. Provide the actual and expected values, as shown in *Figure 11.20*:

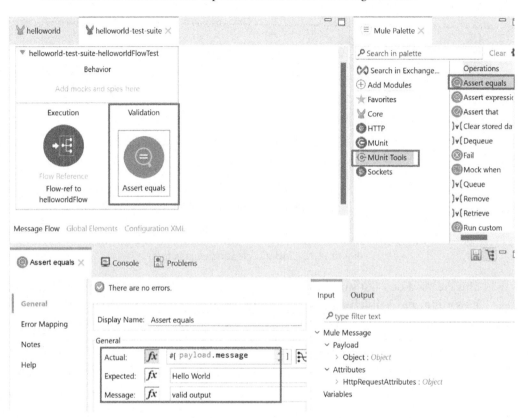

Figure 11.20 – MUnit – test suite Validation

What will happen is, when the test suite is run, the **Execution** section calls the `HelloWorld` flow and provides a result of `{ message: "Hello World" }`. At this time, the **Validation** section compares the flow result with the expected value of **Hello World**, as mentioned in the **Assert equals** condition. If the value matches the actual result, then it will give a **valid output** response.

3. In the canvas, right-click and select **Run MUnit test suite**. The application runs and is compared to the assert condition provided. If the condition matches, then it will show the success result, as shown in *Figure 11.21*:

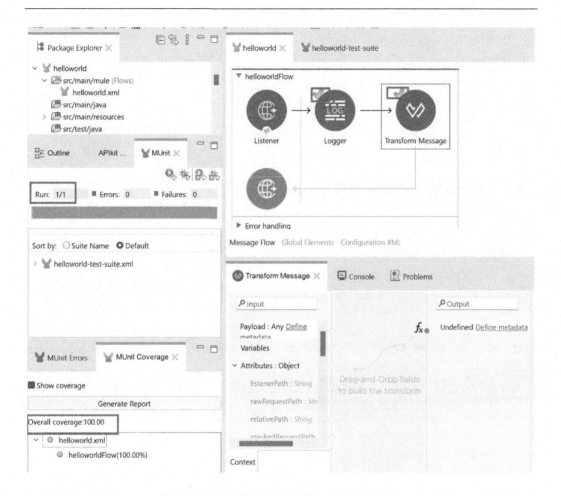

Figure 11.21 – MUnit – test suite coverage report

If all the flow steps are executed in a Mule application, then it will show 100% coverage. As our test suite is successful, the **Failures** count is **0**. This coverage report is also very useful when we have **continuous integration** (**CI**) and **continuous deployment** (**CD**) set up in MuleSoft. it checks the coverage report percentage to decide whether to continue with deployment to the target environment. For example, if the coverage is around 40%, then it will not proceed with deployment to the target environment. If the coverage is more than 80%, then it will proceed with deployment to the target environment.

4. The previous scenario is for a successful test case. Now, let us try a failure scenario. In the **Validation** section, set the expected value as Hello World1 and try to run the test suite again. It fails as our expected value does not match the actual output of **Hello World**.

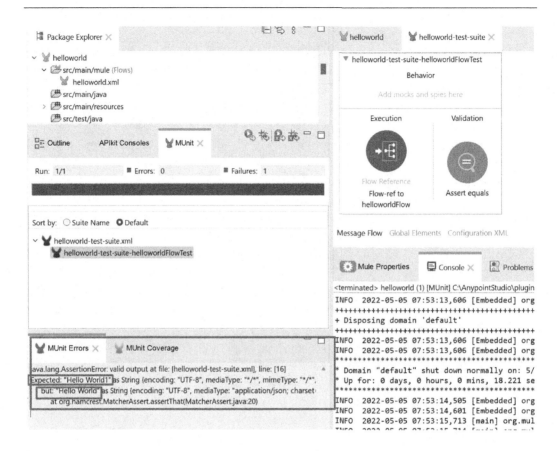

Figure 11.22 – MUnit – test suite MUnit Errors pane

Also, here, it will show 100% coverage as it has executed all the steps in the Mule application. As this test suite failed, it shows the **Failures** count as **1** and it also shows more details about the error in the **MUnit Errors** view.

In the preceding example, we saw a Mule application with just one flow. If we have two flows in the same Mule application, then the test suite file will have two different flows to handle the unit test cases, as shown in *Figure 11.23*:

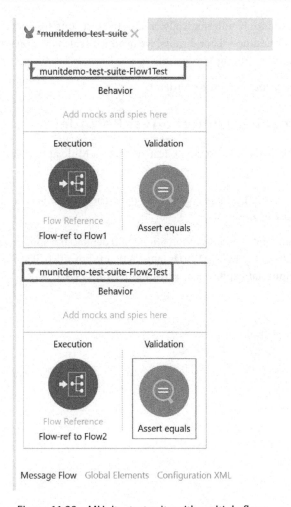

Figure 11.23 – MUnit – test suite with multiple flows

With this, we have understood how to create and run a test suite in Anypoint Studio.

Next, let's explore the MUnit Test Recorder in Anypoint Studio.

Exploring the MUnit Test Recorder

It is time consuming to write each and every test suite manually. Hence, we will use the MUnit Test Recorder to create automated test suites and capture the input.

In a Mule application, we can use the **Record test for this flow** option in the flow to create the required test suites and also start the recording to capture the inputs. The input can be query parameters, URI parameters, or the request payload.

The MUnit Test Recorder only automatically creates the test suite for successful scenarios. For any failure test scenarios or additional conditions, we need to create additional test cases manually. We can debug the test suites by adding breakpoints.

Let's create a test suite using the Test Recorder.

Creating a test suite using the Test Recorder

In this section, we will learn how to create test suites in a Mule application using the MUnit Test Recorder:

1. Open the `HelloWorld` Mule application, right-click on the flow, and select **MUnit** and then **Record test for this flow**.

    It starts the Mule runtime in Anypoint Studio and deploys the application. Once the application is deployed, it shows the **DEPLOYED** status. A dialog box titled **Test Recorder** with the message **Waiting for input data** appears, as shown in *Figure 11.24*:

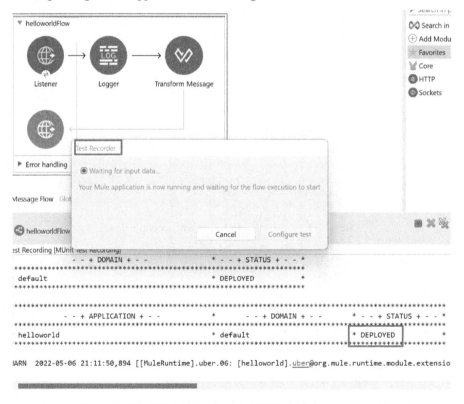

Figure 11.24 – MUnit – Test Recorder "Waiting for input data…"

In order to capture the input, let us send a request from Postman to our Mule application endpoint.

2. Open the Postman application, set the URL endpoint as `localhost:8081/hello`, and click **Send**.

Figure 11.25 – Postman – sending a request to a Mule application

Once you send the request, it reaches the Mule application and executes all the steps there. We can see the **Logger** message in the console, which confirms the execution of the Mule application. Finally, it saves/records the input/output, as shown in the **Test Recorder** pop-up dialog box in *Figure 11.26*:

Figure 11.26 – Test Recorder – "Input recorded"

3. Click **Configure test** to create the test suites.

    Once we click **Configure test**, the **New Recorded Test Welcome** dialog box appears.

4. On the **Welcome** screen, leave **File name** and **Test name** as is and click **Next**.

Figure 11.27 – New Recorded Test Welcome screen

In *Figure 11.27*, we have given the default values for the test suite's filename and test name, but we can change it to any name as per our naming convention. Upon clicking **Next**, the **Configure Test** dialog box appears.

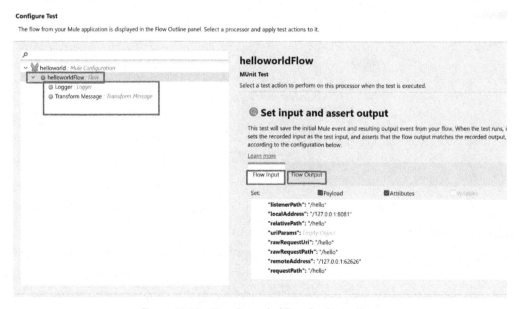

Figure 11.28 – New Recorded Test Configure Test

It shows the name of the Mule application and its flow steps. The **Set input and assert output** section shows the input and output captured and recorded during an earlier run from Postman. The **Flow Input** tab captures the input received through attributes and the payload. As we have sent the request as a `get` method, we don't have any input payloads in the **Flow Input** section.

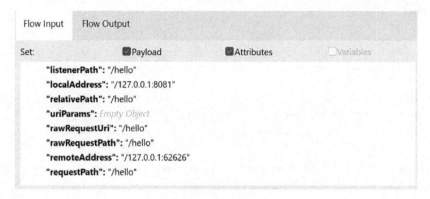

Figure 11.29 – Flow Input

We can use these as test suite input. Now, let us see what information is available in the **Flow Output** tab.

The **Flow Output** tab captures the output (attributes and payload) received after the execution of the Mule application.

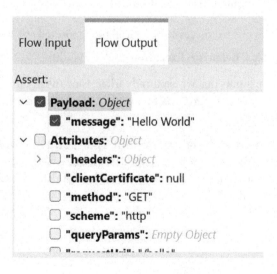

Figure 11.30 – Flow Output

We can use these output values for validation in our test suite.

5.   Click the **Next** button on the **New Recorded Test -> Configure Test** screen (see *Figure 11.28*).

6.   Click **Finish** on the **Test Summary** screen (see *Figure 11.31*) to complete the test suite creation using the MUnit Test Recorder:

Test Summary

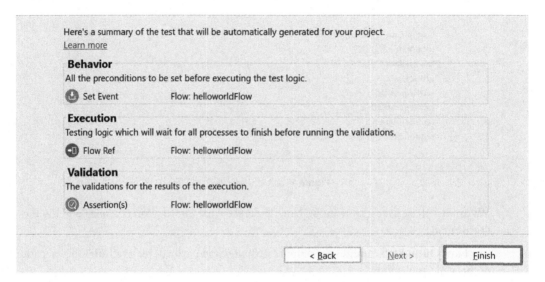

Figure 11.31 – New Recorded Test Test Summary

Now our test suite is created successfully with all the supported test suite .xml and .dwl files. The test suite has three steps: **Behavior**, **Execution**, and **Validation**.

The **Behavior** step sets the inputs that we captured earlier using the MUnit Test Recorder. This input data will be taken from the set-event-attributes.dwl and set-event-payload.dwl files, as shown in *Figure 11.32*.

set-event-attributes.dwl and set-event-payload.dwl have all the attributes data and payload data, respectively. As it is a get method, the set-event-payload.dwl file will be empty. If it were a post method, then it would have had input data in JSON or XML or any other format captured in a .dwl file.

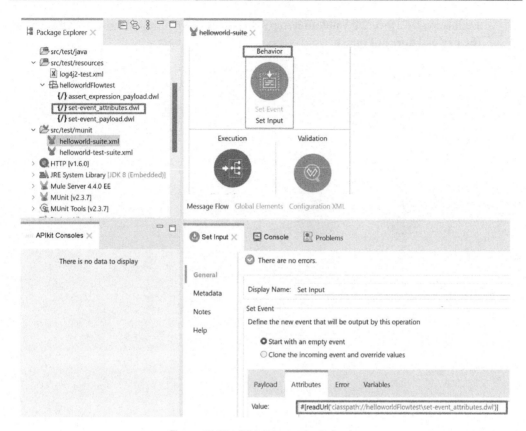

Figure 11.32 – MUnit test suite Behavior

The **Execution** step calls the flow and passes all the values received from the **Behavior** step.

The **Validation** step compares the Mule application output against the captured output that is available in the recorded file (`assert_expression_payload.dwl`).

Figure 11.33 – Recorded output payload

If validation fails, then the **Validation** step in the test suite will throw an error with the message **The payload does not match**.

Figure 11.34 – MUnit test suite Validation

With this, we have understood how to record input and output in a Mule application and use those captured inputs and outputs in our tests using the MUnit Test Recorder.

Summary

In this chapter, we had a look at the basics of testing and the various types of testing tools that are available.

We created a Mule application using a `.jar` file, tried to create a test case using the MUnit framework, and carried out tests using MUnit.

We also saw how the MUnit Test Recorder helps to create test cases automatically.

On completing this chapter, you expanded your knowledge of how to test a Mule application using the MUnit testing framework and I am sure that you are now confident enough to test your own Mule application.

In the next chapter, *Chapter 12*, *MuleSoft Integration with Salesforce*, we'll explore one of the ways to integrate with Salesforce using the Salesforce connector.

Assignments

Try the following assignments to explore more on MUnit.

- Download the Examples asset (*Testing APIKit with MUnit and Unit Testing with MUnit – Tutorial*) from Anypoint Exchange in Anypoint Platform (`https://anypoint.mulesoft.com/exchange/`), and import it into Studio, and practice MUnit testing with this asset

- Explore different MUnit Tools operations that are available in your test cases

- Explore the limitations of MUnit

Questions

Take a moment to answer the following questions to serve as a recap of what you just learned in this chapter:

1. What are the different tools available for load/performance testing?

2. What is MUnit?

3. What is MUnit Test Recorder?

4. When would we use **Mock When** operations in MUnit Tools?

5. What are **Sleep** operations in MUnit Tools?

6. In which path are MUnit test cases stored?

Answers

1. There are many tools available in the market for load/performance testing. For example: JMeter, SoapUI, LoadRunner, and Gatling.

2. MUnit is a unit testing framework for testing Mule applications.

3. The MUnit Test Recorder is a tool to record inputs and outputs in a flow. It also creates automated test suites and those captured inputs and outputs can be used for your tests.

4. **Mock When** is used to mock the data when the flow calls the external system. When unit testing, we cannot expect the external system to be available for our tests. Instead of calling the external system, we must mock the data to continue our testing. To achieve this, we need to use **Mock When** MUnit Tools operations.

5. Sleep operations help to create a delay during a test. For example, during test execution, to wait `10 seconds` before proceeding with the next step, we can use a **Sleep** operation. Here, `10` is the time value and `seconds` is the time unit, which are configurable in the **Sleep** operation.

6. MUnit test cases are stored in `/src/test/munit/` under the Mule application package.

Part 3: Integration with Salesforce and Other Connectors

Part 3 covers how to integrate with Salesforce and also covers different MuleSoft connectors, certification paths, and interview tips.

At the end of this part, we will be familiar with how to integrate with Salesforce and use different connectors, such as File, FTP, SFTP, Database, Slack, Web Service Consumer, VM, and JMS connectors.

Having read all the chapters, by the end of this part you will have a thorough knowledge to pass the fundamental certification and interviews and to work on MuleSoft-based projects.

The following chapters are included in this part:

- *Chapter 12, MuleSoft Integration with Salesforce*
- *Chapter 13, MuleSoft Connectors and Use Cases*
- *Chapter 14, Best Practices, Tips, and Tricks*
- *Chapter 15, Certification and Interview Tips*

12
MuleSoft Integration with Salesforce

In the previous chapter, we learned how to test your Mule application. We also studied several testing tools and a few testing mechanisms and explored MUnit and how to create an MUnit test suite. In addition, we explored the MUnit test recorder, which automates and eases the creation of test case jobs.

Testing is an integral part of an application development life cycle, hence it's important to understand the fundamentals of testing your Mule applications.

In this chapter, we'll be mainly focusing on integrating your third-party applications and Salesforce with the help of MuleSoft. We will study different connectors and templates available to speed up your integration.

Apart from the basics, we'll focus on some of the Salesforce capabilities with MuleSoft. As a Salesforce developer/architect, this chapter will help you to integrate Salesforce and MuleSoft. It'll also help you to explore all the capabilities of integrating MuleSoft with respect to Salesforce.

Here's what you can expect to cover in this chapter:

- Exploring Salesforce connectors
- Discovering accelerators and templates for Salesforce
- Getting started with MuleSoft Composer
- Salesforce capabilities with MuleSoft – the Bulk API, CDC events, and analytics tools
- Quiz and practice

Technical requirements

- Anypoint Studio installation (see *Chapter 3*, *Exploring Anypoint Studio*, for Studio installation guidance)

- An Anypoint Platform account (see *Chapter 2*, *Designing Your API*, to create a 30-day free trial account)

- Sign up for a Salesforce Developer trial account: `https://developer.salesforce.com/signup`

Exploring Salesforce connectors

Ever since the acquisition of MuleSoft by Salesforce in 2018, there has been a major advancement in terms of integrating MuleSoft and Salesforce. Several connectors and templates are offered to users that help to ease Salesforce and MuleSoft integration. This also helps us to unlock data present in silos and benefits in retrieving, transforming, and analyzing the data. We can pair MuleSoft with several Salesforce tools and components such as Tableau, Slack, Einstein Analytics, Service Cloud, Sales Cloud, and so on. This enables us to solve complex transformations. We can also receive Platform Events and publish Platform Event messages with the Salesforce connector. This helps us to stream API events.

Let us understand the different types of Salesforce connectors and how to use them.

Connectors, by far, are the most used and easiest means of integrating Salesforce with MuleSoft.

Let's have a look at the connectors in Mule Palette, which are confined mainly to Salesforce integration. By default, you will have the Salesforce Connector module available in your Mule Palette, which will help you to perform operations on your Salesforce APIs (see *Figure 12.1*).

Figure 12.1 – Salesforce connectors in Mule Palette

To use these connectors, drag and drop the suitable connector in your Mule flow.

We have seen different Salesforce connectors in Mule Palette. Let's understand how to configure a Salesforce connector.

Configuring a Salesforce connector

Let's configure one of these connectors from the Salesforce Connector module. The configuration for all the Salesforce connectors is similar. Let's follow these simple steps to configure a Salesforce connector in Anypoint Studio.

In order to use these connectors, you need access to a Salesforce Developer account. You will also require valid credentials, a security token, and an authentication/authorization token.

1. Choose any connector as per your requirements. We will select the **Get user info** connector from the Salesforce connector module. Drag and drop the connector in your Mule flow (see *Figure 12.2*).

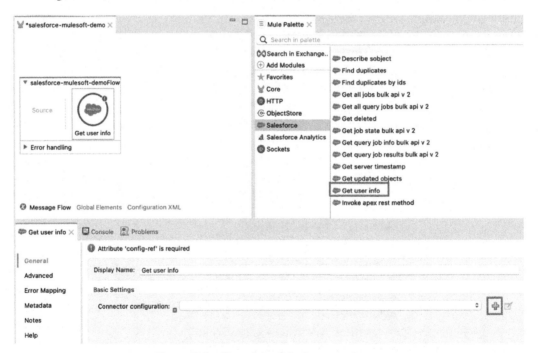

Figure 12.2 – Choosing a Salesforce connector

2. Click on the + symbol as shown in *Figure 12.2*. Fill in the **Username**, **Password**, **Security token**, and **Authorization URL** fields (see *Figure 12.3*). Test your connection and click **OK**.

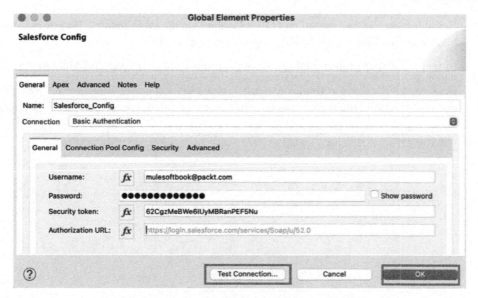

Figure 12.3 – Configuring the Salesforce connector

Note

You can extract the configuration details from your Salesforce Developer account.

---

3.   Once you've entered all the credentials, click **Test Connection…** and **OK** (see *Figure 12.4*).

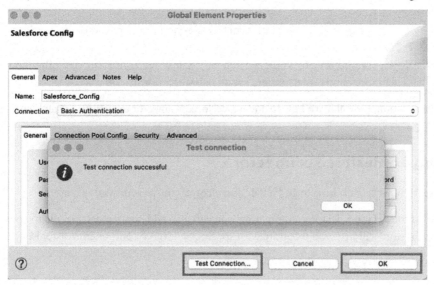

Figure 12.4 – Salesforce connector configured successfully

4. Now complete the flow by adding **HTTP Listener** (as the event source), **Transform Message** (to convert payload to JSON), and **Logger** (to log the payload).

5. Now run the Mule project. Right-click on the project and select Run As | Mule Application.

Once you see the status as **Deployed**, trigger the application from Postman or any web browser and you should see the response as User info from the Salesforce account (see *Figure 12.5*).

Figure 12.5 – User info from the Salesforce Developer account

We have now understood how to configure a default Salesforce connector. Try other connectors in the palette to get more hands-on experience with Salesforce connectors.

In the next section, we will learn how to add a Salesforce connector explicitly to match your particular use case.

Adding a Salesforce connector

In this section, we'll learn how to add a Salesforce connector to your Mule Palette.

Apart from the default Salesforce connectors, you can also add connectors specific to your use case. These connectors will help you integrate with specific Salesforce components or tools.

In order to add these connectors to your Mule Palette, follow these steps:

1. Click on the **Search in Exchange** option in your Mule Palette.

2. Log in to your MuleSoft Anypoint Platform account and add your account if you haven't already.

3. Search `Salesforce` or any specific service for which you want to use the connector.

4. Select the connector you want to add to your Mule Palette.

5. Click on the **Add** button. You can add and remove multiple connectors.

6. Once done finalizing the connectors you wish to add to Mule Palette, click on the **Finish** button (see *Figure 12.6*).

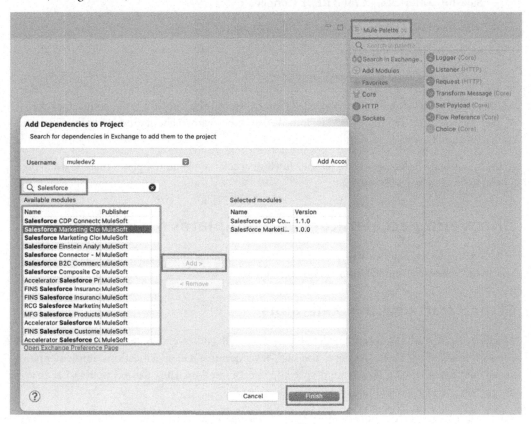

Figure 12.6 – Adding Salesforce connectors to Mule Palette

We have now understood how to add a Salesforce connector explicitly to Mule Palette. Let us now review the list of connectors that are available in MuleSoft's Anypoint Exchange:

- **Salesforce Connector**
- **Salesforce Commerce Cloud Connector**
- **Salesforce Composite Connector**
- **Salesforce Einstein Analytics Connector**
- **Salesforce Marketing Cloud Connector**
- **Salesforce Marketing Cloud REST Connector**
- **Salesforce B2C Commerce Cloud Data Connector**
- **Salesforce CDP Connector**
- **Commerce Cloud B2C Shop Connector**

And there will be a few more added to the list in the future. Similarly, there are connectors available to integrate Slack and Tableau with MuleSoft. We have now learned about different types of Salesforce connectors and how to add Salesforce connectors.

In the upcoming section, let's learn about MuleSoft accelerators and templates that are available for Salesforce integration with MuleSoft.

Discovering accelerators and templates for Salesforce

In this section, we'll mainly learn about accelerators and templates for Salesforce. We will also understand how to leverage these templates for easy integrations.

Getting started with accelerators

Accelerators are ready-to-use and predefined use cases with end-to-end implementation. They provide you with detailed use cases, low-level and high-level designs, API specifications, implementations, documentation, and so on. Accelerators speed up integration time. They also exemplify what an actual integration use case would look like.

You can access these accelerators from Anypoint Exchange. One such instance is **MuleSoft Accelerator for Salesforce Service Cloud** (see *Figure 12.7*): `https://www.mulesoft.com/exchange/ org.mule.examples/mulesoft-accelerator-for-salesforce-service-cloud/ minor/1.5/pages/home`.

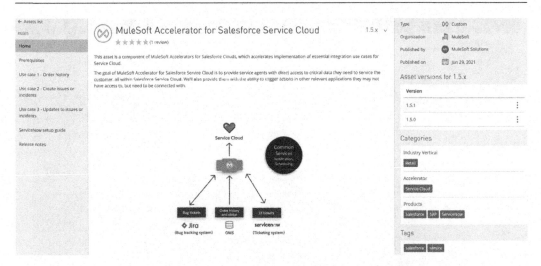

Figure 12.7 – MuleSoft Accelerator for Salesforce Service Cloud

Review all the use cases in Anypoint Exchange mentioned to get a fair understanding of accelerators. In order to get hands-on, you can download and import the use cases in Anypoint Studio.

We have learned about accelerators in MuleSoft and their functionality. Now let's deep dive into templates and learn how to use them.

Exploring templates

MuleSoft provides out-of-the-box templates available on Anypoint Exchange. **Templates** are pre-built integrations that provide you with a skeleton for your integration. They are readily available implementations. Templates can be considered a subset of accelerators as the latter has a lot more to offer.

You can download these templates, configure them, and get started without having to build the integration from scratch.

Let's now learn how to access and configure templates with simple steps:

1. In order to access templates, go to MuleSoft's Anypoint **Exchange**, go to the **Provided by MuleSoft** tab, and select **Templates**. You can find all the templates available (see *Figure 12.8*).

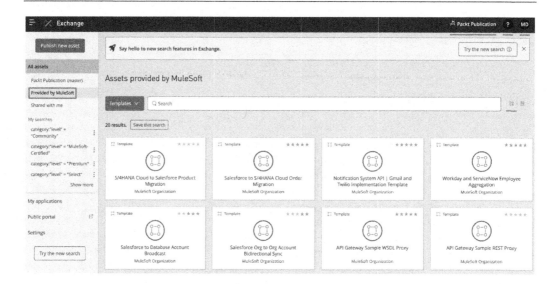

Figure 12.8 – Templates provided by MuleSoft

If you have a particular use case, then you can search for a specific template. For instance, if you want to integrate **NetSuite** with Salesforce, you can simply search for `NetSuite to Salesforce` and you'll get a list of templates available (see *Figure 12.9*).

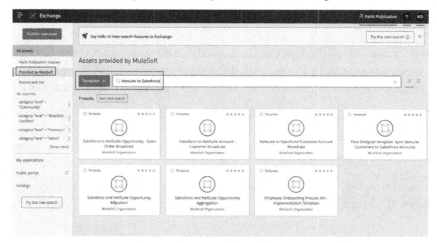

Figure 12.9 – NetSuite to Salesforce templates

You can review all these templates, go through the information documented, and choose the template that is relatable to your use case.

2. Once you've chosen the template, click **Download**. A `.jar` file will be downloaded (see *Figure 12.10*).

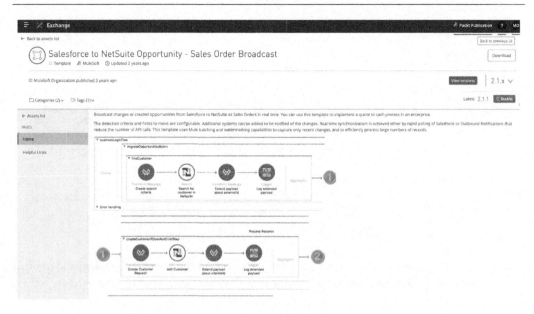

Figure 12.10 – Reviewing and downloading the template

3. After downloading the .jar file, import the file into Anypoint Studio (see *Figure 12.11*).

    Go to **File | Import**, click `Packaged mule application(.jar)`, navigate to the file directory, click **Finish**.

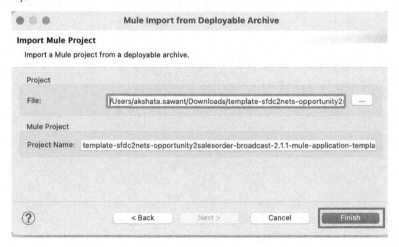

Figure 12.11 – Importing a .jar file into Anypoint Studio

4. Once the file is imported into Anypoint Studio, review all the files, flows, configurations, and so on (see *Figure 12.12*). You can make changes to the flow and the transformation logic as per your requirements.

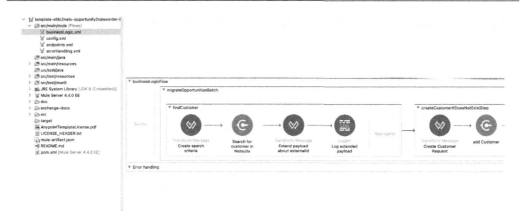

Figure 12.12 – Reviewing the template in Anypoint Studio

You can navigate to the `.properties` file in the `src/main/resource` folder and configure your end systems – NetSuite and Salesforce, in this case (see *Figure 12.13*).

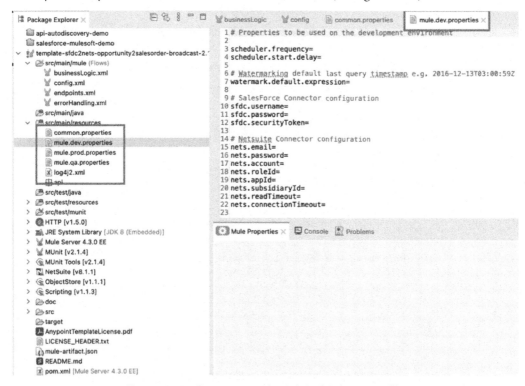

Figure 12.13 – Connector credentials in the properties file

We have now successfully reviewed and added the template to Anypoint Studio.

> **Note**
> The configuration of accelerators and templates implementation-wise is similar.

Let's now review a few advantages of accelerators and templates:

- As they consist of pre-built implementations, it reduces development time as you don't have to build everything from scratch

- If you're new to MuleSoft, you can use them as a reference if you're not already aware of the best practices and coding standards

- You can focus more on the transformation logic and building new integrations

- You can reuse, extend, and customize them as per your needs

We have now learned and understood how to utilize accelerators and templates efficiently to simplify our integrations and reduce our development time.

MuleSoft Composer helps Salesforce admins to integrate data and apps with ease and hence it's essential to learn about it. In the next section, we'll learn about MuleSoft Composer and explore its capabilities.

Getting started with MuleSoft Composer

As a Salesforce developer, you are already aware of how essential it is to unlock the data present in silos. MuleSoft Composer is a tool available in the Salesforce ecosystem that helps you to connect, transform, and integrate various end systems.

It's a no-code platform that is accessible from a Salesforce developer account. Currently, it has around 14+ in-built connectors to connect with different end systems directly, such as Workday, NetSuite, Slack, Jira, Stripe, Asana, and so on. This list will continue to grow over time.

Before deep diving into the configuration of MuleSoft Composer, let's understand its capabilities.

Capabilities of MuleSoft Composer

Let us now review the capabilities of MuleSoft Composer, in order to leverage it better:

- Connects different end systems easily

- You can synchronize, retrieve, and transform data from different end systems

- No-code data transformation with `if-else` blocks, routers, and filters

- Manage the application life cycle (build, test, debug, deploy, and so on) with the help of flows

We've seen the capabilities of MuleSoft Composer, so now let's learn when we can leverage it:

- When you want to map/transform data from different systems (such as NetSuite, SAP, and legacy systems) without implementing complex logic

- When polling data from one end system, adding logical conditions, and transforming the data

- For data migration and data transformation

We have now understood the capabilities of MuleSoft Composer and when to use it. Let's get some hands-on practice and set up MuleSoft Composer with some easy steps.

Configuring MuleSoft Composer

In order to configure MuleSoft Composer, you need to have valid admin access. Let's assume you have the required access and get started with installing and configuring MuleSoft Composer.

In this use case, we will poll the data from Salesforce every 15 minutes. Based on the information retrieved from Salesforce, we will apply conditional logic and fetch data from Slack. Let's follow these steps to get started with MuleSoft Composer:

1. Log in to your Salesforce org. Go to **Setup**, enter MuleSoft Composer in the **Quick Find** search, and click on **Install the Managed Package for MuleSoft Composer**. You will be automatically granted permission to access MuleSoft Composer (see *Figure 12.14*).

    As a first-time user and an admin, you can also change the required permission set and configure OAuth authorization and IP address restrictions by clicking **Change the Type of Permitted Users and Relax IP Restrictions**.

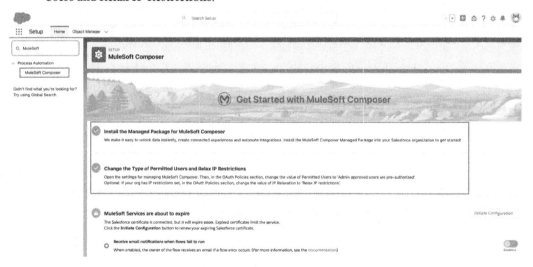

Figure 12.14 – Installing MuleSoft Composer

2. Once the installation is complete, you'll be redirected to MuleSoft Composer's home page. Click on the **Create New Flow** option in order to create a new flow (see *Figure 12.15*).

3. The flow consists of triggers and a series of events that show the execution of the process.

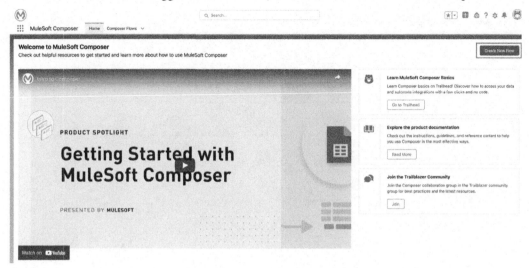

Figure 12.15 – Creating a new flow

4. To start the execution flow, we need to define flow triggers. The flow can either be started by an event triggered from any of these predefined end systems or you can poll the flow using a scheduler. In this case, we'll select **Scheduler** (see *Figure 12.16*).

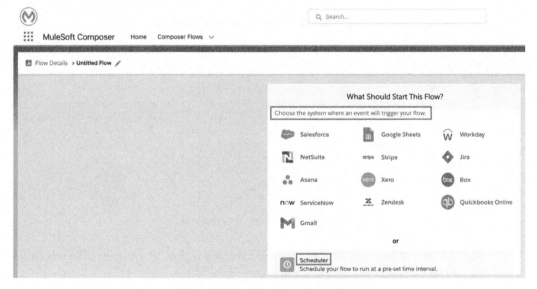

Figure 12.16 – Choosing a flow trigger

5. Configure the end system. As we have selected a scheduler here, you can choose the frequency of events (see *Figure 12.17*).

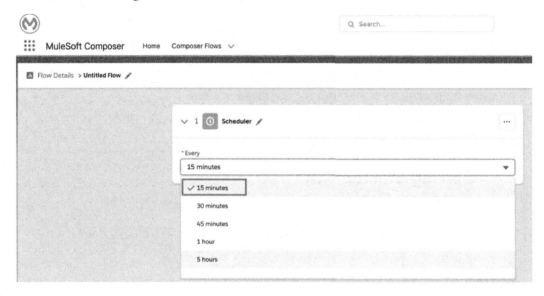

Figure 12.17 – Configuring Scheduler

Note

The configuration of any other end system is similar and easy, provided you have valid access to it.

---

6. You can add the next step by clicking the + sign (see *Figure 12.18*).

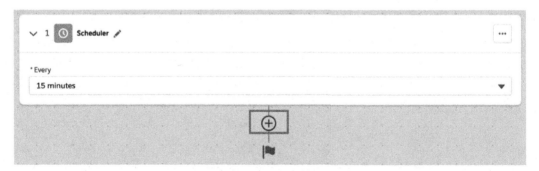

Figure 12.18 – Adding the next step

7. Similar to flow trigger selection, you can select the next action. This action will be responsible for the execution or processing of the flow (see *Figure 12.19*).

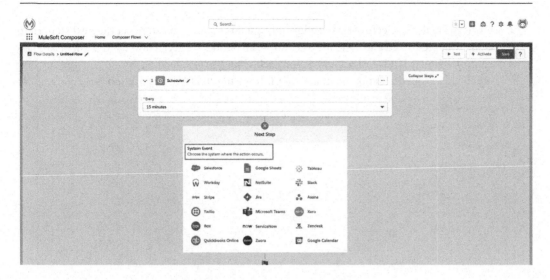

Figure 12.19 – Selecting the next action

8. In this case, we're choosing Salesforce as the actionable end system. Authorize Salesforce and select the connection that you wish to integrate (see *Figure 12.20*).

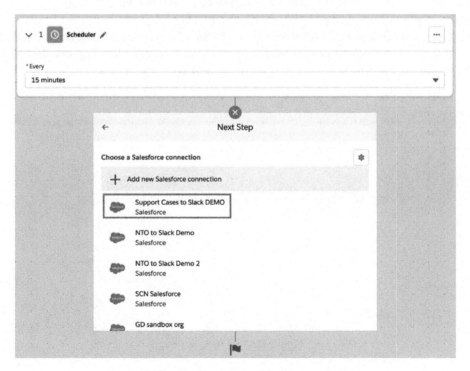

Figure 12.20 – Configuring the Salesforce end system

9. Once you're done selecting and configuring system events, you can select the next step. Here, along with predefined end systems, you also get an option to select a flow control out of two flow controls, namely **If/Else Block** and a **For Each** loop. You also have an option to connect to any other end system that is not mentioned in the list using an HTTP connection (see *Figure 12.21*).

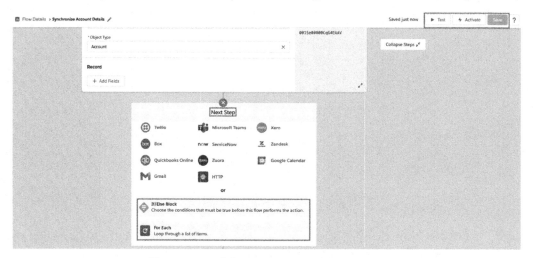

Figure 12.21 – Selecting routers in the next step

10. Once you're done selecting all the steps, you'll have a flow outline describing the activity of the flow. Click **Test** to test the flow. Once you're done testing and are satisfied with the integration result, you can activate the flow by clicking **Activate** (see *Figure 12.22*).

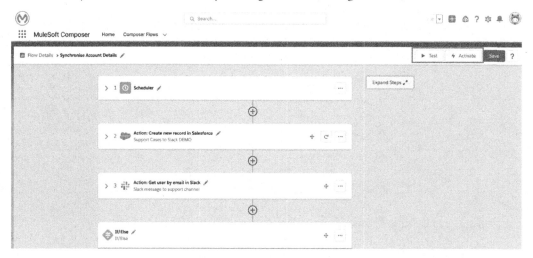

Figure 12.22 – Flow overview

We have studied MuleSoft Composer and its features. We have also learned how to install and configure MuleSoft Composer and create a flow.

In the next section, we'll further explore the integration capabilities of MuleSoft with Salesforce.

Exploring MuleSoft's integration capabilities with Salesforce

We have previously studied connectors, accelerators, templates, and so on to integrate with Salesforce. These are the most commonly used mechanisms. Let's now explore other integration capabilities that can be leveraged with MuleSoft and Salesforce.

The Bulk API

In order to process voluminous data efficiently, you can make use of the Bulk API v2.

You can perform operations such as creating, getting, deleting queries using the MuleSoft connectors for the Bulk API v2 (see *Figure 12.23*). This helps you to easily integrate Salesforce objects and process large volumes of records asynchronously. You can process these records in one go and thus optimize your integration. For instance, if we want to retrieve and process the personal details of all customers, we can use the **Create job bulk api v 2** connector from Mule Palette.

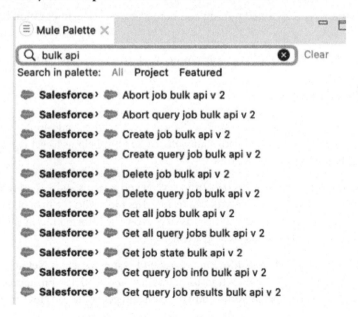

Figure 12.23 – Bulk API v2 connectors

We have now learned about the Bulk API. Let's explore more about CDC events.

CDC events

Change Data Capture events (CDC events) are used to keep external end systems in sync. As the name suggests, they keep track of event changes and hence are useful in real-time integration.

With the help of MuleSoft and Salesforce, you can publish an event change in a Salesforce object.

We can use the MuleSoft connector from the Salesforce module **Replay channel listener** (see *Figure 12.24*). In this case, we can use the publish-subscribe pattern. We can subscribe to the event published by the Salesforce object to capture the data change. For instance, in the case of the Order Management system, as soon as the status changes from Processing to Shipped, the customer should receive communication via email and SMS. This change should be reflected across all end systems involved. In such situations, using CDC would be appropriate to keep all the end systems in sync.

Figure 12.24 – Replay channel listener

By using this pattern, we can avoid polling and hence optimize the integration by confining it to change events.

We have now studied CDC events. Let's learn more about the data analytics tools.

Data analytics tools

Data analytics and visualization tools such as Salesforce Analytics, Salesforce Einstein Analytics, and Tableau can be easily integrated with MuleSoft. These tools help us to get real-time results with customized dashboards and visual reports.

We can extract, transform, and process data from several end systems and   perform transformation logic. Further, we can send such processed data to analytics tools with the help of connectors present in the Mule palette. Analytical tools will help us to portray the information in the form of metrics, charts, reports, customized dashboards, and so on.

For instance, if we have our data residing in several end systems such as NetSuite, Salesforce, and several other legacy end systems, we can transform this data and send it to Einstein Analytics. Further, we can create a customized dashboard to study the data and generate leads for our marketing team.

We have now understood several out-of-the-box integration capabilities of MuleSoft. In order to further understand them and get hands-on experience, review and try out these connectors.

Summary

In this chapter, we have learned about Salesforce integration with MuleSoft. We have studied different approaches to tackle integration such as the use of connectors, accelerators, and templates. We have explored MuleSoft Composer for Salesforce, learned about its capabilities, and created flows using it. We have also studied other integration capabilities such as connecting with a topic listener, the Bulk API, CDC events, and so on.

Learning about various integration techniques with Salesforce will help you to choose the best integration approach.

In the next chapter, we'll learn more about commonly used MuleSoft connectors such as file-based modules, SOAP connectors, VM queues, and so on. We will also understand some industry-based use cases and how to optimize integrations. In order to ace industry-based integration challenges, it's essential to learn about frequently used connectors and some best practices.

Assignments

1. Download the Salesforce accelerator, review it, and import the implementation into Anypoint Studio. Go through the Integration logic and best practices.

2. Integrate Salesforce's Einstein Analytics with MuleSoft using the connector available in the Mule palette.

3. Try out the Bulk API v2 connectors and process data using Salesforce and MuleSoft.

Questions

1. What are the details you need to know before configuring Salesforce with MuleSoft?

2. What are templates and accelerators?

3. What is the purpose of using MuleSoft Composer?

Answers

1. We need to be aware of the username, password, security token, authorization token (if authorization is enabled), and valid access.

2. Templates consist of built-in implementation code and accelerators consist of end-to-end use cases, API specifications, and implementation code.

3. It helps to build no-code integrations inside the Salesforce ecosystem.

13
MuleSoft Connectors and Use Cases

In the previous chapter, we learned how to build and deploy a Mule application using a Salesforce connector. We know that a **connector** is a resource that helps connect different systems. In general, each system will have its own way to connect. For example, to connect SAP, we need to use the tRFC protocol. Similarly, while connecting to databases (such as Oracle, MSSQL, and MySQL), we need to use the JDBC protocol. In order to simplify the connectivity across different systems, MuleSoft provides connectors. So, we need not worry about underlying protocols or methods used to connect different systems. Using these connectors, we can simply configure the connection details, such as the system hostname and URL, username and password, and other required details to connect different systems.

There are many connectors in MuleSoft that can talk to different systems, databases, **Software as a Service (SaaS)** applications, cloud infrastructure services, and protocols.

In this chapter, let us explore the different connectors available to connect different systems.

After reading this chapter, you'll come away with knowledge of the following topics:

- File-based modules – File Connector, FTP Connector, and SFTP Connector
- Database Connector and watermarking
- Web Service Consumer Connector (SOAP)
- Messaging – VM Connector and JMS Connector
- MuleSoft accelerators

Technical requirements

The prerequisites for this chapter are:

- The supported file (`Math.wsdl`) used in this chapter is available on GitHub in the `Chapter13` folder: `https://github.com/PacktPublishing/MuleSoft-for-Salesforce-Developers`

- Go to `https://www.postman.com/downloads` to download and install Postman

Introducing connectors

Connectors are stored in **Exchange**, which is an online catalog that stores all the reusable assets, such as APIs, connectors, templates, and examples. To learn more about Exchange, refer to *Chapter 5, All about Anypoint Platform.*

Connectors are divided into the following four categories:

- **Select**: There are 170 connectors available in Mule 3 and Mule 4 under this category. MuleSoft provides standard support for these types of connectors. They are available to anyone who has a subscription to Anypoint Platform. Some examples are Salesforce Connector and Workday Connector.

- **Premium**: There are 35 connectors available in Mule 3 and Mule 4 under this category. MuleSoft provides standard support for these types of connectors. They are available to licensed users only. Some examples are AS2 Connector and SAP Connector.

- **MuleSoft-Certified**: There are 73 connectors available in Mule 3 and Mule 4 under this category. These types of connectors are developed by MuleSoft partners and reviewed and certified by MuleSoft. In order to get support for these types of connectors, the customer has to contact the partner who created the connector. Some examples are AS400 Connector and SMB Connector.

- **Community**: There are 44 connectors available in Mule 3 and Mule 4 under this category. These types of connectors are developed by community developers and reviewed and certified by MuleSoft. If any issues arise, MuleSoft professional services can be engaged or the customer can reach out to the developer who developed the connectors. Some examples are Slack Connector, Twitter Connector, and PayPal Connector.

Some of these connectors are as follows:

- File Connector, FTP Connector, and SFTP Connector
- Database Connector
- Web Service Consumer Connector
- VM Connector and JMS Connector

- SAP Connector

- Salesforce Connector

- AWS Connector

- Workday Connector

- Apache Connector

- LDAP Connector

- HDFS Connector

- MQTT Connector

- Object Store Connector

If we need to connect different systems, then we need to download the appropriate connector from Exchange in Anypoint Studio.

A list of all the connectors is available in Exchange (**Exchange** | **All assets** | **Provided by MuleSoft**).

Figure 13.1 – Connectors

In *Figure 13.1*, we can see the **Connectors** asset type selected to list the connectors that are available in Exchange. Similarly, we can choose other asset types, such as templates, examples, policies, REST APIs, SOAP APIs, and API spec fragments, to see the list of available assets in Exchange, which are contributed by MuleSoft, MuleSoft partners, and community developers.

We can check the category of connectors from Exchange by searching for the category level, for example, `category:"level" = "Premium"`.

Let us start exploring some of the connectors now. To begin with, we will see file-related connectors.

Exploring File Connector, FTP Connector, and SFTP Connector

File Connector, FTP Connector, and SFTP Connector are related to file processing.

Using file-related connectors, we can read and process files from one location to another, as well as creating directories and lists and copying, moving, renaming, and deleting files. Additionally, we can also fetch files using specific file patterns.

For example, if we need to find a file that starts with `purchase`, then we can use the `purchase*` filenaming pattern in the connector configuration.

In order to handle or process files, we have three types of connectors in MuleSoft. They are as follows:

- **File Connector**: This processes the files from the same system where the Mule application is running.

- **FTP Connector**: This helps to connect to the **File Transfer Protocol** (**FTP**) server. Using this connector, we can get the files from the FTP server for processing and also, send the files to the FTP server folder path.

- **SFTP Connector**: Similar to FTP Connector, this connector helps to connect to the **Secure File Transfer Protocol** (**SFTP**) server in a secured way. Using this connector, we can get the files from the SFTP server for processing and also, send the files to the SFTP server folder path.

Let's see each connector in more detail.

File Connector

File Connector provides the capabilities to process files either from the same system or which are mounted/shared to that system. Let's see the different operations that are available in File Connector.

File operations

In order to perform a specific action in a file, we will use operations. We have similar operations available in FTP Connector and SFTP Connector.

These operations are as follows:

- **On New or Updated File**: Triggers a Mule flow whenever a file is created or modified.

- **Copy**: Copies a file from one directory to another.

- **Create directory**: Creates a directory.

- **Delete**: Deletes a file from the mentioned path.

- **List**: Lists all the files from the specific directory based on a file-matching pattern. If we set the **Recursive** property to `true`, then it lists all the files from the subfolders as well.

- **Move**: Moves a file from one directory to another.

- **Read**: Reads a file from a specific path and returns file content as a payload, as well as file-related information in the attributes. It sets the `MIME` type from the file extension. If we need to override it to different `MIME` types (such as `application/json`, `application/xml`, or `application/csv`), then we can set it from the **Properties** section.

- **Rename**: Renames a file.

- **Write**: Writes file content to the specific path. We can create a new file to write the file content, overwrite file content in the existing file, or append the file content to an existing file using the **Write Mode** option.

File attributes

Whenever we receive a file for processing in a Mule application, we can get all metadata of a particular file from the **Attributes** section of the Mule event. It includes the file creation time, filename, last modified time, full path of the filename, size of the file, and other information related to the file. Let us look at the following screenshot to get a clear idea:

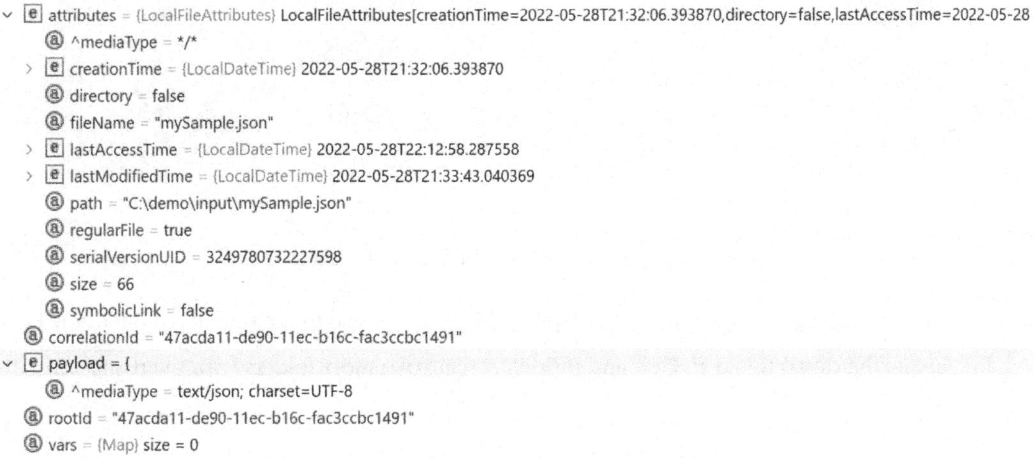

Figure 13.2 – File attributes

As shown in *Figure 13.2*, we can see the metadata of file information and use these attributes in the Mule application.

With this, we have understood the different file operations and attributes. Let's see how to use the **On New or Updated File** file operation in a Mule application.

Creating a Mule application with File Connector

In this section, we will see how to create a Mule application with File Connector. Mainly, we are going to explore the **On New or Updated File** operation in this exercise.

We are going to add **On New or Updated File** as a source, which will help pick up the file whenever it arrives in the `input` folder. After completing all the steps in the Mule application, it will move the file to the `output` folder.

Let's follow these steps to create a Mule application with File Connector:

1. In Anypoint Studio, go to the **File** menu, click **New**, and select **Mule Project**. Provide the project name as `FileConnectorDemo` and leave the remaining settings as is, then click the **Finish** button.

2. Drag and drop the **File** module from **Add Modules** to the Mule palette.

3. Drag and drop **On New or Updated File** from the Mule palette to the canvas.

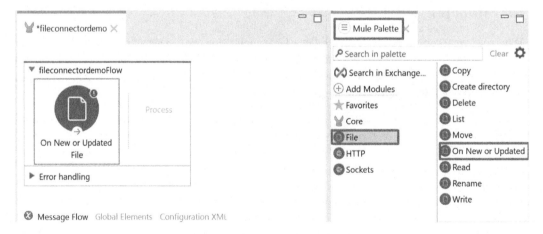

Figure 13.3 – File Connector – On New or Updated File

As shown in *Figure 13.3*, **On New or Updated File** gets added to the source section of the flow.

4. Create the `demo` folder in `C:\` and inside it, create two more folders with the names `input` and `output`.

5. Add the connector configuration to **On New or Updated File**. In the connector configuration, select the checkbox for **Connection** and provide the working directory as C:\demo, then click **OK**.

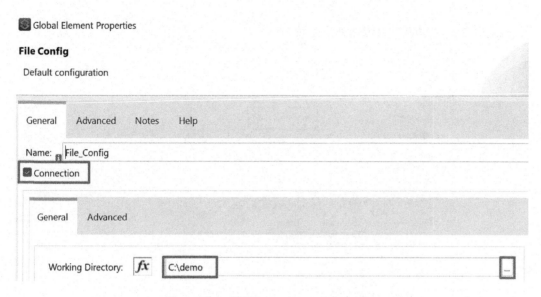

Figure 13.4 – File Connector – configuration

In *Figure 13.4*, we have selected the demo folder as a working directory. Similarly, we can use any directory from the filesystem to process the files. For example, in the Linux system, we will specify the path in the /Users/myFolder format.

6. Provide C:\demo\input as the directory name (**Directory**) and C:\demo\output for **Move to directory**. **Frequency** should be set to 10 and **Time unit** should be set to **SECONDS**.

Figure 13.5 – File Connector – General configuration

We have set the configuration to poll the files every 10 seconds by setting **Fixed Frequency** for **Scheduling Strategy** (refer to *Figure 13.5*). This means our Mule application monitors the files every 10 seconds and whenever a file arrives, it picks up the file and provides it to the next steps in the same application. Once the entire flow is complete, it deletes the file from the source folder (input) based on the **Auto delete** configuration and moves the file to the output folder.

7. Add a **Logger** step after **On New or Updated File**. Set the **Message** value to `payload` in **expression mode**.

8. Place any sample file in the `input` folder.

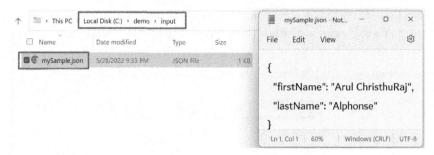

Figure 13.6 – File Connector – input file

In this example, we have placed the `.json` file, as shown in *Figure 13.6*. But we can use any format of file (`.xml`, `.txt`, or `.csv`).

9. Run the project from the canvas.

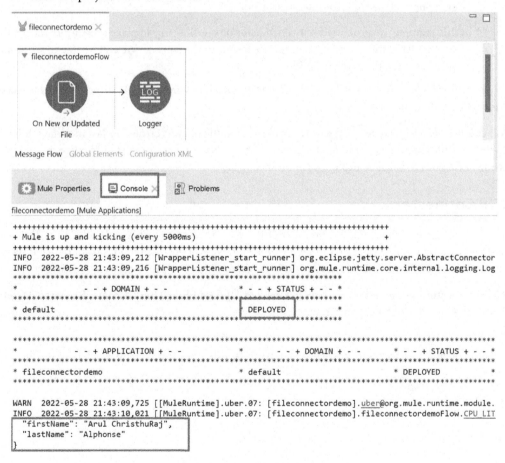

Figure 13.7 – File Connector – run project

When the application is deployed, the file gets picked up and received by the Mule application. Then, it calls the **Logger** step to print the payload content in the console, as shown in *Figure 13.7*.

10. Go to the `C:/demo/output` folder. We can see the `mySample.json` file, which has been moved from the `input` folder as a part of the postprocessing action.

Figure 13.8 – File Connector – output path

11. Check the `C:/demo/input` folder. We will not find the file in the `input` folder as it got deleted due to us setting **Auto delete** to `true`.

In this example, we processed only one file for our testing. Try to place a few more files in the `input` folder at the same time and see the results in the console. We will be able to see all the files processed in the `output` folder.

Try to explore other operations from File Connector, such as **Copy**, **Create directory**, **Delete**, **List**, **Move**, **Read**, **Rename**, and **Write**.

We can also set a **watermark** of the timestamp of when the file was created or last modified. It helps to filter the file after the execution of the last poll. With this, we have understood how to process files using File Connector. Let us explore FTP Connector now.

FTP Connector

FTP Connector is similar to File Connector. In File Connector, we process the files from the local system or mounted filesystem, but in FTP Connector, we will process the files from the FTP server using the FTP protocol. This connector is useful when we need to process files from another server.

FTP Connector has operations such as **On New or Updated File**, **Copy**, **Create directory**, **Delete**, **List**, **Move**, **Read**, **Rename**, and **Write**.

Let us see the details required to configure FTP Connector. It requires the FTP hostname, port (the default port is `21`), username, password, and working directory from where we pick up the files.

Global Element Properties

FTP Config

Default configuration

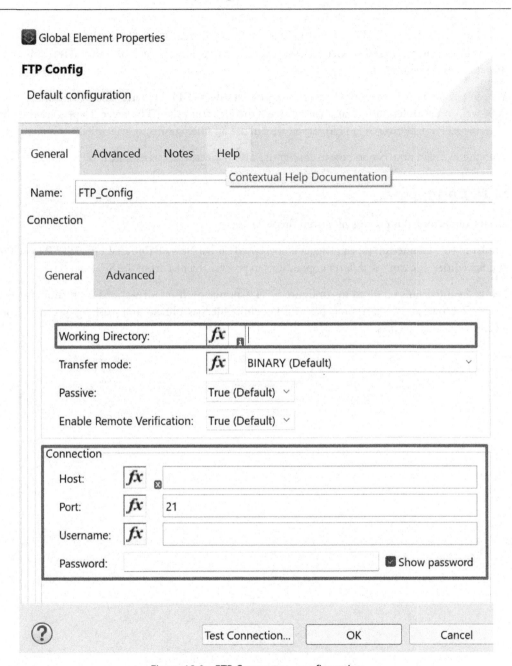

Figure 13.9 – FTP Connector – configuration

In addition to FTP server configuration details, we can configure the file-matching pattern, watermarking, scheduling strategy (**Fixed** or **Cron**), and postprocessing actions such as **Auto delete, Move to directory**, and **Rename to**.

We can trigger a flow based on **On New or Updated File**, **HTTP Listener**, and **Scheduler**. In that flow, we can use different operations to process the files from the FTP server. To process the files from the FTPS (FTP over SSL/TLS) server, we can use another connector called **FTPS Connector**.

With this, we have understood how to configure FTP Connector. Let us explore SFTP Connector now.

SFTP Connector

SFTP Connector helps process files from the SFTP server.

Similar to FTP Connector, we can trigger a flow based on **On New or Updated File**, **HTTP Listener**, and **Scheduler**. We can use different operations to process the files from the SFTP server.

Let us see the details required to configure SFTP Connector. It requires the SFTP hostname, port (the default port is 22), username, password, identity file, passphrase, and working directory from where we pick up the files.

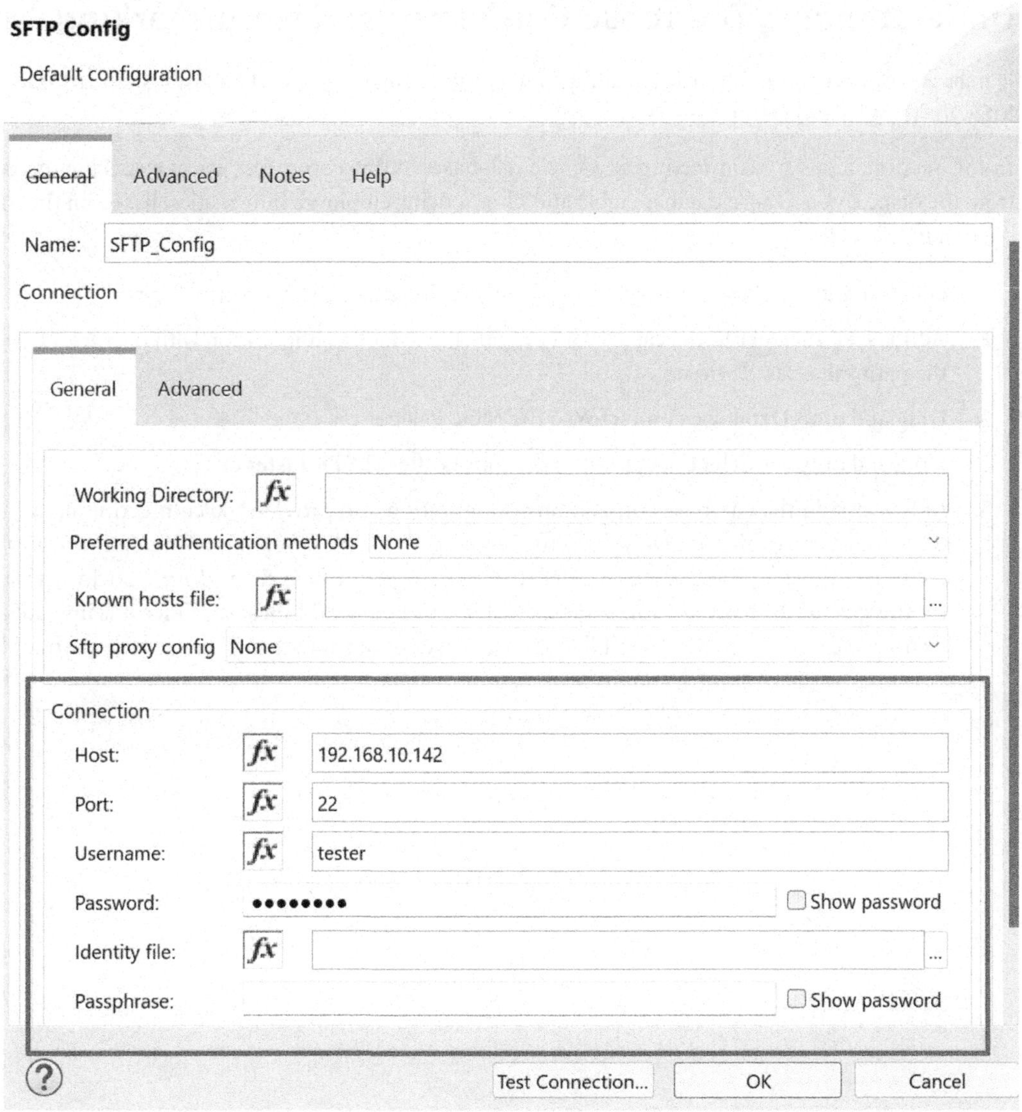

SFTP Config

Default configuration

General   Advanced   Notes   Help

Name: SFTP_Config

Connection

General   Advanced

Working Directory: *fx*

Preferred authentication methods   None ⌄

Known hosts file: *fx*   ...

Sftp proxy config   None ⌄

Connection

Host: *fx*   192.168.10.142

Port: *fx*   22

Username: *fx*   tester

Password: •••••••••   ☐ Show password

Identity file: *fx*   ...

Passphrase: ☐ Show password

?   Test Connection...   OK   Cancel

Figure 13.10 – SFTP Connector – configuration

This is how we configure SFTP Connector to process the files from the SFTP server.

With this, we have completed exploring different file-related connectors, such as File Connector, FTP Connector, and SFTP Connector, to process files.

Let us get familiar with how to connect a database using Database Connector in order to retrieve records from the database table.

Understanding Database Connector and watermarking

Database Connector provides the capabilities to connect any relational databases, such as Oracle, MSSQL, MySQL, and Derby.

In this section, let us try connecting an Oracle database. In this demo, let's select a specific record from the `employee` Oracle database table and filter specific employee information based on the `ID` column in the table:

1. Create a Mule application project with the name `databaseconnectordemo`.

2. Add **HTTP Listener** to the canvas and provide the default configuration with port `8081` and the path value as `/dbdemo`.

3. Drag and drop **Database connector** to the Mule Palette.

4. Drag and drop the **Select** operation to the canvas after **HTTP Listener**.

5. In **Select**, add the database connection configuration and provide the connection name as `Oracle Connection`. Download the required `.jar` file from online (`https://www.oracle.com/sg/database/technologies/appdev/jdbc-downloads.html`) for the specific database version and browse for it in **Required Libraries**. Once it is uploaded, it shows a green tick mark. Now, fill in the database connection details, such as the hostname, port, username, password, and instance name.

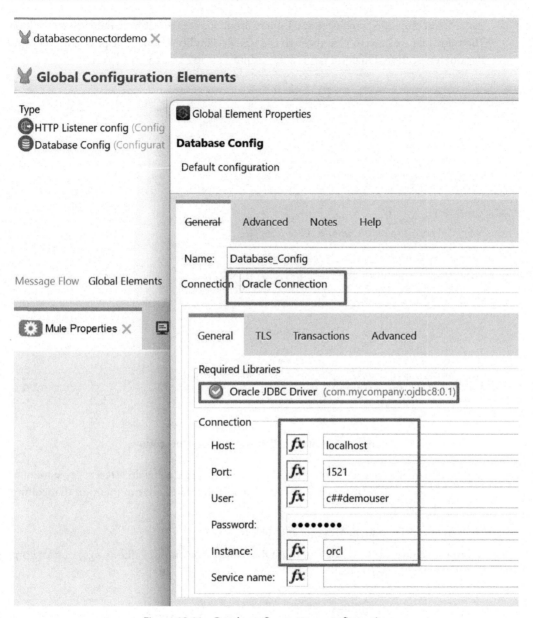

Figure 13.11 – Database Connector – configuration

In **Required Libraries**, we have uploaded ojdbc8.jar, which is related to the Oracle database, as shown in *Figure 13.11*. For other databases, we have to upload the respective .jar files. We have mentioned the instance name as orcl, which is the database name.

6. In the **Select** properties, provide the SQL query details for employee with the where condition. The value that we need to pass through the where condition should be passed in the **Input Parameters** section. Finally, it returns the output as application/java.

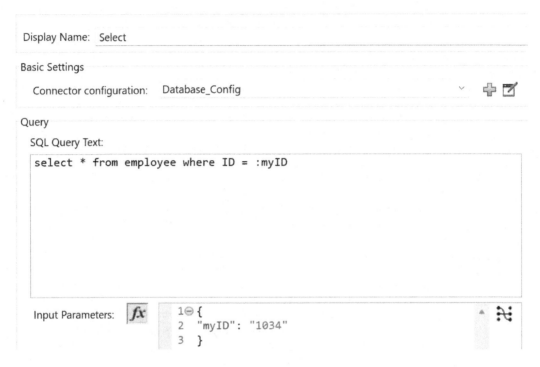

Figure 13.12 – Database Connector – Select properties

In this SQL query, we get all the field values from the table using an asterisk (*) symbol, as shown in *Figure 13.12*. If we need a specific field value, then we can mention that column name in the query.

7. Drag and drop **Transform Message** after **Select**.

8. In order to convert the Java output to JSON, provide the output value as application/json along with the payload.

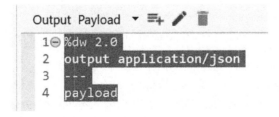

Figure 13.13 – Database Connector – Transform Message

9. From the canvas, click on **Run project**.

10. Once the project is deployed, send a request from the Postman application to trigger the Mule application.

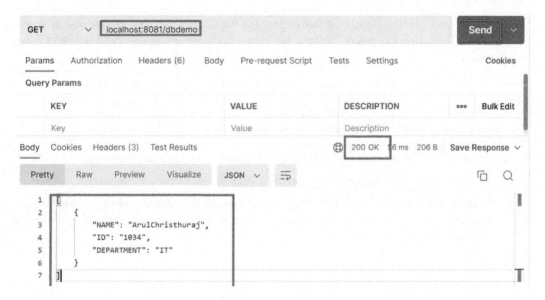

Figure 13.14 – Database Connector – Select response

Once the application receives the request, it executes the `select` query and retrieves the result set that has the value `1034` for the `ID` column field in the database table, as shown in *Figure 13.14*.

With this, we have understood how to use a `Select SQL query` in a **Select** operation.

Other than **Select**, we can also use the **Insert**, **Update**, **Delete**, **OnTableRow**, **Query single**, **Execute script**, **Execute DDL**, **Stored procedure**, **Bulk insert**, **Bulk update**, and **Bulk delete** operations in Database Connector to execute a different query in a database table.

Watermarking

Database Connector provides an out-of-the-box watermarking feature in the **On Table Row** operation. We can configure a **watermark** column in the **On Table Row** properties. A watermark stores the latest processed record ID and, based on that, fetches the remaining records from the table. In this way, whenever there is synchronization between the table and system, we can fetch only the records that are yet to be processed.

With this, we have learned how to use Database Connector to fetch the records from the database table.

Let us begin to explore Web Service Consumer Connector.

Configuring Web Service Consumer Connector

Web Service Consumer Connector is a connector that helps to call a SOAP-based web service using the **Consume** operation.

Let us see the configuration details that are required in the **Consume** operation. We mainly need a **Web Service Definition Language (WSDL)** file. This is the specification file containing SOAP web service details, such as the endpoint, request, and response structure and a list of all its operations.

In this example, we will call a SOAP-based web service that is running on the same machine. But in real time, we will call the actual web service URL to perform a specific operation.

Let us see the steps involved to call the SOAP web service:

1. Create an **HTTP Listener** with /soapdemo to trigger the Mule application.

2. Drag and drop the **Consume** operation from Web Service Consumer Connector.

3. In the **Consume** properties, provide the WSDL location and click the refresh icon in **Service**. It loads the remaining information of **Service**, **Port**, and **Address** from the WSDL specification file. Now, click **OK**.

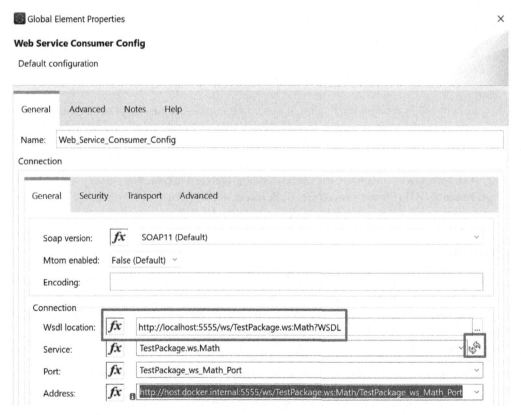

Figure 13.15 – Web Service Consume Connector – configuration

In *Figure 13.15*, we have provided the HTTP URL path of the WSDL file. But we can also provide the local system path of the WSDL file:

Sample WSDL (Math.wsdl):

```
<?xml version="1.0" encoding="UTF-8"?>
<wsdl:definitions name="Math" targetNamespace="http://
host.docker.internal/TestPackage.ws:Math"
xmlns:wsdl="http://schemas.xmlsoap.org/wsdl/"
xmlns:soapjms="http://www.w3.org/2010/soapjms/"
xmlns:mime="http://schemas.xmlsoap.org/wsdl/mime/"
xmlns:tns="http://host.docker.internal/TestPackage.
ws:Math" xmlns:xsd="http://www.w3.org/2001/XMLSchema"
xmlns:http="http://schemas.xmlsoap.org/wsdl/http/"
xmlns:soap12="http://schemas.xmlsoap.org/wsdl/
soap12/" xmlns:soap="http://schemas.xmlsoap.org/wsdl/
soap/" xmlns:soapenc="http://schemas.xmlsoap.org/soap/
encoding/">
  <wsdl:types>
    <xsd:schema targetNamespace="http://host.docker.
    internal/TestPackage.ws:Math" xmlns:tns="http://host.
    docker.internal/TestPackage.ws:Math" xmlns:xsd=
    "http://www.w3.org/2001/XMLSchema">
        <xsd:element name="addTwoNos"
            type="tns:addTwoNos"/>
```

4. Click the refresh icon next to **Operation** and it will list all the operations available in the WSDL specification, as shown in *Figure 13.16*:

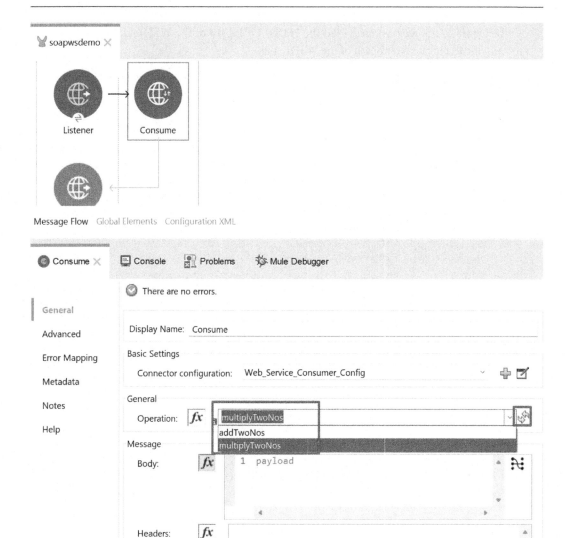

Figure 13.16 – Web Service Consumer Connector – Consume properties

As shown in *Figure 13.16*, we have two operations, addTwoNos and multiplyTwoNos.

5. Choose multiplyTwoNos for **Operation**.

Now we have to map the required input (number1 and number2) for the multiplyTwoNos operation. Hence, we need the **Transform Message** component to map the input fields.

6.   Add the **Transform Message** component before the **Consume** operation.

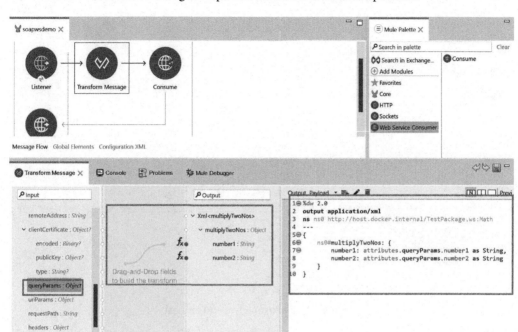

Figure 13.17 – Web Service Consumer Connector – Transform Message

In *Figure 13.17*, we have mapped the number1 and number2 fields from the query parameters.

7.   From the canvas, click **Run project**.

8.   Once the **DEPLOYED** message is displayed in the console, send the request from Postman to our Mule endpoint.

Figure 13.18 – Postman – Send request

In *Figure 13.18*, look at the URL, there are two query parameters such as `number1` and `number2`. We have provided `number1` and `number2` values as 13 and 3, respectively. As these inputs are passed to the `multiplyTwoNos` SOAP web service operation, it has multiplied these numbers and responded with the value in the `output` field.

In this integration, the **Consume** operation calls the SOAP endpoint, which is also running on the same machine in order to calculate and provide the required response. In real-time use cases, we will be calling the SOAP web service running on different servers.

With this, we have understood how to call the SOAP-based web service using Web Service Consumer Connector.

Let us now explore **VM** (which stands for **virtual machine**) Connector and JMS Connector, which provide us with the capabilities to publish and subscribe to a message.

Publishing and subscribing using VM Connector

VM Connector helps to exchange messages in intra- and inter-app communication using queues:

- **Intra-app communication**: Exchanging messages from one flow to another within the same application using queues
- **Inter-app communication**: Exchanging messages from one application to another using queues

We have two types of queues:

- **Persistent queues**: This is the more reliable type of queue, where data gets persisted or retained even though the application crashes. This is slower than transient queues.

- **Transient queues**: This is the more volatile type of queue, where data will not be persisted or retained if the application crashes. This type of queue is faster than persistent queues.

The following are some benefits of VM Connector.

- Distributes messages across the cluster to provide load-balancing capabilities

- Queues messages to process incoming data in an asynchronous manner

Operations

There are four operations available in VM Connector that help to exchange the data or message using the **point-to-point** and **publish-subscribe** patterns:

- **Publish**: Publishes data to the queue.

- **Consume**: Consumes all the data from the queue. This is useful when we need to schedule the interface to pull all the messages from the queue.

- **Listener**: Listens to the queue and immediately picks it for processing.

- **Publish consume**: Publishes the message and waits for the response from the subscribing flow.

Let's move on to see how to publish and listen to a message asynchronously using VM Connector.

Publishing and listening to a message

In this example, let us publish a message to the queue and subscribe to the same message using a listener:

1. Create a new Mule application project called `vmconnectordemo` with the flow name as `publishFlow`, then add **HTTP Listener** with a default port of `8081` and provide the path as `/publish`.

2. Drag and drop **VM connector** from **Add Module** to the Mule Palette.

3. Drag and drop **Publish** to the canvas.

4. In **Publish**, add the connector configuration, click **Queues**, and change it to **Edit inline**, then provide a queue name of `mytestqueue` and set the queue type to `PERSISTENT`.

5. Click **Finish** and then the **OK** button.

VM Config

Default configuration

Figure 13.19 – VM Connector – configuration

6. In the **Publish** properties, click the refresh icon to get the queue name.

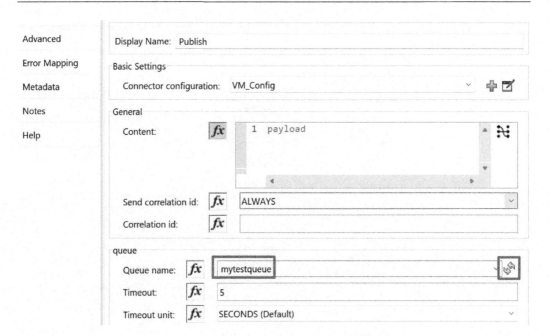

Figure 13.20 – VM Connector – Queue name

With this, the `publishFlow` configuration is complete. This helps to publish the message to the queue, `mytestqueue`.

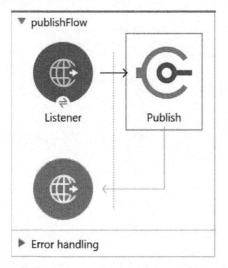

Figure 13.21 – VM Connector – publishFlow

Let's create another flow to subscribe to the message from the queue, which is published from `publishFlow`.

7. Create another flow, with the name `subscribeFlow`, then add **Listener** and **Logger** with a message of `payload`.

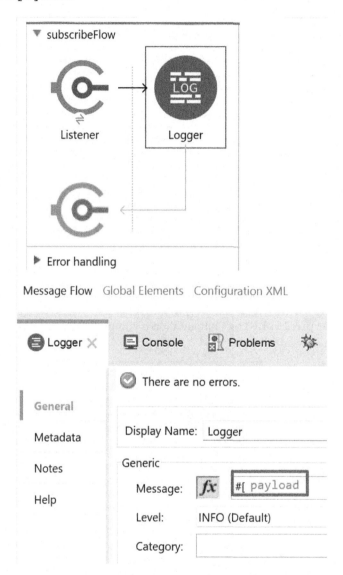

Figure 13.22 – VM Connector – subscribeFlow

In the **VM Listener** config (see *Figure 13.22*), we need not specify any configuration as it gets auto-populated based on the VM configuration that we mentioned earlier in `publishFlow`.

With this, the `subscribeFlow` configuration is complete and helps to subscribe/listen to the messages from the queue, `mytestqueue`.

Now the configurations of both the flows are complete. Let us move on to test the application from Postman.

8. Go to the canvas and select **Run Project**.

9. Once deployed successfully, send the request from Postman to our Mule application endpoint, `http://localhost:8081/publish`.

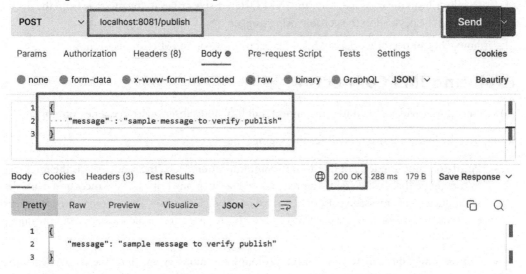

Figure 13.23 – VM Connector – testing from Postman

In *Figure 13.23*, we have specified a sample JSON message in the request body before sending the request.

10. Go to Anypoint Studio and check the console.

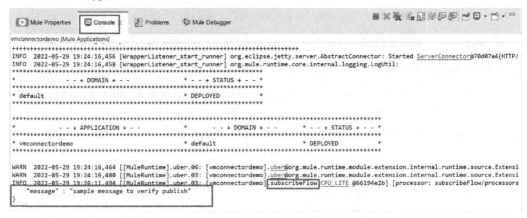

Figure 13.24 – VM Connector – Console

Here, we can see `subscribeFlow` logging the payload that we have sent from Postman, as shown in *Figure 13.24*.

With this, we have understood that when we send a message to a Mule application, the **HTTP Listener** in the application receives it. Then, the application publishes the message to the queue using the **Publish** operation. Now the message is published and is available for the consumer to subscribe to the message. After this, **VM Listener** subscribes to the message from the queue and logs the payload in the console using **Logger**.

This is how VM Connector works in MuleSoft. Let us move on to JMS Connector now.

Exploring JMS Connector

JMS Connector provides capabilities to connect, publish, and subscribe from queues and topics.

It supports the following two models for messaging:

- **Point-to-point queues**: For one-to-one communication. Here, the sender sends the messages to the queue that is specified. The receiver/subscriber subscribes to the messages from the same queue. This message pattern is carried out asynchronously. Even though the subscriber is disconnected from the queue, it will still be able to subscribe to the message from the queue once connected.

- **Publish and subscribe topics**: For one-to-many communication. Here, the sender sends the message to the topic. Multiple subscribers can subscribe to the same message from the topic. Each subscriber will receive a copy of the message.

  If the subscriber is enabled with a durable subscription, it will not lose the message even though the subscriber is not connected. The subscriber can consume the message once the connectivity to the topic is re-established.

There are a few JMS providers available that can connect using JMS Connector. Some are as follows:

- **ActiveMQ**: This is an open source JMS provider from Apache

- **WebSphere MQ**: This is a messaging platform from IBM

- **Solace MQ**: This is a messaging middleware from Solace that supports all forms of publish and subscribe patterns

- **WebLogic JMS**: This is a messaging system that supports JMS, from Oracle

Operations

There are six operations in JMS Connector that help to exchange the data/message:

- **Publish**: Publishes the message to the queue or topic.
- **Consume**: Consumes all the messages from the queue or topic. This is useful when we need to schedule the interface to pull all the messages from the queue or topic.
- **On New Message**: Listens to the queue or topic and immediately picks it when it arrives for processing.
- **Publish consume**: Publishes the message to the queue or topic and waits for the response from the subscribing flow.
- **Ack**: Acknowledges the message while consuming it.
- **Recover session**: Automatically redelivers all the consumed messages that had not been acknowledged earlier before the recover session.
- The following screenshot shows a list of operations of JMS Connector:

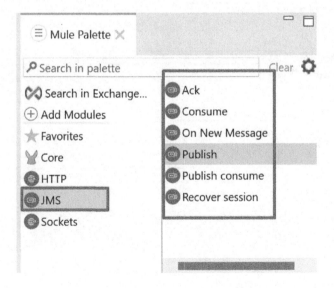

Figure 13.25 – JMS Connector – operations

Now that we have explored all the operations of JMS Connector, let us learn how to configure JMS Connector.

JMS Connector configuration

In order to connect to different JMS providers, we have to configure the required plugin, the plugin version for that particular JMS provider, and also the JMS-related plugins. In addition to plugins, we also have to configure the required repository and dependencies in pom.xml for that specific JMS provider.

Let us see how JMS Connector configuration looks for Solace MQ.

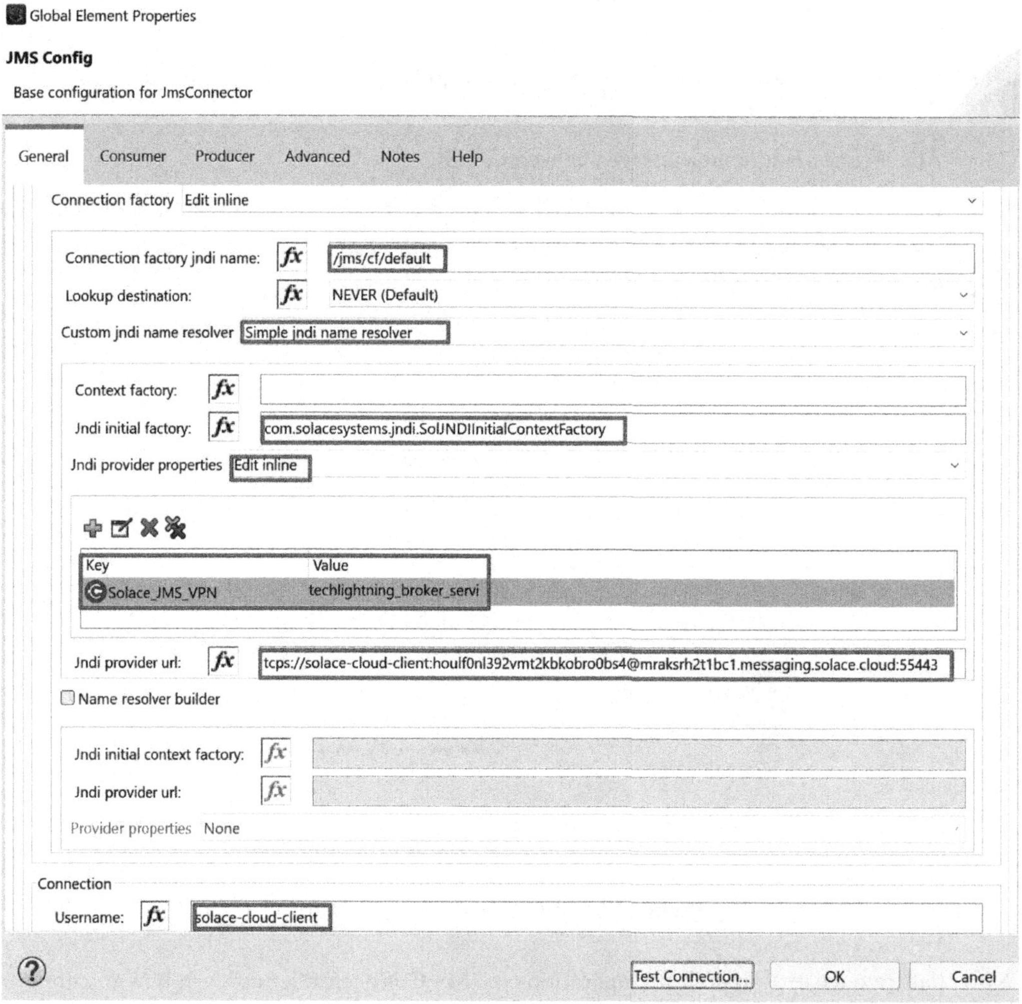

Global Element Properties

JMS Config

Base configuration for JmsConnector

| General | Consumer | Producer | Advanced | Notes | Help |

Connection factory Edit inline

Connection factory jndi name: *fx* /jms/cf/default

Lookup destination: *fx* NEVER (Default)

Custom jndi name resolver Simple jndi name resolver

Context factory: *fx*

Jndi initial factory: *fx* com.solacesystems.jndi.SolJNDIInitialContextFactory

Jndi provider properties Edit inline

| Key | Value |
| Solace_JMS_VPN | techlightning_broker_servi |

Jndi provider url: *fx* tcps://solace-cloud-client:houlf0nl392vmt2kbkobro0bs4@mraksrh2t1bc1.messaging.solace.cloud:55443

☐ Name resolver builder

Jndi initial context factory: *fx*

Jndi provider url: *fx*

Provider properties None

Connection

Username: *fx* solace-cloud-client

Test Connection...   OK   Cancel

Figure 13.26 – JMS Connector – configuration

In *Figure 13.26*, we have configured **Connection factory jndi name**, **Jndi initial factory**, **jndi provider properties**, **Jndi provider url**, **Username**, and **Password**, in order to connect Solace MQ via JMS Connector.

So far, we have seen the connector configuration for Solace MQ. To connect other JMS providers, such as ActiveMQ, WebSphere MQ, and WebLogic JMS, we need to configure the connection details accordingly.

There are predefined templates available to speed up the development of a project. Let us learn more about them.

Introducing MuleSoft accelerators

Accelerators are predesigned Mule applications, API specifications, and documentation that help to speed up the implementation life cycle of a project. These predesigned applications are stored in Exchange as a template that can be downloaded as a `.jar` file in order to create a Mule application project.

When we develop an interface, we can take related templates from Exchange and customize them based on the requirements to speed up the development.

There are different accelerators available in Exchange to support different use cases for different businesses.

Try to download the `SAP ECC Products System API` SAP accelerator from Exchange as a `.jar` file and import it into Anypoint Studio.

It creates a Mule application with all the implementation details, as shown in *Figure 13.27*:

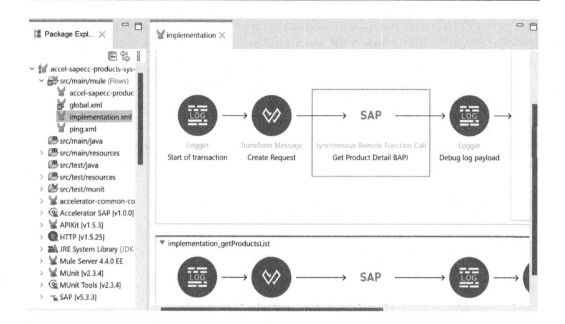

Figure 13.27 – Mule application created using SAP accelerator

Once created, we can customize and configure SAP ECC server details to fetch the product details using **Business Application Programming Interface (BAPI)** from SAP system. This is convenient, avoiding the pain of starting from scratch.

Try to explore other MuleSoft accelerators, such as for Retail, Insurance, Healthcare, Banking, Manufacturing, Salesforce, Coupa, SAP S/4HANA, Jira, ServiceNow, Slack, and PIM, from Exchange and use them in a project.

Summary

In this chapter, we had a look at the basics of connectors, connector categories, and different connectors available in Exchange.

We have understood how File Connector, FTP Connector, and SFTP Connector help to process files across the file system. We have learned how to use Database Connector to connect a database and explored watermarking too. We have used Web Service Consumer Connector to consume a SOAP-based web service. We have also gone through VM Connector and JMS Connector to publish and consume a message asynchronously.

Finally, we have also seen how accelerators help to reduce the work.

On completing this chapter, you have enough knowledge on different connectors to connect various systems.

In the next chapter, *Chapter 14, Best Practices, Tips, and Tricks*, we'll explore the best practices that we need to follow while designing and developing MuleSoft integrations and APIs.

Questions

Take a moment to answer the following questions to serve as a recap of what you just learned in this chapter:

1. How do you read the files from the SFTP server?

2. What is the use of watermarking in File Connector?

3. What connector do you use to call SOAP-based web services?

4. How do you process a message asynchronously in a Mule application?

Answers

1. We can use SFTP Connector and perform read operations to fetch files from the SFTP server based on the configuration of SFTP Connector.

2. It helps to filter the file after the execution of the last poll based on the file created or the last-modified date timestamp.

3. We can use Web Service Consumer Connector to call SOAP-based web services.

4. We can use VM Connector or JMS Connector to process a message asynchronously.

14
Best Practices, Tips, and Tricks

In the previous chapters of this book, we've learned different aspects of designing, developing, and deploying Mule applications. We've learned about the different products that can be found in the MuleSoft suite and their purpose. We learned about Anypoint Platform, Anypoint Studio, Composer, and so on. However, there are still some best practices we'd like to compile for you. This way, you can take these into account when you're working on your future applications.

In this chapter, we're going to cover the following main topics:

- Best practices

- Tips and tricks

Let's start by listing some of the best practices you can apply to your future projects.

Best practices

These are a set of rules you don't necessarily have to follow in order for your applications to work properly, but are a huge help to guide you through what you can do to make your projects better. We will list different best practices ranging from design and development to some security and architecture tips.

As previously mentioned, you are not required to apply these rules to your projects or applications, but they will help you to be more successful with your projects. Feel free to take the ones that apply to you or modify some of them to better fit your needs. The purpose of this list is to help you build your own best practices based on these.

Let's start with some general best practices.

General best practices

Here are some best practices that you can apply to your projects in general.

- **Add a health-check endpoint**: Create a specific endpoint, such as /ping, to get the API's running status. This is helpful to monitor the API from an external tool if needed. You can simply create a new endpoint using the HTTP Listener connector and return a short payload that states this application is up. If the application is not available when you try to call it, it will not return the OK payload. This way, you'll know there's something wrong with the deployed application and you need to double-check it. You can also return more details, such as the name of the host or the time it took to process the response, depending on what you want to see when you send the request to this endpoint to ensure the status of the application.

- **Follow naming conventions**: You can create a set of naming conventions with your team so that APIs, files, flows, properties, and so on share the same standards and can be found more easily. For example, if you're using an API-led connectivity approach, you can add *eapi*, *papi*, or *sapi* to the name of the API in order to easily identify whether it's an Experience, Process, or System API. It can be as simple as naming your project something such as *pshopping* or it can be more complex if you have many APIs and want to be able to differentiate between them.

- **Create unit tests**: Follow the best practice of creating unit tests in MUnit as part of the development cycle. Each developer should be responsible for creating their own set of unit tests to ensure their code works as expected in different scenarios. Of course, you can have a specialized **Quality Assurance (QA)** team that can take care of other types of testing, such as regression or performance, but developers are the ones that are closer to the code, so it should be an expectation for them to create the unit tests for their specific code.

- **Create a CI/CD pipeline**: Whenever the code is pushed to specific branches, a **Continuous Integration/Continuous Delivery (CI/CD)** pipeline should be in place to release the new code in the specified environment. For example, when pushing code to the *dev* branch, a new deployment will be done to the *dev* environment. This should be created by the operations team (or DevOps), but if your company doesn't have the roles, then the responsibility can be that of the developers or architects.

- **Create separate VPNs**: It's a best practice to create a separate VPN for non-production environments (dev, QA, staging, and so on) and the production environment. This is added as a security measure in case anything goes wrong with the non-production environments' VPNs so your production VPN is intact.

- **Do not log sensitive data**: In some cases, the information the API is handling is sensitive data, for example, credit card or social security numbers. It is best not to log these fields for security reasons. You can use other fields to log the information if you need, but make sure they don't contain sensitive data, for example, first name or gender.

- **Use standard logging and error handling**: It's best to use the same standard for all your APIs as much as possible. When developers already know how the logging and error handling works in the whole project, they won't have an issue with working on a different API since the standards are the same. This also helps to keep all logging as secure as possible by not logging sensitive data or masking information. This helps to reduce development time and human error.

As you can see, the previous list was intended for projects or architectures in general. Let's now go a bit deeper and list some of the best practices that you can apply to your Mule projects – the ones you create in Anypoint Studio to create Mule applications.

Mule project best practices

When you start a new project in Anypoint Studio in order to create a Mule application, you're creating a Mule project. You have a `pom.xml` file, a main configuration file where your flows will be, some Log4j configuration, and so on. We will now list some of the best practices to create better Mule projects:

- **Separate global elements**: For easy access, create a file called `global.xml` or whichever naming convention your company has to keep all the global elements in this one file. This will reduce development time when trying to find a specific element and it also serves to not duplicate elements since they're all listed in the same place. You can either create global elements in this file directly or move global elements from other files into this one. For a step-by-step guide, visit the following tutorial: `https://developer.mulesoft.com/tutorials-and-howtos/getting-started/global-elements-properties-files/`.

- **Separate common flows**: For easy access, create a file called `common.xml` or whichever naming convention your company has to keep all the common flows, logic, or functionality in one file. Same as the previous point, this will reduce development time when trying to find a specific common component since they're all located in the same place. When we say *common*, we mean pieces of code (can be flows, subflows, or error-handling pieces) that are used in a number of flows or files across the project. For example, if you have an authorization flow that has to be used before calling an external API, you can consider this authorization flow a common piece since it's referenced by several other flows scattered across different configuration files.

- **Create a folder for each resource**: Under `src/main/resources`, make sure you create a separate folder for each type of resource to find them more easily, for example, `dataweave`, `wsdl`, and `examples`. The same applies to the `src/test/resources` folder to keep your testing files. This is especially useful in bigger projects because you can get lost in so many files. But if you have the correct folders, following intuitive naming conventions, then it won't be that hard to find the files you need by navigating to these folders.

- **Never hardcode data. Use properties instead**: When you *hardcode* certain things in the connectors, it's harder to find and change them later, for example, credentials or URLs. When you use properties to keep this information, there is a single place where the data can be changed. It's also better-looking in your repository at the time of reviewing a pull request. Instead of having to go through the different configuration files, you can just review the properties files.

- **Separate properties files by environment**: When you create properties files (either `.properties` or `.yaml`), make sure you create a separate file per environment to change the values of the properties depending on the environment the application is deployed in, for example, `local.properties`, `dev.properties`, `qa.properties`, and `prod.properties`. You can also separate the secured properties into different files and still separate them by environment, for example, `local.sec.properties` or `dev.secure.properties`, depending on your team's naming conventions. To do this, you need to define a global property to know which environment you're in. This property will change in each environment, which will tell the Mule application to take one file over the other ones. Note that this also applies to `.yaml` files if they are your preference over `.properties` files. For a step-by-step guide, visit the following tutorial: `https://developer.mulesoft.com/tutorials-and-howtos/getting-started/global-elements-properties-files/`.

- **Encrypt secured properties**: Make sure the sensitive properties you add to your Mule projects are securely encrypted. You can encrypt your properties using the *Secure Properties Tool* from MuleSoft and the application will be able to decrypt them at runtime with the *Mule Secure Configuration Properties* module, using the encryption key with which you encrypted the properties in the first place. To learn more about this, visit the following documentation page: `https://docs.mulesoft.com/mule-runtime/latest/secure-configuration-properties`. For a step-by-step guide, visit the following tutorial: `https://developer.mulesoft.com/tutorials-and-howtos/getting-started/how-to-secure-properties-before-deployment/`.

- **Keep the encryption key separate**: Never add the key you used to encrypt the properties (see the previous point) in your Mule application. This can lead to hackers easily decrypting all your properties. Instead, you can pass the key as an environment variable inside the *Run Configurations* section to run it locally and add it directly to the properties in *Runtime Manager* for each environment in CloudHub. For a step-by-step guide, visit the following tutorial: `https://developer.mulesoft.com/tutorials-and-howtos/getting-started/how-to-secure-properties-before-deployment/`.

- **Hide your secured properties in Runtime Manager**: Open your Mule application's `mule-artifact.json` file and make sure you add the properties you want to hide to the `secureProperties` field. This will mask the properties in Runtime Manager so no one can see them from the UI. It won't make a change for your properties in your local machine, but it is helpful from the UI's perspective. For a step-by-step guide, visit the following tutorial: `https://developer.mulesoft.com/tutorials-and-howtos/getting-started/how-to-secure-properties-before-deployment/`.

- **Externalize DataWeave scripts**: When you use the Transform Message component in your Mule applications, the DataWeave script is automatically added to the XML file (or configuration file) where the component is located. It's a best practice to keep an external .dwl file for your script instead of embedding it in the XML file. For this, just click on the **Edit** button inside your Transform Message component, select **File** (instead of **Inline**), add your folder name and filename (for example, dataweave/myscript.dwl), and click **OK**. Your files will be created under src/main/resources. If you have many Transform Message components and you notice it's hard to find the dwl files, it's best you create more folders to separate the script files by folder and find them more easily.

- **Indent DataWeave scripts**: In DataWeave, it's not required to indent properly for the script to work, but it's a best practice to keep the indentation when needed. For example, if you open a parenthesis and then create code on a new line, that new line should be indented to know it's inside the parentheses. The same thing applies to new lines inside a function or a variable even though you might not have opening parentheses or curly brackets.

- **Use data types in DataWeave**: In DataWeave, it's not required to assign data types; however, your code will have better quality if you get used to doing this on a daily basis. You can assign data types to variables, functions, parameters, and so on. This is also helpful to see the potential errors you might have at runtime before even getting to that point. To learn more about this, visit the documentation: https://docs.mulesoft.com/dataweave/latest/dataweave-type-system.

- **Create a Mule project template**: Create a Mule project that can be used as a template with the required structure, configurations, or dependencies. This way, the developers don't have to create a new project from scratch but they can use this template as a foundation to create a new one with the needed structure already added.

- **Use different workspaces**: It's good to keep different kinds of projects in different workspaces, especially if you work with a lot of Mule projects. This is also helpful to save separate settings in your workspaces, for example, personalize your own debug view or create a custom view. It's also worth noticing that the cache is stored by the workspace (at least in Anypoint Studio). We will see why when we cover tips and tricks later in this chapter.

Now we have a better idea of what best practices are good to apply to your Mule projects. Some are more critical because of security issues that may arise, while others just provide a more comfortable solution to reduce development time.

Let's now jump into some best practices when working in Anypoint Platform and the different products we can find there.

Anypoint Platform best practices

Anypoint Platform is where most of MuleSoft's products are located. We start by designing APIs in Design Center, we deploy Mule applications in Runtime Manager, we secure our APIs in API Manager, and so on. Let's list some of the best practices we should be using for some of these products:

- **Apply automated policies**: In API Manager, instead of applying policies to one API at a time, you can apply automated policies that will be added to all the APIs you select. This helps to reduce human error and keep a standard across all APIs.

- **Enhance Exchange's documentation**: When you publish a resource to Anypoint Exchange, make sure you add clear descriptions, required images, and supported authentication in the API documentation. This will be helpful for other people who want to use your API.

- **Define common API specification fragments**: When creating the API specification in Design Center, make sure you create fragments for the repeating blocks and reuse them across the specification. This way, you don't have to copy and paste the code every time you need it in a different place, reducing time and human error.

- **Use common headers in the API specification**: When creating the API specification in Design Center, you can use common headers to include the correlation ID, transaction ID, and so on. This way, similar information will be used across all APIs, which is helpful for the development team. This will help to improve tracing and correlation across different APIs.

- **Use nouns for the API specification's resources**: When creating the API specification in Design Center, make sure you use nouns instead of verbs for the names of the resources, for example, `/members` instead of `/getMembers`. You can read more about best practices for your API specifications in this article: `https://developer.mulesoft.com/tutorials-and-howtos/getting-started/best-practices-first-api-spec/`.

- **Use versioning in the API's URL**: It's a best practice to add the version number to the API's URL. There are different ways of doing this, but we recommend using the version before the resource path, like so: `/v1/members`.

- **Create an API specification template**: Create an API specification that can be used as a template with the standardized resources and shared fragments. This way, the developers don't have to create a new API specification from scratch but they can use this template as the foundation to create a new one with the needed resources already added.

Most of these best practices apply to Mule projects in Anypoint Studio because it's where most of the coding happens. The second place where we do most of the coding is when creating the API specification. As you just saw, most of the best practices for Anypoint Platform come from Design Center at the time you're designing your API specifications.

Now that we know some general, Mule project, and Anypoint Platform best practices, let's take a look at some tips and tricks for when working with MuleSoft's products.

Tips and tricks

The following list of tips and tricks is not the same as the best practices list. Best practices are rules or standards that you can choose to follow to create a better developer experience or to avoid common mistakes. The following list gives you some advice that you may or may not be aware of but will help you to troubleshoot your applications more easily:

- **Switch workspaces when needed**: If you notice some weird behaviors with Anypoint Studio, for example, if the breakpoints aren't working properly or the debugger does not work as expected, you can switch to a different workspace and import your project there. This works sometimes because the cache in Anypoint Studio is saved within each workspace. So, if the problem you're experiencing is because of the cache, once you switch to a different workspace, the cache is brand new. This might help to resolve your issue with the IDE.

- **Run more than one Mule project at a time**: In Anypoint Studio, go to **Run** and then select **Run Configurations**. Here, you can create a new Mule application configuration and select more than one Mule project to launch at the same time. This will help you when you need to run the three API layers (Experience, Process, and System) on your local machine. You can use this configuration to either debug or run all applications. Just make sure all the applications you want to run are open in the same workspace.

- **Monitor certificates**: If your Mule application is using certificates, make sure you monitor the expiration date and renew the required certificate before it expires. Otherwise, your application will stop working because of security issues. This is good to keep in mind to avoid any future troubleshooting and save development time.

- **Use the latest version of the connectors**: When you browse for a connector in Exchange, make sure you use the latest stable version of it in your Mule applications. Sometimes there are bugs in previous versions that were fixed in the newest versions, so it's best to keep up to date. If you already have a connector and you want to update it to the latest version, you have to make sure it's a minor version and not a major version. Otherwise, you risk your code breaking or the functionality changing. If your code is compatible with the newest major version, then you can update the connector.

- **Create custom error types when needed**: It's good to use the default error handling, but sometimes you need to provide more details to know what failed in your code. You can create custom error types to handle different scenarios, such as data errors, validation errors, or connectivity errors.

- **Use error codes when needed**: If you create custom error types for your applications and you have different errors for different scenarios, it's useful to use the error code instead of the error description. This way, the calling application knows how to handle the given exception based on the error code, which should be unique.

We hope this list of tips and tricks is useful for your MuleSoft journey and your future projects. These are some things that have helped us in our career and we wanted to share them with you. You can create your own list with more things that have helped you and share it with others to expand the general knowledge on MuleSoft's line of products.

Summary

In this chapter, we listed some best practices and tips and tricks that you will be able to apply to your future MuleSoft projects.

We talked about general best practices that may apply to different projects, such as integrations or APIs, as well as ones that are more high level. Then, we zoomed into actually talking about the things that are implemented in the Mule projects in Anypoint Studio. Finally, we discussed some of the best practices you can apply to your API specifications and other Anypoint Platform products, such as API Manager.

We also provided a list of some tips and tricks that have been helpful for us in our MuleSoft career. We encourage you to take this list and enhance it with your own tips, especially after trying out the new Mule products that we didn't get to try in this book, such as Anypoint Code Builder (MuleSoft's new IDE that hasn't been released yet).

Questions

Take a moment to answer the following questions to serve as a recap of what you just learned in this chapter:

1. What is a health-check endpoint and why is it useful?

2. What is an example of sensitive data that you shouldn't log in your application?

3. What is the `global.xml` file used for?

4. What is the best practice to separate your properties?

5. What is the best practice to keep your properties' encryption keys?

6. What is the file you can use in your Mule project to hide your secured properties in Runtime Manager?

7. In Anypoint Studio, where is the cache for your Mule project saved?

Answers

1. A health-check endpoint is one that you create in your API to get the API's running status. It is helpful to monitor the API when needed to make sure it's up and running.

2. Credit card information or social security numbers.

3. To separate all the global elements into this one file to reduce development time when trying to find a specific element.

4. Separate them by environment, for example, `local.properties`, `dev.properties`, `qa.properties`, or `prod.properties`.

5. Never add the keys to your Mule application's code. You can pass the key as an environment variable in Anypoint Studio for local runs or using Runtime Manager for CloudHub.

6. `mule-artifact.json`.

7. In each workspace.

15
Certification and Interview Tips

You have learned everything we had to teach you on the technical aspects of using MuleSoft's products. After a long journey of understanding best practices and following how-to guides, you might now feel ready to start your career in the *MuleSoft ecosystem*. But where to start?

In this chapter, we're going to cover the following main topics:

- Choosing your career path
- Getting MuleSoft certified
- Expanding your knowledge with the official training
- Contributing to the MuleSoft Community
- Passing your interview

When we say MuleSoft ecosystem, we mean that you don't necessarily have to work at MuleSoft to have a MuleSoft career. You could work for a number of MuleSoft's partners or customers. MuleSoft's customers are those who pay for its products and benefit from generating Mule applications or architectures. While MuleSoft's partners are companies that work to implement solutions for customers. Partners don't necessarily benefit from the final product but from providing consultancy services. They work alongside MuleSoft to make sure the products are being utilized to their maximum and that customers are happy with the solutions. You could also work as an independent professional and lend your services on an hourly basis, although this option is not that popular in real life. Most professionals work with either partners, customers, or MuleSoft directly.

Let's start by understanding the different roles you can have and choosing your preferred one.

Choosing your career path

When you want to start a career in the MuleSoft ecosystem, there are different career paths and certifications that you can follow to achieve a specific role. Each company defines its own roles to work with MuleSoft products, the biggest ones being developer and architect. However, how do these roles differ and what would you prefer to be? If you come from a Salesforce role, it might be easier to choose where to go from there – for example, if you're a Salesforce architect, you might want to become a MuleSoft architect as well. Let's take a look at the most popular career paths in the MuleSoft ecosystem and what they mean:

- **Architect**:

    - Works with clients to gather requirements and understand the required solution

    - Creates diagrams and documentation as an agreement of how the solution will work

    - Decides on security protocols and recommends technology stacks and best practices

    - Works with the developers to build the solution

    Some companies leave the responsibility for the API specification (creation/maintenance) and the deployment to the architect instead of the developers or operations.

- **Developer** – covers almost everything we see in this book:

    - Transforms the business requirements into a solution

    - Is hands-on to create the code, ensure quality testing (unit tests), and troubleshoot any issues

    Some companies leave the responsibility for the deployment to the developer instead of operations.

- **Operations** – widely known as **DevOps** (a combination of software development and IT operations):

    - Creates automated pipelines to reduce development time – also known as **Continuous Integration/Continuous Delivery (CI/CD)**

    - Ensures code reaches the required environments, running automated tests and troubleshooting if the deployment doesn't work

- **Business user** (this is not an official career path): Since MuleSoft's acquisition by Salesforce, a new product combining the two technologies has emerged: **Composer**. This role creates integrations with this no-code tool using clicks instead of code. A great difference from the three previous roles is that you don't necessarily need an IT background. You can be in a business position and still learn how to use Composer to create integrations.

There are some variants from the previous list of roles depending on the company and the size of the project. For example, if it's a very small project (around 1 month of development), they might decide to only use an architect and a developer; but if it's a huge project (more than 3 years of development), they might use more specific roles such as a *designer* who specializes in creating and maintaining the API specifications.

Choosing a specific career path doesn't necessarily mean you'll have to stay on that path forever. A lot of people start as developers and become architects later on, or feel more interested in the operations side. There are plenty of training and resources out there to learn what you need in order to switch to a different path. If you just need a place to start and you have no previous experience, we recommend you start as a developer.

You might have a better idea of what career path you're looking for after seeing this list. Now let's talk about how to get more knowledge and prove it in your resume with a certification.

Getting MuleSoft certified

There are currently four available certifications you can get with MuleSoft to prove your knowledge (at the time this book was written). Some companies may have a requirement of holding at least one certification in order to apply for a position. While not a rule, it might be helpful for your resume to have more certifications (at least one).

There are two certifications for developers:

- MuleSoft Certified Developer – Level 1
- MuleSoft Certified Developer – Level 2

They each test your knowledge of the different products we have looked at in this book. The first one is the entry certification (or the most basic one). The second one was just released in June 2022, so not a lot of people hold this certification yet. It might be a great differentiator when looking for a new position.

The other two certifications are for architects:

- MuleSoft Certified Platform Architect – Level 1
- MuleSoft Certified Integration Architect – Level 1

While they are both for architects, they have different specializations. MuleSoft defines a *Platform Architect* as a person who *lead[s] cross-project design decisions and focus[es] on visibility across systems and clouds to identify issues before they impact the business*. While an *Integration Architect* is a person who *make[s] project design decisions and [is] the bridge between architect managers and developers [...] value[s] architectural repeatability and ensure[s] project quality* (https://training.mulesoft.com/learning-path).

As you can see from the architect certifications, they are only Level 1. Level 2 certifications are still in the works but there's no date to know when they'll be published.

Here are some tips to get certified:

- *Follow the requirements*: If you go to `training.mulesoft.com/certification`, you can see the details of each path. Read them carefully and follow them as much as you can to really be prepared for the exam. All of the following details can be found on each certification's page.

- *Take the training*: Each certification is linked to its own training. For example, to get the MuleSoft Certified Developer – Level 1 certification, it is recommended you take the *Anypoint Platform Development: Fundamentals* training.

- *Finish the do-it-yourself exercises*: The **MuleSoft Certified Developer (MCD)** certifications have their own DIY exercises so you can practice. Practice is one of the fundamental ways to pass the developer exams more easily.

- *Take the practice exam*: Once you feel ready, take the practice exam listed on each certification page. As ready as you feel, make sure you take this exam first. Aim to get 90% or more correct answers. If your score is lower than this, it may mean you're not ready to take the real exam yet.

- *Review the topics*: Make sure you read all the topics that will be included in the exam. If there's any topic you don't feel comfortable taking, make sure you spend extra time on it. A lot of times, people don't pass the exam because of that one topic they left out.

- *Take the first attempt*: If you purchase the training for each certification (or take the free self-paced one for MCD – Level 1), it will include two attempts to pass the exam. When you take the first attempt, don't take it assuming you're going to pass. Rather, take the first attempt as another practice. You will get a better feeling of what the exam is like and discover things you didn't know. Take this opportunity to absorb the information you will need to learn for the second attempt.

- *Manage your time*: You will have 2 hours to finish and there are 60 questions. You have to manage your time effectively or you will run out of time. The exam's platform lets you flag a question to go back to at the end if you still have time. It is better if you skip questions that are too hard and focus on the ones you can answer more easily than spending too much time on the harder questions.

- *Take notes afterward*: You cannot have any notebooks nearby while you are taking the exam. However, as soon as the exam is done, you can take notes of all you need to study for the second attempt. The quicker you write down this information, the fresher it will be in your mind, so try to do this immediately after you're done with the first attempt.

- *Find a quiet room*: Someone will have access to your screen, webcam, and microphone while you take the exam to make sure you're not cheating. You can't look away from your screen or it might be misinterpreted as cheating. You can't have your phone or smartwatch nearby and you can't listen to music. In other words, there must be no distractions whatsoever. This environment might be stressful for some people, so make sure you make arrangements to be in a quiet room where you can't get distracted as easily. Make sure no one will enter the room while you're taking the exam, otherwise, the exam will be suspended immediately and you will fail your attempt.

Each certification exam is different, but they all consist of multiple-choice questions. The developer exams have more practical/technical questions, while the architect ones have more of a use case basis or are theoretical. You will notice the differences when you take the practice exams. Apart from that, the previous tips apply to all certification exams.

So, you chose your career path and your certifications, now let's see how you can learn more things with some training.

Expanding your knowledge with the official training

You can find the complete list of courses at `training.mulesoft.com/course-catalog`. At the time this book was written, there were 16 courses available for you to take. Some of these are free and self-paced, and some are paid and instructor-led.

Let's separate the training by career path to make things easier, starting with the developer training.

Developer training

Let's take a look at the different types of developer training available:

- If you're in a business role and want to see a quick overview of the tools but also get some hands-on experience, you can take the *Getting Started with Anypoint Platform* training. This will give you an overview of the main products in Anypoint Platform and guide you through some exercises so you can see them in action. This training is not aligned with any certification.

- If you want to get started with the MuleSoft products (both Anypoint Platform and Anypoint Studio), especially from a developer perspective, you should take the *Anypoint Platform Development: Fundamentals* training. This is more in-depth training that will get you started as a MuleSoft developer. It teaches you all the basics to get an idea of how to use the different tools to develop applications. This training is aligned with the MuleSoft Certified Developer – Level 1 certification.

- If you want to get more knowledge on RAML and learn some best practices to design your API specifications, you can take the *Anypoint Platform Development: API Design with RAML* training. Even if you're new to designing API specifications, this will help you to get started and understand some more advanced topics to create RAML files. There used to be a certification for this training but there isn't anymore.

- If you want to learn more about DataWeave, but still at a basic-intermediate level, you can take the *Anypoint Platform Development: DataWeave* training. This is especially useful if you have some specific DataWeave questions that you want to clear with an instructor. This training is not aligned with any certification, but it is useful to take it before attempting the MuleSoft Certified Developer – Level 1 certification.

- If you want to learn more about operations and how to get production-ready, you can take the *Anypoint Platform Development: Production-Ready Development Practices* and *Anypoint Platform Development: Production-Ready Integrations* training. This is helpful if it is your first time deploying your applications to production and you want to be familiar with the best practices. This training is not aligned with any certification.

Now let's jump into the next path: architecture.

Architect training

As we previously saw when discussing the two different architect certifications, MuleSoft separates architects into Platform Architect or Integration Architect. There is training for each role:

- *Anypoint Platform Architecture: Application Networks* for Platform Architects
- *Anypoint Platform Architecture: Integration Solutions* for Integration Architects

Each of them will help you to get ready for the architect certifications.

> **Tip**
> Taking the architect training is not enough to get the certifications because there is so much knowledge required to pass the exams. However, they will give you the resources you need to study on your own even after the training is done. You should spend around 3-4 weeks studying the content in detail before attempting the exams.

There is additional training that is specialized in the healthcare industry and it helps you to implement a 360 use case. This is the *Anypoint Platform Architecture: MuleSoft Accelerator for Healthcare* training.

Now let's look at the last path: operations.

Operations training

One of the great things about MuleSoft's products is that you can choose between deployment options for the control and runtime planes, as we saw in *Chapter 9, Deploying Your Application*. With this training, you can learn more about how to achieve different deployment options and learn best practices for different scenarios.

If you want to learn more about Mule-hosted runtime and control planes, you can take the *Anypoint Platform Operations: CloudHub* training for the runtime plane part and *Anypoint Platform Operations: API Management* for the control plane part.

If you want to be more proficient in Runtime Fabric (customer-hosted runtime plane and Mule-hosted control plane), you can take one of the two available types of training, depending on which scenario you want to learn more about: *Anypoint Platform Operations: Runtime Fabric on Virtual Machines* and *Anypoint Platform Operations: Runtime Fabric on Self-Managed Kubernetes*.

There are other products to achieve customer-hosted deployments without having to necessarily have a Mule-hosted control plane. You can learn more about this in the *Anypoint Platform Operations: Customer-Hosted Runtimes* training.

Finally, if you want to learn more about creating custom sites or documentation pages for your APIs, you can try the *Anypoint Platform Operations: API Community Manager* training.

The list of available training is always growing to include more up-to-date information. If you want to work for a MuleSoft partner or customer, make sure they offer a budget for official MuleSoft training so you can keep up with the latest technologies and products. An alternative way of learning new things about MuleSoft is to participate in the MuleSoft Community, which we will look at next.

Contributing to the MuleSoft Community

The MuleSoft Community is supported by the community team at MuleSoft but is completely run by community members (not working at MuleSoft directly). There might be some MuleSoft employees attending or speaking at meetups from time to time, but the focus is on all the developers and architects using MuleSoft in their day-to-day work and sharing their knowledge and experience with the rest of the community.

There are several ongoing initiatives within the community that you can take advantage of. Let's start with meetups.

Expanding your knowledge with MuleSoft meetups

This is one of the biggest (if not the biggest) initiatives of all. For years, professionals have been organizing, attending, and speaking at these meetups around the world. There are in-person and online meetup groups that you can join. In the beginning, all meetups were happening in person, until health restrictions were applied in 2020. At that point, all groups were switched to online meetups. Some groups have returned to in-person meetups now and some others are doing hybrid (in-person and online) events. You can join any meetup of your preference; it doesn't have to be your local meetup group.

The first step you can take is to join your local meetup group or online meetup groups to keep posted about when there's a new meetup. Then, attend more meetups to gain knowledge. Once you feel ready with a topic, you can apply to be a speaker at one of the meetup groups by contacting the organizers of the group. This could be beneficial for you because you might get free training or certification vouchers when you are a speaker. You can apply to speak at a meetup here: `meetups.mulesoft.com/speak-at-a-mulesoft-meetup`.

Find the complete list of meetup groups here: `meetups.mulesoft.com/chapters`. Some examples of meetup groups are the following:

- Online Group – English
- Online Group – Spanish

- Online Group – Portuguese

- Women Who Mule AMER

- Women Who Mule JAPAC

- Women Who Mule EMEA

- MuleSoft for Java Developers

- New York City, United States

- Buenos Aires, Argentina

- Paris, France

- Mumbai, India

- Sydney, Australia

There are more than 120 groups around the world. But that is not all: if your local meetup group is inactive or one has never existed, you can take the initiative and become a MuleSoft meetup group leader to organize the meetups for a specific chapter. You can apply to become a leader here: `meetups.mulesoft.com/become-mulesoft-meetup-leader`.

Becoming a meetup leader comes with very special perks such as getting free training/certification vouchers, access to special community events, free access to some MuleSoft conferences, and more. However, the best perks of the community are awarded to MuleSoft Ambassadors. To become a MuleSoft Ambassador, first, you have to become a MuleSoft Mentor. Let's learn more about this.

Helping others as a MuleSoft Mentor

You can apply to become a MuleSoft Mentor once you feel ready to start contributing in a more formal role to the community. There are quarterly requirements that you'll need to meet to continue being part of this program, but you also get great benefits in return, such as free training, special swag, and coaching with one of the MuleSoft Ambassadors.

This is the first step you can take to become a more recognized member of the community if you don't want to become a meetup leader right away. Being a meetup leader and a MuleSoft Mentor are not correlated. You can be a leader and a mentor or you can apply to be a mentor without having to be a leader. The more you do for the community, the more *points* you'll get in your favor to reach the MuleSoft Ambassador title.

You can find the complete list of requirements and benefits here: `developer.mulesoft.com/community/mentors`. Note that the full list of MuleSoft Mentors is not available yet. There are more than 100 mentors currently.

Once you become a mentor and have been a mentor for a while, depending on your level of contributions, you might look into becoming a MuleSoft Ambassador next. Let's learn a bit more about that.

Becoming a MuleSoft Ambassador

MuleSoft Ambassadors are the top-tier experts in the community. They each specialize in a different area, which is very helpful for the rest of the people trying to learn MuleSoft. Some create high-quality videos on YouTube, some write articles, some help in the forums, and some speak at events and meetups. There's not just one characteristic of being an ambassador that you can copy and apply to yourself since everyone's so different. The thing they all have in common is their passion for helping others and answering questions. You can get in touch with an ambassador for specific questions you may have and they'll be happy to help you.

If you want to become an ambassador and don't know where to start or what specialty to take, you can follow the current ambassadors on social networks and see what they're up to. Maybe you like creating videos or maybe you prefer helping in the forums. You can try a bit of everything until you find what you're more passionate about.

As mentioned before, you first have to be a MuleSoft Mentor in order to have a chance of being a MuleSoft Ambassador. Once you've spent some months or years helping the community, you might have the chance to become an ambassador. MuleSoft Ambassadors are not normally nominated. There is a separate special process for selection. This is why you get coached by an actual ambassador when you're a mentor – to understand the process better and get a plan to become one.

You can find the complete list of MuleSoft Ambassadors here: `developer.mulesoft.com/community/ambassadors`.

There are still more things to do even if you don't want to be part of the meetups or the mentors/ambassadors program. Let's now talk about the MuleSoft forums.

Getting help with the MuleSoft forums

The forums are primarily run by community members. People in the community can ask a question there and it will get answered in less than a day by – at least – one of the community members that are dedicated to helping others solve their questions.

A lot of the current MuleSoft Mentors and Ambassadors are active contributors in the forums. It's a specialty for some of them to answer technical questions or clear some doubts about the products. This is one of the biggest sources of information for the community.

If you want to take advantage of this site, you can access `help.mulesoft.com` and create an account to start posting questions/answers. Please note that it is best to create an account with a personal email instead of your work email. If you change emails, you will no longer have access to your previous account's points and you'll have to start from scratch.

You can use an Anypoint Platform free trial account and even if it expires, you'll still have access to your profile.

Now that we know where we can go with questions we may have and who we can look to for advice, let's look at some interview tips to nail your first MuleSoft job.

Passing your interview

You chose your career path, you got the training, you got the certification, and you know where to go for help; now the only thing missing is to get your first MuleSoft job.

There is no magic formula that you can follow to nail technical interviews, especially since there are different roles and each company focuses on its own priorities. Maybe some companies are more interested in knowing that you can learn new technologies and not so much on your actual MuleSoft knowledge, or maybe they just ask specific MuleSoft questions.

For example, if you're applying for an entry job as a MuleSoft developer, they might already know that you will only answer the questions you saw in your training but you don't have practical experience in real-life projects. So, their questions will be more focused on your understanding of the basic topics instead of real-life complex projects. However, if you're applying for a senior MuleSoft developer role, they'll probably expect you to be an expert on MuleSoft's products and have lots of hands-on experience. They won't ask the same questions of a recent graduate and an experienced architect. There are some tips that we can give you so you can take these things into account.

Most of the questions people generally ask are related to what you saw/will see in the fundamentals training. Some of these are even part of the MCD – Level 1 certification exam. Besides finishing the training or passing the exam, we also recommend that you do some personal projects so you can get more familiar with the products and troubleshoot on your own.

Some general questions you may be asked in your interview may be the following:

1. What is the Mule runtime?
2. What are some differences between Mule 3 and Mule 4?
3. What is API-led connectivity?
4. What's the difference between a RESTful and a SOAP web service?
5. What are the differences between a flow and a sub-flow?
6. What's the Mule message structure in Mule 3 versus Mule 4?
7. What is MUnit?
8. What is a domain project?
9. What are the different ways to deploy an application into CloudHub?
10. What are the differences between CloudHub, on-premises, and Runtime Fabric?

As mentioned before, the questions will be different depending on the type of role you are interviewing for and the total years of experience you already have. The previous questions were some general/basic questions you may get asked for any role, but some examples for a senior or architect position might be the following:

1. When can you use the Object Store Connector and when should you use the Object Store REST APIs?

2. How can you use streaming in connectors such as File and HTTP?

3. What is the threading model in Mule 4?

4. How do you set up a CI/CD pipeline (such as Jenkins) for automated deployments?

5. What are the different encryptions you can achieve in Mule 4?

6. How can you create a custom policy and deploy it to Exchange?

7. What is the difference between a **Dedicated Load Balancer** (**DLB**) and a **Shared Load Balancer** (**SLB**)?

8. What's the difference between a keystore and a truststore?

9. What's the difference between a worker and a vCore?

10. How can you set up a different identity provider for Anypoint Platform?

Most of these questions are answered in the different types of training we previously listed. Some are found in the fundamentals training, some in the operations training, and some in the architect training. Depending on the role you're applying for, we recommend you take a look at the specific training and study as if you were going to take a certification exam.

You should also self-reflect on how you learn best. Some people learn more when doing hands-on, practical exercises. Some people learn more by watching videos. Some people learn more by reading documentation. It is important that you figure out how to absorb this information so you really understand it and don't just memorize it. This will help you in both your exams and your interviews.

Depending on the company, you may be able to ask them to provide a guide for the topics they're going to go through in the interview. This will help you get a better idea of what the questions are going to be about so you can prepare days in advance. Don't take your interviews lightly; always prepare and re-read tutorials/documentation or re-watch videos to give yourself a refresher. Even if they're basic topics, you might forget the details sometimes.

Finally, you can use the networking side of LinkedIn or similar social networks to connect with professionals that are working at the company you're applying to. You can get in touch with them and schedule a meeting to get a better sense of what the interview will be like. Maybe they have some specific pointers about their interview process that will be helpful for you to know beforehand. You can also get in touch with some MuleSoft Community members to ask for their help in having mock interviews. This is especially helpful if you haven't been to interviews for a while and don't quite remember the feeling of being in an interview. Having several mock interviews with others might help you be less nervous in the actual interview and you'll get to practice some technical questions.

Summary

In this chapter, we learned about the different roles you can work in in the MuleSoft ecosystem. The official ones are architect, developer, and operations. We learned that there are some variants of these roles depending on the company, for example, designer.

We reviewed the four available certifications and why they might be important for your resume. There are two developer certifications: MuleSoft Certified Developer – Level 1 and Level 2. And there are also two architect certifications depending on your specialization: MuleSoft Certified Platform Architect or Integration Architect. Both are just Level 1 for now. We also mentioned some tips to get certified, such as taking the training and the practice exams.

We talked about the different official training you can find to expand your knowledge. There is specific training depending on your career path and/or specialization. Some of it comes with free vouchers to try the certification exam and some is just to show you more best practices or give you experience in certain products.

We understood a bit more about the MuleSoft Community and how you can be a part of it. We discussed how MuleSoft meetups work, how you can become a mentor or an ambassador, and how to take advantage of the forums to either ask questions or help others with theirs.

Finally, we listed some example questions you might get in your interview, depending on the role or experience level you're looking for. We also talked about how each company is different and there's no one-size-fits-all guide to guarantee you pass the interview. But you can get a better feeling of what kind of questions you might expect.

Questions

Take a moment to answer the following questions to serve as a recap of what you just learned in this chapter:

1. What are the four different career paths we talked about?

2. What are the four available certifications?

3. List at least three types of training for developers.

4. List at least two types of training for architects.

5. List at least three types of training for operations.

6. What are the three different official roles you can achieve in the community?

7. What is the URL to access the MuleSoft forums?

8. What is the best practice to create a new account for the forums?

Answers

1. Architect, developer, operations, business user

2. The four available certifications are:

   - MuleSoft Certified Developer – Level 1

   - MuleSoft Certified Developer – Level 2

   - MuleSoft Certified Platform Architect – Level 1

   - MuleSoft Certified Integration Architect – Level 1

3. The types of training for developers are:

   - Getting Started with Anypoint Platform

   - Anypoint Platform Development: Fundamentals

   - Anypoint Platform Development: API Design with RAML

   - Anypoint Platform Development: DataWeave

   - Anypoint Platform Development: Production-Ready Development Practices

   - Anypoint Platform Development: Production-Ready Integrations

4. The types of training for architects are:

   - Anypoint Platform Architecture: Application Networks

   - Anypoint Platform Architecture: Integration Solutions

   - Anypoint Platform Architecture: MuleSoft Accelerator for Healthcare

5. The types of training for operations are:

   - Anypoint Platform Operations: CloudHub

   - Anypoint Platform Operations: API Management

   - Anypoint Platform Operations: Runtime Fabric on Virtual Machines

   - Anypoint Platform Operations: Runtime Fabric on Self-Managed Kubernetes

   - Anypoint Platform Operations: Customer-Hosted Runtimes

   - Anypoint Platform Operations: API Community Manager

6. The different official roles you can achieve in the community are:

    • MuleSoft Meetup Group Leader

    • MuleSoft Mentor

    • MuleSoft Ambassador

7. The URL to access the MuleSoft forums is:

    `help.mulesoft.com`

8. To only use your personal email address and not your work email address

Index

Packt.com

Subscribe to our online digital library for full access to over 7,000 books and videos, as well as industry leading tools to help you plan your personal development and advance your career. For more information, please visit our website.

Why subscribe?

- Spend less time learning and more time coding with practical eBooks and Videos from over 4,000 industry professionals

- Improve your learning with Skill Plans built especially for you

- Get a free eBook or video every month

- Fully searchable for easy access to vital information

- Copy and paste, print, and bookmark content

Did you know that Packt offers eBook versions of every book published, with PDF and ePub files available? You can upgrade to the eBook version at packt.com and as a print book customer, you are entitled to a discount on the eBook copy. Get in touch with us at customercare@packtpub.com for more details.

At www.packt.com, you can also read a collection of free technical articles, sign up for a range of free newsletters, and receive exclusive discounts and offers on Packt books and eBooks.

Other Books You May Enjoy

If you enjoyed this book, you may be interested in these other books by Packt:

Salesforce B2C Solution Architect's Handbook

Mike King

ISBN: 9781801817035

- Explore key Customer 360 products and their integration options

- Choose the optimum integration architecture to unify data and experiences

- Architect a single view of the customer to support service, marketing, and commerce

- Plan for critical requirements, design decisions, and implementation sequences to avoid sub-optimal solutions

- Integrate Customer 360 solutions into a single-source-of-truth solution such as a master data model

- Support business needs that require functionality from more than one component by orchestrating data and user flows

Becoming a Salesforce Certified Technical Architect

Tameem Bahri

ISBN: 9781800568754

- Explore data lifecycle management and apply it effectively in the Salesforce ecosystem
- Design appropriate enterprise integration interfaces to build your connected solution
- Understand the essential concepts of identity and access management
- Develop scalable Salesforce data and system architecture
- Design the project environment and release strategy for your solution
- Articulate the benefits, limitations, and design considerations relating to your solution
- Discover tips, tricks, and strategies to prepare for the Salesforce CTA review board exam

Architecting AI Solutions on Salesforce

Lars Malmqvist

ISBN: 9781801076012

- Explore the Salesforce's AI components and the architectural model for Salesforce Einstein
- Extend the out-of-the-box features using Einstein Services on major Salesforce clouds
- Use Einstein declarative features to create your custom solutions with the right approach
- Design AI solutions on marketing, commerce, and industry clouds
- Use Salesforce Einstein Platform Services APIs to create custom AI solutions
- Integrate third-party AI services such as Microsoft Cognitive Services and Amazon SageMaker into Salesforce

Packt is searching for authors like you

If you're interested in becoming an author for Packt, please visit `authors.packtpub.com` and apply today. We have worked with thousands of developers and tech professionals, just like you, to help them share their insight with the global tech community. You can make a general application, apply for a specific hot topic that we are recruiting an author for, or submit your own idea.

Share Your Thoughts

Now you've finished *MuleSoft for Salesforce Developers*, we'd love to hear your thoughts! Scan the QR code below to go straight to the Amazon review page for this book and share your feedback or leave a review on the site that you purchased it from.

`https://packt.link/r/1801079609`

Your review is important to us and the tech community and will help us make sure we're delivering excellent quality content.

Made in United States
North Haven, CT
23 September 2022

24408072R00267